THE GREAT ECONOMISTS

A HISTORY OF

ECONOMIC THOUGHT

THE Great ECONOMISTS

A HISTORY OF ECONOMIC THOUGHT

BY *Howard D. Marshall*

VASSAR COLLEGE

Pitman Publishing Corporation

NEW YORK · TORONTO · LONDON

ACKNOWLEDGMENTS

Figures 5, 6 and 7 are reprinted with permission of the Macmillan Company from *Principles of Economics* by Alfred Marshall. © The Royal Economic Society, 1961. Figures 13 and 14 are reprinted with permission of the Macmillan Company from *The Economics of Imperfect Competition* by Joan Robinson.

To My Mother

The Great Economists:
A History of Economic Thought
is one of a series of textbooks
published in cooperation
with E. K. Georg Landsberger.

PREFACE

This book is not meant to stand by itself. It is the author's conviction—as it must be of any teacher of the history of economic thought—that the student can best learn about the masters by reading their original works. It is obviously impossible, however, even in a year's course, to cover all of the theorists who figure prominently in that history. Furthermore, many of their writings are difficult for the undergraduate student to follow without some guidance. Nor can all of the students be expected to have a command of the historical background and the nature of the theories involved—both of which are necessary for a clear understanding of each writer. This book is intended to fill some of these gaps. Since it is my conviction that students sometimes "cannot see the forest for the trees," this book is selective as to the writers included.

The author's deep intellectual debt to the work of others will be immediately apparent to any reader at all conversant with the material. The process of accumulation of ideas and interpretations involved in nearly fifteen years of teaching economics makes it impossible for me to identify all the sources of insight, even if there were space to do so. My special gratitude goes to Miss Jane Slabaugh, Mr. Patrick de Fontenay, and my wife, Natalie J. Marshall, who combined wifely sympathy and encouragement with an economist's critical eye. Any credit for whatever merits the book may possess must be shared with this group. Since I did not always follow their advice, the remaining faults are my own. I also wish to thank Mrs. Lester F. Tubby for her expert typing of the manuscript.

HOWARD D. MARSHALL

CONTENTS

THE GREAT
ECONOMISTS

A HISTORY OF
ECONOMIC THOUGHT

CHAPTER I: Introduction

> What can we gain by collecting the absurd opinions and rejected theories which deserve oblivion? It would be useless as well as boring to disinter them. Errors must be forgotten, not studied. The history of economic doctrine serves only idle curiosity.
>
> —JEAN BAPTISTE SAY

> It is incontestable that continuity and fecundity are the least doubtful symptoms of all truly scientific conceptions . . . each new work on political economy, [however,] in lieu of presenting itself as the spontaneous sequence and gradual development of previous works, has an essentially personal character according to its author so as repeatedly to put in question the most fundamental notions. . . .
>
> —AUGUSTE COMTE

Any student approaching a course by his own choice, or at the instigation of his academic adviser, has the right to inquire about the reason for the existence of the subject and the benefits from studying it. This introductory chapter is an attempt to provide a preliminary answer to these queries with respect to the study of the history of economic thought.

Before seeking an answer to these problems, however, we must be certain that we agree on our definition of economic theory. When we offer the obvious definition that a history of economic thought traces the evolution of economic theory, the reader receives little enlightenment unless he understands the nature of such a theory. Any student who has successfully mastered the introductory course in the principles of economics should not be a stranger to economic theory. At a somewhat simplified level, he has already been introduced to many economic theories. The theory of national income determination and the theory of marginal utility are perhaps the two most likely to be remembered, but a little concentration will help to recall a number of others also.

Theories of economics or any other subject originate basically through the theorist who searches for a pattern or a semblance of order in what appears at first glance ot be little more than a jumbled collection of facts. He attempts to discover certain features in the situation which are repetitive and to distinguish between those which are causal and those which are merely reactions in response to others. In order to achieve this goal, the theorist makes use of the methods of induction and deduction. Deductive reasoning is the process of developing a theory on the basis of certain generally known facts, causes, and relationships. From these "knowns," the theorist attempts to supply through the use of his deductive powers the missing causes and effect which are less easily perceived. Whereas deductive theorizing involves moving from the general to the specific, inductive reasoning works in reverse. In this method, the theorist examines a multitude of facts and events empirically and attempts to derive certain broad generalizations therefrom. These generalizations can then serve as the basis for new deductive work. Although the need for a close interrelationship between the two methods is obvious, it seems fair to say that through much of the history of economic thought the deductive method has been considered more important. Thus economic theorists have more frequently tended to work from the general toward the specific rather than in the opposite direction. Inductive reasoning, while not completely alien to economic thought, has played a distinctly secondary role. Economic theorists, particularly the early ones, were inclined to believe that the basic principles of political economy could be readily discerned. The charge that they were "armchair" economists is not without some merit.

Simply stated, theory is a matter of observation coupled with inductive and deductive reasoning—like adding two plus two and hopefully arriving at the correct total. When the important elements have been separated out, inevitably a large mass of extraneous data remains. In this sense theory is abstract; it does not attempt to include all of the possible variables but only those most important. Since theory acquires usefulness when it helps us to predict or to explain why things happen as they do, the importance of a proper selection of variables is obvious.

An answer to the question of "why" may prove difficult to achieve at the level of simple observation and deduction, and therefore a more complicated analysis may be necessary. The construction of a theory now develops into an exercise in complicated logic. The theoretician starts with certain basic assumptions and builds, by a process of deductive reasoning, a theoretical model. The theoretician may go astray at two points: Either his basic assumptions may have been incorrect or the reasoning thereafter may prove faulty.

The assumptions may be false because the real world and the actual facts may not be as easy to perceive as might first be imagined. To select the most significant and relevant factors is not always an easy task. Furthermore, if the assumptions are to be of any value in helping the theorist to understand the situation to be analyzed, they must be usable or they must be capable of serving as a sound foundation for erecting his theory. For example, economists were loathe to abandon the model of perfect competition long after it was apparent that it frequently had little relevance to much of the real world about them. It was not that the economists were particularly stubborn forms of human beings, but rather that the model of perfect competition could be so easily developed and analyzed. As the theories of imperfect and monopolistic competition emerged, it soon became evident that many problems were created which even the complicated mathematics of game theory have been unable to solve.

One of the many difficulties which the theorist encounters is an inability to make all of his assumptions known either to his readers or himself. While the theorist, of necessity, should make clear his major assumptions, especially the assumptions which depart from those the reader might normally expect to obtain, the task of enumerating all of them would in many cases require an entire book. The theorist must therefore rely on the sympathetic intelligence of his readers to supply the missing background assumptions. Much wasted effort could be avoided if the critical reader recognized this basis for his disagreement with the stated theory.

Quite frequently theorists solve the problem of multitudinous assumptions by making the blanket assumption that virtually everything except that which is to be examined remains unchanged, thus referring to the assumption regularly used by early and present-day economists alike—the assumption of *ceteris paribus*. This Latin phrase meaning "other things being equal" is both an analytical necessity and a convenient way of ignoring a lot of things that do not fit one's theory. The use of *ceteris paribus* is a necessity because no theory can hope to encompass all the possible variables; instead, we seek those which are most significant. The assumption is then frequently made that other factors are unimportant or, if they are important, they do not change. Thus the importance of variation in any one factor can be separated out and studied in isolation. The obvious problem is, of course, that in the real world other changes do take place and these changes may produce important repercussions elsewhere in the system.

No theoretician in the social sciences pretends, even to himself, that his theory will cover all possible situations at all possible times. At best, the theory can only picture the normal expected pattern of events; it cannot hope to encompass all of the possible exceptional situations as well. This helps to explain why there are no real economic laws. A possible exception is the Malthusian Law of Population, but, as we shall see, this was so carefully qualified and hedged as to retain little meaning as a "law." Rather, the economist, like his fellow social scientists, is content with the discovery of "tendencies" or "propensities," thereby allowing for the exceptional or unusual case.

The economists whose writings appear in this text made frequent use of assumptions and employed them to build a model of the world as they saw it in order to better explain its operation. Occasionally there may be faults in the logic of some of the economists, but even the good students will have difficulty in finding many of these. When the great treatises in economics are read, particularly a difficult, abstract work such as that written by David Ricardo, one must read carefully and search for the writer's assumptions, whether they are explicit or implicit. The great economists rarely neglected or forgot their own assumptions, but the careless reader may miss them much too easily.

The crucial role played by assumptions can perhaps be made clearer if we cite the distinction between static and dynamic theory as an example. A static theory involves a heavy dosage of *ceteris paribus*. Suppose we wish to analyze the nature of the business cycle. We are fearful of confusing our picture with numerous changes not associated with periodic oscillations in business conditions, but with secular growth. We might wish to hold constant in our theoretical analysis such elements as population change, the amount of available capital, the state of technology, or changes in the output of the extractive industries. Holding all of these factors fixed might serve to simplify our analysis and thus help us to discover meaningful relationships that might otherwise be overlooked. But if we hold one or more of these factors constant, we may very well have missed a crucial relationship whose importance may outweigh or negate the theory erected on the assumption that no change in the possible variables occurred.

The concept of static analysis, if rigorously defined, would not even include the variation of the business cycle itself. A static analysis is highly monotonous in the sense that nothing changes; each day is nothing more than a repetition of the preceding day. A dynamic analysis which acknowledges the day-to-day changes is thus more realistic but at the same time less manageable.

As a theory develops beyond the first rudimentary stages, the interrelationships become increasingly complex and a model begins to emerge. In its simplest forms the model constitutes a verbal presentation of the system as the theoretician views it. As the analysis becomes more rigorous and the model more intricate and involved, it frequently becomes useful to express the model in mathematical language. Equations can now be devised for describing the interaction of the component parts of the model. Just as the good logician may make no errors in his deductions but may still fail to solve the problem because of faulty facts or assumptions, so may the good mathematical economist solve his equations with even greater precision but still fail to render a satisfactory solution.

We may summarize by saying that theory is an attempt to provide a meaningful skeleton for what appears at first to be a meaningless accumulation of events and facts. The theoretician generalizes in his attempt to formulate a theory. He seeks certain repetitive causal features and then builds his analysis on them. What he seeks is a method of explaining strange objects as familiar, and unexplained events as occurrences which seem new because they are being seen from a different viewpoint. In his efforts to be concise and to arrive at the crux of the issue, he will treat the problem in an abstract fashion and may, if his intellectual resources permit, utilize various mathematical tools of analysis. Strictly speaking, theorizing does not include the selection of assumptions; rather, the theory is developed on the basis of the assumptions made. Like any job of construction, however, the edifice thus erected is only as sound as the foundation upon which it rests.

At this point we must be careful to avoid a trap into which even good students frequently fall. "After all," they argue, "all of these are just theories and can't really be proved right or wrong anyway, so why worry?" There is, unfortunately, just enough truth in this assertion to make it plausible. As a result, many theories of even a highly improbable nature die extremely hard deaths. New and superior theories frequently become alternatives to rather than replacements for currently existing ones. And yet the good economist, like the good theoretician in general, is not completely without tools for testing.

We have already suggested that the reader should both ascertain the assumptions made in the book he is studying and test the logic of the structure erected on those assumptions. If both of these pass muster, other methods of further testing may be employed. Statistical evidence may be assembled which will either substantiate or challenge the theory's conclusions. No better illustration of this can be found than the extensive empirical data assembled with respect to the nature of the business cycle. Sometimes a case study approach will appear useful. The theory that workers move freely in response to wage incentives has been tested several times by the use of local labor market studies.

Sometimes the historian's services can be utilized. One of the advantages of historical study is to come closer to a controlled experiment. Careful scholarship can bring us to a closer observation of all the actions and reactions involved in a given situation. The most difficult of all tests to employ is the direct experiment itself. The reason for this is so obvious as to need little explanation—people cannot be manipulated in test tubes like bits of chemical particles; their actions are ever subject to the uncertainties of unexpected behavior. Because of the difficulties of applying the "world is my test tube" approach to social science research, the use of historical investigation is frequently resorted to as a means of testing and checking interrelationships and causal patterns. An important *caveat* should be noted, however. It is all too easy to confuse historical sequence with cause and effect. The mere fact that event B followed event A one or more times in the past provides us with no definite assurance that event B was somehow the result or outgrowth of event A. The stream of economic thought has sometimes been cluttered with theories "proved" by the events of history. Further investigation or subsequent events have shown them not to be "proved" at all. Bearing this warning in mind, we note that historical study can help us to confirm or reject some theories.

While these methods of testing have their limitations, students should not be led to conclude from this that as far as a matter of value judgments is concerned, one theory is as good as another. No better antidote to this belief can be prescribed than a careful study of the history of economic thought.

We are now prepared to answer the first of our two basic queries: Why is there a history of economic thought? Or to phrase our question in a slightly different manner: Why didn't Adam Smith say everything that needed to be said? We uncovered a small part of the truth in a preceding paragraph when it was stated that theories frequently become alternatives for other theories instead of displacing them. Life would become much simpler for the student if, when a new theory displaced an old one, all written reference to the previous theory were destroyed.

With no disparagement to Adam Smith, however, we must support the idea that a great deal more has been discovered in the field of economics since he wrote *Wealth of Nations*. While a few present-day economists sometimes talk as if nothing worthwhile in economics had been discovered since the time of Adam Smith or other economists such as John Stuart Mill and Alfred Marshall, they are in a distinct minority. What accounts for this record of progress in theory is the ability of any modern thinker to build on the structure already erected by predecessors such as those mentioned in the text above. Revisions may be nothing more than minor corrections in some previous thinker's line of thought, or they may be more substantial. While studying someone else's work, a reader may be stimulated to produce a whole new line of thought or begin to view the problem in an entirely different manner. New "truths" of the theory being studied may be uncovered. We can find an interesting illustration of this principle if we anticipate some of the material to be covered in succeeding chapters.

Both Adam Smith and David Ricardo offered versions of a labor theory of value which in effect explained the value of products in terms of the amount of labor necessary to produce the product. The manner in which Ricardo developed this analysis beyond Smith's simple presentation is an interesting story in itself, although too complex to be developed at this stage. But one point can be made: Neither Smith nor Ricardo saw any exploitation of labor involved in this explanation of value. Karl Marx, writing three quarters of a century after Smith, seized upon this labor theory of value and fashioned it into a full-blown attack on the injustices of the capitalist system. The thinking of two of the staunchest defenders of a laissez-faire system of free markets was therefore converted into a rationale for its overthrow. Innumerable instances of a less startling nature could also be cited, but it suffices at this point to call attention to their existence. Some of the economists we shall study acknowledge their indebtedness to their predecessors freely and without reservation; others, with as deep a debt, are less generous with their acknowledgments. The author hopes this book will help readers to find some of these links and the student should attempt continually to seek these chains of thought for himself.

New emphases are closely related to our first reason for a history of economic thought. One economist may feel that a previous economist placed insufficient stress on some aspect of the economic system or that he unduly magnified the importance of other factors. Again the names of two of the earliest economists come to mind—Adam Smith and David Ricardo. For example, Smith chose the problem of production as his central theme. Although he did not neglect the question of distribution entirely, the emphasis was clearly on means of increasing output and thus the wealth of the nation. Ricardo, on the other hand, felt that the central problem of an economic system was the issue of distribution and he chose to concentrate on this question to the virtual exclusion of the problem of production.

Thus far we have been talking as if the basic situation remained constant and only the descriptions and analyses of its nature varied from one observer to another. But of course the economic scene is always in a state of flux as well, sometimes changing abruptly and dramatically, sometimes changing slowly and almost imperceptibly. To the extent that the theories are to be models of the real economic world about us, so must they change in response to changing economic institutions. We have already seen the potential conflict in using assumptions which are both realistic and tractable. An inability to resolve this conflict successfully lies at the heart of the old saying that "it's all right in theory but no good in practice." In the final analysis, this adage is nonsense; if an idea does not work out in practice, it is not very good. The theory may be a perfectly good one when applied to a given situation; the difficulty lies in the fact that such a situation no longer exists. If it does exist, it does so with certain important modifications for which the assumptions of theory do not allow. One need not be a profound student of economic history to realize that the economic environment has changed tremendously since Adam Smith gave the operation of a pin factory as an illustration of the benefits of the division of labor. The growth of the large corporation, with its limited discretionary policy with respect to pricing policies, has produced serious qualification to, if not rejection of, Smith's principle of "consumer sovereignty." Modern advertising techniques serve to guide the consumer; his demands no longer guide the productive plans of the businessman. The existence of the corporation has also compelled economists to revise their theories of profit. When stockholders have little or nothing to say about the operation of the business, many of the old theories of profits based precisely on these functions fall by the wayside. Similarly, the expansion of modern banking systems, with their ability to create money, has dramatically altered theories of business cycle behavior and the sources of funds for the payment of wages. Even more striking is the fact that the Ricardian theory of rent came into full bloom at just about the time when agriculture and land ceased to play a dominant role in the English economy. As England became increasingly an industrial society, the importance of explanations of rent diminished.

This last illustration serves to bring us to a final reason for the existence of a continued history of economic thought. Just as situations and institutions may change, so may new and different problems arise. It is not surprising, for example, that no "general theory of unemployment" was developed until the 1930's. As the numerous critics of John Maynard Keynes' views have repeatedly pointed out, many of the seeds of his ideas can be found scattered in the works of numerous writers who preceded him. Writing nearly a century earlier, Thomas Malthus, the famed population expert, suggested that the economy might face the problem of inadequate demand. The fact that his suggestion received so little attention was not entirely, as Keynes has suggested, because Ricardo diverted theory into another direction with his analysis of conditions as they existed under full employment. It is unlikely that Ricardo's views would have won the day had the problem of recurring and persistent unemployment appeared to be more pressing and urgent. The Classical economists in picturing an economy of virtually full employment were but mirroring accurately the real world about them.

It is important, therefore, in gaining a clear understanding of the writings of the great economists of the past, to have a clear understanding of the historical background of the period in which each one wrote. What at first glance appears to be irrelevant or far removed from reality as viewed through modern-day eyes suddenly becomes very clear to the student as the original setting of the writing is given proper recognition. Part of the job of this book will be to provide the student with some of the relevant historical background as a setting for the study of the various writers.

It is now time to turn to the second of the two problems raised in the first paragraph of the chapter, namely, what a student will gain from a study of the history of economic thought. In part, the study of the history of economic thought provides the same function as the study of theory itself. Theory helps us to give facts a meaning and a structure; what at first appears as a meaningless jumble emerges into a meaningful pattern as the theory provides us with a kind of guideline map. In addition, theory helps us to prepare questions and hypotheses capable of being tested by empirical investigation. The study of the history of economics helps us to put these theories in perspective. Not only can we obtain a clear understanding of how we arrived at our current state of economic knowledge, but we hope that this study will help us to avoid making the same errors. Students should get a sense of the development of thought through time and they should simultaneously acquire an ability to apply the principles and techniques of thinking to problems of current interest.

Few, if any, would maintain that the works we are about to study constitute light summertime reading. They include difficult books, written by men with keen analytical minds. Sometimes the books are poorly organized and studded with obscure phrasing. There are two bright rays of hope, however, to console the student lest he become too discouraged before he begins. To a certain extent, these books have been great because they are so difficult. It is not always possible to express important or complex ideas in simple terms and still maintain their quality. Furthermore, the student who has struggled to master Keynes' *General Theory* or Ricardo's *Principles* has a kind of vested interest in them. Not only has he had his intellectual powers stretched and expanded, but the effort involved means that the material and logic acquired is less likely to be ephemeral but to remain with him for years to come.

Although the books are difficult, they are also challenging. The reader finds himself conversing with some of the greatest minds in history as he follows their written conversations with each other. These books were written not merely as scholarly additions to the world's economic literature, although this is what they have proved to be, but they are much more. The books become quite meaningful when it is realized that each contains a plea for reform and change, and the reader who fails to recognize this second feature is missing one of their great qualities. Save, perhaps, for some of the members of the Marginal Utility School, it is difficult to think of a great economist of the past who was not a passionate reformer. One might even go further and argue that the economists' ability to constructively criticize the way in which current problems were being handled was one of the qualities that made their writings so enduring.

Each of the writers we are about to study was concerned with different problems or with a variant of a similar problem. The economic problems of the day as seen by Keynes, for example, are a far cry from those as viewed by Adam Smith. Again, both Smith and Ricardo fought for free trade, but their rationales for doing so were quite different. Even Ricardo's abstract method of discussion becomes more comprehensible when we realize that his theories were styled in such a way as to bring drastic changes in English trade policy.

Judged by the standards of numerous modern-day economic theorists, many of the writers we are about to study were guilty of a cardinal sin. Few of these great economists ever hesitated to make moral judgments whenever they felt the need existed. Even the beginning student is aware that this was true for someone like Marx, whose whole analysis of capitalism, scientific as he may have attempted to make it, was predicated on the judgment that capitalism was evil and must be overthrown. The result blinded him partially, though not completely, to the things capitalism might achieve. As the works of other authors are read, it will become equally evident that they also share in the "sin" of moral judgments.

There is always the danger, of course, that the scholar will be so blinded by his system of values or his ideology as to betray his function as a scientist. If he becomes a special pleader who blinds himself to those facts which do not fit his argument and chooses for his goal the proving of his case rather than the uncovering of the truth, his effectiveness as a scholar is correspondingly diminished. It is also true that some of the economic theories of the past may have been accorded more attention than they merited because of the ideology involved. The appeal of Marxism lies in its moral fervor rather than in its complex economic reasoning; many of Marx's most ardent followers have not even read the *Communist Manifesto,* let alone his ponderous three-volume study, *Das Kapital.*

Those economists who are most critical of their fellow practitioners who make value judgments, and who treat such judgments as a major sin, fear the loss of the scientific character of economics as a social science. As students of one of the social sciences, they prefer to emphasize the scientific rather than the social character of their discipline. To them, it is more fitting for the society to make decisions as to the proper direction of the economy. Should it have a faster rate of growth? Should there be more equal distribution of income? Should the rate of unemployment be held to less than 5 percent? Once the society has decided upon the answers to these and similar questions, these economists would argue, then the economist can, with his theoretical tools of analysis, provide advice as to the best means of achieving goals agreed upon by the economy.

There are, of course, certain areas of investigation in economics where the scholar can feel reasonably assured that his various built-in biases will have no effect on either his choice of assumptions or his subsequent analysis; one can remain safely indifferent as to the moral values of the indifference curve. But the majority of issues in economics can not be confined to matters of fact supported by logic. As the economist Kenneth Boulding once observed, "Science is a process in which unimportant questions which can be answered are substituted for the important questions which have no answers." If economics is to have value as anything more than a pure intellectual exercise, it must inevitably deal with policy issues of a controversial nature. When the economist becomes so blinded by his ideology that he becomes little more than a special pleader, he loses, of course, much of his claim as a scientist. Even then, the loss from the point of view of the discipline or the economy is not fatal. The real safeguard lies not in the economist remaining silent on certain issues, but in the assurance that his views will be criticized and corrected by his fellow economists. We frequently hear of the damage wreaked on capitalism by Marx's savage attack. Yet the very force of this attack not only provoked a spirited defense from other economists but also stimulated the adoption of a number of important reforms which served (in the author's judgment) to strengthen rather than weaken the capitalistic system.

Strictly interpreted, the logic of the group of economists who would outlaw all value judgments would involve forfeiture of much of the educational value derived when economists make recommendations, which are then subject to the criticism of fellow economists. This, of course, was exactly what the great economists of the past were attempting to accomplish, and many of them undoubtedly would have felt that they were grossly neglecting their duty if they did not speak out and offer solutions to issues, solutions which, while not always capable of scientific proof, were nevertheless needed. How could the public otherwise render well-informed decisions if it did not have an opportunity to hear the testimony of those thinkers who were most expert in economic affairs, the economists themselves?

As we have already made clear, not all economists would agree with our assessment of the inevitability of value judgments, but all would be forced to acknowledge that the great economists of the past were more than willing to express their opinions about subjects which could not be scientifically proved. The history of economic thought emerges partly from the fact that these ideas were repeatedly criticized and reformulated by succeeding generations of economists.

At this point we can say that economists do have a sufficient impact on public opinion and legislative bodies to make a sufficient difference. A statement made by John Maynard Keynes is so relevant at this point that it deserves quoting in full. Keyes wrote:

The ideas of economists and political philosophers, both when they are right and when they are wrong, are more powerful than is commonly understood. Indeed the world is ruled by little else. Practical men, who believe themselves to be quite exempt from any intellectual influences, are usually the slaves of some defunct economist. Madmen in authority, who hear voices in the air, are distilling their frenzy from some academic scribbler of a few years back.[1]

Others would argue that Keynes grossly overestimated the power of economic ideas and assert instead that the forces of history would have produced much the same policies even in the absence of any economist's advice. In a sense this issue is merely a variation of the old historical problem: Does man make history or does history make the man? Those

[1] John Maynard Keynes, *The General Theory of Employment, Interest, and Money* (New York: Harcourt, Brace and Company, 1935), p. 383.

who maintain that men make history point to the impact on the world of forceful personalities such as Napoleon, Julius Caesar, and Alexander the Great. Would the present-day world be the same, they argue, if there had been no Hitler, Stalin, Churchill, or Roosevelt? Those critics who would minimize the importance of individual men answer that social and economic conditions existing at the time produce a Napoleon or a Roosevelt, and if they had not been born, someone else would have filled the positions in much the same manner.

Whichever view of history the reader prefers to accept, he should not thereby conclude that the same conclusion can be applied to the field of economic thought. Goverments may be overthrown, wars may be lost only to be rewon another day, but ideas once clearly expressed tend to live with us for generation after generation. This is not to deny that the events occurring around them did not shape the thinking of the writers we shall study: we have already suggested that the response of economists to these changing events serves as a partial explanation of why there is a history of thought. It does suggest, however, that their ideas, once expressed, continue to play an important role in our thinking years after the authors' lifetimes.

Students of economic thought have argued, for example, that Smith's attack on trade restrictions actually had little or no bearing on subsequent Parliamentary action and that mention of Smith's book was rarely if ever heard. Whether such negative evidence is actually conclusive, who can deny that his ideas have continued to be approvingly cited down to the present day? Would the ideas set forth by Smith have survived so persistently if they had been fashioned by a less skillful craftsman? In reading these books, therefore, the students should ask himself not only what contribution the book makes to our understanding of the science of economics, but what was its impact upon the society at the time and on the course of future events. Studied in this fashion, the books cease to be old and outdated and assume a new meaning and dimension.

One final point needs attention before we begin our examination of these great economists. Although we have entitled our book *The Great Economists: A History of Economic Thought,* we will find that many of our early writers make little reference to economics as such; their books are called *Principles of Political Economy,* or some variation thereof. The student must wait until he studies Alfred Marshall before finding a book titled simply *Principles of Economics.* Yet a brief glance through the contents of any of these early books will reassure the beginning economics student that he is studying the proper subject. Political economy is the older term, which encompassed a broader range of study. (Economics it-self had not yet developed all of its multitudinous specialities.) At an earlier time, the link between the analysis of governmental action and economic problems was in some ways even clearer than it is today. It is ironic that the early writers who, in general, believed that governmental action was a drain on the economy and must be kept to a minimum, should see their study as a kind of state bookkeeping.[2] With this qualifica-tion, it remains true that all of the writers we will study would, while defining the nature of the subject in different ways, basically agree on what subject material was appropriate. In doing so they have set the stage for our continuing study of the subject.

[2] The term political economy dates back to the seventeenth century and was ap-plied to the study and writings of the Cameralists. This latter term applied to those economic advisers who served as economic experts for the numerous princely states existing in Europe at the time. As the followers of Adam Smith began to adopt the term as an embracing description of their field of study, the earlier political economists became known as Mercantilists.

CHAPTER II: Early Economic Thinkers

From ivory towers the philosophers looked down on a pulsing economic world and decided that buying and selling were human activities that merited study. . . .

The hope that economics might become a systematic discipline inspired the labors of other scholars not formally trained in philosophy.

—E. A. J. JOHNSON

Economic problems are as old as man himself. The caveman had to make economic decisions, whether he was aware of the fact or not, and anthropologists have developed a special field of economic anthropology from their studies of primitive peoples. Fragmentary passages dealing with the origin of value can be found in the writings of Plato and Aristotle. A consideration of economic questions can also be found in passages of the Old and New Testaments; at least two doctoral dissertations focusing on the subject of economics are known to the author. It would thus be possible to start our study well before the coming of Christ and cite the writings of some early thinkers, but we will comment only on Aristotle's viewpoint in this particular period. We will also briefly sketch the economic views of another early philosopher, St. Thomas Aquinas, and those of a group of economic predecessors called the Mercantilists, before we begin our formal tracing of the development of economic thought with Adam Smith, the "father of political economy."

Aristotle and Aquinas cannot properly be called economists, but the writings of each reflected the economic conditions prevailing at the time, and each raised relevant economic questions. Their writings are interesting forerunners of later economic thinking and also provide a marked contrast with later writings.

ARISTOTLE (384–322 B.C.)

The Greeks disliked any study of economic life. Neither Aristotle nor his teacher Plato could find anything complimentary to say about the process of engaging in business. Both regarded it as a necessary evil not really suitable for the citizens of the state.

The Man. Aristotle was born in Stagira, the son of the court physician for Amyntas II. He later served as tutor of Alexander the Great, the grandson of his father's employer. At the age of 17, Aristotle was sent to Athens, where he enrolled in Plato's school and remained there for 20 years, until his teacher's death. Shortly after leaving Athens, Aristotle married the adopted daughter of Hermias the Tyrant, whom he served for a brief time. Aristotle became Alexander's tutor and returned to Athens to set up his own school when the conqueror set out on his Asiatic conquests. He continued teaching philosophy until a change of government following the death of Alexander led to a charge of impiety against the philosopher. Aristotle then fled to Chalcis, where he died. He was a prolific writer in the field of philosophy, and his major economic views are to be found in his *Nicomachean Ethics* and his *Politics*.

Economic Views. While there were parts of Aristotle's writings on economic maters which later writers could find laudable, much of his views were in sharp contrast to those expressed in later centuries. Unlike his teacher, Plato, for example, Aristotle took a dim view of communal property. This view is fully shared by the Classical School of economists discussed in Chapters III to VI. Aristotle was a good early capitalist, and his defense of private property was couched in the now familiar incentive terms of how the acquisition and ownership of property spurred men on to greater effort. His definition of property dealt mainly with the household. Emphasis was placed on tangibles, and intangibles were virtually excluded. A further mark of the times in which he wrote was Aristotle's endorsement of slavery and his inclusion of slaves as a form of property.

In his defense of property, Aristotle argued that it was not the institution of property that was the evil, but the manner in which it was employed by men. Aristotle agreed with Plato's diagnosis that most men were selfish and avaricious beings. Evidently some of Plato's preachments against property bore fruit, for Aristotle, despite his general championing of property rights, was willing to impose some restrictions upon inheritance.

Much of Aristotle's discussion of economic questions involved household problems. Trade took place because the household was unable to satisfy its wants. This subject inevitably led to Aristotle's topic of value. Through this Aristotle developed a distinction which played a primary role in later economic writing: the difference between value in use and value in exchange.

In keeping with his distaste for trade and business, Aristotle greatly preferred use value to value in exchange. He used a shoe as an example to distinguish between the two. A shoe had value for the use it brought to its owner, but it also could be used to trade for other things. Such exchange arose from the normal course of events, as households found themselves with a surplus of some commodities and an inability to supply others. When exchange took place, it was natural to inquire how the value of the product was to be determined. Aristotle was not too clear on this point, but he seems to have suggested that any two articles should exchange at a rate commensurate with the amount of effort involved in their production, after allowing for disparities in the kinds of work involved. We shall see that this problem of equating different kinds of labor remained a stumbling block for later labor value theorists also.

Aristotle's objections to value in exchange arose from the fact that exchange did not stop when households were able to satisfy their needs, but it increasingly became a way of life and a way to wealth. As such, it was a path that Aristotle would have preferred men not to tread, for when men traded for profit, the principle of getting only a fair and just return from the exchange was lost.

His evaluation of exchange led Aristotle to an examination of the role of money. Money grew out of the inconvenience involved in relying upon barter, and it served all of the functions which we deem most important for money today, as a medium of exchange, a store of value, and a method of account. Offsetting these advantages was the fact that money itself might figure in exchanges over time and involve a cost to the borrower for its use.

Aristotle was even more determined in his opposition to interest payments than he was to exchange. He conceded that some exchange could be useful, provided it was conducted in such a way as to benefit both parties. Interest, however, was a payment for the use of a sterile object—money—and as such could never be justified. Later economists were to object to this attack, pointing out that money as a factor of production could be used to increase the productive capacity of a plant and thus justifiably bear the cost of being borrowed. For such cases Aristotle was clearly wrong, but his error is more a mark of the period than a flaw in his thinking. Virtually all loans in Aristotle's time were for purposes of consumption.

Summary and Evaluation. The intellectual greatness of Aristotle is beyond dispute; he was *the* philosopher of his age. Although he anticipated some of the problems which were to plague later economists, it is difficult to think of Aristotle himself as an economist. No modern economist would be willing to think of his subject matter as being undignified, as Aristotle did. His attack upon interest and his emphasis upon the need for exchange to take place in such a way as to benefit both parties provided a model for subsequent writers such as the thirteeth-century philosopher, St. Thomas Aquinas.

ST. THOMAS AQUINAS (1225–1274)

St. Thomas Aquinas was even less of an economist than Aristotle had been, but he stands alone as the philosopher of his century in much the same manner as Aristotle had during the period in which he lived.

The Man. St. Thomas was born in a castle near Aquino, Italy. His formal connection with the Catholic Church began at the age of 18, when he entered the order of preaching friars founded by St. Dominic. St. Thomas continued the pursuit of his studies at Cologne, where he became a teacher. The remainder of his life was spent teaching and writing on religious and philosophical questions. He taught in Paris and later in Italy at Rome and Pisa. St. Thomas died while journeying to a council at Lyons, to which he had been summoned by Pope Gregory. He was subsequently canonized by Pope John XXII. His most celebrated work was his *Summa Theologica.*

Economic Views. While at Cologne, much of St. Thomas' early writing was an appraisal of the philosophy of Aristotle. It is not surprising, therefore, that many of St. Thomas' economic writings followed along the lines laid down by the Greek master. St. Thomas' contribution to economic thinking is best remembered by his formulation of the concept of "just price" and his attack on usury. At the same time his views represent to some extent a compromise with the economic realities of the world about him, just as Aristotle's views had made pragmatic concessions to the necessity of exchange.

Early Church fathers had expressed strong criticisms of private property, worldly possessions, and the business world in general. By the thirteenth century, however, an economic system based upon an extensive system of local and international trade had developed, and this meant that the heavy religious opposition of early days was increasingly out of step with the world as it then existed. One of St. Thomas' efforts was to reconcile Christian doctrine with the economic world about him.

St. Thomas' solution to this dilemma followed the line of reasoning set forth by Aristotle: It was not the institution of private property that was at fault but the manner in which men employed it. This qualified endorsement of owning private property inevitably led to a reluctant acceptance of trade. Like Aristotle, St. Thomas regarded trade as a blemish on the perfection of things, but went a step further, regarding it as an unfortunately inevitable blemish. Since trade could not be eliminated, it was important to set standards for its conduct in order that its evil could be minimized. The merchant could be justified in his activity when it contributed to the welfare of the society and earned him no more than was necessary to maintain his position in the society.

The concept of "just" price which had been implicit in Aristotle's writings, as well as those of earlier church fathers, was *polished* and *refined*. However, St. Thomas never clearly defined what he meant by "just" price, perhaps an inevitable result of attempting to apply ethical considerations to a business question. He appeared to adopt Aristotle's view that things should exchange at their true value in terms of cost of production, thus rendering the trader's justifiable profit a payment for his efforts.

Price by itself was no assurance that an equitable exchange had been made, St. Thomas observed, since recognition also had to be given to the quality of the product in question. Part of the difficulty in discerning exactly what St. Thomas meant by his "just" price arises from the way in which he was willing to see his standard qualified. Whereas the seller who unknowingly sold a product with a defect committed no sin, he was obligated to reimburse the buyer his purchase price should the latter be dissatisfied. On the other hand, a product with obvious defects could be properly sold if the seller decreased the price, even though he did not call the buyer's attention to these defects. To this extent, St. Thomas was willing to let the buyer's own powers of observation be his source of protection. Further concessions involved the right of the seller to sell above the "just" price where his own valuation of the particular commodity exceeded the fair (cost of production) value. Possible oscillations around the "just" price occasioned by changing market conditions also bothered St. Thomas, but since the market was less fully developed at that time than it was later, this problem was less serious than it might have been.

St. Thomas rested his case against usury on the same grounds advanced by Aristotle. Money was barren and therefore no price for its use was justifiable. St. Thomas saw no sin in borrowing; the sin lay in the interest charged by the lender. For this reason he viewed the "buy now, pay later" schemes, which resulted in a higher price to the buyer, as an evil. Curiously enough, however, he saw no sin in a reduction in price where payment was made in advance of the date specified in the sale. The logic of the second position in the face of his condemnation of interest is somewhat difficult to resolve.

Summary and Evaluation. Neither of the two major tenets in the writings of St. Thomas Aquinas and Aristotle was attractive to the classical economists or to most of the writers who were to follow. We have already noted that the opposition to interest can be more easily rationalized in a time setting when virtually all borrowing is for consumption purposes. Similarly, a "just" price is more easily defended in an era when the forces of the market have not yet been fully developed and the power of competition is too weak to provide adequate protection to consumers.

THE MERCANTILISTS (1500–1800)

Mercantilism was one of the doctrines which played a major role in shaping the development of later economic thinking. Among its adherents are such men as David Hume, John Locke, James Stewart, Thomas Mun, Dudley North, and William Petty,[1] in England; Antoine de Montchré-

---

[1] Although the label Mercantilist can be attached more fairly to Sir William Petty (1623–1687) than to Hume, it is also only fair to add that Petty was a much more profound economic thinker than our general description of the school suggests. If we had not chosen to reserve the honor for Adam Smith, the title "father of political economy" might have been bestowed with considerable justification on Petty. One can find in his writing an anticipation of many lines of thought of be developed by later writers: Adam Smith's division of labor, Böhm von Bawerk's role of capital and his roundabout means of promoting employment. In setting labor as the determinant of value, Petty sought to find some relationship beween value and market price. Here, again, he set a course for numerous economic thinkers to follow. His explanation of rent as a surplus derived from land demonstrated that he saw rent as a result of price rather than a component part. He also anticipated Ricardo on the nature of differential rent. Petty's analysis would have won more recognition, perhaps, if it had not been widely scattered through a number of books.

tien and Jean Baptiste Colbert in France; Phillip von Hoenick in Germany; and Antonio Serra in Italy.

Although Mercantilist thought prevailed for over three centuries in England and on the European continent, with remnants still to be found today, it never succeeded in developing a real theoretical structure. The list of names included above is surprising because most of the members of this school were practical men of business or statesmen. Churchmen and university scholars, with few exceptions, are notably missing.

Because Mercantilism lasted for so many generations and was supported in varying degrees by so many different writers, it is difficult to give a precise and accurate summary of its general content. Many writers have solved this by summarizing the views of four or more writers who exemplify variations in Mercantile thought. Since our objective is to discuss Mercantilism as it affected Adam Smith, we will forego such a detailed discussion. Students interested in more information should consult the bibliography at the end of this book.

The early emergence of Mercantile thought toward the end of the fourteenth and the start of the fifteenth century is connected to two profound historical events—the discovery of the New World, with its vast supplies of gold bullion, and the emergence of the national state. The sudden inflow of gold to England and the Continent made its acquisition and retention of great importance since there was now that much more to be acquired and retained.

The interaction between Mercantilism and the emerging national states was more subtle. The preceding historical period, sometimes referred to as the Medieval Era, was a strange blending of internationalism and petty localism. The Catholic Church dominated all religious life, and Latin was the language of scholars and religious and political leaders alike. At the same time, local baronies and principalities established their own trade rules and restricted the access of foreign merchants to the local markets. A central feature of Mercantilism was the efforts of its spokesmen to overcome these local restrictions and place the power to regulate the economy in the hands of a national sovereign. In so doing, they destroyed the international aspects of feudal society.

Put in its simplest terms, Mercantilist thought emphasized a need for continuous governmental interference in economic affairs to assure the proper functioning of the economy. Countries such as Spain and Holland were cited by the Mercantilists as glowing examples of what could be achieved under such supervision. To achieve this goal, it was deemed necessary to build a strong central government with sufficient power to control the activities of its own citizens and to ward off threatened encroachments from other states. For this reason, later students of Mercantilism such as Gustav von Schmoller, the nineteenth-century German economist of the Historical School, described Mercantilism as little more than "state-making."

The emergence of the national state, with its ability to provide standards for trading, to furnish a national currency and the security of property against attack, was a necessary stage in economic development. Smith and his followers quarreled not with the notion of a central national government, but with the uses to which that central government was put by the Mercantilists. The struggle with local governments was a difficult one, and resistance to national rule was great. If the number of rules and regulations laid down by the central government was great (and it most assuredly was), the violations and general disregard for these rules was also great. Haphazard enforcement meant that stiff monetary fines lost their effectiveness because of the infrequency with which they were imposed.

The Mercantilists, particularly the early members of the school, known as the Bullionists, have been frequently pictured as writers who confused gold and money with true wealth. While a preoccupation with the acquisition of gold was a dominant part of the thinking of all the Mercantilists, it seems only fair to add that they wanted gold for their country for what it would buy—but not for the *finer* things in life. The importation of luxuries was to be prohibited, and where the "finer" things could not be produced at home, the people should forego their enjoyment rather than waste the nation's supply of gold in purchasing them. Rather, gold was important for what it could buy the state—materials of war, equipment, and even soldiers. This, after all, was the era of the paid mercenaries. The state could hire citizens of other countries—even from those countries unfriendly to it—to help fight its wars.

As applied to international trade, this theory led to the imposition of various trade restrictions designed to reduce the volume of foreign competition with home industries, while at the same time it offered active support to those same home industries by means of various subsidies. The Bullionists saw a direct and simple means of maintaining a nation's stockpile of gold—simply prevent its shipment abroad—even if it was worthwhile for trade purposes. If it never left the country, there was no cause to worry whether or not it would ever return. As the volume of trade between countries increased, the handicaps rendered to merchants by such a rule became increasingly obvious. Later Mercantilists, while no less convinced of the importance of maintaining the country's supply of gold, sought a more flexible method. Emphasis was now placed on maintaining a favorable balance of trade. The balance between exports and imports should be tipped in favor of exports. As long as more was exported than was imported, merchants in other countries would have to make up the difference by shipments of gold. The greater the discrepancy between exports and imports, the more gold that would flow into the country and the more favorable the trade balance would become.

The fact that Mercantilist thought was important in so many different countries led none of the writers to the obvious conclusion that not all nations could gain in this way. A favorable balance of trade for one country must inevitably entail unfavorable balances elsewhere. Virtually all of the writers, from whatever country, believed that the betterment of a single nation's economic welfare could come only at the expense of other nations—one country's gain was inevitably another country's loss. The possiblitity that all nations could benefit from a general broadening of international trade was alien to all of the Mercantilists.

Mercantilist policy was not limited to the international scene, however. The Mercantilists saw state action as the most efficient and economical method of raising the nation's produtive levels. In part, state interference was an inevitable product of Mercantilist trade policy. When foreign supplies were cut off, home supplies had to be increased or use of the commodity foregone. Thus the state was faced with a role in assuring the establishment of needed if uneconomical trades. The proper ordering of the system, in the Mercantilists' view, could be assured only by a sizable amount of government intervention and direction. While ownership could remain in private hands, production plans and policies were to be under the direction of the state. Again, we should remember that Smith's attack on Mercantilism was directed not only against its trade policy but against its domestic policy as well.

The relative position of the various groups in the economy as seen by the Mercantilists is also of some interest. They were, of course, most interested in raising the economic position of the merchant class—a fact not too surprising in terms of the number of Mercantilists who were themselves merchants.

The Mercantilists considered agriculture an important but not dominant part of the economy. This general minimization of agriculture can be explained by their feeling that it added little to a nation's export balance and hence little to the supply of gold.

The position of the working classes under Mercantilism was not a par-

ticularly happy one, either. Most of the Mercantilists took a dim view of
the qualities of the working poor. They considered them to be lazy, unsatisfactory workers, who needed constant supervision if they were to produce anything useful. Nor did the Mercantilists conceive of higher wage
rates as a means of creating added incentive. In their view, higher wages
were likely to make workers less industrious (an argument which was an
anticipation of the "backward sloping supply curve of labor" theory of
later years). In order to maintain a favorable balance of trade, it was
important that prices remain stable. Rising prices would quite possibly
lessen the attractiveness of a nation's exports to foreigners, while falling
prices would be attractive to customers in other lands but would discour-
age domestic business enterprise. The best of all possible worlds for a
Mercantilist would, of course, be the opportunity to "buy cheap" and "sell
dear." While some were guilty of confusing the terms of trade with the
balance of trade, the charge cannot properly be leveled at all Mercantilists, and many of them were antagonistic to wage increase on the above
grounds. This limitation on changes in the price level precluded the granting of higher money wages. The usual solution provided today for afford-
ing higher wages is to raise the level of efficiency, but the Mercantilists
had little faith in the possibility of raising the level of average productivity; any increase in productivity a nation might achieve came as a result of
increasing total productivity by expanding the size of the labor force.
Workers were thus perpetually doomed to a low level of wages. Viewed
from the vantage point of the entire economy, this was beneficial, since
low wages served to check the demand of workers for consumer goods,
thus making available a larger volume of products for the consumer. In
addition, it served as a means of keeping the price of export goods attractive.

Herein lay one of the weaknesses of Mercantilism. In its crudest form,
it made no provision for enhancing the welfare of the majority of the
citizens; it was enough that the state and the merchants prospered. The
possibility of economic growth was recognized, but its benefits were extended to a limited few. The one group which gained from growth was the
merchants, but again it should be emphasized that this would be true only
for the merchants in those countries which won the competitive struggle
to export more than they imported.

Mercantile philosophy met with varying degrees of success in Spain,
but was widely accepted in England. In France it was only partially successful, while in Italy and Germany it was a complete failure. The eventual demise of Mercantilism has frequently been attributed to the effec-

tiveness of Smith's attacks, but it is doubtful whether or not it could have survived much longer in any case. Even its supporters came to have more and more reservations about some of its tenets. We have already seen that the crude solution for preserving the gold supply suggested by the Bullionists found little support among later Mercantilists. Increasing sophistication about the gains from trade and the role of money developed through the years.

DAVID HUME (1711–1776)

David Hume was one of the last writers to toy with Mercantilist ideas but his views were in many ways so enlightened as to raise doubts about the propriety of including him with that group.

The combination of David Hume's friendship with Adam Smith and his fame as a philosopher has led many students to overemphasize his contribution to economics. On the other hand, it would be unfair to leave the reader with the impression that he was guilty of all the errors involved in the Mercantilist thought. At the very worst, Hume can be described as an enlightened Mercantilist who favored the merchant class. Hume is best remembered in economics for his early enunciation of a clear if somewhat crude form of the quantity theory of money, and also for his development of the price specie flow. According to the quantity theory, a nation which lost money would suffer a consequent reduction in prices which would so encourage foreign buyers that the supply of money would be speedily restored. An excess of money in a country would work in reverse fashion. His view that this could operate without any need for government intervention was enough by itself to endear him to Smith.

Hume, best known as a political philosopher, was not particularly original as an economic thinker; many of his ideas were borrowed from other Mercantile writers, particularly John Locke. Although he continued to champion the merchant as one of God's great gifts to mankind, he recognized that money was but a symbol of wealth and declared that the amount of money which a nation possessed was not really very important. Furthermore, a strong central government, which had been so appealing at the close of the Medieval Era, when everything was in a state of chaos, became increasingly less so to the later Mercantilists when its restrictions hampered the freedom of businessmen to seek profits.

CHAPTER III: Adam Smith—Beginnings of Political Economy

> . . . the whole of political economy
> might be divided into two parts—before
> and since Adam Smith; the first part
> being a prelude and the second a sequel
> (in the way either of continuation or
> opposition to him).
>
> —WILHELM ROSCHER

ADAM SMITH (1723–1790)

Adam Smith's first name is peculiarly appropriate, since it is generally agreed that he was the "father of political economy" and the first real economist deserving the title. Smith's studies were the first economic works attempting to encompass the range of fields included under the heading economics and to combine empirical observations with reasoned theoretical treatment. Not only was Smith the first economist, but fortunately he was one of the best as well. His work served as an admirable starting point for the economists to follow. Virtually every writer following Smith who treated the subject of wage differentials began his analysis by repeating Smith's five explanations of this difference, to be discussed later in this chapter. A number of these writers amended or qualified these reasons in various ways but acknowledged their indebtedness to Smith. Similarly, Smith's four canons of taxation, also to be discussed later, have served as a model for students in the field of government finance.

Back in the days when the assigning of a date for the start of the Industrial Revolution was done more frequently than it is today, someone remarked that the year 1776 was famous for three revolutions: the start of the Industrial Revolution, the proclamation of the American Revolution against England, and the publication of Smith's book marking a revolution in economic thought. Who was this man Adam Smith, who by publishing his *Wealth of Nations* heralded the beginning of a new social science?

The Man. There has never been a long and lively biography of Smith written, nor is it likely that there ever will be. The sad fact is that Smith, who lived a quiet and rather uneventful life, was poor fodder for the aspiring biographers. In all too many ways Smith fits the caricature of the typical college professor—absentminded to a high degree, apt to sink into reveries of preoccupied thought, able to ignore events taking place about him. A somewhat shambling walk and a shrill voice, both of which were perhaps a product of some nervous ailment, complete the picture.

Nor can one paint a picture of happy domesticity. Adam Smith remained a confirmed bachelor. He was a good son and lived with his mother in her later years until she died at the age of 90.

The founder of the study of political economy was not an economist by profession but a professor of moral philosophy. He was educated at Oxford and upon graduation he was offered a chair of law at the University of Glasgow, which shortly thereafter was converted into a chair of moral philosophy. The breadth of subjects covered by the term moral philosophy was very wide, ranging from theology to political economy. Thus Smith's preoccupation with the wealth of nations is not as strange as it might seem at first glance.

Nevertheless, Smith's first book, published in 1759 and titled *The Theory of Moral Sentiments,* came much closer in content to what we might expect a moral philosopher to write about today. This book provides an interesting sidelight on Smith's thinking and raises doubts about the interpretation of Smith as an individual who conceived of individuals acting only in their own self-interest. Instead, Smith may more appropriately be characterized as the "other directed" David Reisman of the eighteenth century. In *The Theory of Moral Sentiments,* Smith maintained that men were highly sensitive to the opinions of others and acted in such a way as to assure themselves of the esteem and the affection of their fellow men. The contrast between this phase of Smith's thinking and the usual conception of his views is striking and partly of Smith's own making. Attempts to reconcile his two books have never, in the author's view at least, been entirely successful, but we must be careful to avoid the temptation to dismiss Smith's earlier message and accept the popular interpretation at full face value. A careful reading of *Wealth of Nations* reveals that, although Smith warned the consumer not to rely on the kindness of the businessman for protection, he constantly appealed to the capitalists' "better nature." [1]

No biographer would fail to point out that the eighteenth century was truly a century notable for the outstanding minds which flourished during the period. Smith knew a number of these men and got some of his inspiration from them. His contacts with Benjamin Franklin, for example, probably led Smith to his optimistic views about the future of the American colonies. His contacts with the French economists, the Physiocrats, will be considered in some detail shortly. Perhaps most interesting, however, is his close personal friendship with many members of the Mercantilist School. Thus Smith was a warm admirer and friend of David Hume —an admiration, incidentally, which was to involve Smith in some difficulty at the University of Glasgow, where Hume was considered to be a dangerous freethinker. Another person who befriended Smith was Lord Townshend, originator of the infamous Townshend Acts designed to collect revenue from the American colonists. It was arranged for Smith to act as Townshend's stepson's tutor on a trip to France, an arrangement which afforded him close contact with the formulators of Physiocratic thought.

Smith's second book, *Wealth of Nations,* which was to serve as the foundation of economics, was "a long time a-brewing"; it took nearly ten years to assemble and write. It has taken even longer to achieve full interpretation and recognition, despite the fact that virtually every writer in economics for the next century began his analyses with a review of Smith's writings.

It is impossible to fully understand Smith's contribution, however, unless we are aware of the ideas and policies to which he was reacting, so we shall briefly sketch another school of thought which played a major role in shaping Smith's own views, the group called the Physiocrats.

THE PHYSIOCRATS (1750–1780)

For purposes of discussion and summary, the Physiocrats are a far more manageable group than were the Mercantilists. Largely confined to the geographical boundaries of France (although they did acquire a few unlikely disciples such as Empress Catherine of Russia), their influence was

---

[1] The apparent conflicting views of human nature never appeared to disturb Smith. *The Theory of Moral Sentiments* went through six editions, with the final one appearing in 1796. Only in this last edition were there any substantial changes, and even here the changes made reveal no indication that Smith saw any conflict in the two books.

of short duration. The number of major representative figures in the school is correspondingly small, and we will note in detail only two: François Quesnay and Anne Robert Jacques Turgot. Of the two, Quesnay is perhaps the more striking figure, both in his role as the formulator of Physiocratic thought and in his personal life.

FRANÇOIS QUESNAY (1694–1774)

The Man. Quesnay was the son of a lawyer, who died shortly after his son's birth; the younger Quesnay was raised in the country and did not learn to read until he was 12. At the age of 16, he began his life's career as a doctor, when he became an apprentice to a surgeon. Later his success in his chosen career in medicine was assured when he became court physician to Louis XV and Madame de Pompadour. Quesnay's interest in economics came late in his life and he did not begin writing in the field until he was past 60.

Physiocratic Views. Quesnay founded the study of Physiocracy, or the rule of nature, and developed its leading principles. The first principle was the name itself, meaning "the rule of nature." Quesnay believed that there were certain natural laws underlying the operation of human society, just as there were certain laws basic to the physical sciences. The only task was to uncover these laws and make men aware of their existence. The logical persons to achieve this were quite clearly themselves, the Physiocrats. Unfortunately, the "obvious" features of a system of natural law were never made obvious to others ("obvious" is a word of description employed by Physiocrats). The concept, as set forth by Quesnay and other writers of the school, remained a curious blend of preordained laws and free will. Since man had free choice, he was not strictly bound by these natural laws; predestination was not a part of Physiocratic doctrine. Nevertheless, it was inevitable that men paid for their transgressions against these laws.

Since a further pursuit of the concept of natural law would lead us into the field of political philosophy, it will be sufficient if we indicate some of the economic implications arising from the concept. One of the most important of these was the championing of laissez-faire by the Psysiocrats. "Let do and let be and the world goes of itself" was their famous motto. Since man was likely to misinterpret natural law and enact false "positive" laws, it followed that the fewer laws man passed the better. Natural laws, after all, had been enacted by God; how could man presume to improve them? As one reads the Physiocratic literature, one sometimes gets the feeling that the role of the state could have had the Physiocrats' blessing to become highly authoritarian if it would correctly divine and enforce natural law. But the state was likely to do the wrong thing, a fact which led to the conclusion that life would be better if the state did nothing. Not that the state was entirely without functions. In addition to its obvious role of protection of human life and maintaining order, the state was needed to provide protection to private property.

The Physiocrats' endorsement of the government as the defender of the right of private property will remind students of the political philosophy of John Locke's classic, *On Civil Government.* Man had the natural right to private property even before society was organized, and it was important that he not forfeit this right as a price for becoming a member of society. Thus the concept of natural law was closely tied to the right of private property, the right of each man to pursue his own basic self-interest. The product of this pursuit simultaneously by all men was not chaos, but an orderly and smooth-functioning economy. Although the theory was not worked out as completely as Adam Smith's was, it nevertheless represents an interesting anticipation of the heart of Smith's doctrine.

Perhaps the best remembered of the Physiocratic doctrines was the belief that agricultural produce was the only source of real wealth. The formulation of this belief is difficult to understand when viewed in the context of today's modern industrial economy. It must be remembered, however, that the Agricultural Revolution was a necessary forerunner of the Industrial Revolution. At the time when the Physiocrats were developing this doctrine, the Agricultural Revolution was far more evident than any sign of the coming industrial change. We must remember also that France was (and still is) a country with wonderfully fertile soil, and at the time the Physiocrats were writing, tremendous improvements in agricultural output were well in evidence. It is likely, also, that the intellectual flavor of their admiration for things agricultural was influenced by the "back to nature" movement enunciated by writers such as Jean Jacques Rousseau. Nor can the possibility of a reaction to the crass commercialism of the Mercantilists be ignored.

The clearest statement of this insistence on agriculture as the only source of true wealth is to be found in Quesnay's *Tableau Economique* (*Economic Table*). Quesnay predicated the existence of three classes of citizens in any nation; the productive class, the proprietary class, and the sterile class. The productive class were the farmers who cultivated the land, and therefore created the wealth of the nation necessary for the support of the other two classes. The proprietary class consisted of the government officials. They were owners of the land and the collectors of tithes. The third class, designated as sterile members of the society, incorporated all those workers engaged in the supplying of services, such as factory workers, for example, and those who fashioned agricultural produce into finished form. Their labor, said the Physiocrats, added nothing to the wealth of the nation; it merely converted the true agricultural wealth into another form. Quesnay's *Table* did more than state this simple belief, however. It was an attempt to uncover the interrelationships viewed in terms of goods between the above three classes. As such, Quesnay and his disciples conceived of the *Table* as a kind of navigational tool essential for understanding the ebb and flows of income. The arithmetic of Quesnay's *Table* was not difficult to follow. He began with an amount paid to the landed proprietors, the net annual income. Half of this went to cultivators (farm rents at that time in France were set at half of the product) and this was spent productively to earn a new net product in the coming year. The remainder was spent and respent among the various classes. It would be an interesting exercise in arithmetic to continue following Quesnay's allocations, but in light of its faulty base, the assumption that agriculture was the sole source of increments in value, was not particularly rewarding in economic thinking. The important point to remember is that the Physiocrats thought the *Table* provided a guide as to how the flow of income did and should take place. Let too much income flow to the sterile, nonproductive elements in the economy, they warned, and the effect on the output of the economy might be permanently damaging.

A few words of recognition should be accorded to other areas of economics where the Physiocrats anticipated later writers. In keeping with their doctrine of laissez-faire, the Physiocrats were staunch champions of the doctrine of free trade. Quesnay made short work of the Mercantile concept of a favorable balance of trade. Since all trade was sterile, with value emanating from agriculture alone, the notion that a nation could benefit from an export surplus was deemed ridiculous. An export surplus merely meant that a nation had sold more goods than it acquired. The fact that fewer goods were imported only meant that the process of trading was incomplete or suspended halfway toward completion.

Since trade was sterile in the Physiocrats' view, we have cause to wonder why they were such firm supporters of its freedom. Their writings provide us with no one probable answer; simply that it was in keeping with their concept of maximum freedom for the individual to pursue his own self-interest. It may also be the case that the Physiocrats believed that trade would relieve their nation of the necessity of producing many manufactured goods, thereby permitting the economy to concentrate on the true source of a nation's wealth—agriculture.

By their insistence that all labor save agriculture was sterile, they introduced a theme which was to lead to much unproductive discussion by later economists about the distinction between productive and unproductive labor. Earlier, John Locke had also made this distinction, but the Physiocratic doctrine made it much more forcefully and dramatically. Smith was one of the first to adopt and develop this distinction between the two and thereby condemn to secondary status workers who labored in fields where no goods were produced.

The Physiocrats' belief in the sterility of all financial transactions and the uniqueness of agriculture as the source of value influenced their doctrine with respect to the financing of government. Government debt was to be avoided like the plague, since it provided increased activity to financiers who were notorious members of the sterile classes. Furthermore, debt tied up funds which might otherwise possibly have been put to use in augmenting the nation's net product. Since government borrowing was to be avoided at all cost, unavoidable expenses of government should be financed by taxation. Once again the central role of agriculture was revealed. Taxes, no matter at what point in the economy they might be imposed, would eventually fall on the net product. Quesnay concluded, therefore, that the best policy was to impose all taxes immediately at this fount of all wealth. We will return to the issue of the single tax at several points throughout our study, but we should note at this point that later proponents of this system of taxation owe a substantial intellectual debt to the Physiocrats.

The doctrine that no value was added by exchange relieved the Physiocrats of the task of finding a *raison d'être* for exchange value. Some of the fragments of Quesnay's writing suggest that he was a hedonist and a utilitarian, and it is possible that he would have developed the utility theory of value, had not his dismissal of all value save in agriculture precluded his pursuing this subject further.

Quesnay anticipated certain ideas of later economists by setting forth a theory of overexpanding population and an "iron law of wages." He once declared that wages and the enjoyments obtained by wage earners are fixed and reduced to the lowest possible level by the extreme competition among the wage earners.

Among the names of those who can be included as members of the Physiocratic School are the Marquis de Mirabeau, Mercier de la Rivière, and Anne Robert Jacques Turgot. From this list of names only that of Turgot needs to be singled out for special attention. In some respects it is inaccurate to include Turgot with the Physiocrats, and one great scholar of economic thought, Joseph Schumpeter, has denied the validity of his inclusion.[2]

ANNE ROBERT JACQUES TURGOT (1727–1781)

The Man. Turgot was born in Paris and educated at the University of Paris. He originally planned on a life in the service of the Church, but this plan was abandoned and he turned to government service, where he served in various capacities for most of his life. Turgot's first major post was as an executive officer in the district of Limoges. Here and elsewhere he had the opportunity to introduce the tax policies espoused by Physiocratic doctrine. While at Limoges he began the gradual abolition of the corvée (a tax whereby citizens contributed work for the government) and substituted a money tax. As comptroller general of France under Louis XVI, he continued this and other tax reforms. Turgot's efforts at reform won him the enmity of many members of the "sterile" class, including Marie Antoinette, and he was later forced to resign. He continued his writing and research after retirement and in 1777 was chosen vice-president of the Academie des Inscriptions et Belles-Lettres.

Economic Views. True, Turgot did write of the singular characteristics of agriculture and of its unique contribution to the wealth of a nation. But the general tenor of his writing represented a marked advance over the thinking of Quesnay and his disciples. Schumpeter has argued that those passages of Turgot which have been interpreted as Physciocratic were but an acknowledgment by Turgot of his friends' thinking. It is true that Turgot went considerably beyond the other Physiocrats in his thinking about prices, the role of money, and the determination of interest (Physiocratic thought virtually ignored the question of interest), and his own treatise was an admirable predecessor to Smith's. Whether Turgot was really a Physiocrat at heart or "an independent with Physiocratic leanings" is too fine a point to discuss here. What is of interest is that while he

[2] Joseph Schumpeter, *A History of Economic Analysis,* ed. by Elizabeth Boody Schumpeter (New York: Oxford University Press, 1954), pp. 243–244.

served as minister of finance under Louis XVI, he recommended policies
of a distinctly non-Physiocratic nature; his program of protective tariffs is
but one of these.

Summary and Evaluation of Physiocracy. The reign of Physiocracy
was brief. With the death of Quesnay in 1774 and Turgot's retirement
from government service two years later, the school quickly ceased to
exist. Despite its preoccupation with the central role of agriculture, it still
stands as a landmark in the progress of economic thought and the first real
"school" of economics. For the first time, an organized theoretical approach to economic life was attempted; its theoretical superiority when
compared to Mercantilism is notable.

It is difficult to measure the impact of the Physiocrats on Adam Smith's
thinking. Although he was in France and had the opportunity to meet and
talk with its leaders during the period of the school's ascendancy, there is
evidence from his lecture notes that much of the analysis to be found in
Wealth of Nations had already become a part of Smith's thinking prior to
his trip to France. One point is immediately evident; Smith erected no
elaborate theoretical model comparable to Quesnay's *Economic Table.* In
fact, despite a certain lingering fondness for agriculture evidenced in some
of the passages in *Wealth of Nations,* Smith was sharply critical of the
notion that all value was created from agriculture. Nevertheless, Smith
had a great admiration for the Physiocratic doctrine and once declared it
"the nearest approximation to the truth that has yet been published." It
seems likely that at the very least Smith was reinforced in his own beliefs
about laissez-faire and free trade by exposure to the thinking of the Physiocrats.

Smith's Economic Views. Before plunging into a detailed appraisal
of the contents of Smith's *Wealth of Nations,* it might be wise to stop for
a moment and ask what kind of a man he was picturing. Who was the
"economic man" that Smith visualized as populating his system? What
were this man's motives? What psychological and physiological traits
did he possess?

The average man in Smith's system was industrious and hard-working.
Not that the existence of drones was inconceivable to Smith; he was far
too realistic to ignore the existence of nonproductive members of the society. But the lazy individual was not a characteristic part of the English
economy. Men worked so hard partly because it was natural for them to
desire improvement in their economic circumstances. The average man

was deemed to be discontented with the status quo and was pictured as constantly striving for something better. Another answer as to why men were willing to work so hard was to be found in the moral character of the typical Englishman. The Protestant Reformation had long since swept England with its message of salvation through hard work and industry. Smith feared that this natural expression of man's inherent willingness to work and take risks would be destroyed if too much government control was permitted. Part of his opposition to Mercantilism stemmed from his concern about the evil effects government intervention would have on men's moral fiber.

Other characteristics of the economic man were equally promising for the operation of Smith's system. Men were born traders with an inherent propensity to "truck and barter." [3] Modern anthropologists would probably take exception to this as a universal characterization of mankind, but the point was an important one for Smith. As we shall see, the tendency to trade was crucial for a nation's expansion. Without trade and the expanding markets thereby achieved, a nation would never succeed in growing wealthy.

Part of the secret of increasing the wealth of a nation, of course, lies in the ability to retain a part of the wealth once it has been produced. When a society consumes all that it produces, increases in production become virtually impossible. The role of capital accumulation in Smith's system will be explored in more detail below; it suffices here to point out that capital accumulation in Smith's view was aided by the propensity of individuals to save. As Wesley Mitchell, the American economist, used to say, Smith's economic man was "a wee bit Scotch." Once again Smith recognized the existence of the profligate but remained confident that such cases were in a decided minority.

The belief that man was both capable of recognizing and anxious to pursue his own self-interest was also important to the operation of Smith's economic system. In the light of his previous book, *The Theory of Moral Sentiments,* one should probably not overstate Smith's position in representing men's actions as being framed exclusively toward selfish ends with complete insensitivity to the interests of their fellow man. Yet it is abundantly clear throughout *Wealth of Nations* that Smith considers man to be basically selfish and working to his own self-interest.[4] In fact, the miracle

[3] Adam Smith, *Wealth of Nations* (New York: Modern Library, 1937), p. 13.

[4] Although the author has used self-love, self-interest, and selfishness as if they were synonyms, it may be that Smith felt that the first two terms did not need to involve the third.

of Smith's system is how order and the maximization of the public welfare is achieved from this apparent state of anarchy.

Most surprising is Smith's postulation of the basic equality of men's abilities. Why is one man a philosopher while another is relegated to the menial duty of street cleaning? Smith states that in all probability both men were born with the ability to do either kind of work. Only the whims of chance in terms of family background and opportunities for education differentiated the two. As time wore on, of course, the lack of training would render the street cleaner unfit for anything but similar lowly tasks. At birth, however, the mental faculties of both men were equal. As stated by Smith, this concept pushed the proposition of men's equality to the extreme and exposed Smith to numerous criticisms by later writers.

SMITH'S MODEL VERSUS THE MERCANTILE SYSTEM. The reader can often learn a great deal about the central theme of a book by studying its title; this is particularly true of Smith's pioneer study in political economy. Its full title, *An Inquiry into the Nature and Causes of the Wealth of Nations,* provides us with as neat and accurate a summary of the essence of his book's message as could be desired. For all its wandering onto other themes, the book remains basically a study of how the wealth of a nation can be increased. Smith was motivated to undertake this exploration by his belief that the Mercantilists in their preoccupation with gold had fastened upon an incorrect measuring rod. Where, then, did the true wealth of a nation lie? Judged by most of our current definitions of wealth, Smith's definition failed to include a number of important items. No mention is found, for example, of a nation's supply of natural resources or its stockpiles of capital goods and equipment. Actually Smith's definition of wealth came close in meaning to what we refer to today as our national product. The wealth of a nation lay in its ability to produce, and available resources were a valuable but insufficient prerequisite for expanding development.

Smith's neglect of those factors by which we customarily measure the wealth of a nation came not only from his rather special definition of "wealth" but from the absence of reliable statistical evidence as to the relative availability of resources throughout the world. Not only was the state of knowledge of the extent of resources in England little advanced over what we know about the resources of some of the underdeveloped nations today, but the existing level of industrial technology was too primitive to make clear what resources would assume major importance in the future. In neglecting these usual measures of wealth, Smith (probably unwittingly) emphasized a point that has become increasingly apparent to students of economic growth in recent years: a country may attain a high standard of living even in the absence of many of the resources deemed crucial for proper economic development.

The key to the growing wealth of a nation in Smith's view lay in its ability to expand production by an ever increasing division of labor. Smith argued that the division of labor aided productive effort in three ways. It increased the dexterity of workers, it encouraged the development of inventions, and it saved time wasted, as the worker otherwise was forced to go from job to job. Smith's use of a pin factory as an illustrative example points up the fact that the Industrial Revolution was only beginning to get under way.[5] Nevertheless, two of the key time savings claimed by Smith for the division of labor are basic to the efficiency found in modern assembly-line production. The second of the claimed benefits, the stimulation of workers to invent because their minds are freed by the performance of routine tasks, is open to greater question. Modern industrial plants have had rather mixed results with their use of suggestion boxes into which workers deposit their suggestions for increasing plant efficiency. Not only are workers likely to regard such plans as a threat to their job security, because of possible displacements caused by increased efficiency, but the stultifying nature of routine work, as seen by Smith himself, casts doubts on the likelihood that workers will be stimulated to concoct worthwhile improvements in efficiency.

In addition to the deadly monotony occasioned by work that has been repeatedly subdivided, Smith noted two other limitations to the division of labor. One of these, the fact that some goods by their nature are desired because they are in the nature of specialty goods and thus purchased because they are handcrafted, is too obvious to need any elaboration. But the third limitation to the division of labor is more significant and bears on Smith's attack on the Mercantilists.

Smith noted that the division of labor could be limited by the extent of the market. Unless the market was sufficiently broad, increases in productive efficiency would not be made, since they would simply go to waste. Therefore, it was important that manufacturers be free to sell their goods

---

[5] While there had been a decline in the iron trade in the middle of the eighteenth century due to the threatened exhaustion of wood as a fuel, it may be that Smith underestimated the importance of technological change in expediting growth. Consider, for example, the rapid pace of innovations taking place at the time Smith wrote his book:

1765—use of steam—Watt
1769—roller spinning—Arkwright
1770—spinning jenny—Hargreaves
1779—spinning mule—Crompton

in as wide a market as possible. A major basis for Smith's opposition to the Mercantilists now becomes clear. The Mercantilists, with their proposals for limiting trade, would narrow the extent of the market. In doing this they were endangering the force which Smith saw as the chief means by which a nation's wealth was augmented: the opportunity to carry out increasing subdivisions of labor. While Smith's opposition to the Mercantilists was not based on this fact alone, it did play an important role in stimulating his attack.

The reason for Smith's retention of a somewhat revised version of the Physiocratic distinction between productive and unproductive labor now becomes apparent. No invidious comparisons were implied, and Smith freely acknowledged the contribution that the providers of transportation and other needed services and scholars made to the society. These groups were unproductive only in the sense that they did not contribute directly to the stockpile of material goods and thus the wealth of the nation. It has become fashionable to poke fun at this distinction, but we still draw many of the same lines of demarcation today. Few people, for example, would question Smith's plea to reduce armaments as wasteful expenditures, and we still occasionally hear complaints about the growing proportion of white-collar workers in relation to productive workers in our factories. In making this distinction, Smith was not disagreeing with the Mercantilists; much that he deemed unproductive they would have deemed likewise, if only because it couldn't be exported.

Another basis for Smith's rejection of Mercantilism was its concept of the manner in which the economic system functioned. To the Mercantilists, governmental supervision was an absolute necessity if the economy was to be guided along the proper channels, whereas Smith, with few exceptions, held that the less government interference the better.

Smith developed his now famous concept of the "invisible hand" when he formulated his idea that the economy could operate more efficiently in the absence of government controls. There has been much discussion since Smith's coining of the phrase as to exactly what he meant by the term. Did it possess metaphysical overtones or was it to be interpreted in purely secular terms? Whatever may have been Smith's intent at the time, it is quite possible to explain the concept in strictly economic terms.

Basic to the idea was the belief that there was a harmony of interests in the society. This harmony was produced, however, not by the solicitude of each person for everyone else's welfare but by the concentration of each on his own economic good. At the center of the system was the consumer, who made careful buying decisions based on quality and price. Each consumer wanted to maximize his total consumer satisfaction. Producers, in turn, responding to the pressure from rivals to win consumer demand, lowered their prices to the lowest possible level. Businesses were free to set their prices at whatever level they chose, but since consumers would seek out the best offers, this freedom was largely meaningless. The businessman was at the mercy of the consumer.

The operation of the system can best be seen if we consider a simple example. Let us suppose that Mr. Jones decides to open a butcher shop and sell steak for a dollar a pound. Whether he will be able to maintain this price will depend on whether the housewife is willing to pay this price. Maintaining the price depends upon how badly households want to eat steak and also on the available alternative supplies. Assuming that the housewife finds she can buy her steak from Butcher Brown for $.90, she will surely switch her trade to this less expensive shop. Butcher Jones, to woo customers, will now find it necessary to lower his price to perhaps a shade under $.90. How low will the price fall? Smith answered this by distinguishing between the natural and the market price. The natural price was that necessary to cover the costs of producing the product, including an average rate of profit. The market price, on the other hand, was determined by the interaction of the market forces of demand and supply. Smith's expectation was that the market price would oscillate about the natural price; the market price might remain above the natural price for considerable periods, but rarely could remain long below it. If a normal rate of return in any line of business was not achieved, the businessman would quickly shift to another field.

Note the simplicity of the system: High prices act to attract new competitors, thus acting to correct themselves automatically. Similarly, when prices are too low, enough producers are driven from the field so that prices are restored to their proper natural level. Note also that, at the same time, the system has solved the vexing problem of proper output of various products. Students of economics will recognize the above as the standard introductory textbook description of the way in which a free-price system is supposed to operate; for indeed, that is exactly what Smith was describing!

Smith's faith in a natural harmony of interests may have been derived in part from the Physiocrats' notion of a natural order. He may also have been influenced by Bernard Mandeville's *The Fable of the Bees*. According to Mandeville's thesis, each bee, by pursuing its own self-interest and busily storing a supply of honey, actually worked toward the total welfare of the hive. The analogy to be drawn to human society is obvious.

There were two basic assumptions imbedded in Smith's concept of the operation of the price system. One was the belief that the consumer was rational and capable of correctly judging his own best interests. But the concept of consumer rationality has been subject to vigorous attack for the past century. The critics have pointed to the volume of impulse buying or purchases made through inertia, the extent to which consumers are ill informed about standards of quality and price, and the fact that consumers may be misinformed and misled by devious advertising.

It would be a serious mistake to attack Smith as the one who accepted the doctrine that the theoretical model of perfect competition, as it eventually developed, assumed perfect knowledge on the part of consumers. He was far too much of a realist to have ever adopted such an heroic assumption, for his assumption of consumer rationality was a much more modest one. Smith insisted only that the consumer was a far better judge of his own best interests than any governmental planning board could ever be. Mistakes might be made by the consumer, but still, the extent of the error was likely to be less and to be made less frequently. While Smith might see fit to amend his doctrine somewhat in the light of some of the recent developments in the field of consumer economics, it is doubtful whether he would feel that his basic premise was vitiated.

Smith might be somewhat more shaken in his belief in the validity of the second of the two assumptions basic to the operation of the "invisible hand." If consumer choice is to be meaningful, a state of vigorous competition must exist. Smith warned the consumer not to rely on the goodwill of the butcher or the baker to assure him of satisfactory prices.[6] What brought prices down to the proper level was the competition of the butchers or the bakers among themselves. This principle, of course, applied to the pricing of products in all other trades as well. Despite Smith's realism with respect to the many imperfections in the market, he never faced up to the fact that monopolies might develop, with a part or all of the competitive model thereby destroyed. Smith's explanation for the emergence of monopolies was not completely irrelevant by the standards of some modern economists. According to him, monopolies were a product of government interference. Again responsibility was placed at the door of the Mercantilists, who, by their policy of restricting foreign competition and subsidizing certain companies, were rendering competition

[6] Whatever Smith's departure from the thesis of his earlier book at this point may be deemed to be, his deviation from the teachings of St. Thomas Aquinas about the principle of just price was even greater. St. Thomas had argued that merchants should charge no more than would earn them a fair profit, and that to take advantage of a market situation to charge high prices was a sin.

helpless. It should be remembered that this was the era of the big trading companies such as the East India Company, which had acquired exclusive trading rights in certain areas of the world. When Smith studied these giant trading monopolies, he simplified the problem by asserting that the removal of these special privileges would solve the problem of monopoly. Part of Smith's distaste for Mercantilism stemmed from the top-heavy bureaucracy which it helped to fashion and the inefficient manner in which that bureaucracy functioned.

Smith's aversion to Mercantilism was based on three additional issues. He objected to the threat raised to the continued division of labor; Mercantilism's sponsorship of monopolies, with its confusion between gold and true wealth; and the trade practices created by other evils of the system. Smith pointed out that in the first place it was foolish for a nation to produce anything which could be purchased more cheaply elsewhere in the world. Yet this kind of production was exactly what the Mercantilists were encouraging in order to avoid importations. The result was to impose a double burden on the consumer, one in the form of a tax to subsidize production and exportation of the product, the other in the form of the higher prices the consumer had to pay for the goods. Smith was eager to condemn Mercantilists' practices, and he appeared at times to overstate the case. He argued, for example, that bounties on goods to be exported were far more harmful than bounties on goods destined for domestic consumption. (Neither, of course, was to be considered desirable.) Yet, to the extent that a bounty on exports enabled the importation of cheap foreign goods, the greater evil associated with this bounty became less striking than Smith made it appear.

The real heart of Smith's aversion to Mercantilism, however, has always been alleged to lie in his espousal of a laissez-faire economy. Smith has been heralded as the champion of business interests, and support from his writings has been sought by quoting relevant passages in support of maximum freedom for the businessman to carry on his business without outside interference. Such a reading of Smith is not entirely incorrect. It is evident from what we have already said that Smith was highly critical of government intervention as exemplified by Mercantilist policy. However, several serious qualifications to this widely accepted view are necessary.

In the first place, Smith was highly suspicious of the tendency of businessmen to undertake collusive action whenever possible. At one point he remarked that businessmen can seldom come together in even casual meeting without conspiring to control prices or wages. The notion that the businessman, without his government regulation, would do the honorable and correct thing (from the economy's point of view) was alien to Smith's thinking. But the logical expectation that monopoly would follow collusive action did not occur to Smith. Those who prefer their economics in terms of heroes and villains will point out that just as the merchant was the hero for the Mercantilists, so the small businessman was the hero of Smith's opus. This picture, accurate as far as it goes, overlooks the fact that Smith's businessman was a somewhat tarnished hero.

Smith was unduly pessimistic about the economic results of monopolies. He remarked that a monopolist tended to set his price at as high a level as possible so that he could sell *any* of his product.[7] Part of his theory of exorbitant price levels instigated by monopolies can be explained by the quality of analytic tools available to Smith. He had no knowledge of monopolistic and imperfect competition as it was to be later analyzed; even marginal cost and marginal revenue were unknown terms. Part of the explanation lies also in the fact that monopolies in Smith's time were much more complete. Today, products are far more interchangeable and the consumer has greater latitude of choice. If the present-day consumer should find glass containers too expensive, he can always find firms who will readily supply him with metal containers. Similar opportunities for consumers in the eighteenth century were less frequently available and the monopolist had far less to fear from rival products.

Since the businessman cannot be characterized as the unblemished hero of Smith's study, we can view him more accurately by considering him a model for Smith's system of decentralized power. No businessman or groups of businessmen should have the power to impose standards of price or quality. Unquestionably, the power should not be held in the hands of any other group, either. Because it was the government which was the greatest possessor of economic power at the time, and because in Smith's view it was so seriously misusing this power, his attack centered on the evils of governmental economic power. But what Smith really wanted was an atomistic society with numerous small units, each incapable of controlling the market. In order to assure this kind of atomistic society, a high degree of government intervention would be necessary in order to prevent corporations or unions from developing undue market influence. Even in a modern world where few economists would defend the concept of laissez-faire, only a small number would pursue a policy designed to dismember many of our large corporations. Adam Smith, however, never had to squarely face the full implications of his cherished model. The technologi-

[7] Smith, *op. cit.,* p. 61.

cal efficiency to be found in the giant corporation had not yet been un-covered.

However, Smith would never have drawn the moral from his doubts about the ethics of businessmen that the government could perform the task better. Not only did excessive governmental activity create a still more dangerous power bloc, but it was likely to be less efficient as well. Even in a field such as public education, which is almost universally ac-knowledged today as a proper function of government, Smith had reserva-tions and felt that some of the costs, at least, should be borne directly by the parents whose children were to be educated.[8]

Smith's ambiguity with respect to government action can be seen by contrasting his proposal for education noted above with his reaction to defects in the Scottish banking system. Basically, his solution for these abuses is one familiar to most of us today—"there ought to be a law." This seeming inconsistency and ambiguity is not as marked as it appears to be at first glance. Smith was willing that the government intervene to cor-rect malpractices. In all fairness to him, however, we must note that even here he had his doubts. The Poor Laws,[9] to Smith, were a good example of how a well-intentioned government might not succeed in correcting an evil, but only make it worse. We will discuss the Poor Laws in more detail in Chapter IV when we consider the reactions of one of their strongest critics, Thomas Robert Malthus. The only point we need to make here is that Smith's opposition to the Poor Laws was based on somewhat different grounds. He saw those laws, with their residency requirements for relief eligibility, as a major impediment to the free movement of labor. What was clearly unacceptable to him was that the government removed one malpractice merely to replace it with another. Not only was government less efficient, but it was likely to be far less responsive to the wishes of consumers than the private sector.

Smith found a prime example of the similar harmful effects which an-

---

[8] Smith, *op. cit.,* pp. 716–740.

[9] These Poor Laws had a long history in England. Prior to 1601, the laws had pro-vided that the care of the truly poor was the responsibility of the churches, the guilds, and private charity. After 1601 care for the lame, the blind, and the aged was still to be provided, but the rest, including children, were to be put to work. Dole was to be administered through the local parishes with funds raised by compulsory taxation. Be-cause treatment differed from parish to parish, there was a tendency for the poor to flock to those parishes that provided the best treatment. As a result, Laws of Settlement were passed making it impossible for a worker to move to another parish without per-mission and the promise of a definite job. It was these Laws of Settlement to which Adam Smith objected so strenuously, since they limited the free movement of labor.

other form of government interference had on the proper functioning of
the market in the domestic policy of the Mercantilists. In his chapter on
inequalities in wages, Smith explored the reasons why wage differentials
continue to persist from decade to decade. One of his reasons advanced
therein is relevant here. Smith argued that Mercantilists, by erecting various barriers to the free movement of labor, prevented labor from shifting
about in response to wage differentials. Through the use of licensing laws
and prolonged apprenticeship regulations, employment in some places
was restricted while it was overly abundant in others. In recent years we
have come to think of apprenticeship regulations—the prolonged periods
of training required before the worker is admitted to full status in the
trade—as a feature of certain labor unions. But in the time that Smith was
writing, unions were nonexistent and the seven-year training period required for admission to some trades was enforced by the government.
When Smith attacked these restrictions, he argued that the old guild techniques of production were declining and that "modern" methods of production required much shorter periods of training. In addition, he questioned whether the protracted periods of training had been necessary even
at an earlier time.

In addition to all of these theoretical reasons for rejecting the economic
system of Mercantilism, Smith had a moral objection as well. The period
just prior to Smith's book was one of extremely high protectionism, with
results somewhat comparable to those in our own Prohibition days.
Smuggling had grown to sizable proportions, and a general resistance
to the forces of law and order, which were attempting to enforce
the restrictions, met with little public disapproval. Such gross and widespread disregard of the law shocked Smith's moral sensibilities and accounts for some of the savagery of his attack on the Mercantile system. In
Smith's opinion, no system which resulted in such flagrant violations of
the law should be permitted to continue to exist.

Considering the forcefulness of Smith's criticisms, it is surprising to see
how moderate his demands for change proved to be. Instead of asking for
an overnight abolition of tariff barriers and the immediate institution of a
program of free trade, Smith indicated that progress in this direction was
likely to be slow and time-consuming. In reality, one might even speculate
that England emerged as a champion of free trade at a much earlier date
than Smith would have been willing to predict. Smith was willing to concede that there were certain situations such as war where trade restrictions
were a desirable policy. His belief that trade restrictions might be imposed
in retaliation to the trade barriers of other nations is even more disliked

than protection for defense by current proponents of free trade policy. The possibility that such a policy might lead to ever-rising trade barriers did not seem to concern Smith. In many ways this willingness to accept a slow pace of reform and to acknowledge the need to make exceptions was one of the strengths of the man. Too often, needed reforms flounder because their proponents adopt an "all or nothing" policy. Smith's economics was good enough to enable him to see that an overnight change would involve violent upheavals in the economy, thus strengthening the forces of opposition to the change and rendering the process of adaptation that much more difficult.

There is more to achieving a smoothly functioning economy, however, than merely knowing how the market operates and the role the government plays with respect to that market. If an economy is to expand, some method of assuring an accumulation of capital must be devised. Neither the Mercantilists nor the Physiocrats provided their readers with very much in the way of a theory of capital accumulation. In his concentration on technology and the division of labor, Smith also neglected the problem of capital accumulation, and his analysis of this question is weak and unsatisfactory. The motives for saving and the function of the interest rate in encouraging savings receive scant attention in *Wealth of Nations*. Evidently Smith saw no close connection between the interest rate and the volume of savings, since he spoke of the decline in the rate of interest, historically, without making any reference to the effect on savings. Perhaps Smith's confidence in the inherent thriftiness of the economic man precluded his displaying any great concern on this issue.

The role of population expansion in fostering economic growth was recognized by both the Mercantilists and Smith. The Mercantilists saw little opportunity for increasing the average productivity of workers. Thus, if total production was to be augmented, it had to be done by increasing the size of the labor force. The most obvious way to achieve this goal was through an expanding population. For Smith, population increases served a somewhat different function. First of all, the increasing amount of capital bidding for labor would threaten to drive wages up to impossible levels if the rising wages did not permit parents to raise more children, thereby adding to the size of the labor force. Nor was the time interval between birth and entrance into the labor force the extended period that it is today. Children at work in the factories before the age of ten were not at all an uncommon sight, and cases of their performing light work by the age of seven were not infrequent. Smith appeared to have no objection to the early employment of children, providing only that they have some opportunity for an education. The education of the young was important to prevent their becoming completely stultified by factory routine. The possibility of a widow in North America faring well through the employment of her several children was noted by Smith, but without any word of disparagement.

Not only were wages thereby prevented from rising to the point where they threatened profits, but the expanding population served another useful function in Smith's system. It will be remembered that Smith saw the expansion of markets as the key to the further division of labor. What more assured built-in method of widening the market could there be than an expansion of the number of consumers by the growth of the population?

It is therefore clear that the possibility of technological unemployment held no fears for Smith. The growing accumulation of capital equipment would produce a shortage of labor rather than cause its displacement. However, this optimistic view was not shared by all of the economists who followed Smith. The issue of technological unemployment arose repeatedly in the economic literature of succeeding decades, and many of the writers treated the subject in a far more detailed fashion than did Smith.

THE DETERMINATION OF VALUE. Smith found it necessary to set up another standard for measuring the value of the goods produced, since he rejected gold as a standard of wealth and focused upon the production of physical goods as the true measure of a nation's wealth. Note again Smith's concentration of tangible goods that could be seen and physically measured. Whereas we include in our current figures for national income and gross national product all of the intangibles in the form of personal services, education, and entertainment, Smith was careful to exclude all such items. Instead, he concentrated his discussion of value on tangible goods.

A second point to note in the following discussion is Smith's rejection of utility as a basis for the explanation of the value of goods. By concentrating on a cost-of-production explanation of value, Smith delayed the emergence of modern value theory for nearly a century. One can point to Smith's formulation of a theory of value as a diversion from a simultaneous expression of the utility concept. A contemporary French writer, E. B. Condillac, developed the notion of utility as an element in the determination of a productive value in a book published the same year as Smith's book. Smith, however, was either unaware of or completely ignored this contribution, with the result that he struggled to find a solution to the comparative value of water and diamonds. Ignoring the possibility of examining the problem in terms of marginal utility, Smith compared the two products' values solely with the measuring rod of total utility. The result was to leave Smith baffled and uncertain. Why should diamonds bring a price so much higher than that of water, when obviously water was far more important to man's survival? Smith was never able to solve this question, and after some slighting references to the value of diamonds to society, he abandoned the question as unanswerable. Smith observed that there were two kinds of value—value in use and value in exchange. These concepts were never developed further, as he settled down to concentrate on the question of determining the value of products in exchange.

As we noted earlier, the problem of why products exchange with others in certain set proportions was one of the first questions posed by early observers of economic life. It is a question that has continued to intrigue economists down to the present time. Adam Smith began his analysis of the question by examining what he considered a typical primitive situation of exchange. It might be noted in passing that few anthropologists would award Smith a very high grade for his interpretation of the primitive society. However, Smith began by using two hunters as an illustration. One of the hunters trapped beaver while the other hunted deer. Assuming that both hunters had reasonable luck in their respective hunting, at what rate would exchange between the two woodsmen take place? Smith attempted to provide an answer by formulating two interpretations of a labor theory of value and thereby exposed himself to sharp criticism from later writers. Let us assume, said Smith, that the fruit of the two hunters' efforts exchange at the rate of two deer for one beaver. Why should the hunters exchange (assuming that each found exchanging to be desired) at this ratio rather than some other? Why not three deer for one beaver or four deer, or for that matter, why not two (or more) beaver for one deer? Smith answered by stating that the ratio of two deer for one beaver measured both the comparative amounts of effort required in the catching of each of the respective animals and also the amount of labor that the animals were able to command in the process of exchange. Smith argued that there was no real distinction between these two interpretations and that both represented the value of the product. The first of these — the amount of labor involved in producing one product in contrast to the amount required in the production of another—can be described as the *labor jelly* theory of value. The second—the amount of labor a product can command—may best be referred to as the *labor command* theory. Although Smith was content to treat these two concepts as identical, this can be true only so long as the laborer receives the full value of the product he produces. When profit (and rent) recipients are brought into the picture, the scene changes.

While some commentators have sought to rationalize this dichotomy, most students of Smith agree that he was somewhat befogged on this point. While agreeing in general with this second group, the author feels it only fair to point out the factors that probably abetted Smith's entrapment. Smith's emphasis on a labor command theory can in part be explained by his stress on the importance of the division of labor. Man was a trading animal; no one could produce all of the things necessary for his own existence. Hence, it was important to determine value in exchange and not simply in an abstract sense. We should also note that part of the confusion stems from Smith's discussion of two separate questions. We have already discussed the first of these: determining the value of a product. The second has quite a different meaning: knowing what the best standard of value is. Smith, having rejected money because it fluctuated and did not remain constant, toyed with the idea of using corn, but abandoned this standard as also being subject to wide variation. Smith then turned to labor as the best standard of measurement of value over space and time. When we remember the utilization by present-day economists of comparisons of work hours necessary to buy products when measuring living standards between different countries, Smith's justification for employing a labor command theory as one of his standards becomes readily understandable.

It can easily be seen why so many students of economic thought blame Adam Smith and David Ricardo for setting the stage for Marxian thought. If the value of a product can be measured solely in terms of the quantity of labor involved in its production, then why is the landlord or the capitalist entitled to share in the final selling price of the product? No such dangerous thoughts ever entered Smith's mind, however. As society moved from a primitive to a more developed state, said Smith, a reward for both of these parties was reasonable and to be expected. As production became increasingly complex, the services of landlords and particularly of capitalists grew increasingly important, and so repayment for their services was necessary. Thus, what had commenced as a labor theory of value had now been converted into a straightforward cost-of-production theory. Once again, however, Smith exposed the weakness of his theoretical analysis. He simply straddled the issue and suggested in less than one hundred pages that rent was to be considered a part of the cost of production and treated as some kind of surplus quite irrelevant to the question of value determination.

Although Smith's primary interest was in analyzing ways to increase production and stimulate the growth of the nation's wealth, his exploration of the nature of the value of a product and his resulting cost of production theory led him into an examination of the nature of distribution.[10]

WAGE DETERMINATION. In seeking a theory to explain the level of wages, Smith anticipated most of the theories of wages that were to be developed by succeeding generations of economists. Thus he offered as possible explanations of the general level of wages a subsistence explanation, a wages-fund theory, a productivity theory, and the theory that wages were established by bargaining between combinations of labor and employers. Typically, Smith did little to explore the ramifications of these various theories, but contented himself with a summary listing of the possible explanations. We shall reserve consideration of these theories until they become more prominent in the writings of later economists. There is one important exception to the above observation on Smith's somewhat casual treatment of theories of wages, however, and this exception illustrates Smith's powers as an acute observer of the contemporary scene. Smith observed that the subsistence theory of wages did not always appear to equate with the facts, even though he assumed that in the long run there was a positive correlation between the price of corn and wages.

Put in the simplest terms, the subsistence theory of wages is virtually self-explanatory. Wages cannot rise above bare subsistence levels; otherwise population expansion would augment the labor supply and therefore push wages back down to their previous levels. Variations on this theme played a major role in the thinking of economists for the next hundred years.

In appraising the validity of the subsistence wage, Smith observed that workers frequently received equal wages even when they lived in various parts of the country with varying costs of living. Obviously, if wages were determined by the needs of subsistence alone, the rates would fluctuate with the variations in the cost of living. Furthermore, wages varied little from one season to another, although Smith noted that living costs were obviously much higher in some parts of the year than others. Apparently Smith neglected the possibility that wages might be at subsistence levels when computed on an annual basis and that workers saved the excess in seasons when costs were low for use in periods of high prices.

[10] Smith placed his discussion of distribution in the middle of his chapter on prices. His relatively brief treatment of distribution has been cited as evidence that his book was virtually formulated prior to his visit to France and his contact with the Physiocrats.

In listing the possible explanations for the general level of wages, however, Smith missed the various theoretical inconsistencies. Note, for example, that if wages as a part of the cost of production help to determine the
value of a product, while at the same time wages are thought to be determined by the haggling of the forces of labor demand and supply, a round
robin is established with all of the variables dependent on each other.

Smith was on surer ground when he came to the analysis of why wages
differed from one occupation to another. Five causes of wage inequalities
were given: (1) agreeableness of the work; (2) difficulty of learning
the trade; (3) regularity of the employment; (4) amount of trust to be
given the person performing the task; and (5) the possibilities of success
in the trade. These factors listed by Smith need little, if anything, by way
of explanation. It might be noted that later writers who examined the
question almost unanimously began with a restatement of these five explanations. Sometimes, however, they did not agree with Smith's reasoning. Nassau Senior, who wrote some sixty years after Smith, argued that
workers did not prize regularity of work, since work was so irksome by
nature. He said that as a result, seasonal or other irregular work paid little
more, even in terms of hourly rates, than those occupations where the
work pattern was more consistent. John Stuart Mill, in his chapter on
wages, acknowledged the contribution that Smith had made, but then
maintained that Smith was incorrect in arguing that the less agreeable
work was recompensed by higher than average wages. Surely, said Mill,
the reverse condition prevails; the more disagreeable the task, the lower
its reward is likely to be.

Other qualifications and comments about Smith's five reasons for wage
inequalities can be made. Was Smith correct in feeling that workers were
inclined to be too confident of their own abilities and too willing to accept
relatively low rates of remuneration in trades where the chances of loss or
failure were abnormally high? While this characteristic may have
changed through the years as workers became more realistic about opportunities, the continued high rate of failure of small businesses suggests
that some of this same phenomenon still exists today.

By saying that the amount of trust to be imposed had a bearing on the
wage level, Smith may have meant that one must pay individuals a great
deal so that they will have no temptation to misuse funds they are en-
trusted with. Such cynicism, however, seems not to be in keeping with
Smith's general view of human nature. It is more likely that what he had
in mind would be a reason for the difference in the incomes of teachers as
contrasted with those of doctors. The income of the typical doctor is con-

siderably higher than that of his educational counterpart, even when roughly corresponding amounts of intelligence and training are required. Obviously, even a poor student can survive the ministrations of a poor teacher more easily than he can those of a poor doctor.

Even with these minor qualifications, however, Smith's five factors still stand as guideposts for the commencement of an analysis of wage differentials. Smith did not stop here; he enunciated a sixth factor contributing to wage differentials—the immobility of labor. Smith clearly recognized that human beings do not always respond in the manner his model of the market suggested when he remarked that "a man is of all sorts of luggage the most difficult to be transported."[11] Workers failed to shift to areas where wages were higher because of ignorance or a reluctance to leave familiar surroundings. Again it was Smith the painstaking observer, not Smith the careful theoretician, who glimpsed the truth.

PROFITS. Smith's examination of profits was brief and fragmentary in comparison to his extensive treatment of wages. The justification for profits in Smith's view lay in the necessity of providing a means of subsistence to the workers during the interval before their product was ready for market. As such, he was enunciating the rudiments of a wages fund theory of wages; this theory was to be picked up and elaborated upon by Ricardo, Mill, and other writers. Despite the importance that Smith attached to savings as a factor promoting economic progress, his analysis of the manner in which capital accumulation took place was not particularly satisfactory. Profit could be divided into two parts: the first and the largest part was an interest payment made for the use of the money advanced, while the second part was a payment for the risk involved. Note that "wages of superintendence" played no part in Smith's explanation of profits, as they did with some later economists.

In the short run Smith argued that profits varied far less than wages, since they were subject to only two of the factors producing variations in wages. Only risk and the agreeableness of the trade were important considerations in producing profit differentials. As in the case of workers, however, the consumers' ignorance of opportunities elsewhere could produce lengthy periods when profits in one field might remain at above normal levels. Merchants, commented Smith dryly, were unlikely to publicize their good fortune if the result would attract rivals.

Over a longer range of time, profits were likely to continue to fall. Smith cited the declining rate of interest as evidence in support of this thesis. This was important since interest accounted for a sizable propor-

[11] Smith, *op. cit.*, p. 75.

tion of profits. Because predictions about a declining rate of profits continued to play a major role in the thinking of many of the economists who followed in Smith's footsteps, it is important to examine more closely why Smith, who was generally optimistic in tone, also took a dim view of the future of profits. Part of the answer lay in the fact that because wages and profits were part of the same value "pie," each could only improve its relative position at the expense of the other. As wages rose, the rate of profits would eventually decline. This theme was developed far more extensively by later writers and we will reserve our commentary until we encounter them in coming chapters. However, Smith saw population increases as a possible deterrent in preventing wages from rising too sharply, but he emphasized another factor as contributing to the decline of profits. Profits were likely to decline because of the amassing of constantly increasing amounts of capital through continued accumulation. By this process of accumulation, capital became more and more plentiful and gradually would be put to less productive uses. Smith felt that the process was likely to be long and drawn out but eventually England would come to the stationary state where no further growth would take place. "Sufficient unto the day was the evil thereof" might well have been coined by Smith, and he devoted no analysis to the consequences of this ultimate development. The scanty vision he did provide of this future event suggests that he did not think the final story would be too terrible.

RENT. Rent was the reward to the third party of production and land. It received the least satisfactory treatment of all at Smith's hands. Again, Smith's eclectic approach is evident as he provides us with three separate explanations for the existence of rent. Rent could be explained as a monopoly return paid because land was scarce and owned by only a relatively small proportion of the population. Almost directly opposed to this was a second explanation; rent came as the result of the bounteous generosity of nature. Nature, by its excessive fertility, produced a surplus, and this surplus was thus available for payment to the landlord for his service in providing the land. A third explanation received equally brief treatment at Smith's hands, but was adopted and developed by Ricardo as the sole explanation. This third explanation involved consideration of the fact that different pieces of land had different degrees of fertility. The most fertile lands, having produced a surplus of output as compared to the less fertile sections, were in a position to bear a charge for their use and this charge was rent. Partly because Smith never attempted to make a selection from among these three explanations, he was confused as to the role rent played in the determination of price, and he succeeded only in presenting both possible views: (1) that rent did enter into the setting of price; and (2) that rent was a result, not a cause of price. Whereas Smith had warned against confusing wages and profits—unduly high profits might be a result of this confusion—he maintained no such clear distinction between rent and the return to other forms of capital. Improvements on the land, for example, became incorporated into the item rent.

ROLE OF GOVERNMENT. Book V of *Wealth of Nations* has only three chapters but encompasses nearly one third of the pages in the volume. It deals with the issues of the proper functions of the government and the means of supporting those activities. The appeal of Smith's views to businessmen and conservatives (and combinations of the two) has already been noted. Smith's prescription was to keep all government activity to the necessary minimum. He viewed the expenses of government as falling into three large categories: the expenses of defense, the expenses of justice, and the expenses of public works and institutions. The last of these three functions involved certain activities that private business could not or should not perform, such as providing education, roads, and bridges, and the coinage of money. Smith thought that all such actions were essential to maintain the commerce of the nation. A good network of internal transportation was necessary to maintain the volume of trade, and the increased amount of trade which came with the broadening of the market was essential as a means of securing continuing divisions of labor. But even though these internal improvements could properly be assigned to the government for performance, Smith felt that all too often the expenses were simply financed from the proceeds of the general revenue. Smith noted that roads and bridges could be financed much more frequently than was currently the practice by the levying of small tolls and fees.

For those activities such as national defense, where the costs of government could not be made self-liquidating, it was necessary to discover the best means of raising revenue. Smith devoted the second chapter of Book V to solving this problem, and laid down four canons of taxation which have served as maxims in the field of public finance down to the present day.

Before we tackle the problem of what made for a good tax, first it is necessary to emphasize that these two words in Smith's view were basically contradictory. There was no such thing as a good tax! All taxes must inevitably limit individual initiative and hamper the proper functioning of the private sector of the economy. The best one could do was to devise the least harmful tax system possible. Smith proposed that a tax be judged on the basis of the following four criteria: (1) Did it provide equality of treatment? (2) Could people be assured of its impact, i.e., did it possess certainty of burden? (3) Was it structured so as to be as convenient in payment and collection as possible? and (4) Was it an economical tax to administer? The last three maxims were accepted by later writers with little or no reservation, but the principle of equality was to cause endless dispute and to raise many problems of interpretation. What did Smith mean by equality? Was he leaving the door open for at least a modified form of progressive taxation?

Smith ended his mammoth study with a concluding survey of the problem of national debt. As might have been expected, Smith concluded that debt, while not always avoidable, was usually not desirable, and his general attitude can best be summarized as one of caution. After describing the circumstances usually surrounding the creation of debt—the advent of war, and the willingness and ability of merchants and manufacturers to lend—he warned that no nation had ever completely repaid its debt and even devices such as sinking funds were of no avail. Of equal importance in Smith's reasoning was his observation that taxation to meet government expenditure probably involved the diversion of funds from one unproductive use to another unproductive use, but borrowing would involve the diversion of funds from productive to unproductive uses. As a large debt was borne for a long period, the multiplication of taxes necessary for interest and attempts at repayment might well hinder the ability of a society to accumulate.

An Overall Appraisal. Wealth of Nations as a contribution to the study of economics was not a vastly original book. Smith himself acknowledged his indebtedness for ideas to nearly a hundred persons, and there were probably still more who went unacknowledged. Writers such as Petty, Law, Hume, Condillac, and Quesnay had already investigated topics in a manner similar to that undertaken by Smith, and in some instances had arrived at sounder conclusions. Numerous critics of Smith have accused him of being little more than an eclectic or one who went about "hanging other people's laundry out to dry."

Nor did Smith develop a rigorous theoretical model. Time and again we find him assembling sufficient data to reach at least a preliminary conclusion, only to back off, either leaving the answer inconclusive, or partially developing an alternative line of reasoning. The book is nearly a thousand pages long, and Smith permitted himself numerous bypaths and diversions from his mainstream of thought. One might question whether the book would have received the recognition and study it has been accorded had it not contained the attack on Mercantilism. If it was this aspect that brought recognition to Smith, does it deserve careful study today? And again, has the economic system so changed in its structure as to make virtually all of the principles set forth by Smith of little value to us today? Even in the absence of such dramatic changes in our economy's structure, wasn't Smith's optimism so great as to vitiate much of his analysis, even when applied to his own times?

Smith offered a remarkably cheery view of the world about him in comparison to many of those economists to follow. The problem of high wages and population growth were seen as being capable of resolution or incorporation into his system. The benevolent direction of the "invisible hand" assured an automatic regulation of market forces. And yet with all of his optimism, Smith was a stern realist as well. He noted many imperfections in the nature of man and the operation of the market system. His cheerfulness with respect to production was tempered by caution in regard to the suitability of distribution as guided by the market forces.

It is true that as the problems and the setting changed, some of Smith's prescriptions became less usable. But this has always been true for all theories and will so continue. Criticism might better be directed at adherents of Smith's philosophy who fail to recognize the changing times, rather than at Smith himself. Later economists, not Smith, forgot the dictum that all production was for the purpose of consumption, and they relegated consumers to a secondary position under the assumption of an always existing demand.

Although much of the criticism is justifiable and there are serious weaknesses in Smith's analysis, this should not lead us to conclude that Smith's works have no value. Smith's originality lay in the manner in which he interwove a broad variety of material so that it formed a rational if not always vigorous whole. No previous writer had attempted to construct so ambitious a study of economic problems. While *Wealth of Nations* may not meet all the standards of a treatise in economics, surely the defense can be made that Smith never intended his book as such. Smith was a cautious reformer and he saw his book as a study of the nature of human economic welfare rather than a study of economics alone. It was this feature in addition to its philosophy of government that made the book so universally appealing. Although Smith never developed his theories of value and distribution fully by setting forth in an orderly fashion the variety of possible explanations, he did act as a stimulant to future economic thinking.

Nor should we belittle Smith's powers of observation. Whatever un-
kind words may be said about his ability as an economic theorist, the fact
remains that he was an astute student of the world about him. The book
abounds in statistical references and allusions to actual events. As we proceed to an examination of some of the writers to follow Smith, we will
find cause to regret that they did not share in Smith's appreciation of the
importance of facing things in a realistic manner. Later economists should
also have learned how to hold the reader's attention. Even with its mean-
dering and discursive style, Smith's book, even two centuries later, remains
enormously readable.

CHAPTER IV: Malthus—
Pessimism Personified

> *. . . Mr. Malthus, as was natural, never cleared his mind entirely of the dismal theory with which he began. Scarcely any man who has evoked a striking and original conception of a subject ever gets rid of it; long after he himself fancies that he has cleared his mind of it, everyone sees that it haunts him still. Mr. Malthus was peculiarly little likely to get rid of his errors; he had published his original theory, had made a name by publishing it, and he never admitted even to himself how complete a change the foundation of his ideas had undergone.*
>
> —WALTER BAGEHOT

> *There are perhaps few subjects on which human ingenuity has been more exerted than the endeavour to meliorate the condition of the poor; and there is certainly no subject in which it has so completely failed.*
>
> —THOMAS ROBERT MALTHUS

THOMAS ROBERT MALTHUS (1766–1834)

Few students of economics would fail to recognize the name of Thomas Malthus. Indeed, concern over the Malthusian specter of overpopulation has become so widespread that many laymen could probably identify him equally well. After nearly a century, during which Malthus' warnings were generally dismissed as no longer relevant, the threat of hunger and starvation resulting from overpopulation has again returned to the fore in economic writing on the problem of underdeveloped nations. If Adam Smith was the father of political economy, then Malthus was the man who earned for it Thomas Carlyle's appellation, the "dismal science." For where Smith had foreseen the possibility of increasing productivity leading to material improvement in the conditions of the working classes, Malthus foresaw continued misery and suffering. Smith had counseled the payment of higher wages because higher wages would enable workers to buy more goods, thereby producing a further widening of the market, and because he believed that higher wages made for healthier, more efficient workers. Malthus denied the likelihood of either of these predictions ever coming true and in fact found partial inspiration for his own dissenting views in the writings of Smith. While painting a dismal picture of the future of mankind, Malthus was to formulate one of the few "laws" of economics—not his Law of Population, which still has questionable stature as a "law," but rather the Law of Diminishing Returns.[1] Later economists were to revise and polish Malthus' first crude formulation until it took its present form, with the more precise terminology, the Law of Variable Proportions. Before turning to a more orderly consideration of Malthus' contributions, however, let us pause briefly to look at the man himself.

The Man. Malthus was one of a family of eight children, whose father was an English country gentleman. Malthus knew little, personally, of the living conditions of the poor about whom he wrote. As a young man, he came by his love of philosophical dispute naturally. His father was an avid reader of philosophy and a friend of Jean Jacques Rousseau and other contemporary philosophers. Malthus received the impetus for writing his *Essay on Population* from discussions with his father on some of these writings. His father encouraged him to do so, even though the elder Malthus strongly disagreed with his son's conclusions.

Although Malthus is usually pictured as a stern minister of the Anglican Church, he was in fact a rather jolly individual who liked a good joke, whether told by him or a companion. Nor was he a minister for all his life; he served in this capacity for only a short period of time after his ordination in 1797. It is true that he was a practicing clergyman at the time he first published his *Essay on Population,* but shortly after the appearance of the second edition, Malthus accepted a post as a professor of history and political economy at Haileybury College, which had been established with funds donated by the East India Company and dedicated to the training of young men for service in that company. Although hampered by a speech defect, Malthus is generally reputed to have been a popular lecturer, giving clear, concise lectures. Malthus did not marry until he was thirty-eight, and the three children who were a product of this happy marriage were of a number in keeping with Malthusian doctrine. He believed that the average marriage tended to produce six children, of whom four survived to have children of their own. Malthus' contribution

---

[1] It would be more accurate to say that the seeds of the Law of Diminishing Returns were embedded in Malthus but that it was John Stuart Mill who cultivated them and presented their growth to the world as Malthus' contribution.

to the pressure of overpopulation was partly coincidental, because only two of Malthus' children were living at the time of his death.

The Book. There was nothing original in the statement that the increase in population had a tendency to outstrip the means of subsistence. Many eminent writers had warned of this danger long before Malthus set pen to paper. Plato, Aristotle, the Physiocrats, John Steuart, John Locke, and Benjamin Franklin are some of the writers who quickly come to mind. Only the comparative ratios between the expansion of population and foodstuffs was new, and this was perhaps the least valid part of Malthus' contribution.

How, then, are we to explain the impact which this new statement of an old idea achieved? Why did it on the one hand convince William Pitt, a former staunch advocate of the Poor Laws, to withdraw in 1800 a bill for Poor Relief, and on the other hand, produce such a violent storm of criticism? It is true that the events of the time gave fuller support to Malthus than they had to his predecessors; the population of England was rising sharply after a long period of virtual stability, and two great wars had demonstrated the effectiveness of this means of checking population growth. We will have occasion to refer to the expansion in population later in this chapter, but for the real source of Malthus' impact we must look elsewhere.

Malthus wrote the first edition of his *Essay on Population* in 1798 and had it published anonymously. It was written as a vigorous protest against certain utopian dreams, with all the moral fervor and indignation capable of being expressed by the young.[2] Criticism was not long in coming, and William Godwin, one of Malthus' targets, referred to it in an answering book—*Political Justice*— as the "black and terrible demon that is always ready to stifle the hopes of humanity." The Malthusian doctrine was as controversial in its day as its more modern versions have remained until this very moment. The issue was warmly discussed in social, economic, and political circles alike. Malthus realized that his position had been too hastily taken, but he was convinced of the basic accuracy of his thesis despite the attacks of his critics. He sought to buttress his arguments by undertaking a tour of the Continent in search of supporting evidence. Malthus traveled abroad for three years, visiting Russia, the Scandinavian

[2] The full title of Malthus' first edition was *An Essay on the Principles of Population As It Affects the Future Improvement of Society with Remarks on the Speculations of Mr. Godwin, M. Condorcet and Other Writers.* By the second edition an equally formidable title had been composed, but all reference to the utopian philosophers had disappeared.

countries, France, and Germany. In addition to experiencing this firsthand exposure, he also collected and read a large volume of statistical data on population and birth-control practices in countries all over the world. He made extensive use of his travels and research to strengthen the factual content of the first edition's statement. He was now in a position to furnish the reader with all too numerous illustrations of methods used in various parts of the world to check overpopulation. One reads of abortions, infanticides, and the exposure of the older members of the society to the forces of nature. All of these practices helped to explain, said Malthus, why a population explosion had not occurred long ago. In the process of collecting and reporting this data, Malthus anticipated some of the subsequent work of modern anthropologists. His search for evidence in other lands was in sharp contrast with the methods of contemporary English economists, who were content to establish England as a model for the rest of the world.

Fortified with this evidence in support of his original thesis, Malthus presented to the public in 1803 what he considered a greatly strengthened version of his work. This second statement was a more complete new book, rather than a second edition, and this time Malthus' authorship was clearly identified. What had been gained in the way of statistical support had been lost in the way of literary charm, and some of Malthus' more challenging refutations of Godwin had disappeared. Although the new book was more in keeping with the investigative techniques of a social scientist, it is doubtful whether Malthus' theory, if first advanced in that form, would ever have created the stir that it did. Four subsequent editions of this new version of the *Essay,* including some modifications, were to appear.

Economic Views. The basic thesis contained in both versions of the Malthusian doctrine can be very quickly summarized. To use much the same language employed by Malthus—the argument consisted of an assertion that human progress was incapable of being maintained because a nations' population always tended to increase at a more rapid rate than its supply of food. The argument, as developed by Malthus, consisted of two basic propositions: (1) That passion between the sexes was mutually enduring and tended to lead to an expansion of the population at a geometric rate of progression (2, 4, 8, 16, 32, etc.) and (2) The means for sustaining this expanding population were capable of increasing only at an arithmetic rate (1, 2, 3, 4, 5, 6, etc.).[3] Unless something acted to check

    3 While the arithmetic ratio remained a part of the second and subsequent editions,

the tendency of population increases to outstrip the growth in the means of subsistence the inevitable result would be death by malnutrition and starvation.

Malthus's first edition provided little hope for a solution to this dilemma in the way of possible checks to population growth. If population failed to expand at a geometric rate of progression, it was because certain positive, natural checks acted to restrain population expansion. War, disease, famine, and vice acted as positive checks. When all else failed, the ultimate check was the shortage of food. Before the economy reached this state, however, the expansion in population was likely to be halted by the prevalence of various diseases which played an increasingly lethal role as the means of subsistence became less and less.

The outbursts of indignation and the fiery criticism to which this early statement was subjected led Malthus not only to search for statistical evidence to support his conclusion, but also to qualify this grim conclusion with another possible check to overpopulation which would be less annoying to his critics.

Malthus, in the second and subsequent editions, distinguished between the *positive* and the *preventative* checks to overpopulation. The positive checks remained as listed above. But now Malthus stated that there was another possibility; people might exercise sufficient moral restraint. If people would postpone marriage until a late age in life, the number of children produced by the typical marriage could thereby be sharply reduced. Now men were given an opportunity once again to guide their own futures.

The inspiration provided by Malthus to the writings of Charles Darwin has been frequently noted by students of the history of ideas. The first edition of Malthus' *Essay* definitely had the seeds of Darwin's approach: Men, in their tendency to reproduce themselves, were compared with plants and animals. In the second and succeeding editions, however, Malthus recognized the possibility that man, with his superior mental abilities, might be capable of intelligently forestalling the dread effects of overpopulation. Man could be more than merely blindly adaptive to his environment. This concession did little to still the more vociferous of Malthus' critics, and, indeed, even today it is unclear how seriously Malthus himself took his own qualifications to his original doctrine. It seems quite possible that Malthus offered this concession for purposes of making his theory

---

Malthus was much less dogmatic about the possibility of the means of production expanding at more than an arithmetic rate. He continued to maintain that it held true for Great Britain but recognized that it was inapplicable for the colonies.

more complete and exact, and less subject to challenge. The fact that moral restraint was now offered as a possible solution does not mean that Malthus himself took this possibility very seriously.

In a way, this is one of the irritating aspects of the Malthusian doctrine. In essence, Malthus has presented his readers with a kind of "Heads I win, tails you lose" proposition. His message can be interpreted somewhat as follows: Population tends to expand without end unless something acts to check it, in which case it does not. In either event the Malthusian prediction has come true. With such assurance of accuracy, it is little wonder that the Malthusian doctrine became the *Law* of Population. Such an interpretation of Malthus undoubtedly ignores the serious message that he attempted to convey. The fact that his lesson can be reduced to the principle that something will happen unless it doesn't should not blind us to the possibility that the worst of Malthus' fears could conceivably come true.

Many commentators on Malthus' work have seen a connection between Malthus' *Esssay* and his training as a clergyman. It has been argued, for example, that Malthus saw man as generally sinful by nature after his fall from grace, and that, being sinful, man was incapable of achieving perfectability here on earth. But as we shall see shortly, part of Malthus' motivation for writing his *Essay* lay in his rejection of this possibility. Nor was it as difficult to combine a faith in a just God with a belief in an eternal future of misery and suffering for man on earth as it might seem today.

Without minimizing the moral overtones of Malthus' *Essay,* it is also important to bear in mind that the book was written by an economist. Malthus was one of the two economics writers of any importance between Smith and Ricardo (the other was Lord Lauderdale, a minor figure in economic thought), and the first of those we have studied to hold a university post in economics. It will be remembered that Smith, the so-called "father of political economy" was a moral philosopher. Malthus' attempts to verify his theory with careful statistical research is in the best scientific tradition as set forth in our introductory chapter. Nor did Malthus fail to recognize the economic implications of his thesis.

It is now time to delve into what prompted this outburst of pessimism. Why did Malthus feel impelled to warn people about the imminent dangers of overpopulation? In part, the answer lies in Malthus' reaction to the optimistic tone contained in the writings of a number of contemporary philosophers and indeed in the opinions of Malthus' own father. In France, Condorcet had written *An Essay on the Progress of the Human Mind,* which asserted that man was capable of improving through the functioning of his own mental capabilities until he reached a state of virtual perfection. Meanwhile in England, William Godwin, the clergyman-turned-philosopher-and-writer, preached much the same gospel of progress. If anything, the future as envisioned by him was even rosier. The bane of man's existence, said Godwin, was bad government and faulty institutions. Godwin pictured a future society in which private property was abolished, the need for government ended, and men forced to work only for half an hour a day in order to earn a living. What men were to do with the remaining twenty-three and a half hours was never made completely clear, but evidently the additional time was not to be spent in amatory dalliance, since Godwin declared that in the future society man would learn to control his sexual passions. Even so, Malthus had reason to suspect that the idyllic scene described by Godwin would soon become overpopulated, for Godwin suggested that the additional free time would help to prolong men's life almost indefinitely.

The concept of a future utopia was not revolutionary, and the question had been examined by a number of earlier writers (Plato is one obvious example). Part of the success of Godwin and Condorcet in renewing this dream lay with their ability as writers. Even so, their views probably would have received far less attention from later generations if they had not both been the subjects of Malthus' vigorous attacks. Malthus could see little prospect that man would ever achieve such a golden age here on earth. His reasoning is apparent in the message conveyed in his *Essay* as outlined above; long before man had arrived at any such happy condition, the expanding population would have wiped out all traces of progress.

In part, Malthus was probably also prompted by the sudden upsurge in population taking place in England at the time he wrote. Thus, there was already clear evidence that improvements in man's condition led to sudden increases in the population. The accompanying table presents some rough estimates on the size of the population in England for the decades when Malthus' *Essay* was written.

POPULATION OF ENGLAND BY DECADES[4]

Decade	Population in Millions
1781	8.9
1791	9.7
1801	10.686
1811	12.147

[4] Phyllis Deane and W. A. Cole, *British Economic Growth 1688–1959* (Cambridge: Cambridge University Press, 1963), p. 8.

The population figures given for each year represent the most recent esti-mates made, and they differ by as much as a million from some earlier studies. Estimates are even more approximate for the period prior to 1770, but most students of English history agree that England's population re-mained virtually stationary at somewhere between six and seven million for over a hundred years. Thus the upsurge from 1770 on represented a sharp departure from the population pattern of the past. It seems likely now that Adam Smith was closer to the correct reason for this sudden up-surge in population than Malthus was. Smith had argued that there was always a tendency for a high birth rate among the laboring classes, but that no expansion in population resulted because of the simultaneous existence of a high death rate. He argued that rising wage rates would make possible better standards of health and therefore lead to reductions in the death rate. Most of our statistical evidence for the period, faulty as it is, suggests that Malthus, in stressing the rise in the birth rate induced by improved living standards, was emphasizing the wrong thing.[5] What apparently happened was much as Smith had prophesied—the betterment in eco-nomic conditions led to a marked reduction in the death rate.

Malthus was a reformer, like so many of the other writers we will study. Although his confidence in the power of his suggestions to cure the problem was markedly less than Smith's, he did advance one suggestion to improve public policy. Malthus concentrated his arguments on the Poor Laws.

Malthus' objections to the Poor Laws were couched in somewhat differ-ent terms from Smith's. He agreed that individual improvements in the conditions of the poor might be at least temporarily gained, but he as-serted that such improvements would not be lasting or conducive to the general welfare. Malthus noted that the more money collected for the alleviation of poverty, the worse the situation of the poor seemed to be-come. He questioned this apparent contradiction. The seeming inconsist-ency proved, on careful examination, to be easily solved. The more sup-port given to the poor, the greater the increase in the numbers of the poor. Furthermore, the funds given to the poor would simply push up the price of the means of subsistence, ultimately leaving the poor no better off than they were before. The real problem was a shortage of the necessities of

[5] A modern supporter of Malthus' position is Professor H. J. Habakkuk. See his article entitled "English Population in the 18th Century," *Economic History Review,* 2d ser., VI (1953), 117–133. Habakkuk argues that medical science was at the time not yet that much improved and that the lower death rate statistics were unreliable and probably produced by the increased proportion of the population in the younger age brackets.

life, not of the money with which to buy them. In modern terms, Malthus saw the Poor Laws as a solution operating much like the suggestion to cure wartime shortages of goods by the issuing of more ration coupons. Basic to Malthus' opposition to the Poor Laws was his view of human character. In his opinion, most men were naturally lazy and unwilling to work hard except when forced to do so. Without the protection of the Poor Laws, men might be driven to greater effort to support their expanded families, but with the security provided by the Poor Laws, no compensating increase in effort to offset the expanded numbers would be forthcoming.

Malthus' opposition to the Poor Laws was predicated also on their sharply rising cost. From a figure of £689,000 in 1750 the expenditure for poor relief had risen to £3,861,000 by 1800. Within a period of fifty years the cost of supporting the poor had grown fivefold, and it continued to grow for several decades thereafter. During this time the population had little more than doubled. It is a tribute to the persuasiveness of Malthus that by 1834 substantial reform of the Poor Laws had been achieved. Despite this achievement, however, Malthus cannot really be congratulated for providing dramatic solutions for the problems he posed. In reality, Malthus saw no humane solution to the problem of excess numbers save the practice of moral restraint. A passage from Chapter 3 of Book IV of his *Essay* is instructive on this point.

I do not see how it is possible for any person who acknowledges the principle of utility as the great criterion of moral rules to escape the conclusion that moral restraint, or the abstaining from marriage till we are in a condition to support a family, with a perfectly moral conduct during that period, is the strict line of duty. . . .[6]

The passage is interesting not only for the recommendation it contains, but also because it makes obvious that Malthus was not opposed to children as such. When a man was able to earn sufficient income to support his family properly, the propriety of raising a family was unquestioned.

As Malthus continued, it becomes evident that he placed little faith in the effectiveness of even this recommendation for moral restraint. The following brief passage makes this doubt quite clear.

At the same time I believe that few of my readers can be less sanguine than I am in their expectations of any sudden and great change in the general conduct of men on this subject: and the chief reason why in the last chapter I al-

[6] T. R. Malthus, *An Essay on Population* (New York: Everyman's Library, 1933), Vol. II, 168.

lowed myself to suppose the universal prevalence of this virtue was, that I might endeavour to remove any imputation on the goodness of the Deity, by showing that the evils arising from the principle of population were exactly of the same nature as the generality of other evils. . . .[7]

We have suggested that Malthus' work was both warmly supported and bitterly attacked. The opposition of those whom Malthus had questioned can be readily comprehended, but the groups who praised Malthus' views were business groups who found the Malthusian explanation for the existence of poverty particularly appealing. For who was to blame for the existence of the poor in Malthusian terms? Not the capitalist or the factory owner who paid low wages; if wages were low and the poor numerous, the fault lay with the poor themselves. By their thoughtless tendency to overproduce themselves, they were condemning themselves and their children to these miserable conditions. As various Parliamentary committees undertook studies of the working conditions in English factories, the appeal of the Malthusian explanation of poverty grew increasingly attractive to the upper-class employers. Note that the implication of the doctrine was that if workers would only behave in a prudent fashion, there was almost no limit to the improvement in their conditions which could be obtained. Indeed, James Mill, the father of John Stuart Mill and a devout disciple of Malthus, made exactly that observation in attacking the schemes of the Socialists. Without population control, James Mill said, all plans to redistribute income would accomplish nothing; with checks on population, improvement of the condition of workers would proceed automatically.[8]

CRITICISMS. We have already seen that the first and succeeding editions of Malthus' *Essay* were criticized. These criticisms were not all of the name-calling variety; many of them were based on sound economic principles. Critics were particularly dubious about the validity of the two ratios. They argued that Malthus never made it clear whether he regarded the geometric increase in population a tendency or an actuality. Malthus' references to the United States as illustration of the principle were discredited on two grounds. It was pointed out that a substantial part of America's rapid increase in population was due to immigration—a fact for which Malthus never allowed. The further claim was made that the United States was unrepresentative of conditions elsewhere because such a large proportion of its population was of child-bearing age, thus fostering

[7] *Ibid.*

[8] James Mill, *Elements of Political Economy,* 7th ed. (London: Longmans Green, Reader and Dyer, 1871), Vol. I, p. 201.

a more rapid expansion of population than would normally occur. The arithmetic increase in the means of subsistence was subjected to even great challenge. Critics maintained that Malthus offered no empirical evidence to support his conclusion that food production could proceed at no more rapid a pace. At their most naïve state, critics suggested that every additional birth meant not only one more mouth to feed but an additional pair of hands to help produce. More sophisticated critics emphasized the wonders of the revolution in agriculture.

The lowest criticisms of all, however, came with the charge that Malthus was not only a bad economist but a poor theologian as well. Some critics cited the biblical admonition to "be fruitful and multiply." Others recalled the words of Saint Peter that it was better to marry than burn, and suggested that Malthus' prescription of late marriages would but increase the already excessive amount of vice.[9]

Summary and Evaluation. In summary, there is much of value in the Malthusian doctrine. Malthus was not only the founder of a new field of study—demography—but a significant contributor to the history of economic thought as well. His theory of population had a profound effect on the thinking of economists for the next half century. By the turn of the twentieth century, however, the Law of Population was considered to be obsolete, as applied to modern industrial nations, at least, and the pendulum was beginning to swing in the opposite direction. Concern was now expressed about the possible depopulation of certain countries. A quotation from an old history of economic thought by Charles Gide and Charles Rist is illustrative of this point. Speaking of the validity of the Malthusian Law they comment "The fears of Malthus have vanished: the other spectre, race suicide, is now casting a gloom over the land."[10]

If we stopped at this point, the critics of Malthus would appear to have won the day. The rate of population growth, instead of increasing geometrically as Malthus had predicted, was actually decreasing. In part this may have been due to urbanization, but it appears also to have been the result of parents' deliberate choice to forego added children in order to raise further their standard of living. New and convenient methods of birth

[9] An interesting criticism from an opposite viewpoint came from a man named Francis Place who argued that birth control was the only answer and who criticized Malthus for failing to recognize this. In 1823, following his criticism of Malthus on this point, Place offered one of the first handbooks providing specific information on the means of avoiding conception.

[10] Charles Gide and Charles Rist, *A History of Economic Doctrines* (London: D. C. Heath, n.d.), p. 133.

control made it easier to put this plan into effect. Malthus, of course, included all of the then known methods of birth control under the heading "vice" and would have deplored society's reliance on these techniques.

Since the time of Malthus, startling progress has been made in uncovering new techniques for producing foodstuffs. Also, Malthus was guilty of a failure to appreciate sufficiently the significance of the Agricultural Revolution. His critics were correct in maintaining that he was far too pessimistic about the potentialities for further expansion in the rate of output, as the United States secretaries of agriculture for the past thirty years have been all too well aware. Far from holding to the arithmetic increases predicted by Malthus, a smaller and smaller number of farmers have been able to oversupply a larger and larger population. Nor is the end of the growing efficiency in agricultural production even now in sight; the Law of Diminishing Returns with its assumption of a fixed state of technology, has had little scope for operation in United States agriculture. The law has been refined and reworked through the years, but its application in the manner envisioned by Malthus has proved to be inaccurate.

Despite these encouraging signs, recent years have witnessed a resurgence of interest in the Malthusian doctrine. Economists, who for fifty years had been treating the Malthusian Law purely as a matter of historical interest, have suddenly found cause to examine his writing more carefully. One reason for this renewed interest has been the impact of the "revolution of rising expectations" noted by Adlai Stevenson in connection with the problem of underdeveloped countries. Many of these countries, eager to move overnight from the thirteenth to the twentieth century, have been threatened with engulfment by population explosions. The name of Malthus inevitably arises in conjunction with these countries; the battle between high birth rates and the forces of famine, misery, and disease are more than faintly reminiscent of Malthus' thinking—although in some cases it seems evident that the problem of rapidly expanding population is more nearly one of a falling death rate than a rising birth rate.

Malthusian doctrine has also received a wider hearing in the more advanced countries. Dire predictions about the exhaustion of our natural resources or the evil effects of the more recent upsurge in the birth rate have haunted the thoughts of even an "affluent society" like the United States. Neo-Malthusians such as William Vogt and Fairfield Osborne deplore the wasteful habits of modern society, even without an expansion in population. Further increases in numbers only render the situation more difficult. Many of the present-day Malthusians recommend the dissemination of birth control information—a policy that even Malthus was never able to recommend, because of moral reservations. Men and women, said Malthus, should exercise restraint by postponing marriage until they were older. Malthus had no constructive recommendations for those who were married; presumably he regarded the rearing of children as a natural and proper result of any marriage.

Thus, by exaggerating the danger of overpopulation, Malthus failed to convey clearly an important lesson to be drawn from his *Essay.* Current alarmists on the subject of population also sometimes overstate their case. There is little danger that the earth will someday become so crowded that we (or more properly, our descendants) will have no room in which to move. The real danger is in the uneconomic balance between resources and population. Let the number of people exceed some optimum total, and productivity and efficiency will decline. When this occurs, retardation and retrogression, rather than growth, begin.

OTHER VIEWS. Although Malthus was most famous for his *Essay on Population,* he wrote a number of other works as well. Among these were studies of the Poor Laws and the Corn Laws, *The Principles of Political Economy, Considered With a View to Their Practical Application; Definitions of Political Economy,* and his *Inquiry into the Nature and Process of Rent.* A few of the ideas contained in these studies are worth our examination. We have noted that Malthus' view of natural law was far less optimistic than that of Smith. Nevertheless, he was generally a firm supporter of the concept and its concomitant principle of laissez-faire. An important exception to this generalization was Malthus' recommendations with respect to the Corn Laws. Ignoring Smith's plea for freer trade, Malthus took issue also with Ricardo's recommendation (see Chapter V) for the gradual abolition of the Corn Laws. England's Corn Laws were a holdover from the days of Mercantilism, and they had been employed as a means of stabilizing the internal supply and price of corn. Corn was alternately imported or exported, depending on the success of the harvests, and a system of import duties and export duties was devised to prevent excessive flows of corn in either direction. Through the years England had become more and more dependent upon foreign sources for part of her supply of corn, and her own exports, had dwindled to nothing. As a result, the import duties became increasingly onerous and produced much public protest. However, Malthus supported a continuation of these import duties. In defense of his position, Malthus argued that their abolition would unduly penalize the landlords by reducing their rent. More important, the result would be a lessening in agricultural activity, as the less fertile pieces of land were unable to meet foreign competition. Malthus considered this undesirable since he felt that agriculture and industry should remain equally important.

In the light of Ricardo's subsequent emphasis on the importance of rent, which will be discussed in Chapter V, the views of Malthus on this subject are also of some interest. Malthus saw three basic explanations for the existence of rent.[11] Two of his explanations were identical to those of Smith. Rent could be the product of the bountifulness of labor—the fact that the land produced enough to more than compensate the cultivators for their efforts—or it could result from the comparative scarcity of the most fertile lands. This second explanation was developed further by Ricardo. Malthus' third explanation was new and will lead us to an appraisal of another important part of his thinking. This explanation was that food, unlike other products, produced its own demand. As the food supply expanded, so did the population, thereby assuring an ever-ready demand for additional food. The contemporaries of Malthus were willing to concede the possibility that a particular product might be overproduced (although here they even tended to minimize the problem), but they denied the possibility of general overproduction. It was Malthus' other great contribution to the history of economic thought to suggest the possibility of a general glut of all nonfood market goods. Before we can appraise the significance of Malthus' suggestion, however, we must pause briefly to introduce the founder of the opposite school of thinking—Jean Baptiste Say.

JEAN BAPTISTE SAY (1767–1832)

Say's principal work, *Treatise on Political Economy,* was first published in 1803. The book was readable and highly popular at the time of its publication, and it was widely read as a simple exposition of the views of Adam Smith. After a delay of eleven years, the second edition appeared in 1814 and in the next twelve years three additional editions were published. Due in part perhaps to its popular success, Say's work was never taken very seriously by later economists, who usually relegated it to the status of a popularization of Adam Smith. Probably few of today's economists could correctly state the title of Say's work, although all of them could state the essence of Say's Law of the Markets.

[11] T. R. Malthus, *An Inquiry into the Nature and Process of Rent* (London: J. Murray, 1815).

The Man. Born in Lyons, France, Say became an economist after a career in journalism. For a brief time he served as the editor for *Décade Philosophique Littéraire et Politique.* A career in government followed when Say was appointed to the Committee of Finance by Napoleon. His book displeased Napoleon, and as a result Say returned to journalism from government service. Thereafter he served as a professor of political economy at the Conservatoire des Arts et Métiers and later at the College of France. A grandson, Léon Say, earned further distinction for the name of Say in French economic circles.

Economic Views. The tendency to disparage Say's contributions is not completely just. It was Say's book which sounded the final death knell for the Physiocrats. Although Physiocratic thought was in a state of disorder after the death of its founder, Quesnay, remnants of the school were still to be found throughout France. Say's espousal of industrial capitalism was far more complete than Smith's had been. Where Smith had continued to place agriculture in a high if not dominant position in the economy, Say moved industry into the driver's seat. The change in tone between Smith's and Say's books is a mark of the strides made by the Industrial Revolution. The simple pin factory no longer provided an accurate picture of industrial production.

Recognition should be accorded also to Say's attempts to fashion political economy into a true science. All of the previous writers we have studied (and many of those still to come) had treated political economy as a kind of guide to political and economic action. Say insisted that political science should be studied in the same manner as the natural sciences; there were certain natural laws to be discovered and it was the function of the student of political economy to uncover these rather than to prescribe therapeutic remedies for the day's problems.

The principle which has assured Say of lasting immortality, however, is his famous Law of the Markets, frequently referred to today as simply Say's Law. The principle enunciated in it has remained an important part of economic thought throughout the years and is still widely discussed today; John Maynard Keynes "revolution" in economic thought in the 1930's consisted largely of an attack on this "law."

The seeds of doubt about the ability of an unplanned economy to assure a maintenance of full employment were sown early, and Say was anxious to uproot these doubts before they did further damage. The heart of his argument is found in the following passage: "The total supply of products and the total demand for them must of necessity be equal, for the total demand is nothing but the total mass of commodities which have been produced; a general congestion would consequently be an absurdity." [12] Thus, more briefly, "supply creates its own demand." When products are produced, the various factors of production receive payments for the services they contributed. With the money thus earned, the persons controlling the three factors of production—land, labor, and capital—are able to buy back the goods they have helped to produce. A particular product may be overproduced—that is, it cannot be sold at a price sufficient to cover its total cost of production. But this means that some other product has been produced in insufficient quantities and the operation of the automatic price mechanism will soon act to rectify this error. The nature of the circular flow involved can be seen in Fig. 1.

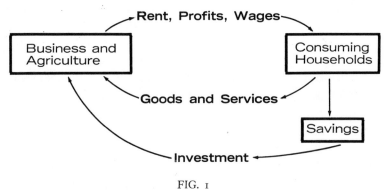

FIG. 1

Note in Figure 1 that while savings might be thought to constitute a problem, such is not really the case. Money saved is returned to the businessman for reinvestment into the economy and thus retained in the income stream.

   Malthus was the first in a continuing string of heretics who challenged the validity of Say's Law, but whose views, in turn, were never really admitted to the mainstream of economic thought. Not until Keynes wrote his *General Theory* did these economists receive any respectful attention. Malthus predicated his doubts about the correctness of Say's Law on an acceptance of Smith's labor command theory of value, and a rejection of Ricardo's adoption of the labor jelly theory. Malthus argued that the productive workers in society were not paid the full value of the product; the discrepancy between the wage paid and the price at which the product was

   [12] Jean Baptiste Say, *A Treatise on Political Economy,* trans. by C. R. Prinsep (Boston: Wells and Lilly, 1821), Vol. II, p. 175.

sold was accounted for by the profit.[13] The profits could not be relied upon to augment demand since capitalists tended to save their money and invest it for still further production of goods. Thus deprived of adequate support from either the productive workers or the capitalists, the market was likely to suffer a general glut of products as the level of *effective* demand failed to match the outpouring of goods into the marketplace. Malthus saw as the only solution to this dilemma the bolstering of demand by the "unproductive" workers in the economy. While acknowledging the importance of capital accumulation to the progress of a nation, Malthus thought there could be too much of a good thing. If capital was accumulated too rapidly or in excessive amounts, it would penalize "unproductive" consumption, and unproductive consumption was ". . . absolutely necessary" if a country with great productive capacity was to succeed in consuming all that produce.

The list of unproductive consumers was an interesting one. It included lawyers, soldiers, doctors, servants, statesmen, and clergymen. First and foremost, however, were the landlords with their incomes of rent to spend.

Malthus was thus an interesting forerunner of a whole school of "underworld" economists known as the underconsumptionists. We will postpone an examination of the validity of this school's doctrines until later. We can point out here, however, that Malthus' version rested on a questionable explanation of value and it is startling in view of his exposition of the Law of Population. Why Malthus did not place greater stress on the role of expanding population in maintaining effective demand is difficult to explain.

[13] Malthus, *Principles of Political Economy, Considered with a View to Their Practical Application* (Boston, 1821), p. 119.

CHAPTER V: Ricardo—
The Pessimistic View
Continued

*Had Ricardo had a typewriter and had
he circulated copies of his manuscript
for criticism, the world might have been
spared Marx.*
—ARTHUR SMITHIES

*. . . one would suppose from his [Mal-
thus'] language that I considered them
[the landlords] enemies of the state.*
—DAVID RICARDO

DAVID RICARDO (1772–1823)

The works of both Adam Smith and Thomas Malthus suffered from one serious defect. Each man demonstrated great powers as a recorder of the current economic scene, but lacked the ability to develop a rigorous theoretical model without which economics could not become a true science. David Ricardo had that ability. His technique is interesting, not only for his abstract, analytical way of thinking, but because of the manner in which he built on the work of his precedessors. His book is a difficult one to read. Subjects are taken up in no meaningful order; for example, an issue may be partly analyzed in one chapter, only to be dropped and then picked up again several chapters later. Subsequent editions of the book were expanded simply by the addition of chapters at the end; they did not undergo complete revision. Ricardo's illustrations are all hypothetical, and at first reading appear to bear little resemblance to the real world even as it then existed. Whereas *Wealth of Nations* contained endless numbers of quotable passages, there are few lines in *Principles of Political Economy and Taxation* to attract the student. Despite all these blemishes few books have done more to set a pattern for the proper study of a subject than Ricardo's brief book did for economics.

The Man. Both Smith and Malthus had been members of the academic profession throughout most of their lives, but Ricardo made his career in the world of business. As a result, Ricardo received less formal academic training, a fact which may explain his problems in defining his position. In a sense Ricardo had been born to a career in business, since his father was a banker. The father, having moved to England from Holland, took Ricardo into his firm when the boy was 14. Ricardo showed his independence of mind at a young age by marrying a gentile woman and breaking with his family, who were Jewish. Ricardo, who also wrote extensively about the condition of the poor, was even more removed from their position than Malthus had been. Years before his classic study was written, Ricardo had amassed a sizable fortune on the exchange, and he did not turn to a study of the problem of economizing until the question was no longer a personal issue. By that time he had become a member of the landlord class—a group which received much criticism in his *Principles.* Ricardo was elected to Parliament in 1819, where he served until his death in 1823. While a member, he took an active role both in instigating and in opposing numerous reforms. He was an active participant despite the handicap of being a poor speaker. Although he was unable to express his thoughts clearly, either verbally or in written form, Ricardo's intellectual prowess was evident despite these faults, and his mental capabilities assured him of a respectful audience, though sometimes a puzzled one. While his *Principles* was to be the basis for his enduring fame, Ricardo wrote numerous other articles and tracts. Thanks to the patient efforts of Piero Sraffa, an Italian economist who now resides in England, these writings have all been collected and indexed for the use of students wishing to explore further the thinking of this complex mind. Ricardo died at the age of 51 from an ear infection.

Economic Views. Basic to an understanding of Ricardo's system is his distinction between the long and the short run. In discussing the issues of market and natural price, the nature of value, and the problem of distribution, we need to remind ourselves constantly that the solutions with which Ricardo provided us were applicable only to the long run. The entire concept of equilibrium as a kind of norm to which the economy constantly tended to return, no matter what forces were diverting it, was predicated on this distinction. Short-run deviations were recognized, but they were by definition temporary aberrations which had no lasting impact on the economy. The unwary reader who does not remember Ricardo's concentration on the long-run solution will find himself frequently quarreling with Ricardo for the wrong reason.

Ricardo's emphasis upon the importance of the long run, with its accompanying concept of equilibrium, is important not only for an understanding of his system but because it set a standard for the analysis of the economists who were to follow. It provided a convenient means of dismissing some of the more pressing problems of the day, such as business cycles and unemployment, as short-run problems which would soon correct themselves as the economy returned to its long-run equilibrium position. As Keynes not too profoundly remarked in criticizing this concentration of Classical economists on the long-run solution, "In the long run, we are all dead."

This distinction between the long and the short run provided Ricardo with fresh insight into the operation of natural law. Like so many of his contemporaries, Ricardo believed that the economic system was guided by the operation of certain natural laws; once the operation of these laws had been discovered, the operation of the system *in the long run* could be understood. Smith and Ricardo chose different problems to attack in their search for a natural law of economic behavior. Whereas Smith had concentrated on the problem of production, Ricardo was preoccupied with the problems of distribution. How were the payments to land, labor, and capital determined? What was happening to the relative share of each of these three?

In seeking an answer to these questions, Ricardo borrowed solutions from both Smith and Malthus. From Smith, Ricardo developed the concept of capital accumulation, and from Malthus the principle of population expansion. Important alterations were made in Malthus' doctrine, but the basic contention remained the same.

The capitalist saved his money and put it into his business because of the profits to be made. Variations in the rates of profit were considered unlikely to exist for any sustained period, because other businessmen would seize upon the opportunity and the differentials would thus be quickly erased. Ricardo was far more willing than Smith had been to assume virtually perfect knowledge and perfect mobility of labor and capital. If Smith's economic man had been "a wee bit Scotch," Ricardo's man was somewhat of a stockbroker—eager to seize upon the slightest economic advantage and react accordingly. Ricardo saw the result of this accumulation in terms that, in their preliminary stages, resembled Smith's views. As the capital accumulated, the demand for labor increased, bringing with it an inevitable rise in money wages. This increase in the market price of labor would lead in turn, just as Smith had suggested, to a rise in the population, with an eventual expansion in the labor force.

But here Smith and Ricardo parted company. For where Smith had seen the rise in the supply of labor acting as a restraint on higher wages, Ricardo saw the expansion of the total population as impinging on the means of subsistence. Just as Malthus had pictured the growth of the population as leading to an ever rising cost of living, thus worsening the standard of living for the majority of population, so also did Ricardo fear the effects of this expansion in population.

Wages would not be restored to their previous lower levels by the increase in the size of the labor force. Why not? Because the added numbers made necessary a permanent rise in the cost of living. Since the natural level of wages was geared to this cost of living, a rise in that cost would inevitably produce a rise in the natural level of wages. As the natural rate of wages was thereby increased, the rate of profits would inevitably decline. The time would eventually come when the rate of profit would decline to the point where no further accumulation of capital would take place. When this happened, all economic growth would cease and the stationary state would emerge.

The capitalist would not benefit from this process because his rate of profits declined steadily as the process continued. The worker would not benefit in the long run either, although he might benefit for indeterminate periods as the market price for his services soared above the natural subsistence wage. In the long run, wages would settle to the subsistence level. It was the third class, the landlords, who really benefited. As the demand for the means of subsistence rose, increased cultivation of both an intensive and extensive nature became necessary. The more fertile lands were increasingly capable of yielding a surplus paid to the landlord in the form of rent.

In capsule form this is the essence of Ricardo's famous theory of rent. Note its dependence on the Malthusian principle of population. If higher wages did not produce an expansion in population faster than the means of subsistence were able to be increased, the entire picture would change. In fact, Ricardo himself was hopeful that if Parliament adopted his recommendations, the dismal picture he painted could be postponed for an indefinite period of time. One of the problems he and his followers faced was to explain why England continued to grow at a rapid pace even though trade restrictions were not removed until the mid-nineteenth century.

VALUE. Before filling in some of the details of this sketchy outline of

Ricardo's system of distribution, it is necessary to begin as Ricardo did with a consideration of the definition of value. Students of Ricardo have debated whether he developed his theory of value to help explain the question of distribution or whether the reverse was true. Our own interpretation leans to the former belief—that Ricardo was most concerned with the question of distribution and that his concept of value was developed accordingly. Whichever interpretation is the correct one, however, the fact remains that the question of value was never resolved to the satisfaction of either Ricardo or his readers. Near the end of his life Ricardo wrote to Malthus confessing that the theory of value as he (Ricardo) had explained it in his book no longer completely satisfied him and that he found the question to be more troublesome than at first.

As one begins the chapter "On Value," the first impression is a return to the early picture given by Adam Smith. The value of a commodity is again determined by the quantity of labor involved in its production. Certain refinements have been introduced. The uncertainty of choice between the labor jelly and the labor command theories has been resolved in favor of the former. (Ricardo criticized Smith for treating the two as if they were identities.)

Ricardo began by discarding value in use as a personal issue; the real question was the value products had in exchange for other products. Furthermore, it was relative values over time and space which were important, not absolute values. Certain nonreproducible items, such as rare paintings, which were too few in number to merit attention, were also discarded from the analysis.

Ricardo was thus seeking a way to determine the relative values of reproducible commodities. For such commodities, the amount of labor that needed to be expended under the most difficult conditions of production determined their value. This last sentence is an important key to a preliminary understanding of Ricardo's explanation of value. Note that while labor determined the value of a product, it was not just any labor but that labor expended on the final unit of the product necessary to satisfy demand, even if labor employed on the last unit was unable to produce as much of the product as previous applications did. Suppose that one unit of labor was capable of producing two bushels of wheat but that the demand for wheat was such that still more wheat was required. If further production of wheat meant that only one bushel of wheat could be produced with one unit of labor, the value of wheat would have risen relative to all other products where the amount of labor required for their production had remained unchanged. This is true because it would now take more labor to produce a unit of wheat than previously. How could this happen? Because of the principle of diminishing returns as laid down by Malthus. According to Ricardo, attempts to expand production, particularly in agriculture, were likely to encounter less and less satisfactory conditions, thus leading to the necessity to employ more and more labor. As increased quantities of labor became necessary, the relative value of the product would thereby rise. Note the role played here by demand. Although Ricardo devoted little of his analysis to the role of demand in determining value, nevertheless it was important. Without the expanded demand for wheat, production would not have been pushed to the point where more than proportionate amounts of labor were required for the additional units of output.

Ricardo's first statement represented a marked improvement over the treatment given by Smith. Ricardo had perceived the fallacy of treating the labor jelly and the labor command theories as identities and had rebuked Smith along much the same lines as we noted in our discussion of Smith's concept of value.

Nor did the question of the division of the pie (the nation's output) create any more problems for Ricardo than they had for Smith; if anything, the problem was made simpler by the fact that the landlord was clearly excluded. Ricardo argued that the value of a product, although determined by the quantity of labor necessary to its relative production, constituted a pie capable of being divided into two parts—between the laborer in the form of wages and the capitalist in the form of profits. Rent, for reasons to be explained later, did not enter into the determination of value, but instead was an outgrowth of that value. Since wages and profits were component parts of a pie of fixed size, any change in either could come only at the expense of the other. Therefore, an increase in wages meant a decline in the rate of profits, not an increment in the value of the product. While the capitalist might try to correct this deplorable turn of events by raising the price of his product, such actions would be doomed to failure. Since all capitalists would attempt to recoup their losses in this manner, the result would be a general rise in prices, thus bringing the relative value of the products back to where they started.

Unfortunately for both the reader's and Ricardo's peace of mind, the problem of value involved far more complexities than were apparent at first inspection. Many of the qualifications and exceptions to the primitive model were necessitated by the existence of capital as well as labor. According to a first answer by Ricardo, the appearance of the labor theory of value created no real problem when capital was introduced. After all, capital was merely "stored-up" labor. Once capital had been so defined, it also could be reduced to the same common denominator.

Ricardo began his appraisal of the exceptions by noting wistfully that his theory as originally stated worked fine in a primitive society where members exchanged beaver for deer and the weapons used were of equal durability, requiring equal quantities of labor for their production. When these assumptions were removed however, changes in value were produced, not just by changes in the necessary quantity of labor but by changes in the cost of labor and by unequal quantities of stored-up labor or capital of unequal durability. None of these was by any means a minor qualification. As we saw in our brief sketch of the operation of Ricardo's system of distribution, he fully expected money wages to rise. Indeed, this was an integral part of his theory. Therefore it became necessary for Ricardo to take account of the impact of wage rate changes in formulating a theory of value. In his *Principles,* sections IV and V of Ricardo's first chapter were devoted to an exploration of the importance of varying quantities of fixed capital and changing wage rates to the determination of value when the capital involved in producing different products was of unequal durability or yielded a return to the employer with varying rapidity.

Let us assume, said Ricardo, that two products produced with varying proportions of fixed capital in period 1 are compared in value. Even in the absence of a change in wages, they will not be of equal value since the commodity produced by means of more machinery or stored-up capital will also have to return an interest payment to the employer for the forfeiture of control over the capital invested in the machinery. Thus, if corn were to have a value of $500 because 100 men produced it, a machine produced by the labor of 100 men would also have a value of $500. But if that machine were then devoted during the following year to the spinning of cloth, with the employment of an additional 100 men, the cloth would be more than double the value of the corn. This excess was necessary to provide the capitalist a return on his investment in the machine. For the sake of simplicity, Ricardo assumed one-year intervals, both in the raising of the corn crop and in the construction of the machine. On the basis of a pure labor theory of value. the cloth should be exactly twice the value of the corn, but as we have just seen Ricardo admitted this would not always prove to be true.

Now let us further suppose, continued Ricardo, that a general rise in wages occurs. Remember that previously Ricado had maintained that a change in wage rates had no effect upon value. According to Ricardo, the result would be that the commodity with the greatest amount of stored-up labor would decline in value relative to other commodities. Similar variations in value would occur for other commodities in accordance with the amount of capital involved in their production. The reason for this change can be seen from our previous numerical illustration. Since wages cannot rise except at the expense of profits, any general rise in wages would depress the general rate of profits. Those products which were produced with large amounts of capital would experience the greatest reduction in the amount of profits contributed to value. A 1-percent reduction in the rate of earnings on $20,000 produces a greater absolute reduction than a 1-percent reduction in the rate of earnings on $10,000.

The student who has labored thus far will perhaps be somewhat exasperated to learn that Ricardo did not consider the alteration in value from changes in wage rates likely to be very significant; if it was, Ricardo remarked, the resulting change in the rate of profits would speedily put an end to all further investment. His analysis of the effect on value of capitals of unequal duration was similar to the above analysis.

In summary, value in most cases could be explained as being determined by the amount of labor in a product. It could be conceived of as a pie allocated to two component parts—wages and profits. Under normal circumstances, a change in one acted to the detriment of the other without having any effect upon value. Under certain circumstances, however, changes in either wages or profits could produce variations in value.

Many students of Classical economic thought have sought a solution to the problem of why these early writers of the Classical School clung to the labor theory of value, when its retention left so many other problems unresolved. Part of the answer may lie in the fact that labor in those times played such a dominant role in the process of production. Even today, the labor costs account for approximately two thirds of all costs, and the percentage was probably higher at the time Ricardo and others were writing. Note, however, that it was the *amount* of labor, not the *cost* of labor, that mattered. As long as labor was such a dominant factor, it was tempting to seize upon it as the sole causal factor. Other writers have suggested that the importance of labor in determining value was stressed because of a desire to justify the existence of private property. If a man worked hard and amassed ownership of a considerable amount of property, then surely he had the right to retain possession of that property. If this interpretation is a correct one, the use to which the labor theory of value was put by Marx becomes even more ironic.

Today, economists and consumers alike tend to talk in terms of price rather than value. The concept of price was not unknown to Ricardo, but he tended to grant it scant consideration. Price was merely the worth of commodities measured in terms of gold. Since Ricardo was interested in a more stable and less varying standard than gold was likely to be, he discarded it in favor of labor as a most suitable measuring rod.

DISTINCTION BETWEEN WEALTH AND VALUE. Ricardo felt that Smith had been confused not only in the proper choice of a labor standard to measure value but in his treatment of the distinction between value and wealth. Ricardo argued that Smith had treated the two terms as if they were interchangeable, and furthermore that Smith believed that increases in the wealth of a nation correspondingly produced increases in the value of its products. Ricardo denied this relationship. As the wealth of a nation increased, value inevitably declined. The reason for this inverse relationship becomes clear as we review Ricardo's definition of value. The value of any product was determined by the amount of labor expended in its production under those conditions where it was precisely at the point of being worthwhile to continue production—that is, no surplus, beyond the amount required for the payment of wages and profits in order to assure continued production, was forthcoming. But if wealth increased, it must mean that the production of goods was becoming easier rather than more difficult, and that less rather than more labor was being expended in production. As the amount of labor needed to produce commodities was reduced, of course, the value of the goods also declined. But if the value of all commodities declined, wouldn't this in effect leave their relative values unchanged? While at a given time in a given country this might appear to be the case, it is important to remember that Ricardo was concerned with the question of values between different countries and between different periods of time.

It was typical of Ricardo's style of writing that, having excluded rent from the components of value, he next turned to the task of explaining the existence of rent. We will postpone our consideration of rent until we have explored in more detail the issues of wages and profits.

WAGES. Ricardo spoke of two types of wages—the market wage and the natural wage. The distinction was much the same as he had made with respect to the natural price and the market price. The market wage was a temporary price set by the interaction of the market forces of supply and demand. The natural wage was the wage necessary for the support of the worker and his family. Defined as such, it became nothing more than the subsistence wage. Just as the natural price of a commodity was the true cost of producing the commodity in terms of the quantity of labor involved, so the natural wage was the true cost of assuring a reproduction of the labor supply. Again, the natural wage, similar to the natural price, provided a norm about which the market wage could oscillate.

Although the general tone of Ricardo's analysis was pessimistic, he was not dogmatic in his pessimism. There were several ways in which wages might continue to rise for an indefinite period.

The first method was by an acceleration in the process of accumulating capital. Minus some of the refinements which were to embellish later versions of the theory, Ricardo's theory can best be described as a wage-fund doctrine. The demand for labor was the product of the capitalists' collective laying aside of part of their income for the employment of workers. This money, which was advanced to the workers to provide their support while the commodity was being produced, was returned to the capitalists with interest when the period of production had ended. The concept comes closest to reality in agricultural production for the period between the planting and the harvest, and it may very well have been the observation of this process that stimulated both Ricardo's and Smith's thinking. Now if wages were paid from some previously accumulated fund, the obvious moral to be drawn was that the faster the fund could be made to accumulate, the greater the possible increase in wages.

Ricardo felt that the possibility of the accumulation of capital outdistancing the growth of population for considerable periods was by no means remote. At such times, the demand for labor would grow faster than its available supply; the money wages would stay above the natural wages and the condition of laborers would correspondingly experience marked improvement.

Another hopeful sign was the fact that the principle of diminishing returns was not operable everywhere in the economy. Indeed, Ricardo thought that labor and foodstuffs were exceptional in that their natural price tended through time to drift upward. Other products were likely to experience a decline in their natural price because of the introduction of machinery and more efficient means of production. Ricardo placed little reliance on this change, however, to better the lot of the working classes. Laborers were too dependent on agricultural produce to benefit greatly from the decline of prices elsewhere. This dependence explains why Ricardo attached so much importance to the removal of the Corn Laws, which imposed high protective duties on the importation of foreign grains. If cheap food could be imported into England, many of the dire results deemed otherwise inevitable could be postponed almost indefinitely. Even with a continuation of the Corn Laws, Ricardo was not completely pessimistic about the prospects of augmenting the food supply.

Improvements in agriculture were less likely to overthrow the Law of Diminishing Returns than were counterpart gains in industry, but the possibility of augmenting agricultural output was clearly recognized by Ricardo. He even divided the possible improvements into two kinds—those making the land itself more productive, and those improving machinery —thus reducing the necessary amount of labor. Both types of improvements would reduce the value of foodstuffs as well as rent. Despite Ricardo's inclusion of this last possibility in his book, the general tone of his analysis suggests that he placed little reliance on its ability to solve the problem of rising food costs.

Perhaps the most famous and often quoted passage in Ricardo's book is one in which he noted the possibility that the future might not be as black as he had pictured it. Here Ricardo suggested that workers might eventually require higher standards for their subsistence wage.

It is not to be understood that the natural price of labour, estimated even in food and necessaries, is absolutely fixed and constant. It varies at different times in the same country, and very materially differs in different countries. It essentially depends on the habits and the customs of the people. . . . Many of the conveniences now enjoyed in an English cottage would have been thought luxuries at an earlier period of our history.[1]

Critics who have pictured Ricardo as postulating an "iron law of wages" tend to overlook or minimize the significance of this passage. If Ricardo can be accepted at his word, however, the above statement suggests that his view of wages could more appropriately be described as a "steel" law of wages, with the greater flexibility implicit in the word "steel." Clearly, Ricardo recognized the possibility that workers might learn to limit the size of their families in order to enjoy higher subsistence wages. It is impossible to judge, however, how seriously this passage should be taken. Perhaps, as we suggested may have been the case with Malthus, Ricardo was only acknowledging the existence of the possibility without foreseeing much likelihood of its occurrence. Whatever may be the correct interpretation, the fact remains that later writers were to place a much greater emphasis on this possibility, and that the possibility did in fact prove to be the case, thereby quieting some of the alarms occasioned by Malthus' predictions.

One thing seems certain: Even with all of these reservations, Ricardo

[1] David Ricardo, *Principles of Political Economy and Taxation* (London: Everyman's Library, n.d.), pp. 54–55.

cannot be classified as a sunny optimist. A brief passage from his *Principles* will demonstrate the validity of this conclusion:

> In the natural advance of society, the wages of labour will have a tendency to fall, as far as they are regulated by supply and demand; for the supply of labourers will continue to increase at the same rate, whilst the demand for them will increase at a slower rate.[2]

Ricardo joined forces with Malthus in expressing opposition to the Poor Laws. These laws, in Ricardo's judgment, did nothing more than make the rich poor and the poor more miserable. Their only current saving grace was in the fact that each parish raised its own funds and was thus encouraged to keep the rates as low as possible. If the funds came from a general tax, Ricardo remarked, the result would be still worse. Although he argued that the only workable reform was the ultimate abolition of these laws, Ricardo was enough of a realist to foresee that the change could not come overnight but must instead be a gradual one.

PROFITS. Ricardo's failure to accept completely the labor theory of value was based on the difficulties arising when capitals of unequal durations were employed. The existence of profits by themselves never appeared to cause him concern. After all, the capitalist had a right to a part of the "pie," for it was he who contributed the machinery and advanced workers their wages. The possibility that these acts might contribute to the value of the commodity was not explored.

Ricardo's general conclusion that the general rate of profits was inevitably doomed to decline was based on several considerations. Foremost was the assumption that the economy was sufficiently competitive to assure equality in rates of profit between quite different lines of economic activity. The role of differentials in risk and character of the business emphasized by Smith received scant attention from Ricardo. It was true that new techniques of production or new products could produce temporary rewards, but these excess profits would be quickly eliminated as new capital moved to these fields to take advantage of the extra rewards to be earned.

Having postulated that profits tend toward equality in all trades, Ricardo thus tied the fate of the increasing return industries to those industries experiencing diminishing returns. The importance of this tie should be noted.

When the costs of cultivation of the necessities of life rose because of diminishing returns, the wages of labor would have to rise as well. Wages,

[2] *Ibid.,* p. 57.

it will be remembered, were usually at the natural subsistence level, and a rise in the cost of necessities would have to lead a proportionate increase in wages. A rise in wages for such products as corn would serve to lower the rate of profits in corn production but would leave the value of corn unchanged. But the decline in the rate of profits in the field of corn output must be matched by declines in the rate of profits throughout the economy, since rates of profits have been assumed to be equal in all lines of activity. No matter how efficiently the pin factory owner subdivided his labor and increased his output, he was still faced with the declining rate of profit.

Note that in this chapter and throughout the entire book, Ricardo was speaking of the *rate* of profit, not the total profits. In fact, Ricardo felt that the rate of profit could continue to decline for a considerable period while total profits continued to mount. The arithmetic of this seeming paradox is not difficult to understand. As long as the total amount of capital upon which the rate of profit was to be earned increased at a more rapid pace than the profit rate declined, total profits would continue to rise. The important variable in determining continued investment and economic progress was the rate of profit. When the rate of profit fell too low, capitalists would be unwilling to bear the risks and uncertainties of further investment.

Numerous references to Ricardo's rent theory are to be found scattered throughout the chapter on profits. This was not only characteristic of Ricardo's style of writing, but it served a useful function as well. Ricardo was anxious for the reader not to confuse returns in the form of rent with returns in the form of profits. Even though the farmer owned land fertile enough to earn a rent return, he should not consider all of his earnings as profits. His profits could be no more and no less than those earned on the least fertile piece of land worth cultivating. This insistence on the proper allocation of returns to the factors of production set an example for other economists to follow.

RENT. From the four explanations advanced by Smith and Malthus for the existence of rent, Ricardo selected the differentials in fertility as the correct one, and devoted his entire last chapter ("Malthus on Rent") to an appraisal of Malthus' alternative explanations. Ricardo argued that Malthus was wrong in ever attributing rent to the bountifulness of nature. Increased fertility of a piece of land, Ricardo maintained, simply made it capable of yielding additional rent at some future time. Rent was a result not of the fertility itself but of the fertility of one piece of land when compared with others also under cultivation. If Malthus' view was correct,

Ricardo asked, why was it true that rents were frequently lower in countries with much fertile land than in countries with soils of generally lower fertility? The problem with "the enhanced fertility explanation of rent," said Ricardo, was that the augmented quantities did not accrue to the landlord as they would if they were true rent; instead, consumers benefited through lower prices.

Ricardo also dismissed Malthus' second explanation—that rent was created because food was the one commodity that automatically, through the expansion in population, was assured of a ready demand. In assessing this explanation, Ricardo argued that Malthus was placing too much stress on the need for the prior provision of food as a condition for a rising birth rate. On the contrary, said Ricardo, as long as living costs are low or wages are high, there will be a tendency for the population to expand even without a preceding accumulation of food. As Ricardo put it, "In America, population increases rapidly because food can be produced at a cheap price, and not because an abundant supply has been previously provided." [3]

Ricardo was not being particularly original in developing the differential theory of rent. Not only had Smith and Malthus mentioned it, but at an even earlier date Hume had anticipated the conclusion that rent was not a determinant of price. Nor did Ricardo's contribution lie in his ability to intertwine the differential theory of rent with historical fact and current events. On the contrary, Ricardo's analysis made virtually no reference to either. What did distinguish Ricardo's explanation of rent from those of his predecessors was its concentration on a single well-developed explanation, to the exclusion of alternative explanations, and the inclusion of implications to be drawn from the theory.

Rent was a tribute exacted from the economy as a price for its growth, and particularly for the expansion of its population. The payment of rent became necessary when the demand for agricultural produce expanded to the point where less fertile land was brought into cultivation. When a country was first settled, land was abundant relative to the population, and only the best and most fertile pieces needed to be cultivated. With such abundance, Ricardo remarked that there was no more need to pay a fee for the use of the land than there was at the present time to pay for the air we breathe. If land were as unlimited in quantity and as equal in quality as the air, there would be no need to pay rent even as the population expanded. The unhappy fact, however, was that neither of these conditions prevailed; land was obviously limited in supply and its quality was known to vary markedly from one acre to another.

[3] *Ibid.,* p. 279.

The result was that as the population expanded, recourse to the less fertile lands became necessary. Let us assume that on the most fertile land one man was able to produce an output of 50 bushels per acre. The same man (or his equivalent—men were assumed to be of equal ability), on a slightly less fertile piece, was capable of producing only 45 bushels. The result was to give the cultivator of the more fertile piece of land a surplus of 5 bushels over his competitor tilling the second piece. But was it the cultivator who really benefited?

Since the value of the commodity was determined by the quantity of labor necessarily applied at the margin, the farmer on the second piece was assured of receiving full reward in terms of wages and return on his capital. The extra 5 bushels produced by the most fertile land would go to the cultivator, declared Ricardo, but only if he was the owner of the land. Even if it did go to him, however, he should be careful not to think of this as profits. Profits, after all, were kept equal throughout the economy by the forces of competition. But more likely the land was not owned by the person cultivating but by a second party. In this case, of course, any rent payments would accrue to the owner rather than to the tiller of the land.

The process as described above continued to operate as successively less fertile pieces of land were brought under cultivation. If a third piece, capable of yielding only 40 bushels, were now to be cultivated, the rent of the first (most fertile) piece of land would have been increased to 10 bushels, while the second piece would now yield a rent of 5 bushels. Note that the marginal piece of land just worth cultivation yielded no rent. When only the first, most fertile strip needed to be cultivated, rent payments were zero. As the second piece was cultivated, rent was now earned on the first piece. The process would continue, each successive piece of land bringing increasing returns of rent for the more fertile pieces. As each additional less fertile piece of land was cultivated, the formerly marginal piece of land which bore no rent now produced a rental return.

The reason why Ricardo felt that rent did not enter into the determination of price now becomes clear. Value was determined by the quantity of labor necessary for the production of a given amount of output. The ability to produce more bushels on the fertile land was the equivalent of the ability to produce the same amount with more labor on less fertile soil. Thus the value of the product was determined by the amount of labor required on the marginal or least fertile soil to be cultivated. The rent earned by the more fertile acres was a surplus and had no bearing on the value of the product itself.

The existence of several assumptions basic to Ricardo's explanation of rent should be noted. One was the proposition that land itself was in limited supply; the validity of this conclusion, particularly in a relatively small country such as England, was subject to little challenge. Equally important, perhaps, was the assumption of varying degrees of fertility among different pieces of land. The implications of this varying fertility as developed by Ricardo were later questioned by some of his critics. Subject to even stiffer criticism was the implicit assumption that the level of agricultural productivity remained constant. A consideration of the general validity of Ricardo's theory of rent can wait until we have finished surveying its structure. Note should be made, however, of one assumption sometimes incorrectly attributed to him.

Students sometimes infer that Ricardo's explanation of rent involved an attack on the form of land ownership. Let land ownership become more widely disseminated and the problem of excessive rent would solve itself. If the cultivator owned his own land, the rent of his land would be paid to himself and thus nothing would be lost. But there is a serious objection to this line of reasoning, of which Ricardo was well aware.

It was true that in Ricardo's system the landlords were growing wealthy at the expense of the other members of the society. Not only did their share of the nation's output grow in size as the payments in rent grew larger and larger, but the payment of rent in produce meant that the absolute value of the rental payment was also increasing. Remember that the value of agricultural output was steadily advancing because it was necessary, through the pressure of demand, to cultivate increasingly less fertile pieces of land.

However, we must also remember that rent was not a determinant of value. Ricardo was very specific on this point. Let the landlord be so generous as to return all the rents to society and the price of agricultural output would be lowered not one iota. The reason for this seemingly curious result lay in the fact that rent did not cause value. Thus, whether rent payments were made or not, the cost of agricultural products would remain high. Ricardo might have added, as Malthus had, that the redistribution of wealth would only worsen the problem by leading to still higher bidding for the necessities of life.

The casting of the landlord in the role of villain is not completely inaccurate, however. Although rent did not contribute to the high cost of the necessities of life, the landlords undertook to augment these rents by encouraging Parliament to maintain high protective tariffs on agricultural produce. The pressure by landlords for the maintenance of the Corn Laws served to keep prices artificially high, thereby aggravating the problem posed by Ricardo.

Ricardo defined rent as "that portion of the produce of the earth which is paid to the landlord for the use of the original and indestructible powers of the soil." [4] Viewed in the light of our preceding discussion, this definition of rent did little justice to Ricardo's subsequent discussion. There seems no reason for thinking, even in Ricardo's time, that the soil was "inexhaustible," or, as the definition suggests, that rent was paid to all owners of land rather than only to those holding lands of above marginal quality. Marginal land, as Ricardo himself later asserted, bore no rent, and land of still lower quality was for the moment not worthy of cultivation.

Ricardo never made completely clear why the marginal land would be placed into use if it yielded no rent. Why should the landlord provide land free for someone else to cultivate? If the land stood idle, it might still bring its owner some benefits in the form of hunting and other recreational uses. Despite Ricardo's own silence on this question, a number of possible explanations may be advanced. Some marginal land might have been held by independent landowners, who would be lured into cultivating it once the average profit return for its use was assured. It might also happen that the marginal land, having no rental value at the moment, would be included as a package deal with the rental of lands of superior quality. If this reason is accepted, obvious conclusions about the relative bargaining strengths of the renter and the landlord can be drawn.

Ricardo illustrated the inability of marginal land to earn rent when he discussed briefly the implications of intensive as well as extensive cultivation. Since rent was defined as the excess yield over and above that yield which was necessary to make an application of capital barely worthwhile, it made no difference whether a second application of capital was made on another but inferior piece of land or was applied to the same piece of land as had received the first dose of capital. In either case, the total output could be expected to be less for the second application, with the result that the first dose would yield a rent return. The nature of the rent return from either intensive or extensive cultivation will perhaps be clearer if we make reference to a simple diagram. Fig. 2.

When only the first piece of land or the first dosage of capital as represented by bar I is needed, Ricardo's theory suggests that there will be no rent. When the second and third less fertile pieces of land or dosages of capital become necessary, the rent produced would be indicated by the cross-patched areas. Although the task of developing the distinction be-

[4] *Ibid.*, p. 33.

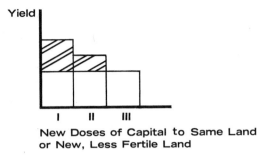

Yield

I   II   III

New Doses of Capital to Same Land
or New, Less Fertile Land

FIG. 2

tween intensive and extensive cultivation on a more complete basis was left to John Stuart Mill (Chapter VI), Ricardo not only recognized both possibilities but noted that where the differences in fertility between various pieces of land were very great, the cultivator might find it more advantageous to cultivate his existing holding more intensively rather than bring new (marginal) land under cultivation.

One point of warning needs to be inserted here. Rent was measured, not in terms of acres of land, but in amounts of applied capital, although it was the result of differences in the fertility of different pieces of land. When capital was applied to fertile land, it yielded a bigger surplus than when applied to less fertile tracts. The principle of differentials in fertility or ability permitting a special return has for this reason remained an integral part of economic theory, and the term "economic rent" has become an accepted part of the economists' language. Although Ricardo defined rent primarily in terms of agriculture, by measuring rent in terms of an above-normal yield on invested capital, he was able to apply the principle to other situations as well. On this principle, Ricardo analyzed the earnings of mines, for example. Like that of agricultural products, the price of ores was unaffected by the level of the rent; rent was again the product, not the cause of price. Its source was also the same—a shortage of mines and differentials in the quality of their ores.

Although the principle of quality differentials was generally accepted by economists, the applications as devised by Ricardo were subject to numerous criticisms. An American economist, Henry C. Carey (1793–1879), argued that the theory of agricultural rent could not be applied to the United States. In the United States, Carey maintained, farmers had been compelled by the threat of Indian attack to cultivate first the hilltops, where protection from attack could be more easily assured. The result, Carey claimed, was to reverse the process as described by Ricardo; cultivation of the most fertile land, in the valleys, came last, only after the threat of Indian attack had ended. This was one of the first of a series of attacks centering on the argument that English classical theory had limited applicability in other parts of the world. In this instance, the reason why Ricardo's analysis would not become valid once the fertile lands had been settled was never made clear. The United States was a poor selection for criticism of Ricardo's thesis in any case, since for a considerable period Ricardo's assumption of limited land was not satisfied.

A more important criticism of Ricardo's theory was the advancement of technological discovery in the field of agriculture. Dramatic new methods of cultivation made it unnecessary to push cultivation to the margin and suspended operation of the Law of Diminishing Returns. By assuming that increases in productivity affected all tracts of varying fertility equally, Ricardo ignored this possibility. Much of the pessimism of Ricardo's system stemmed from the fact that he conceived of agriculture, with its feature of diminishing returns, as calling the tune for the rest of the economy. At the very time Ricardo's book was on the presses, however, the scene was already changing and the dominant role agriculture had held so long in the British economy was rapidly disappearing. Adam Smith and his pin factory had won the day!

Just as Ricardo in later years became dissatisfied with his solution to the problem of value, so also did he become less certain (but for reasons different from those outlined above) about the precision with which rent could be measured. In his *Essay on the Influence of a Low Price of Corn, on the Profits of Stock* he generally repeated what he had said in his *Principles,* but in a passage on the Poor Laws he noted that the return on capital invested in improving land was inextricably entangled with the return in the form of pure rent.

PROCESS OF GROWTH. Ricardo found little with which to quarrel in the model of growth devised by Adam Smith; only the ending was changed to conform with Ricardo's more pessimistic views of the future of the economy. The role of the capitalist in accumulating capital was precisely the same, although perhaps somewhat more fully developed. The role of the government was if anything even more carefully circumscribed. Ricardo saw even fewer flaws in the functioning of the price system than Smith had foreseen. Both Smith and Ricardo foresaw the possibility that wages might rise and the condition of the working classes be improved for considerable periods of time. Whereas Smith saw the resulting increase in population as still contributing to the natural harmony of forces, Ricardo saw this population expansion as sowing the seeds of friction and discontent.

Ricardo saw the growing population forcing increases in the natural wage, with the result that the rate of profits would be squeezed to the point where all further capital accumulation would cease. When this happened, all economic growth would halt and the stationary state would have been reached. None of the classical economists wrote extensively on the nature of this stationary state; perhaps the subject was too distasteful to them. It seems clear, however, that its arrival was no cause for rejoicing. Of all the writers in the Classical School, only John Stuart Mill saw the stationary state as an opportunity to concentrate on the finer things of life. Although the picture of the stationary state is blurred, some of its expected characteristics were revealed. A general cessation in economic growth would take place, no further new investment of capital would occur, the population would remain stationary, and wages would stay at the natural subsistence level. How low wages and the general condition of the laboring class would therefore be would depend upon the willingness of laborers to choose a higher plane of living in preference to more children. Both Ricardo and Smith made reference to China as illustrative of the state which England would eventually achieve.

While the picture was not a particularly cheery one, the outlook was not completely black. Neither Smith nor Ricardo foresaw unemployment as a result of arrival at the stationary state. All factors of production would be assured of full employment but probably at very low levels of income. Both Smith and Ricardo were bothered with the possibility of low levels of income when combined with the cessation of the process of economic growth.

Smith foresaw the emergence of the stationary state as an event somewhere in the distant future. Nor is the immediacy of the threat as seen by Ricardo, even if there was a failure to follow his advice, clearly evident. At some points, Ricardo implied that the possibility of the stationary state was on the immediate horizon. In his discussion of the effect of rising wage rates on the value of commodities, for example, he noted that even where the capital compositions differed, the change in value could not be too great. This was so because a rise in wages sufficient to produce such a change would, by reducing the rate of profit, choke off all investment.

One interesting question posed by Ricardo's analysis was what the capitalists, and particularly the landlords, did with all of their money. As the opportunities for investment disappeared and as total profits and rents continued to mount, to what use was this capital put? The notion of utilizing it in riotous living would have been equally repellent to both Smith and Ricardo. The most probable solution which they would offer was that the capital would be sent to other countries where the prospective earnings for capital were more favorable. Ricardo made reference to the diverting of capital abroad in his discussion of the impact of taxes, and it seems likely that he would have seen the same result from encroaching wage rates.

In keeping with his generally less optimistic view of economic life, Ricardo saw some threat to the welfare of the workers from the widespread adoption of machinery. Actually, the adoption of this position represented a reversal of Ricardo's earlier views and created dismay even among his most loyal followers. Ricardo's chapter "On Machinery" is one of the more baffling parts of his book, and it is difficult to summarize his argument briefly.

Put in simplest terms, Ricardo saw the threat to workers from machinery in terms of the possible impact on the wages fund. When the capitalist chose to invest in machinery, some of the money normally advanced to workers would be tied up in this capital investment. The first year the capitalist would continue to hire workers to construct the machine, but in subsequent years, while the machine continued to operate, funds which would otherwise be free for the employment of labor were then held frozen—that is, invested in the machinery. An ability to predict the result was complicated by the possibility that the increased profits made by the capitalists through the use of their machinery might be plowed back in the total wages fund, thus creating employment elsewhere. Ricardo offered this possibility as a possible offset to the other more gloomy possibilities.

Ricardo's critics were dissatisfied with this concession. Some of them, like Professor J. R. McCulloch, had, after all, previously maintained the position that machinery might displace workers, only to be persuaded to the contrary by Ricardo's earlier reasoning. Now their master had seemingly reversed his position and wound up back on the other side of the argument.

The simplest grounds for attacking Ricardo's doubts about the effect of machinery on workers was to question the validity of the wages-fund concept. Unfortunately, from these opponents' viewpoint, they also were strong adherents to the wages-fund doctrine. Thus barred from this line of attack, they argued that Ricardo had failed to take full account of Say's Law. If wages were lowered by the reduction in the size of the wages-fund, the costs of the commodities would either be reduced or profits increased. In either case real purchasing power was therby increased and full employment of workers assured.

It has always seemed to this writer that Ricardo's critics were unduly concerned by his suggestion about the possible impact of machinery. Ricardo did not deny that the profits thus gained might not be put to use elsewhere in the economy. The general tone of Ricardo's analysis, with its emphasis on the perfect mobility of labor and capital, suggests that Ricardo had little doubt that the problem would be resolved in this fashion. Certainly the permanent displacement and unemployment of workers gave him little concern. He never accepted Malthus' contention that there might be a general inadequacy of demand. In fact, Ricardo was highly critical of Malthus on precisely this point and has been blamed for helping to deflect theorists toward a blind acceptance of the concept of a full-employment equilibrium.

TAXATION. The title of Ricardo's book, *Principles of Political Economy and Taxation* is interesting in that it singles out for special attention the issue of taxation. None of the other contemporary writers gave taxation such a prominent position, although a number devoted equal space to its consideration. Whether Ricardo did this because of the importance he attached to the question of taxation or because he felt the subject was not properly a part of the study of political economy is unknown.

The emphasis on the word taxation is proper, however, for he did not concern himself with the other facts of public finance such as expenditure and debt creation. In the latter of these two fields he can most probably be termed a conservative; the less spending and the less debt creation, the better.

A discussion of various aspects of taxation occupied roughly one third of his volume, and it has been said that an interest in determining the incidence of taxes prompted Ricardo's inquiries into the rules governing the distribution of income. Some comments from his letters seem to bear this out. Whatever the case, his major concern with taxation was the determination of the principles governing the shifting of the tax burden and the determination of its final incidence.

His conclusions were simple (although, typically, not expounded in a clear-cut fashion) by modern-day standards, and logical in relation to the rest of his theory. The incidence of taxes on the three factors of production —labor, capital, and land—was determined by the same principles that governed the particular factor share. So long as one could agree with Ricardo's analysis of income distribution, his further conclusions would follow.

Because Ricardo believed in the "iron law of wages," he observed that any tax which fell on wages, whether a tax on the wages themselves or on the necessities to be purchased by the expenditure of the wages, must in turn bring about a diminution in profits. The effect of a reduction in profits was somewhat less clear, although Ricardo recognized that any impairment of capital would tend to diminish the demand for labor. Such a step might hasten arrival at the stationary state.

In a similar fashion he examined the results of taxes on profits. If the tax was a general one, imposed on profits obtained from all forms of activity, he concluded that the burden could not be shifted. It would remain on profits. On the other hand, if the tax were partial, imposed on profits from certain enterprises, it would cause a rise in the price of the commodities concerned. Unless such a price rise occurred, capital would be attracted away from the taxed industries which had suffered a reduction in rate of profit to other more lucrative fields. If the commodities whose prices rose were necessaries, then wages would be forced up in order to maintain life at a subsistence level. This would then lead to an eventual cut in profits. In the case of the nonnecessity the burden would remain on the consumer.

As might be expected, Ricardo concluded, after regarding the various forms of taxation on land, that a tax imposed on rent remained a burden for the landlord. However, a unit tax on raw products which would be applied to the products produced at the margin, would add to the price of the commodity. This, of course, assumed an inelastic demand for the products. As the cost of living was forced upward, so, too, would wages have to rise; the latter rise again would be at the expense of profits.

In addition to examining taxes directly imposed on the three factors of production, Ricardo explored a variety of taxes, such as those on manufactured goods, with predictable results. His theories of incidence could stand so long as his wage determination theory received credence. When the latter was destroyed in the late nineteenth century his analysis of taxation, with the exception of taxes on rent, also collapsed. His analysis of rent and the effect of taxation on it lent support to later proponents of the single tax.

TRADE. Both Ricardo and Smith were strong advocates of a policy of free trade but for somewhat different reasons. By the time Ricardo wrote, many of the more objectionable trade restrictions condemned by Smith had already been abandoned. A major exception was the case of the Corn Laws. Advocates of the retention of these restrictions argued that they really were to the general interest of the entire English population. Not only would protection prevent undue reliance by England on foreign supplies, which might for reasons of war suddenly evaporate, but the duties would encourage domestic production and thereby augment the supplies and reduce the price of provisions.[5]

We have already seen Ricardo's answer to this defense: The principle of diminishing returns meant that any further reliance on domestic agricultural production would inevitably involve higher costs of production and thus higher cost to the consumers. The chain of higher money wages, higher rents, and lower rates of profit was thus forged. Barring unexpected changes in the rate of population increase, the only way to break this chain was by abolishing the Corn Laws and thus permitting cheap foreign agricultural products to enter the English markets.

Ricardo's analysis of the advantages of free trade was not confined solely to this highly pragmatic basis, however. Typical of his superior theoretical analysis over that developed by Smith was his formulation of the comparative cost doctrine. Smith had seen the gains resulting from free trade solely in terms of absolute advantage. If one country could produce item A much more cheaply than a second country, while the second country was able to produce item B more cheaply than the first country, there were obvious gains to be achieved for both countries if they elected to enter into free trade. Ricardo in his analysis chose to consider the more complex case where one country was more efficient in the production of both commodities (the word "all" may be substituted here, although Ricardo confined his analysis to a two-country, two-commodity situation). The benefits to the less efficient country in obtaining cheaper goods is obvious. Ricardo used one of his familiar arithmetic examples to answer the question of what gain, if any, would the more efficient country experience. Assume, he said, two countries, England and Portugal, each engaged in the production of cloth and wine. Let us also assume that Portugal can produce both commodities more efficiently (*i.e.,* using less labor).

NUMBER OF UNITS OF LABOR REQUIRED TO PRODUCE I UNIT

| | Commodity | |
Country	Wine	Cloth
England	120	100
Portugal	80	90

Given these ratios, each country would benefit by concentrating its production on that commodity which it produced best and exchanging it for the needed amount of the other commodity. It took 20 more units of labor

[5] There was good reason to debate the impact of the Corn Laws on the price of corn. Corn, which had never been over 61 shillings from 1711 to 1794, was up to 171.5 shillings by 1801 and from 1808 to 1813 never fell below 96 shillings.

to produce one unit of wine in England than one unit of cloth. Thus, if England could trade on a one-cloth-to-one-wine basis with some other country, it could, by concentrating on the production of cloth, save 20 units of labor per unit. Similarly, Portugal, although more efficient in the production of both commodities would improve its position if it concentrated on the production of wine. Assuming it also could enter into a 1 to 1 exchange with another country, it could save 10 units of labor. Ricardo never sought an answer to the question of how the benefits of trade would actually be divided between the two countries; instead, he merely assumed an arbitrary equal sharing of the benefits. Later economists refined this comparative cost doctrine and supplied a solution to the problem of the division of the spoils.

Summary and Evaluation. A drama student once described Ricardo's *Principles* to the present author as "Thirty-seven chapters in search of a book." The author replied that the chapters might be searching, but Ricardo was not, because he had not really intended to write a book when he started. The result is a kind of hodgepodge, with the final chapters tacked on as an afterthought. Despite the problem of organization and the defects in the style of writing—both of which result in difficulties in comprehension—Ricardo's *Principles* attracted much attention at the time and has remained a landmark in the history of economic thought. Whether the reader interprets Ricardo as a compatriot of Malthus and a heartless appraiser of humanity or as the founder of the dispassionate analysis of political economy, his name continues to be accorded great respect.

If Smith is to be accused of eclecticism, the same charge can be leveled at Ricardo with equal justification. Of the main outlines of his system of distribution, with its determination of wages, rent, and profits, Ricardo said little that was new. Aspects of his theory of value had also appeared before, and his defense of laissez-faire had been made earlier and better by Adam Smith. The essence of Ricardo's contribution lay in his ability to build an integrated model of the economic system with these earlier ideas. In spite of the bad grammar, the faulty sentence structure, and the poor organization of chapters, Ricardo managed to discard a number of hitherto accepted theories. No longer is the reader exposed to three different explanations of rent, with the invitation to take one's choice.

Ricardo's was the shortest of the many treatises bearing a similar title; its brevity is explained by the fact that Ricardo had no desire to retread ground already covered by Smith. Part of the brevity was due to his own distaste for writing. He once wrote Malthus that he was thankful for the miserable English climate, because it kept him at his desk writing. But another came from the singleness of Ricardo's objective—to explain how the value and distribution of a nation's output was determined. The debt of later economists to Ricardo is substantial even though his theory of value has been substantially altered and his treatment of rent has proved in many respects outmoded. His impact on later thinkers such as Marx is universally recognized. Most important, however, he added a technique of rigorous analysis to the stream of economic thought which has remained an essential part of economics down to the present time.

CHAPTER VI: Mill and the Close of the Classical System

A person is not likely to be a good economist who is nothing more.

—JOHN STUART MILL

Mill and Cairnes undermined the adequacy of the system as a basis for the political precept of laissez-faire, the former by admitting a qualitative element in the pleasures (utility) to be secured from goods, the latter by divorcing the system from a beneficient order of nature and emphasizing the "hypothetical" character of its laws.

—PAUL T. HOMAN

The Classical School draws to a close with our review of the writers cited in this chapter. Of the major writers we shall study hereafter, only Marx retains the flavor of the Classical School, even while he is bitterly assailing it. The dissolution came as a result of pressures both from outside and within. New developments in the stream of economic thought were making themselves felt in England and on the Continent. (Economic thinking in the United States was still at a relatively undeveloped stage.) At the same time, members of the Classical School such as John Stuart Mill were beginning to entertain heretical thoughts which at best caused grave concern on the part of colleagues. We begin our survey of these disciples of Smith and Ricardo with a brief assessment of the contributions of Nassau Senior.

NASSAU SENIOR (1790–1864)

Nassau Senior's contributions to the history of economic thought can be summed up very quickly as dealing primarily with the issues of the character of political economy, the role and nature of capital formation, and the determination of value. Before examining these three questions more closely, however, let us look very briefly at the man himself.

The Man. Born the son of an English vicar, Senior was educated at Eton and Oxford. He took his B.A. in 1811 and eight years later was admitted to the bar. In 1825 a professorship of political economy was established at Oxford, and Senior was asked to fill that post. He did so for five years, retiring to serve in various government posts, but he returned to Oxford in 1847, retiring after a five-year term. Senior served in a similar capacity for a brief period at King's College. He also served on many government commissions investigating the conditions of the working classes, the role of trade unions, and the problems of universal education. He was also a member of the Poor Law Inquiry Commission of 1832. In addition to his best-known work, *An Outline of the Science of Political Economy,* Senior also wrote numerous articles and a series of social studies based on his travels in other countries; the latter, however, proved to have little lasting value.

Economic Views. In light of Senior's repeated participation on various government committees and his frequently stated criticism of certain economic institutions such as trade unions, Senior's views on the proper role of political economy and of the economist are somewhat surprising. Senior argued that political economy should stand apart from the practical questions of the day, for such issues "no more form part of the Science of Political Economy . . . than Navigation forms part of the Science of Astronomy."[1] In part, this wish to disassociate the two stemmed from a desire on Senior's part to make political economy more scientific, and it provided inspiration for similar views by John Elliot Cairnes and others on the subject. Part of Senior's reluctance to combine the two can be explained by his belief that economic factors were not always the sole or even the primary determinants, and thus consideration of other elements must also be made; on these issues the economist was deemed by Senior to be incompetent. Policy issues were a matter for the statesman, and Senior may have felt he was acting in this latter capacity in his service on government committees.

In so designating the scope of political economy, Senior pictured the discipline as primarily a "science" of reasoning. Deductive rather than inductive theorizing was to be the proper approach. We are entitled to ask

[1] Nassau Senior, *An Outline of the Science of Political Economy* (New York: Augustus M. Kelley, Inc., 1951), p. 2.

what this reasoning is to be based on. Senior postulated four basic propositions, which were discoverable as "a matter of observation" [and] "consciousness." [2] These were: (1) Men sought additional wealth but with as little effort as possible; (2) The Malthusian Law of Population; (3) Increasing returns to industry; and (4) Decreasing returns to agriculture. None of these has proved to be as exact as Senior suggested, and some, like the Malthusian Law, have been open to serious question.

ABSTINENCE. Senior's attempts to keep political science aloof from moral and public issues became particualrly ironic in light of the contribution which has been his major claim to fame—the concept of abstinence. The Classical economists from the time of Adam Smith on had found it difficult to justify the payment of a reward to capital; all of them concurred in their agreement that such payments were necessary and proper but their justifications were at best feeble and unconvincing. Senior provided an attractive, if not altogether satisfactory solution to this dilemma. Just as the worker experienced pain in the performance of his work, so did the capitalist sacrifice enjoyment by foregoing an immediate consumption of his money; Senior believed that the pains of postponed consumption were just as real as the pain and discomfort of labor. Since such suffering should not go unrewarded, the capitalist deserved the return which his investment of money brought him.

In stating the concept of abstinence, Senior achieved two things. First, he provided a rational examination and justification for the existence of profits. The word capital (a term which Senior tried to avoid using wherever possible, because of its ambiguous meaning) carried no connotation of human sacrifice and privations; the term "abstinence" in this sense was a loaded one and conjured up a mental picture of forfeiture and sacrifice. Critics were able to make light of the sacrifices borne by the very rich from their failure to consume immediately all of their income, but the term still served as a defensive weapon for the spokesman of the capitalist system. Second, although Senior did not really develop the point, the idea of "abstinence" has imbedded in it the time-preference explanation of the interest rate.

VALUE. Senior's employment of his concept of abstinence to develop more fully a cost of production theory of value has usually led students to place him in the Classical School of economic thought. While this is an essentially correct view and we have also included Senior among the last members of the Classical School, his views on value mark a distinct break with those of earlier economists.

[2] *Ibid.*, p. 26.

Even his cost of production theory, after allowing for the amendment with regard to abstinence, was somewhat different from that of earlier writers. Senior argued that the value of a product was only a reflection of its cost of production (labor plus abstinence) when the bounties of nature were equally accessible to all producers. But such was rarely the case. More frequently certain factors differed in their quality or were in short supply. When this happened the price of the commodity (its value in terms of money) was above the true cost of production and afforded an additional return in the form of rent to the possessor of the factor. This explanation extended the Ricardian version of rent in two important senses. Rent became a tribute paid not only to the landlord but to the possessor of any monopoly, such as a surgeon's skill or a singer's talent. Senior thus developed the concept of economic rent to a point much closer to the sense in which it is used today. Furthermore, Senior observed, differentials in quality were not essential for rent to exist. Let only the object in question prove sufficiently scarce and a rent return would be bound to emerge. Rent existed whenever a payment was made for something which involved no sacrifice; both work and abstinence involved a sacrifice for which they were properly rewarded.

At times, however, Senior's discussion of value hinted at an even more radical departure from Classical thought—the concept of marginal utility soon to be developed by others. In his chapter on value, Senior made little mention of this idea, but his later chapter on distribution contained numerous references to it.

Whereas earlier writers had taken implicit note of the role of demand in determining value, the cost of production would be borne only for those commodities people demanded. Senior developed the concept of demand far more explicitly. One can, for example, find hints of diminishing marginal utility in the following passage:

It is obvious, however, that our desires do not aim so much at quantity as diversity. Not only are there limits to the pleasures which commodities of any given class can afford, but the pleasure diminishes in a rapidly increasing ratio before those limits are reached. Two articles of the same kind will seldom afford twice the pleasure of one and still less will ten give five times the pleasure of two. In proportion, therefore, as an article is abundant, the number of those who are provided with it, and do not wish, or wish but little, to increase their provision, is likely to be great; and so far as they are concerned, the additional supply loses all, or nearly all, its utility.[3]

[3] *Ibid.*, pp. 11–12.

The significance of the above passage will become more evident later when we turn to an examination of the Marginal Utility School. In this connection, we should also note that Senior's discussion of value made frequent references to the pleasure and pain philosophy developed by Jeremy Bentham, mentioned later in this chapter.

POPULATION. Brief mention of Senior's views of the population issue should be made, since they mark him as distinctly less pessimistic than his contemporaries. Senior's position basically was that the worst of Malthus' predictions *might* come true, but that they were not *bound* to occur. In two lectures given at Oxford in 1828, Senior suggested that the problem of population was affected by the wisdom of society's institutions. If the institutions were properly organized and managed, the population problem need never arise. Although Malthus had also suggested a similar solution, evidently he felt that Senior placed too much confidence in the beneficial results. For some reason Malthus refused to grant his approval when Senior sent him a copy of his lectures, inviting Malthus' endorsement.

SENIOR'S IMPACT ON ECONOMIC THEORY. Considering Senior's relatively small part in the history of economic thought, we have perhaps already devoted too much space to a consideration of his views. Our story would be incomplete, however, if we did not take some note of the criticisms his views aroused among the capitalist and socialist critics alike. Senior's intentions were honorable, he considered his position basically a defense of laissez-faire (in a somewhat modified form) and the capitalistic system. In noting monopoly elements as the explanation for the divergence between cost of production and value, he tended to divert criticism away from the system and to those faults which could be corrected without overthrowing the entire mechanism. Unfortunately for his purpose and the taste of some of his capitalist-oriented critics, Senior conceded too much. Inherited wealth was included as a rent return because it had not really been earned by its current possessor but only acquired through chance. Thus the whole system of property inheritance—crucial to the concept of capitalism—was placed in jeopardy. As we shall see in Chapter VII, the Marxian critics of capitalism were not satisfied by Senior's concession and refused to be diverted into seeking only a correction of its evils; for many of them the complete overthrowal of capitalism was the only answer.

The economists who were willing to develop Senior's views, when his ideas were compatible with their own, became highly indignant at other parts of Senior's thinking. While serving on a government commission, for example, Senior had espoused the notion that the capitalists' profits were made only during the last two hours of the working day. The obvious conclusion to be drawn from this view was that any reduction in the length of the working day would quickly eliminate all profits. Marx, as we shall see in Chapter VII, was also highly critical of this concept and developed his own theory of surplus value, partly as an answer to this claim.

Senior's major impact on the non-Socialist economists will become evident as we proceed; basically it was his concept of abstinence which had enduring fame.

JOHN STUART MILL (1806–1873)

John Stuart Mill's *Principles of Political Economy* provides a convenient transition between the Classical School of economics and one branch of its numerous critics. His book maintained a foot for him in both camps; while Mill provided his readers with a remarkably clear and well organized statement of Classical thought up to 1848, at the same time he presented a sympathetic view of the merits of ending private property and establishing some form of socialism in its place. Mill's views were summarized in his famous declaration that the laws of production were fixed but the laws of distribution were mutable. In suggesting that the laws of distribution could be altered to meet the demands of society, Mill aligned himself with believers in the reality of social reform. The question of reform now assumed quite a different coloring. Smith and Ricardo had also been reformers, but their reforms were different in nature. Both of them saw the capitalistic system as operating in terms of certain natural laws. Reforms were necessary in those situations where the economic laws of nature were being contravened. Mill's attitude toward reform was quite different. In some cases there were no fixed, immutable principles. Where this was the case, a society could make changes to suit its needs.

The Man. Who was this man who challenged the accepted doctrine that the laws of production and distribution were equally immutable? The student who feels himself to be unduly plagued by excessive assignments from overdemanding teachers should be comforted by hearing of Mill's early education. In his *Autobiography,* Mill recounts his childhood training under the tutelage of his father. The elder Mill was surely as demanding a taskmaster as ever guided a young mind in its pursuit of learning. By the age of three, Mill was already beginning the study of Greek, and at eight he was studying Latin. Before he was fourteen, Mill was studying Ricardo's *Principles* by listening to readings of it by his father, then writing essays of criticism. These essays were then defended and discussed in detail with his father during long afternoon walks. Perhaps from an overloading of his still youthful mind, Mill suffered a nervous breakdown at the age of twenty-one.

Although it is Mill's economic views which are of most interest to us, we would be remiss if we failed to take note of his interest in a variety of subjects. Indeed it is these other writings, rather than his work in economics, which has brought him much of his enduring fame. Among the more famous of his essays were *On Liberty, Utilitarianism,* and *The Subjection of Women.* Although political economy was one of the last subjects to which Mill was introduced, it was one of the first in which he made a contribution of his own. *Two Letters on the Measure of Value* was published when Mill was only sixteen. A year before that he had written the marginal notes to his father's *Elements of Political Economy.* In fact, to an unknown extent, his father's book had been the product of the earlier critiques the boy had made of Ricardo's work when he was thirteen years old.

Mill served for a period of time as editor for the *London Review* and then later as editor of the *Westminster Review.* His interest in India had been roused at an early age by a study of his father's history of that country. The younger Mill served in India House for a number of years and wrote extensively on the economic problems of that country. Mention should also be made of the influence of Mrs. Taylor, a lady to whom Mill was deeply attached for a number of years and whom he married after the death of her husband. Mill acknowledges in his autobiography the deep intellectual debt he owed her, although it is doubtful whether she had much of a part in shaping his economic principles.

Mill was generally acknowledged as the leading economist of his period, and he was called to testify before the Select Committee of the House of Commons on the Income Tax when a revision was being considered in 1852. His *Principles of Political Economy* earned him an outstanding reputation. For a book which is so well written and organized, it took a remarkably short period of time to write. The book was begun in the fall of 1845; by February, 1846 the third part was complete, and the first draft was completed in spring of 1847. The achievement becomes even more impressive when we remember that during this same period Mill was also doing other writing and working a six-hour day at India House.

Mill's marriage to Mrs. Taylor was happy but all too brief; she died a few years after their marriage. Following her death, Mill ran for Parliament and was elected despite his aversion to any campaigning. His record there was unimpressive, partly because his reluctance to campaign resulted in his defeat three years later, and also for those three years while he was in Parliament he preferred to adhere " . . . to his lifelong principle of doing only work that needed to be done, and that nobody else seemed equally able or willing to do." [4]

It is difficult to assess the importance of all the different people with whom the younger Mill came in contact. His father was a personal friend of Ricardo and the latter invited the young Mill to his home for discussions on political economy. Jeremy Bentham was also a friend of James Mills, and the son again received much intellectual stimulus from Benthams' philosophy. Mill once marked his reading of Dumont's *Traités de legislation* (a French version of Bentham's philosophy) as one of the major turning points in the development of his own mental powers.

Prior to doing the marginal abstracts for his father's book, Mill traveled in France with Jeremy Bentham's brother, and while there visited for a while with Jean Baptiste Say. One important result of this visit was to instill in Mill a permanent interest in Continental liberalism. It was Mill who organized a Utilitarian Society consisting of about a dozen economists and philosophers, who met weekly at Bentham's home. Because of the major role played by Utilitarian philosophy in shaping Mill's attitudes, it becomes necessary to take a brief look at Jeremy Bentham, the founder of this school.

JEREMY BENTHAM (1748–1832)

Although Keynes once denied the propriety of identifying Bentham as an economist, it was also Keynes who suggested to the Royal Economic Society the sponsoring of a survey of Bentham's hitherto unpublished writing. This task, undertaken by Dr. W. Stark, resulted in the publication of numerous additional economic writings by Bentham.[5] However, because these economic writings had remained largely buried, they contributed little to the mainstream of economic thought. Before turning to the

---

[4] William Minto, "John Stuart Mill," *Encyclopedia Britannica* (1897), Vol. XVI, p. 313.

[5] Jeremy Bentham, *Economic Writings*, ed. by W. Stark (London: Burt Franklin, 1952).

sources of Bentham's influence on Mill and others, however, we should note briefly his biographical background and some of the popular misconceptions about Bentham's economics.

The Man. Bentham was born in London, the son of a prominent and wealthy lawyer. His early educational achievements may have set the standard for the training of J. S. Mill. At the age of three the young Bentham was studying Latin and a year later began the study of music and French conversation. Bentham received his advanced training at Queen's College, Oxford University, and was called to the bar in 1772. Despite his family's long tradition in the practice of law, Bentham was more interested in criticizing the practices of others than in practicing law himself. His first book, *Fragment on Government,* for example, was a biting critique of Sir William Blackstone, the famed legal scholar, while a second book criticized prevailing methods of punishing criminals. During his lifetime, Bentham's advice was widely sought by governmental officials in France and the United States as well as in England, and he was later made an honorary citizen of France. His total literary output was tremendous—some eleven volumes of closely printed text published in 1843—but there is considerable evidence to suggest that Mill and others did a sizable amount of the final editing and rewriting. In addition, Bentham was the founder of the *Westminster Review,* a magazine later to become an important vehicle for economic discussions.

Because the other Classical writers of the time championed laissez-faire, it has been generally assumed that Bentham's utilitarianism also embraced the laissez-faire philosophy. Actually the 18-year period (1786–1804) when Bentham was interested in political economy saw a marked change in Bentham's attitude. He began by "out-Smithing" Smith, arguing against any restrictions on usury (*Defense of Usury,* 1787), and ended by writing *The True Alarm,* a book which neither Ricardo nor Mill considered worthy of publication because of its serious "defects." These defects consisted chiefly of assertions that unemployment and deflation might be corrected by government issues of more money. Even more interesting, in view of later developments under the leadership of Keynes, was Bentham's belief that the interest rate might fail to adjust the volumes of savings and investment to each other.

We should note also that although Bentham solved in part the Smith dilemma of water versus diamonds, he never really applied his concept of utility to economic affairs. Nevertheless, to some degree his development of the "felicific calculus" for the measurement of pleasure and pain had an impact on later Marginal Utility theorists.

However, Bentham's greatest impact on Mill came with his discussion of the need for social reform. Bentham applied his concept of the "felicific calculus," with its five measures of pleasure and pain, to the question of legislative reform. His classic statement of this was his *Introduction to the Principles of Morals and Legislation* (1789). Mill was attracted to the idea of running society on the principle of "the greatest good for the greatest number" but was critical of Bentham's failure to draw distinctions between different kinds of pleasure and pain; the pleasures of pinball and Pushkin could be equated on the same scale. It was this concept that led Mill to remark, "Better a dissatisfied Socrates than a satisfied pig." Mill argued that there were qualities of pleasure and pain, as well as quantities, to be considered.

Mill's Economic Views. After an exposure to the awkward writing of Ricardo, Mill's style is a relief, as it is better written and topics follow each other in an orderly sequence. Successive books in the treatise are devoted to topics of "Production," "Distribution," and "Exchange." Two additional books follow these three big topics. They are devoted to the effect of the progress of society on "Production and Distribution" and the "Influence of Government." The treatise is a big book; earlier editions were published in two volumes and it closely resembles the scope of Adam Smith's *Wealth of Nations.*

The resemblance to Smith's book was not purely coincidental. Mill had begun a reworking of Smith's tome under his father's guidance. His intention was to bring Smith's book up to date with the necessary revisions needed in the light of Malthus, Ricardo, and others. In part, Mill was attempting to write a modern version of Smith's book. As such, Mill selected the same issue Smith had chosen as his focal point—the problem of wealth. In addition, Mill undertook a defense of Malthus and Ricardo, with some reservations and modifications to be noted shortly.

Other motives may also have prompted the publication of Mill's *Principles.* Mill was a reformer, just as were those economists who had preceded him. If anything, he showed even more pronounced leanings in this direction than they had, influenced as he was by Jeremy Bentham and the Utilitarian School of philosophy. Mill was also motivated by a desire to integrate further the various social sciences. He was not solely or even primarily an economist, as our brief outline of his life has indicated, but instead, a moral philosopher in the sense in which the term was applied to Adam Smith. The full title of this book is illustrative of this point: *Principles of Political Economy with Some Applications to Moral Philosophy.*

Finally, the attacks by Socialist writers had done much to discredit the writings of Malthus and Ricardo. Mill attempted to rehabilitate their theories in the light of the protests of their critics, so that the views of these economists, which Mill regarded as essentially correct, would appear more presentable. The obvious inadequacies in Ricardo's style of presentation must have also convinced Mill of the need for clarification and restatement.

Since Mill regarded his task as primarily one of clarification and modernization of established theory, we should not be too disappointed at the relatively meager supply of new economic concepts with which he supplies us. We will find little that is truly new in Mill's book; his debt to Smith, Malthus, and Ricardo is a heavy one. Yet the clarity with which he presented these familiar doctrines has helped to preserve the sanity of many a beginning student in economic thought. Furthermore, as we shall see shortly, the charge that Mill contributed nothing new is not completely fair.

The nature of his indebtedness to earlier writers can be quickly demonstrated if we examine his views on some of the issues which also preoccupied his predecessors. We can begin our comparison with the subject of population expansion. Mill accepted with little qualification the premises of the Malthusian doctrine; if anything, he was even more pessimistic than Malthus had been. Numerous passages can be cited where Mill deplored the lack of restraint displayed by the laboring classes and stated his lack of confidence in their ability ever to learn to act in a prudent fashion. Furthermore, it was Mill rather than Malthus who berated the poor for their failures and who likened the folly of excessively large families to the "crime" of drunkenness, and who suggested that the bearing of too many children should be a punishable offense. Mill's pessimism on this score may have been reinforced by his own family background. Mill was the eldest son of a large family, and early in his *Autobiography* he commented on the folly of his father's early marriage and siring of a large family, when he had little to support himself except the income from his writings. In the light of this youthful recklessness, James Mill's own emphatic support of the Malthusian Law becomes an interesting contrast.

Our concentration upon the major figures in the history of economic thought omits an important change in views about the nature of the population problem. There had been a period of revulsion from the implications of Malthus' doctrine. Several economic critics had argued that the situation was improving or that the danger had never been as great as Malthus had pictured it. The younger Mill's views thus represent not simply a continuation of thinking already firmly accepted by all of his contemporaries, but a reversion to the earlier gloom of Malthusian forecasts.

Mill argued that it was much more difficult for people to adjust to improved living standards and to accept them as a new norm than it was for people to adjust to a deterioration in standards. Thus, workers would respond to any improvement in their living standards by having additional children, while failing to restrain their reproductive tendencies in the face of worsening conditions. Mill's judgment contradicts the empirical evidence about the current patterns of consumption of present-day workers. Many economists today would conclude that the reverse was true —workers adjust their standards of living rapidly to improvements in income while clinging tenaciously to accustomed patterns even in the face of sharp reductions in earnings.

Part of Mill's deep pessimism about the course of population expansion lay in his enthusiastic adoption of the Law of Diminishing Returns. Population growth was a deadly menace because, as Malthus had pointed out, nature was unable to match the numerical expansion in mouths to feed with offsetting supplies of food to feed those mouths. Mill described the Law of Diminishing Returns as "the most important proposition in political economy." [6]

The dangers of an overexpanding population were further emphasized in Mill's mind by his adoption of the wages-fund theory. We have already seen that this theory entered into the thinking of Mill's predecessors, but it is with Mill's name that the term is usually linked. Mill's claim to fame with respect to the wages fund is in many respects ironic, for it was Mill, to the consternation of some of his followers, who eventually confessed his error, and in later writings he bowed to the objections of his critic, William Thornton. Prior to that famous recantation, however, Mill had done much to polish and refine the theory.

Mill borrowed the concept of abstinence from Nassau Senior. The theory as presented by Mill was similar to that postulated by Senior; capital was made available for the employment of workers by the willingness of the capitalist class to forego immediate enjoyment of their capital. Since the capitalists had forfeited some of their immediate pleasures, they also

[6] John Stuart Mill, *Principles of Political Economy,* Ashley ed. (London: Longmans, Green, 1920), p. 177.

made a contribution to the value of a product. We will have more to say about Mill's views on value, but we should reemphasize that much of the labor theory of value was predicated on the concept that labor was an unpleasant activity. The more labor that was involved in the production of an item, the greater the total suffering and pain experienced in its production, hence the greater its value. With the concept of abstinence as a sacrifice borne by the capitalist, employers were now elevated to a comparable status with the workers. The concept of abstinence provided defenders of the capitalist class with a convenient rebuttal to those who protested the exploitation of labor.

Mill's conception of the wages fund is not difficult to understand. The money which the capitalists had stockpiled by their abstinence constituted the demand for labor. The total wage bill could not be in excess of this fixed amount of capital. Nor was it difficult to determine the average wage; all that was needed was to divide the amount in the fund by the number of workers to be employed: Wages Fund/No. of Workers. The moral to be drawn was obvious. Since the size of the wage fund was at any given moment of time predetermined by the amount of capital accumulated for wage payments, the level of wages depended on the size of the denominator. The larger the denominator employed, the lower the level of wages.

Mill's concentration on the wages-fund explanation of wages, to the exclusion of alternative theories, led him to make some interesting exceptions to the theory of wages as set forth by Ricardo. Mill denied, for example, that wages could respond positively to changes in the cost of living. Wages did not rise with upward shifts in the cost of living; if anything, the relationship tended to be an inverse one. Since no more capital was available for wages in Mill's view, it is easy to see why he would deny the possibility that wages would rise with living costs. During periods of rising prices, the pressure to work harder and longer was correspondingly increased, with the result that the workers competed against each other more intensively, forcing wage rates downward. Although Mill made no mention of the possibility, presumably he also had in mind the likelihood that women and children would be driven into the labor force by the rising cost of living, thus supplying additional downward pressure on wages.

There was one possible way in which higher prices might lead to higher wages in Mill's system. This was for the higher prices to produce a rise in profits. If profits rose, capitalists would be in a position to save larger amounts of capital and these added savings might be directed to increasing the wages fund.

The early formulations of the wages fund probably stemmed from observation of agricultural practices. The need to accumulate a stockpile of produce, both for planting the following season and for the maintenance of the laborers until the next fall's harvest, was accurately mirrored in the wages-fund theory. As the English economy became increasingly industrial, Mill and others continued to accept the theory as if it described the industrial scene equally well. With the industrial system, the time span between the start and the finish of the production cycle was shortened, and it now became possible to consider wages as coming out of current production. The ability to define production into discrete intervals of time and connect wage payments with previously accumulated capital became more difficult. During this same period in English history the role of the banks in extending credit also became increasingly apparent; employers were thereby able to pay wages from funds borrowed from the banks for the purpose of completing production plans. The issue of whether this was anything more than an empty victory for workers and whether higher wages thus obtained would merely result in higher prices was still left open for debate; the "confession of error" was not followed by all of Mill's supporters.

The wages-fund theory's heaviest criticism, however, came from those who felt that the theory negated the usefulness of trade unions and condemned the workers to an indefinite continuation of low wages. As mentioned earlier, one of Mill's most vocal critics was William T. Thornton. Another critic of Mill was Francis D. Longe. The criticism as set forth by these two would be familiar to any modern champion of labor unions. They argued that the forces of competition were on the side of the employer rather than on that of the worker, and that the overcrowding of the labor market was the result not so much of expanding population as the necessity for women and children to work in order to assure the family's survival. They also noted that low wages tended to make for low efficiency, and that Mill, who had observed that wage rates should not be confused with the cost of labor because of variations in efficiency, took no account of this factor in his statement of the determination of wages. Longe weakened the force of the attack by confusing the question of general level of wages and wage differentials. The idea that there could be such a thing as a general level of wages while still allowing for wage differentials was an impossibility to Longe, and he likened it (not too happily, in view of our modern price indices) to the futility of constructing a general price index. While we might view these criticisms by Longe as evidence of a serious defect in Mill's analysis, it is doubtful whether the question crossed Mill's mind or indeed that Mill was ever influenced at all by Longe's criticisms. Longe wrote bitterly of both Mill's and Thornton's failure to acknowledge the existence of his writings and pointed to the sending of his criticisms to Mill. Whether Mill ever read them or not is unknown, but in any case it was Thornton's attack which triggered Mill's eventual retraction. Thornton's analysis was somewhat superior to Longe's in that the former emphasized the possibility of basing wages on anticipated expansions in consumer demand.

Mill's recantation first appeared in the *Fortnightly Review* when Mill was reviewing Thornton's book, *On Labour, Its Wrongful Claims and Rightful Dues; Its Actual Present and Possible Future.* Mill never included his revised views in the eighth and last edition of his *Principles,* although his previous statement was added as an appendix by the editor, William J. Ashley.[7] In his review of Thornton's book, Mill wrote, "I must plead guilty to having, along with the world in general, accepted the theory without the qualifications and limitations necessary to make it admissible." Mill conceded that expansions in the demand for labor could be obtained from other sources than a cheapening of labor.

Mill's altered position can be explained in several ways. The change can be attributed partly to his growing realization that a dogmatic defense of the wages-fund theory conflicted with his views about the possibility of reform. The conflict grew increasingly important as Mill became more and more willing to entertain proposals for social and socialistic reform. Furthermore, as was indicated above, his theory of wages fund as he had originally outlined it constituted a convenient argument for the opponents of labor unions. Mill recognized the merits in Thornton's query: How was a labor union to win increases in wages for its members when there was only a fixed sum of money available for the payment of those wages? Worse yet was the corollary conclusion implicit in the wages-fund theory that if a union should succeed in getting a greater share for its membership, this gain could only work to the detriment of other workers, who would have a smaller remaining amount for their support. The logic and arithmetic of this argument is not difficult to follow. Granting that the wage fund at any point in time is fixed by the amount of savings previously set aside for that purpose, unions could do nothing to augment the

[7] *Ibid.,* pp. 991–993. Mill's statement first appeared in the *Fortnightly Review* of May 1, 1864, p. 515.

absolute size of the fund. The result of their wage increase would be to carve out a larger piece of the pie for their members, thus leaving a smaller share for other workers. In this way the interests of one group of workers were played off against those of another. The pattern is a familiar one and the assertion is still heard today (not altogether without foundation) that wage increases in the unionized sectors of the economy come at the expense of nonunion employees. Mill never went to the trouble to correct all of the relevant passages in his *Principles,* but confined his recantation to the previously mentioned.

In his analysis of wages, Mill discussed not only the determination of their general level but also the causes for wage differentials. Although he based his analysis on the explanation advanced by Smith, as noted earlier, he departed from Smith's explanations at several important points. Mill observed, for example, that instead of the inverse relationship between working conditions and wages postulated by Smith, there was actually a positive correlation—the more disagreeable the work, the lower wages were likely to be. In explaining this, Mill emphasized the immobility of labor, which had been mentioned but not greatly emphasized by Smith. Not only were workers likely to be rendered immobile through custom, inertia, and preference for particular trades, but they were also handicapped by the lack of opportunities for social mobility.

Mill set the stage for later economists like John Elliot Cairnes, who likened the path to social mobility to a flight of stairs having periodic landings; those on the steps below a landing were unlikely to be able to move to a set of steps higher on the occupational ladder. The impediments of lack of training and education, and even requirements of dress all acted to hold workers to the station to which they were born. Even more depressing, their children faced almost insurmountable obstacles in the attempts to improve themselves. Although Mill explained wage differentials largely in terms of these handicaps to the free movement of labor, he was not unduly pessimistic about the future. He thought it probable that conditions were likely to improve rather than to worsen and that there were already signs of improvement. The extension of public education was fitting the children of the laboring class for a wider variety of jobs, thus making it possible for them to compete in fields previously completely closed to them.

RENT. Mill followed Ricardo's lead in his discussion of the determination of rent. The key element in explaining rent was again the differences in fertility. Mill added little that was new to this thought. He began by stating that rent was a monopoly price made necessary by the scarcity of fertile lands. He attempted to explain the absence of rent on the marginal land by advancing many of the explanations suggested in the discussion by Ricardo. Mill also helped to clarify the relationship between the alternatives of intensive and extensive cultivation. Finally, Mill raised the question of the distinction between those returns on capital which should be treated as profits and those which could more properly be regarded as a rent. Mill argued that capital invested in permanent improvements in the land really earned a rent rather than a profit return. This question was to be revived and modified later by Alfred Marshall.

PROFITS. Mill began his discussion of profits with a justification for their existence: "As the wages of the labourer are the remuneration of labour, so the profits of the capitalist are properly, according to Mr. Senior's well-chosen expression, the remuneration of abstinence." [8] As he developed his explanation of profits further, however, the source of profits became more intricate; Mill suggested three reasons for their existence. First of all, they were partly an interest payment made for the sacrifice involved in abstinence; second, they were a payment for the risks incurred in the investment of the capital; and last, they were partly the wages of superintendence. This explanation for the existence of profits was adopted in whole or in part by succeeding generations of economists. Mill restated the principle laid down by earlier economists, which was to be the crux of Marx's attack. The cause of profits, Mill said, "is that labor produces a surplus." The size of profits was dependent on the absolute size of the pie to be shared by labor and capital and on the relative proportions of the pie gained by the two parties.

Mill found some of the same factors creating differences in profits between different employments as occasioned differences in wage rates. Rates of profit varied with the degree of risk, the agreeableness or disagreeableness of the trade, and the extent of natural or artificial monopolies. Save for these influences, however, Mill agreed with Ricardo that profits of different trades tended to be equal.

One final point in Mill's discussion of profits is of interest. Mill distinguished between two methods of computing the rate of profit. Profits could be computed as a percentage of sales or as a percentage of the owner's investment. In Mill's view, the path to a healthy economy lay in the direction of concentration of capitalists on the latter rate. Low profits per unit of sale encouraged production and economic growth, while at the same time assuring the capitalist a reasonable return on his investment.

VALUE. Mill's discussion of value was begun with a note of opti-

8 Mill, *Principles*, p. 405.

mism: "Happily, there is nothing in the laws of value which remains [1848] for the present or any future writer to clear up; the theory of the subject is complete. . . ."[9] In the light of the continued preoccupation of later economists with the topic of value, Mill's assessment can only be judged as being excessively optimistic. Critics of Mill have been too apt to hold this youthful assertion up to ridicule and to ignore the very real contribution Mill made to the subject, for even judged in the light of modern theory, Mill's statement appears amazingly fresh.

Mill's emphasis on a cost of production theory of value and the virtual exclusion of the role of demand was in keeping with the theories of the earlier writers whom we have already encountered. His failure to take fuller account of the role of demand and utility, however, is somewhat more surprising in light of his belief in the Utilitarian philosophy. Either Mill was convinced by the crude cost-of-production theories of value as expounded by Smith and Ricardo, or his unwillingness to adopt Bentham's "felicific calculus" led him to place little stress on the importance of utility; in either case the inconsistency was more apparent than actual, for it will be remembered that Bentham himself made scant use of his utility theory in explaining value. Not that the importance of utility was completely overlooked—Mill recognized that an item must be desirable or no one would purchase it. Furthermore, irreplaceable items might have their value determined by utility alone; Mill gave as an illustration a musical snuff box which was suddenly desired by a passenger on a boat on Lake Superior. Since the passenger wanted it very badly and only one was available, the owner would be in a position to charge a price far in excess of its cost of production. Such instances were rare, however, and could be discarded, much as Ricardo had dismissed rare paintings and works of art. Mill also recognized the importance of elasticity of demand in controlling price during short-run periods.

> If the article is a necessary of life, which, rather than resign, people are willing to pay for at any price, a deficiency of one-third may raise the price to double, triple, or quadruple. Or, on the contrary, the competition may cease before the value has risen in even the proportion of deficiency. A rise, short of one-third may place the article beyond the means or beyond the inclinations of purchasers to the full amount.[10]

Mill's failure to make further use of the concept of demand may have stemmed in part from the lack of the geometry of the demand schedule.

[9] *Ibid.,* p. 436.
[10] *Ibid.,* p. 447.

The strength of Mill's analysis of value lay in his ability to differentiate between different time periods and different conditions involved in the production of a commodity; he separated those cases where increases in the supply were difficult or impossible from those where increases could be achieved without limit, and devoted the bulk of his consideration to commodities in the latter category. Value for those items easily reproducible was determined by the cost of production plus an "ordinary" rate of profit. Thereafter, we find successive chapters devoted to the role of wages and rent in the determination of value. Mill agreed with Ricardo that, generally, high wages could not produce high values. To assume otherwise, said Mill, would lead to the conclusion that there could never be a *real* rise in wages. Nevertheless, a rise of wages in a particular industry unaccompanied by similar increases elsewhere in the economy could produce alterations in value. In treating rent as a surplus, Mill excluded it as a contributor to value; the analysis, with some minor refinements for urban properties, was similar to that made by Ricardo. Only if rent were paid to prevent the land being used in some other employment might rent properly be included as a cost of production.

One final point of interest in Mill's discussion of value should be noted. He had little faith in the ability of consumers to discriminate wisely in their purchases. Both the wealthy and the poor frequently paid more than the products purchased were really worth, either from lethargy or from ignorance. In an economic system where the consumer reigned as king, dictating the operation of the market, this confession of the monarch's weaknesses was a startling admission and removes much of the sting from those criticisms which suggest that the Classical economists all conceived of a system of perfect competition.

VALUE AND TRADE. Mill carried his discussion of value into the field of international trade. The need to treat international values was explained, said Mill, by the immobility of the variable factor of production; land quite obviously could not be moved, but labor and capital also experienced impediments in their shifts from one country to another. Mill reasserted the position in favor of free trade laid down by Smith and Ricardo and developed the concept of comparative advantage in its defense. Ricardo's statement of comparative cost represented a substantial improvement over Smith's analysis, but Ricardo's analysis failed to provide a solution of the terms on which trade might take place; it was to this task that Mill devoted his efforts. Mill labeled his formulation the Equation of International Demand. Using a numerical example similar to Ricardo's, Mill set forth the familiar two-country, two-commodity example. Instead of holding the output constant, as Ricardo had, and considering how much labor would be required to produce a given output, Mill held the amount of labor constant and considered the variations in output as outlined below.

Country	Broadcloth	Linen
England	10	15
Germany	10	20

Thus, in England, a fixed quantity of labor could produce either 10 units of broadcloth or 15 units of linen, while the same input of labor could produce in Germany 10 and 20 units respectively. Both countries would benefit from trade: England, if it could acquire something more than 15 units of linen for 10 units of broadcloth, and Germany, if it was able to give up something less than 20 units of linen for 10 units of broadcloth. The problem to be solved was where, within these limits, exchange would actually take place. Mill's answer was that the ratio of exchange would depend on the relative strength and elasticity of demand of each country for the other country's product. How badly England wanted linen as compared to how badly Germany desired broadcloth was the key determinant.

ECONOMIC GROWTH. Mill shared the widespread conviction of his contemporary economists that the ultimate future of the economy was one of stagnation. The reasons assigned for this eventuality were also familiar ones. As the population increased, the cost of the means of subsistence would gradually rise. With this rise would come the need for higher real wages and such rises could be achieved only at the expense of profits. Even if population did not grow—an unlikely event in Mill's view—wages would still rise at the expense of profits as a shortage of labor developed. As the rate of profits declined, a point would come when further new investment would be unprofitable and at this point progress would cease. The stationary state pictured by Mill, however, was less in the nature of a catastrophe than as had been viewed by Ricardo, for Mill saw the cessation of economic growth as an opportunity to concentrate on the finer things of life. Mill had little taste for the more crass evidences of commercialism which appeared about him. He had once described the United States as a land where the men chased dollars and the women gave birth to dollar chasers. In the stationary state this kind of nonsense would cease. Mill envisioned a state where people would be able to devote themselves to the arts, to reading, and to the support of cultural institutions. Human and cultural values could assume a dominant position over commercial values.

Meanwhile, until the stationary state was reached, the path to be trod was much the same as previous writers had described it; the motives for and process of capital accumulation showed little variation from previous descriptions. In the case of the introduction of machinery, Mill did little more than support the conclusions reached by Ricardo. Mill answered Ricardo's critics, who had argued that Ricardo had temporarily forgotten the importance of Say's Law by saying that while the purchasing power of those still employed would have been increased, this would be offset by the decline in purchasing ability of those who had been displaced by the machine.

Mill's acceptance of the inevitability of the stationary state should by no stretch of the imagination be interpreted as an acceptance of Malthus' concern over gluts. On this point Mill was as firm in his rejection as Ricardo had been before him. "The doctrine appears to me to involve so much inconsistency in its very conception, that I feel considerable difficulty in giving any statement of it which shall be at once clear, and satisfactory to its supporters." [11] As his subsequent discussion of the question made clear, Mill was a firm believer in Say's Law.

At only one major point did Mill depart seriously from the principles of economic growth set forth by Adam Smith. Mill was willing to accept the notion that it might be necessary for a country just beginning its economic development to encourage the undertaking of new business. Capitalists might be reluctant to start new businesses in the face of competition from already well-established firms in other countries. Thus it might at times be desirable to interfere with the general principle of free trade and institute protective tariffs for newly established businesses. Mill was convinced of the ultimate desirability of free trade, however, and warned that the government must be careful not to continue the protection once the business was established and should avoid continuing protection for firms which showed no prospects of ever "getting off the ground floor."

Mill's views about the future fitted well with those of his predecessors. In fact, it was probably this heritage from his father and Ricardo which induced Mill to cling to his pessimistic views about the future just prior to a tremendous improvement in the standards of wages and conditions for the working classes. Between 1850 and 1900 real wages rose nearly 94 percent, while during this same period England's population rose by over 17 million. Mill thus stands as a poor forecaster of the future, and his confirmed pessimism is difficult to understand except as a holdover from his early exposure to the doctrines of political science as set forth by David

[11] *Ibid.*, p. 557.

Ricardo. Another important fact was that Mill developed his entire theory of production and distribution around the concept of diminishing returns. Mill's insistence that this was the most important principle in political economy also helps to explain his continued pessimistic forecasts. Again we find it necessary to emphasize Mill's consuming fear of expanding population. Already in 1850, in Mill's view, England and other "populous nations had . . . reached the density needed for proper combinations of labor." In light of subsequent growth in both population and standards of living in these "populous nations," Mill's undue pessimism becomes readily apparent.

TAXATION AND GOVERNMENT EXPENDITURES. Mill's treatment of public finance in his treatise can be best termed encyclopedic. It would be difficult for the modern economist to find a single topic in public finance that Mill had not at least fleetingly mentioned. In some ways the discussion is parallel to that given by Adam Smith, and Mill used Smith's canons of taxation as a starting point.

He adopted Smith's joint-tenants concept of government: Government is so preeminently a concern of all, that "to determine who are most interested in it is of no real importance." Thus we have a reason to tax everyone. The benefit principle of taxation was disposed of by Mill when he pointed out that definite values cannot be assigned to things essentially indefinite.

Thus the stage was set for Mill's adoption of ability to pay as a standard for taxation. Each individual would contribute to the government in proportion to his ability. The latter term was taken to mean income. Mill observed that the least sacrifice to all would come from equal sacrifice by each. This usage of the terms "equal" and "least sacrifice" was very loose as compared to the rigorous definitions worked out by the Marginalists at the end of the century, and Mill's terms have been variously interpreted. He stressed the importance of equality of pressure from taxation, and frequently reiterated that the fact that equality was not attainable was no reason to dismiss it as a goal.

To achieve equality of pressure, or to attempt to achieve it, Mill believed that a system of taxes was necessary—no one tax would suffice. Mill pointed out in his correspondence with the Italian writer, Constantino Baer, that one's means of paying taxes consisted of income or of capital, but not of both. He found the income tax itself suitable for use in time of need, although he preferred the other direct taxes: on houses, rent, legacies, and inheritances. The income tax he saw as one way of making the rich pay their share, but he feared it as being a particular burden on the most conscientious. He did not espouse the idea of a graduated rate for the income tax, however, believing that such arrangement would kill incentive. But he did favor making allowances for income saved up to one fourth of the total amount of income.

Although Mill did not pursue the topic of shifting and incidence to determine definite laws or rules governing these phenomena, he was very interested in tracing the burden of each tax, as Ricardo had been. Mill used the soon-to-be-discarded terminology of "direct" and "indirect" to differentiate between those taxes which cannot be shifted and those which can. In doing this he assumed that a distinction could be drawn, but then he proceeded to list the house tax with the direct taxes, which he said could be shifted.

Although Mill recognized the need for indirect taxes to complete his system, he could not be called a strong advocate of taxes on commodities. He particularly criticized such taxes on the grounds that they could only be administered through increased governmental regulation, that businessmen would need to advance more capital initially, and that this last would limit innovation by cutting demand through high prices. Nonetheless, he admitted their convenience. His recommendations, therefore, included taxes on luxury commodities, with exemption of the basic necessities. He advocated the taxation of foreign-made goods when such goods were not in competition with domestic products. Under no circumstances did he accept taxation for protection of well-established domestic industries.

One exception to Mill's acceptance of the principle of equality in taxation ought to be noted. He recommended the taxation of all unearned increments in the value of land. This proposal has received a great amount of discussion, although it has rarely been attempted in practice.[12] It was enlarged upon by the American economist, Henry George.

To round out the taxation picture, Mill mentioned local taxes only fleetingly. This topic was to receive greater attention from the writers in the latter part of the nineteenth century. Mill's comment reflects the relatively minor importance of local expenditures. He favored special taxes for all local spending, that is, a separate tax or percent of a tax would be allocated to each item of expenditure.

Mill was farsighted, for the mid-nineteenth century, in his attitude toward public debts. He did not share the extreme fears of some of his

[12] The single exception to this generalization of which the writer is aware is the case of the Labor Party in England which, upon gaining power after World War II, imposed such a tax; it was repealed when the Conservative Party regained control.

predecessors, although he favored debt reduction when possible on the theory that money was more likely to fructify in the pockets of the ex-bondholder than in the pockets of the taxpayers. His recommendation to devote the proceeds from one tax—his suggestion was the successions tax —to debt reduction has occasionally found favor by legislators. One explanation for his more moderate view of debt might be his feeling that some government expenditure is productive. Such an idea was foreign to most of Mill's predecessors.

DISTRIBUTION. Mill's views on taxation reflected rather neatly his basic irresolution about redistribution. Mill, far more than any of his predecessors, was confident of the opportunity for society to alter the existing patterns of distribution. But at the same time, he recommended caution lest the resulting alteration in income upset the willingness and ability of the capitalists to abstain and invest.

Mill's thoughts on the variability of the laws of distribution are contained in the following frequently quoted passage:

The laws and conditions of the Production of wealth partake of the character of physical truths. There is nothing optional or arbitrary in them. . . . It is not so with the Distribution of wealth. That is a matter of human institution solely. The things once there, mankind, individually or collectively, can do with them as they like. They can place them at the disposal of whomsoever they please, and on whatever terms.[13]

Taken at its literal face value, the statement is sheer economic nonsense. A society cannot expect to alter its patterns of distribution without incurring some repercussions in production. This apparent flaw in Mill's logic has served as the basis for attack by a number of his critics.

Yet the summary of Mill's views on taxation just presented makes it clear that Mill was not unaware of this danger; his opposition to the progressive income tax was based on precisely this objection. The real problem lay in the attempt of Mill to embrace simultaneously two different economic philosophies. While flirting with Socialistic reform, Mill remained an unregenerate defender of individualism and laissez-faire.

SOCIALISM. Given Mill's identification with individualism and his ambivalence about the proper distribution of income, it is surprising to find Mill identified as a sympathizer with socialist ideas. Nevertheless, such an identification is essentially correct and Mill became increasingly impressed with socialism's virtues with the passing years. While the opponents of socialism may attribute Mill's flirtation with it to increasing age

[13] *Ibid.*, pp. 199–200.

and the resulting degeneration of his mental faculties, a more likely explanation can be found. Mill supported the system of free enterprise and private property as a model. Ideally it provided the best possible results. The difficulty was the numerous flaws and imperfections which existed. In view of these blemishes, however, "all the difficulties, great or small, of Communism would be but as dust in the balance." [14] We must remember also that Mill's dalliance with socialism remained but a flirtation and never involved a passionate embrace. Until the day when some form of guild Socialism might emerge, the current system still appeared to Mill to be the better way.

Summary and Evaluation. We have already seen cause for challenging Smith and Ricardo on grounds of eclecticism. Such a charge can also be leveled against Mill and perhaps with even greater accuracy. There was comparatively little in Mill's analysis which was novel. Only his theory of comparative advantage in international trade can be termed completely new. His major contribution was one of classification and clarity of exposition. In addition, he served as a link between the Classical School and its Socialist critics. Mill was too thoroughly exposed to the teachings of Ricardo and his father to be able to throw off their theories on rent, profits, and population. But he found it increasingy difficult to accept the grim implications of their doctrines, as his eventual rejection of one of his own concepts, the wages fund, clearly demonstrates. As time went by, the possibility of social reform became increasingly appealing. An examination of the position of those less reluctant to abandon the Classical model will be found in the next chapter devoted primarily to Karl Marx, but before hearing from these later critics we must first meet briefly two other members of the Classical School, Cairnes and Fawcett.

JOHN ELLIOT CAIRNES (1823–1875)

If Mill can be described as one who, despite his sympathy for social reform, still clung to the concept of individualism and laissez-faire, Cairnes may best be described as one who never had any doubts about the undesirability of opposing any proposal for interfering with the free operation of the market. Long after Mill had abandoned his wages-fund doctrine, Cairnes was still defending the concept against all attacks. His *Some Leading Principles of Political Economy Newly Expounded* was intended as a

[14] *Ibid.*, p. 208.

defense of Ricardian economics, but was interpreted by later writers such as Marshall as weakening rather than bolstering Ricardo's position.

The Man. Cairnes as an economist played "second fiddle" to Mill. In part, this was due to Cairnes' own acknowledgment of Mill's superiority and in part, from Cairnes' poor health. In the later years of his life he suffered from a serious and painful muscular debility and by the time of Mill's death Cairnes was bedridden. In spite of this handicap, Cairnes became generally acknowledged as one of the leading British economists of his time. In addition to his *Some Leading Principles of Political Economy,* Cairnes is best remembered for *The Character and Logical Method of Political Economy.* Two volumes of his collected essays also were published. Of these essays, perhaps the most notable was his criticism of slavery, *The Slave Power,* which has been described by some as one of the most forceful criticisms of slavery ever written. Cairnes served for sixteen years as a professor of political economy, until his retirement in 1872. During that period he taught both in England and in Ireland, the latter country being where he had received much of his early training.

Economic Views. In addition to his continued defense of the wages fund after its abandonment by Mill, Cairnes gained recognition for other (and sounder) economic concepts. He further developed the relationship between the cost of production and the value of a product. In doing so, Cairnes raised questions about the advisability of considering wages as a cost of production. Wages were a cost, Cairnes pointed out, for the capitalist, but for the workers they were a remuneration. More appropriately, the cost of labor and abstinence was borne by labor and the capitalist respectively, while the cost of risk fell chiefly but not inevitably on the capitalist. It is evident from this brief description that Cairnes patterned his thinking along the lines laid down by Nassau Senior. The element of risk distinguished his presentation from that of Senior's.

Cairnes' objection to the equating of remuneration and cost was based on several points. First of all, the two were frequently direct antitheses to each other; it was often possible to have a large payment and a small cost. Here Cairnes was enlarging on Mill's distinction between the earnings of labor and the cost of labor. But Cairnes' emphasis on this point led to his rejection of Mill's explanation of cost of production. Cairnes believed that it was impossible to talk of wages as always being a measure of the disutility of work, when so clearly they bore no close relationship at all. More important, he detected a flaw in one of the arguments then being offered

in the defense of trade barriers. Incidentally, this argument is still dear to
the hearts of protectionists. If value could be related to the cost of production in terms of high wage rates, Cairnes observed, then there was no way
to attack those who urged protective tariffs as a device for protecting high
wage rates.

Cairnes' attack on Mill's formulation of a cost of production theory of
value was also closely tied up with another important contribution. In
developing his attack, Cairnes presented the concept of noncompeting
groups. Although competition was free and vigorous between workers in
similar lines of work, Cairnes was more pessimistic than Mill about the
opportunities for workers to move freely from one station in life to another. Unlike the capitalist who had relatively wide freedom of choice as
to where to invest his capital, the laborer had little latitude. The essence of
Cairnes' position may be seen in the following passage:

> What we find, in effect, is, not a whole population competing indiscrimi-
> nately for all occupations, but a series of industrial layers, superimposed on one
> another, within each of which the various candidates for employment possess a
> real and effective power of selection, while those occupying the several strata
> are, for all purposes of effective competition, practically isolated from each
> other.[15]

The result was that the products of workmen in competing groups were
exchanged for their cost of production, but the value of products produced
by noncompeting groups rested instead on a theory of reciprocal demand
analogous to the analysis developed by Mill with reference to international trade.

Cairnes' discussion of this alternative explanation of value is noteworthy on two counts. First, it helped to undermine the Classical School's
theory of value; it was in this sense that Marshall maintained that Cairnes
weakened rather than supported the Classical School's case. Second, the
value of products produced by members of a noncompeting group assumed a more subjective character, which could not be measured by the
level of payments to the factors of production. Cairnes' subjective treatment of disutility is somewhat surprising in the light of his firm if somewhat questionable rejection of William Stanley Jevons' utility theory of
value, discussed in Chapter IX. When Cairnes stated his concept of noncompeting groups, he pushed the possibility of social immobility to the
foreground much farther than Mill had been prepared to do.

15 J. E. Cairnes, *Some Leading Principles of Political Economy Newly Expounded*
(New York: Harper & Brothers, 1874), p. 66.

Cairnes' other major contribution was made in his book titled *The Character and Logical Method of Political Economy*. Here he developed the proposition stated earlier by Say and Senior that political economy should develop as a science freed from moral and ethical judgments. As long as it was directed toward the attainment of certain specific ends, it could never become a science. Cairnes suggested that political economy should stand ". . . neutral between competing social schemes; neutral, as the science of Mechanics stands neutral between competing plans of railway construction . . . as Chemistry stands neutral between competing plans of sanitary improvement. . . ." [16] Cairnes was thus overzealous in his efforts to reshape economics as a science; while there was room for improvement in this direction, Cairnes perhaps overstated his case. The contrast with Mill is striking. Mill had appended to the title of his book the words *"With Some Applications to Moral Philosophy."* Such applications were exactly what Cairnes was preaching against.

Cairnes may be criticized also for his belief that the "laws" of economics were all hypothetical and could never be tested by an appeal to empirical evidence. To disprove an economic "law" it became necessary to demonstrate that the formulator had either incorrectly assumed the basic "principles" of human action or had committed errors in logical deduction from the basis of these "principles." As a result of this philosophy, Cairnes was vociferous in his opposition to statistical methods. Like Senior and Say before him, Cairnes provided a useful warning to those who would stock the discipline with an oversupply of value judgments. By overstating his case, however, some of the force of his argument was lost.

HENRY FAWCETT (1833–1884)

The Man. As in the case of Cairnes, one can but wonder what additional contribution would have been forthcoming if Fawcett had not suffered a major physical handicap. He was blinded on a hunting trip at a time when he was just beginning to study law. Earlier, he had displayed his ability as a student by winning honors in mathematics. Fawcett is perhaps best known as the famed postmaster general of William Gladstone's cabinet. Much of his reputation was founded on his ability as an administrator and as the husband of a famous English suffragette. Fawcett owed his intellectual inspiration to three people—Henry Thomas Buckle, the

[16] J. E. Cairnes, *The Character and Logical Method of Political Economy* (New York: Harper & Brothers, 1875), p. 37.

scientific historian, Charles Darwin, and John Stuart Mill. He wrote his
Manual of Political Economy as a simple introduction to the more complicated analysis of Mill's *Principles* with the hope that the lay reader,
thus introduced to the subject, would be encouraged to read Mill.

For this reason Fawcett's life makes for more interesting reading than
does his *Manual*. His thoughts varied little from those of Mill; the book
was more tightly organized, with none of the minor inconsistencies about
public finance that Mill had allowed. Fawcett's major disagreement with
Mill came when he felt that Mill departed too readily from the Classical
tenets. Thus, Fawcett continued to cling to the wages-fund doctrine after
its abandonment by Mill and criticized Mill for accepting any form of
factory legislation. To Fawcett, all attempts at legislative reform of factory
conditions were wrong! He opposed the nine-hour day on the grounds
that there was no end to the further reductions in hours that workers
would seek. Once granted a nine-hour day, they would seek an eight-hour
day, and when that was won, would push for a limitation to seven hours,
and so on. Already, Fawcett argued, England was growing uncompetitive
in some fields of world trade where she had traditionally reigned supreme.
Fawcett denied that a shortening of hours would pay for itself by increasing workers' efficiency to the point where total output would be as great or
greater than it was prior to the reduction. If such were the case, Fawcett
argued, employers could be counted upon to reduce hours on their own
initiative in order to maximize profits. We have included Fawcett in this
book not because he made any great contribution to the history of economic thought; he did not. We include him because he marks the close of
the Classical School as we have described it in preceding chapters. While
he did depart from Mill at some other minor points of organization—by
adding chapters on subjects which he considered to be of current interest,
such as strikes, gold discoveries, and cooperative societies—in most respects he remained a devoted follower of Classical economic thought.

And so the dominating position of the Classical School drew to a close.
It was virtually unchallenged for nearly a century, but from this point on,
it met increasing attacks from all sides. Indeed, the following chapters of
this book are devoted to the views of those who reacted against the Classical viewpoint. There are a few exceptions, such as Alfred Marshall, and
even he, while apologizing for his predecessors' inadequacies, acknowledged and corrected their deficiences. The reasons for the dissent from the
Classical School are many and varied, but no group was more vocal or
determined in its criticism than that to which we turn next—the Socialist
and Communist group.

CHAPTER VII: Marx
and the Socialist Critics

> *Capitalism is an economic system
> where one individual exploits an-
> other; under Communism and
> Socialism, it is just the opposite.*
> —ANONYMOUS

> *The bitter argument between
> economists and human beings has
> ended in the conversion of the
> economists.*
> —ARNOLD TOYNBEE

It would be a serious mistake to picture the emergence of Socialism as simply a reaction to Classical economic thought. As all beginning students of philosophy know quite well, Plato presented a basic part of the Socialists' program in his picture of a utopia. Other outstanding examples could be cited of early Socialist thought in England and elsewhere.[1] What distinguishes the Socialist writers whom we are about to review in this chapter is that each of them, in his own way, was reacting to and protesting the attitude of the Classical writers toward human welfare. Although it is difficult to provide a definitive answer as to whether the members of the Classical School supported or opposed factory legislation,[2] at the very least it can be said that their economic philosophy held little appeal to the working classes. Either it maintained, like Smith, that the existing system was the best of all possible worlds and that everything would turn out well in the end, or else it argued that the problems facing mankind were the workers' own creation and that if wages were low, workers had no one to blame but themselves. Whether true or not, this message was not particularly comforting to the workers so situated.

[1] Our neglect of these earlier socialists is justified since they founded no system or added to the stream of economic thought.

[2] Mark Blaug, "The Classical Economists and the Factory Acts—A Reexamination," *The Quarterly Journal of Economics* (May, 1958), p. 212.

Among the many problems virtually untouched by the analyses of members of the Classical School was the business cycle. Only John Stuart Mill examined it in any detail, and one gathers no sense of urgency even in his analysis. Given their faith in Say's Law, it is not difficult to understand this neglect. Disposed by their theoretical underpinnings to minimize the importance of the cycle, they did not find it difficult to brush away its significance. At the time when Adam Smith was writing, the problem of the cycle had not yet fully emerged. Although oscillations in prices were already noticeable, the cycle as we know it today began its history only after industrialization was in full bloom. Later, when evidence of the cycle's existence became unmistakable, it was easy for economists to rationalize it as the product of the mismanagement of bank credit or errors in trade policy or internal governmental programs. Whichever explanation was adopted, the argument always concluded in the same fashion—the market would speedily react to restore conditions of full employment. While the Classical economists were piously mouthing these assurances, workers bore the brunt of the periodic "disturbance." It is little wonder, therefore, that they sought aid elsewhere.

Despite the casual treatment accorded business cycles by the earlier writers, it was the conditions resulting from these periodic crises which acted as a fulcrum in expediting reform legislation. Space does not permit us to recount the conditions against which workers protested through the Chartist and similar movements, nor the slow, painstaking progress made through reform. The reader can get a clue when he realizes that in the early part of the nineteenth century, boys of five were working a 12-hour day in Smith's beloved pin factories. The business crises merely emphasized what were problems even in the best of times—the low wages, the long hours, the ruthless employment of children, and the displacement of skilled craftsmen by modern machinery. As someone has said, it was not the use but the abuse of machinery which was one of the roots of the problem. The current chapter deals with two quite different groups of men—both Socialistic in philosophy—who appealed to and on behalf of the workers. Those in the first group, for the most part, sought relief by devising elaborate schemes for the reform of society, while the second group found hope only in the eventual complete overthrow of the capitalistic system. The second group offered no clear program for a future society, suggesting only that the eventual collapse of the system was an inevitable part of history. Both groups shared, however, a disdain for the central theme of the Classical School—the doctrine of individualism. The doctrine of liberty and freedom, fostered by opposition to the restrictions of Mercantilism and set forth by Rousseau in politics and Voltaire in philosophy, had been shaped by the Classical economists into a set of principles used to protect factory owners against any attempts to curb their excessive power. Ricardo, for example, once proposed legislation designed to forbid forced patronage at company stores. Not that the Socialists were opposed to the doctrine of freedom! Rather, they saw the freedom of a society as being achieved through collective action. As the Socialist critics saw it, the trouble with individualism as the way to maximize freedom was that it led to freedom for a few and misery and exploitation for the many. Interestingly enough, only one of the critics we are about to review came from the ranks of the underprivileged classes whose cause was being championed; instead, most of the critics came from well-to-do middle- or upper-class families. The range and breadth of Socialist thought is quite lengthy. The most we can hope to do in this chapter is touch briefly on some of the major figures; not even a list of names of those who might have been included will be provided. Students interested in pursuing the subject further should consult a good history of socialist thought.

JEAN CHARLES LEONARDO SISMONDE DE SISMONDI (1773–1842)

Inappropriately enough, we begin our survey of the Socialist critics with a man who was not really a Socialist at all, and who, though frequently included among the opponents of private property, did not carry his criticism of its employment to the usual conclusion. For critical as he was of the way in which the economic scene about him operated, Sismondi, despite some scattered sentences in his works to the contrary, never supported the abolition of all property income. Nevertheless, he was a passionate critic of the injustices wreaked by the capitalist system and many of his ideas furnished a model for subsequent writers. For this reason, he is included here.

The Man. Sismondi was born in Geneva of upper-class parents; his father was a property holder and a pastor. His parents were of the Protestant faith and had left Italy to settle in France, but following the repeal of the Edict of Nantes, they moved to Geneva. Sismondi was well educated, but at the behest of his parents (who had lost considerable money in defaulted bonds) gave up the study of literature to pursue a commercial career; he began as a bank clerk in Lyons. Political upheavals in Europe

led to a move by the family to England, but they found the English climate unattractive (although Sismondi himself loved England), soon returned to Geneva, and after selling their property, returned to Italy. The
proceeds of the property sale in Geneva furnished the means to purchase a
farm. By working on this farm, Sismondi obtained a firsthand background
for his first book on the problems of agriculture. Soon afterward, Sismondi
returned to Geneva, where he worked on his two major historical studies
—a 16-volume *History of the Italian Republics* and a 29-volume *History
of the French*. During this period, Sismondi became involved in local society and later became a supporter of Napoleon—events not altogether to
be expected from someone protesting the conditions of the poor. In 1819
he married an Englishwoman, a marriage which from all reports was a
reasonably happy one. Throughout his life, Sismondi maintained a curious
blend of liberal views combined with a respect for nobility and wealth.
Symptomatic of this mixture was his change in the spelling of his last
name from Sismonde to Sismondi, after a well-known Italian family. Biographers tell us that he grew increasingly conservative in later years.
Sismondi was quite a hypochondriac, and since he died a victim of cancer,
his fears may not have been without foundation.

Economic Views. Sismondi's first book in political economy proved
to be little more than a panegyric on Adam Smith's *Wealth of Nations.*
Later, when asked to write an article for the *Edinburgh Encyclopedia,*
Sismondi had cause to reconsider his ideas and discovered that his thinking was at many points considerably different from that of Smith. The
conclusions reached by Sismondi in this article were elaborated upon in
a second book entitled *Nouveaux principes d'économique politique.*
Smith's failure to recognize that his assumptions could not always be applied to a real world beset with such problems as the maldistribution of
property, the introduction of machinery, and the business cycle, without
causing undue suffering and distress for the masses, was the basis for Sismondi's dissent. Sismondi's questioning of the method of the Classical
economists was of less importance. Let us turn to a brief appraisal of each
of these issues, bearing in mind that Sismondi wrote his book as a warning
to the rest of the world not to follow England's example.

Sismondi felt that the Classical economists, including Smith, had placed
too much faith on the ability of capital and labor to move quickly in
response to changing market demands. Not only did workers find it difficult to give up chosen fields and geographical locations (a point clearly
recognized by Smith but unstressed by many of his followers), but it was

also difficult to uproot capital, once it had been invested, for reinvestment in more lucrative employments. It was not that simple to uproot capital invested in heavy capital equipment. This inability of factors of production to adjust played an important role in Sismondi's explanation of the business cycle.

Sismondi saw two major evils in the existing economic scene. One was the low level of wages and the general misery and suffering experienced by the majority of the working classes even in times of prosperity, and the second was the periodic recurrence of the business cycle. The poverty of the working classes stemmed from their separation from property. Without land or other means to sustain themselves, they were forced to depend on others for a livelihood. Sismondi thus anticipated Marx by picturing society as being divided into two classes—those who had property and employed others and those who were employed. Sismondi combined this picture of a basically two-class system with the Malthusian doctrine. When workers owned their own land or other means of support, they were able to gauge properly the size family which they were best able to support. But when the bulk of workers became dependent upon others for their means of support, workers lost their sense of prudence and restraint. With caution thrown to the winds, workers tended to raise larger families than they could afford to support, thus increasing the size of the labor force and depressing wages still further. Why the loss of property destroyed the worker's "moral restraint" and made him submissive to the demands of employers for more or fewer workers was never made clear. Whether a reader would accept or reject this hypothesis depended in large part upon how convinced he was as to the correctness of the Malthusian doctrine.

Adding to the misery of the workers, in Sismondi's view, was the displacement effect of machinery. As a historian, Sismondi was interested in short-run transitional effects as well as long-run effects, and his powers of observation suggested that workers frequently experienced short-run difficulties augmented by their tendency to be immobile. Furthermore, the capitalists (supported by the Classical economists) concentrated their justifications for the machine on the increases in output and reductions in prices made available to the consumer. But Sismondi warned that except as consumers, the workers did not share in the benefits of machinery. To be fully protected, workers should also win gains in the form of shorter hours and improved working conditions, and this all too rarely happened.

THE BUSINESS CYCLE. Although the immobility of labor and capital was an important explanation provided by Sismondi for the existence of cycles, it was not the only one. Part of Sismondi's explanation rested on his conviction that the economic system was continuously threatening to out-run its ability to consume all of the goods which it was able to produce. According to Sismondi, the purchasing power to buy today's output (more strictly speaking, this year's) came from a previous period's production. Thus when an economy was expanding, current production would outstrip last year's generated purchasing power and thus some of the goods would go unsold, wreaking bankruptcy and ruin on their producers. His theory is reminiscent in many respects to the wages-fund theory, and like this theory, seems to take as its model an agricultural economy where the pre-ceding harvest made possible consumption during the following year. Sis-mondi's own lack of clear analysis at this point did little to clarify or strengthen his argument, and this explanation of the business cycle found little favor among contemporary or later economists.

Other elements of Sismondi's analysis of the cause of cycles (and more particularly crises) found wider support. Sismondi suggested that part of the difficulty arose from the inability of producers to forecast accurately the changing demands of the market. This problem became increasingly difficult as the market broadened. When this inability to forecast was combined with the aforementioned immobility of factors of production, the opportunity for the economy to go seriously astray was apparent. Fi-nally, Sismondi foreshadowed the underconsumption school, who argued that maldistribution of wealth made it impossible for the consumers to buy back all of the goods they had helped to produce. Sismondi, however, unlike later underconsumptionists, emphasized not the general lack of de-mand for all production but rather that any expansion in demand for products which did occur was for luxury goods (since only the revenue of the wealthy was expanding). This was matched by a relative decline in demand for ordinary goods. The inability of the economy to shift quickly into new lines (because of immobilities) led to the importation of the luxury goods from other nations and the dismissal of workers in industries where demand had failed to grow. The resulting unemployment of workers reduced their ability to consume nonluxury goods still more, thus leading to further reductions in employment. Although these last two ex-planations of the business cycle won some favor with later underconsump-tionists, they suffered (as do underconsumption theories of the cycle in general) from the fact that they explain more clearly why a crisis might occur than why a recovery would materialize.

METHODOLOGY. Sismondi felt that political economy had deterio-rated badly after Adam Smith as the result of the abstract theorizing of

Ricardo and his followers, with their unwillingness to examine closely the real world about them. Smith, Sismondi pointed out, ". . . attempted to study every fact in the light of its own social environment. . . ."[3] All facts must be taken into consideration, Sismondi believed, and to theorize on the basis of single facts taken in isolation was to insure that one would inevitably go astray. It was Sismondi the historian who was speaking at this point, and his criticism of the Classical School's approach set the stage for the German Historical School.

Summary and Evaluation. Sismondi's impact on later economists was twofold: (1) He set the stage for the critique of method followed by the Historical School; and (2) his criticism of the capitalistic economy set the stage for later socialist critics—particularly Marx. Marx liked Sismondi's view of a two-class system and the process by which it emerged, and also Sismondi's description of the growing concentration of wealth. Marx may have also found inspiration for his economic interpretation of history from Sismondi's three stages of history—slavery, feudalism, and modern industry. Unlike Marx, however, Sismondi did not urge or predict the overthrow of the capitalist system. Rents and profits might be unduly high, but neither one was deemed completely unjustified. Sismondi's strength lay in his recognition of many of the social and economic evils about him, to which the Classical economists had closed their eyes. As a formulator of possible reforms, however, Sismondi was irritatingly vague. The state was to intervene to assure a more equitable distribution of income and to prevent a too rapid shifting by the economy from one line of activity to another, thus softening the problem of shifting factors of production. He urged the government to legalize associations which would act to widen the distribution of property. Meanwhile, he rejected both the communism of Marx and the utopian schemes of Owen and Fourier, and at times appeared to despair of ever achieving any worthwhile reform. Sismondi looked forward to a day when somehow the great concentrations of capital would be reduced and employers were required to exercise a social conscience with respect to their workers, thus assuring shorter hours, better pay, and improved working conditions. Unfortunately the details for achieving this dream were not provided.

[3] Sismonde de Sismondi, *Nouveau principes d'économique Politique,* Vol. II, No. 56, as quoted in Charles Gide and Charles Rist, *A History of Economic Doctrines* (London: D. C. Heath, n.d.), p. 174.

ROBERT OWEN (1771–1858)

Whereas Sismondi had limited impact on the thinking of his contemporaries and has been rediscovered only recently, our next critic, Robert Owen, is more famed for his immediate accomplishments than for his writings. Whatever one may think of his economic philosophy, the change in English industrial society which he helped to produce must be acknowledged. Owen was largely responsible for the provisions in the Factory Act of 1819 which set standards of hours, education, and employment of young children. Owen also pushed for something far more grandiose, helping to spark the cooperative movement in England. Finally, but just as important, Owen later disassociated himself from the movement and helped to organize a nationwide trade-union movement.

The Man. The early years of Owen's life were like a page from a manual of "How to Succeed in Business." Born in Wales of poor parents (his father was a saddler), Owen attended school until the age of nine. He started his career in business at an early age and made rapid progress in the textile industry. At the age of nineteen, he was already manager of a plant employing a hundred workers, and he developed it into one of the leading textile plants in the country. Owen's technical knowledge about spinning techniques and grades of cotton led him to a position of leadership in the industry. By 1799 he had become a partner in the business, and in that year he persuaded his partners to aid him in buying a plant of his own in New Lanark. By happy coincidence, he also succeeded in marrying the daughter of the previous owner. It was at New Lanark that Owen introduced his social reforms, designed to better working conditions and to convert Lanark into a model community. In 1812, having achieved great success in this one community, Owen launched a nationwide program for reform. This was stepped up through the years and produced its first results with the enactment of the Factory Act of 1819. Although the factory at New Lanark had continued to be a profitable enterprise, some of Owen's reforms, such as improved housing, infant education, and the operation of a company store at virtually cost prices were expensive and caused criticism by some of Owen's partners. As a result, he withdrew from the firm and organized the first of a series of new firms. One of his partners in the first enterprise was Jeremy Bentham.

Owen borrowed not only Bentham's money but his philosophy of "the greatest good for the greatest number," and until 1817 Owen can best be characterized as "businessman and philanthropist." In that year in his *So-*

cial System he first set forth his socialist views for the reorganization of society into cooperative communities. Owen did more than merely write about these—he also spent a major part of his fortune attempting to establish them, one near Glasgow and the other at New Harmony, Indiana. Both of the communities failed soon after being set in operation.

After the striking success of Owen's early years, the later years of his life were not as happy. At first a public hero, he came to be an object of scorn and derision. This was not because of his Socialistic views, but rather because of his outspoken antagonism to all formal religion. Also, his views on marriage were somewhat lax by the then existing standards, and he was charged by critics of seeking a community of women. Owen's early leadership in the organization of a labor union movement, when he presided at a convention of the Grand National Consolidated Trades Union, was forfeited when he withdrew his support because he felt the other leaders were too militant. As a result, labor leaders rallied to support the Chartist movement. In his last years Owen became even more unorthodox in his views. He dabbled in the field of spiritualism and proposed a floating community to be established on large barges on the Thames River.

Economic Views. In some ways it is presumptuous to describe Owen's writings as economic; he was not an economist and some of his difficulties stemmed from this fact. Nevertheless, his writings are of interest to economists in that they anticipate views held by later critics of capitalism. Owen's writings were patterned closely after his own activities: The early essays reveal the philanthropist and philosopher, while the later writings spell out the details of his program of reform. In his *A New View of Society*, and *Essays on the Principle of the Formation of Human Character*, Owen set forth his belief that a man's character was the product, not of his own actions and choice, but of the society about him. It was society and the forces which surrounded man which determined whether he was to be good or bad. Two important conclusions emerged from this by no means new philosophy: (1) Man could not properly be judged responsible for his own actions—the responsibility could be placed more properly with society; and (2) Such being the case, it was important to put man under the proper moral, physical, and social influences at as early an age as possible. One of the most important things society could do was to assure each man of a job. No man was fated to be a pauper if society would ensure employment for all.

In his report to the Committee on the Poor Laws and in his later books and his newspaper *The Crisis,* Owen continued his diagnosis of society's economic problems and the recommended prescription. In these later writings, Owen saw the profit motive as the root of all evil. It was the drive for profit which led to the indiscriminate introduction of machinery, which displaced workers and brought overproduction and business crises. Basic to his discussion of profit was Owen's concept of value and the role of money.

VALUE. Like all true Socialists, Owen adopted a labor theory of value. Owen's theory was simple—all one had to do to determine the value of a product was to total the number of hours involved in its production. Little or no recognition was given to differences in the quality of varying types of labor or the relative efficiency of different workers. It was not such considerations but the drive for profit that distorted the relative exchange value between commodities of equal value—measured in labor time—and pushed prices up to the point where workers could not afford to buy back the goods they had produced. Goods, said Owen, should always sell for the cost of their production in terms of labor hours required, and nothing more. Stated as such, Owen's definition of a "just price" went far beyond what St. Thomas had set forth. Any excess in price above the true cost of production was defined as profit, and since profit was both measured and gained in the form of money, it was necessary in Owen's view to eliminate money and substitute paper representing labor units.

Owen actually attempted to put this scheme into practice by organizing a National Equitable Labour Exchange. Members could sell their products to the exchange for pieces of paper stating the number of hours of work they had performed. These pieces of paper could then be used by their holders to buy other products priced at the number of hours needed to produce them. The Exchange lasted for only a short time and even the beginning economics student should be able to spot some of the reasons for its failure. With no allowances for the quality of the labor or differences in its efficiency, the exchange soon found itself burdened with commodities of high labor cost but little exchange value, while the stocks of worthwhile products were depleted. We might note also that since each worker traded for things of like value, and thus got back theoretically only what he contributed, the plan did not meet the standards of Communism "from each according to his ability and to each according to his need." Thus the plan did not appeal to those who wanted a more drastic revision of economic affairs. Owen himself recognized this failing but justified his program as a step in the right direction.

Owen's plans for reforming society also included provisions for a set of model communities, each containing some 1,200 persons. Barracks-type homes, with common eating facilities but private living quarters, were provided, and arrangements for the care of children over three were included. An elaborate system of rules and regulations was prescribed, with minute details for their enforcement. Owen called these villages, which were to provide a blend of factory and farm work, "villages of paupers." Owen meant to demonstrate by this title that those men who were currently held in contempt as paupers could become good and worthy citizens if only given work and the means to prove themselves.

Summary and Evaluation. Despite the numerous defects in his analysis and the repeated failure of his schemes when put into practice, Robert Owen deserves a place in any survey of socialist criticism of Classical economic writings. Like other Socialist critics, he attacked the Classical School at their most vulnerable point—their virtual disregard for the plight of the industrial workers. Unlike his fellow Socialists, he took some constructive actions to improve the situation. Many of the important steps taken by the government and private employers to improve the miserable conditions of the working classes can be attributed to Owen's persistent efforts. There seems little doubt that the consumer cooperative movement and the Rochdale Plan received partial inspiration from Owen's writings even though they were a far cry from the cooperative villages envisioned by Owen. That Owen has not won wider acclaim among economists is explained by the weakness of his analysis. That he did not win greater favor among the working classes at the time is explained by his persistent denunciations of religion and his unwillingness to adopt a spirit of militancy and revolt. He remained active until his death, however. He had a breakdown at the age of 69 while presenting a paper before the Social Science Association of Great Britain. The motto of Owen's principal journal, *The Crisis,* serves well as a lasting memorial to the man, "If we cannot yet reconcile all opinions, let us now endeavour to unite all hearts." It is also appropriate that he has been called by many "the father of British Socialism."

HENRI DE SAINT-SIMON (1760–1825)

In many ways, it is as dangerous to classify Saint-Simon with the Socialist critics as it was Sismondi. Although he championed the cause of the poor and urged reforms in the distribution of private property, he never explicitly endorsed the abolition of private ownership. Nevertheless, his fol-

lowers regarded him as an ardent foe of the capitalist system; his concept
of government as an economic rather than a political organization was
hailed by the Marxists as an important contribution to Socialist literature.

The Man. Claude Henri de Rouvroy, Comte de Saint-Simon, was
born in Paris, the son of a French nobleman and a direct descendant of
Charlemagne. Despite this illustrious family background, Saint-Simon was
an ardent democrat and earned distinction in battle during the American
Revolution. Upon his return to his native land, he surrendered his title
and was elected to the National Assembly. Despite his democratic stance,
he fell under suspicion during the revolution in France and was imprisoned because of his associations with foreigners. After his release from
prison, he attempted to instill in his mind all of the world's knowledge. In
his attempt to learn everything about everything he even undertook an ill-
fated marriage. This mad thirst for knowledge proved to be too expensive
even for the son of a nobleman, and Saint-Simon's last years were spent in
abject poverty. Near the end of his life, he attempted suicide but only
succeeded in blinding himself in one eye. He died two years later. Most of
his writings appeared in little-known journals or as pamphlets, but his
views attracted an ardent band of disciples who pushed his philosophy to
its logical conclusion. One of his better-known supporters was the philosopher Auguste Comte. Saint-Simon's three principal works are *Industrial
System, Catechism of Industry,* and *New Christianity.*

Economic Views. If one were compelled to summarize Saint-Simon's
views in a single word, the proper word to select would be "industrialism."
In what has become known as "Saint-Simon's parable," he contrasted the
effect upon the economy if it lost its leading industrialists, bankers, and
craftsmen with the effect if it lost its government officials and its landed
gentry. In the first case, Saint-Simon argued, the effect would be cata-
strophic, while in the second, regrettable as the loss might be, the effect on
the functioning of the economy would be nil. In pursuing his analysis,
Saint-Simon, like Sismondi, took a historical perspective of the changes in
society. By a careful study of the path which society had followed in the
past, it was possible to project into the future and find out what lay ahead.
As Saint-Simon saw the future, the arrival of the industrial state was inevitable.

How was the new industrial state to be achieved, and what would it be
like once achieved? One does not get the sense of inevitability of the final
goal that comes with reading Marx. Nevertheless, Saint-Simon clearly

thought that the signs of history pointed toward an industrial state and that no revolution was needed in order to produce it; moral persuasion and exhortation would suffice. As to conditions once the industrial state had been established, Saint-Simon was not extraordinarily clear. Only two classes would survive—the workers and the idlers—and this second class would gradually disappear as it became evident that all must work. Included in the ranks of the first group were not just industrial workers and artisans, but manufacturers and bankers as well, since these groups also made a definite contribution to the productive efficiency of a nation. The capitalists deserved a return for their contribution just as did other workers.

Saint-Simon's own views on private property were unclear; he spoke of the need to reform property ownership to make its contribution to production more meaningful, but never spelled out the implications of this doctrine. It was Saint-Simon's followers who converted this position into one of opposition to hereditary rights and argued that inheritance frequently left property in the hands of persons unsuitable for utilizing it in the most effective manner.

One other feature of the industrial state deserves mention. The role of government was to be changed. Once France had been turned into a gigantic workshop, the function of government would be to organize rather than govern industrial forces. The details of governmental reorganization need not concern us here, but it should be noted that like the Classical economists before him and Marx later, Saint-Simon saw the role of government at a minimum. Just as the task of policing a factory could be delegated to subordinates, so could the traditional functions of government be minimized. Leaders from business, labor, and agriculture would serve as legislative representatives and assure the passage of legislation designed to promote industrial activity. A chain of command democratically selected but otherwise similar to that in any factory would pass upon day-to-day decisions in regard to wages and working conditions.

Summary and Evaluation. In many respects, Saint-Simon was even less an economist than Robert Owen. Many of the central issues preoccupying economists, including the problem of value, were slighted or completely ignored. Like Owen, Saint-Simon's impact stemmed more from his personality and his example. But whereas Owen left behind him an impressive list of accomplishments, Saint-Simon left behind a devoted, if small band of followers. Saint-Simon expressed in France the same sense of dissatisfaction with the inadequacies of the Classical system that Owen had in England. Although Saint-Simon directed his sharpest attacks on the landed nobility, his emphasis on "the exploitation of man by man" and his dissatisfaction with current methods of distributing property provided a model for later Socialist writers. His prescription of a government with minimal regulatory functions was later embraced by Marx and Engels.

FRANÇOIS MARIE CHARLES FOURIER
(1772–1837)

The Man. Born in Besançon, France and educated at the university located there, Fourier was the son of a middle-class tradesman, whose career the son followed with extreme reluctance. Upon the the completion of his formal education, Fourier traveled for some time in Germany and Holland as well as in his native France. When his father died, Fourier inherited considerable property, but it was lost during the French Revolution, and in order to earn a living Fourier embarked on a career in the army. His stay in the armed services was of short duration, however, since he was discharged after two years for reasons of ill health. The remainder of Fourier's career was spent in commerce and in writing books setting forth his philosophy of cooperation. All of his life was spent in genteel poverty, with an annual income of 1,000 to 2,500 francs a year. This comparatively uneventful life is in striking contrast to the strangeness of Fourier's well-known ideas. Some of his more imaginative writings of the future society read like pages from a writer of science fiction, and even Fourier's followers have attempted with difficulty to rationalize his writings in terms of allegories. Following the publication of his second book in 1822, Fourier moved to Paris and advertised that he would wait at his home for any rich philanthropist who was willing to subsidize his planned communities. No such offer was forthcoming, despite several years of patient waiting each noon at his home.

Economic Views. Saint-Simon is reputed to have received the inspiration for his life's work from a vision received while he was languishing in jail, but Fourier received his in a more prosaic fashion. Early in his working career, while employed by a merchant in Marseilles, Fourier was ordered to destroy a stock of goods in order to maintain its market price. Appalled at the waste involved in this early variation of later-day agricultural price supports, Fourier concluded that some better system could be devised than the wastefulness of the free-market economy. He began with the idea that God had a plan to ensure man's happiness—the problem was to find this plan. Fourier's solution resembled in many ways that of Robert Owen; Fourier also proposed a system of model communities which were to operate on a cooperative basis. These communities he called phalanxes.

The resemblance of the phalanx to Owen's villages of paupers is striking, although the extent to which Fourier consciously copied the English Socialist is unknown. It has been suggested, for example, that Fourier may have received part of his inspiration from observing conditions about him when he was working in Lyons; the contrast between the strife, poverty, and unemployment existing in that relatively well-developed industrial city and the tranquillity of the smoothly operating agricultural cooperatives outside the city may have been the source of Fourier's ideas. In any case, many points of similarity with Owen's model communities can be found. Provision was made for a central residential building which was to serve as a base for much of the community's social activity. Arrangements within this central building (phalanstery) were also much like those in Owen's. Provision was made for a central dining room where members could eat, if they chose. Clearly, however, Fourier felt that meals eaten in common were preferable, not only for reasons of economy, but because in the process of constant association the distinctions between rich and poor would in some magic way be reduced. Again, like Owen, Fourier believed that man was a product of his environment and that given the opportunity to free himself from the necessity of drudging for a subsistence and to have contact with others, he would be able to blossom and achieve his true potential. Fourier took infinite care in planning his communities down to the last detail; this insistence on detail and symmetry was a mark of his "old maid" propensities.

Fourier drew no sharp distinctions between labor and capital. Indeed, the output of the phalanx, after providing an abundant subsistence for all of its members, was to be divided into twelve shares. Five of these shares went to labor, four were to go to capital, and the remaining three were a reward for "talent." By talent Fourier meant the managers of the phalanx, who were to be elected by the members. Instead of proposing the abolition of private property, Fourier urged the dispersion of it, giving all members a sense of ownership by having each member own shares in the phalanx. In the light of current enthusiasm for employee stock purchase plans and the wonders of a wide stock ownership (referred to by stock exchange officials as People's Capitalism), Fourier's plans for broadening property ownership now look less improbable than some of his early critics made them out to be.

Fourier observed that work, although a necessity, was a satisfying feature of primitive men's lives; one of the central goals of his scheme, therefore, was to remove some of the burden of modern work. To do this, he provided a number of ingenious solutions. Much of the sting of work could be removed, Fourier said, if men were not absolutely dependent upon it for their subsistence. If workers could be assured of a basic standard of living, they would choose to work as a means of expressing themselves. Stated in this way, Fourier's reasoning came close to Veblen's "instinct of workmanship." Even so, Fourier admitted that some work was inevitably a drudgery, and the best thing to do was to reduce the amount of all work to an absolute minimum and particularly to minimize the more unpleasant varieties. The use of machinery was one way to provide a release from the drudgery of work. Since children enjoyed getting dirty, jobs unable to be performed by machines but involving a certain amount of untidiness could be reserved for them. Finally, Fourier suggested, the new society must devote itself to the task of making work more enjoyable and challenging. Workers should be provided with a variety of tasks so that the change of pace would make their work more interesting. The gains in efficiency stemming from Adam Smith's gospel of labor were judged to be less important than the stultifying effects of monotonous, routine work.

Fourier was not particularly helpful in spelling out the means by which these cooperative communities of work were to be established, but he did argue they should be the product of men's initiative rather than of action by the state. He also suggested that the men who were to join such communities would have to be exposed to a preparatory stage where they learned to cooperate under conditions assuring them of subsistence and security. Unlike Owen, he was not wealthy. Therefore he hoped for outside support to establish some model communities, whose success would then set an example for the formation of similar communities throughout the country. Even without philanthropic aid, several dozen such communities were established in France and the United States; the best known of these in the United States was the famous Brook Farm. Only one of these experiments, however, proved to have any lasting success.

Summary and Evaluation. Although there have been several attempts to implement Fourier's plans by establishing model communities, none of Fourier's three books, *Théories des quatre mouvements et des destinées générales, Traité de l'association domestique et agricole,* and *Le nouveau monde industriel et sociétaire,* had a deep impact on the history of economic ideas. In large part this was due to the fact that the keen and perceptive analysis of the current ills of the world contained in these books was mixed with wild and fanciful predictions about other worlds and the eventual changing of all sea water to a delightful beverage. Other predictions sounding equally wild at that time, such as his forecast of the melting of the polar caps, have become less fantastic in terms of current scientific discussion about a warming trend in the earth's atmosphere. Even so, some of Fourier's predictions outdid Jules Verne! Furthermore, even the most rational and sensible of Fourier's ideas were frequently expressed in such an awkward and involved manner that they were unintelligible to the average reader. Fourier never married, and some of his ideas on the subject of love and marriage were unorthodox even by present-day standards. His insistence that men should express fully all their passions, including the sexual ones, found little favor in religious circles. His abhorrence of life in the large industrial city and his plans for widespread dispersal of the population throughout the countryside provided a model for future architects in England and on the continent. The most conservative economist can also comment favorably on Fourier's position that the basic problem was not the inequality but the insufficiency of wealth, while arguing with Fourier's means of achieving greater wealth.

PIERRE JOSEPH PROUDHON (1809–1865)

Like most of the critics we have reviewed thus far, Proudhon saw definite evils arising from the institution of private property; his views on the subject can be summarized succinctly in a three-word quote—"Property is theft." His remedy, however, was quite different from that prescribed by Owen, Saint-Simon, or Fourier. Not only did Proudhon not espouse a utopian society, but he was as critical of utopian schemes as he was of the capitalistic system. When he moved from the realm of criticism of others' views to a positive program of his own, however, his Exchange Bank proved to be every bit as utopian as Owen's Exchange Bank, and bore at first glance many marked similarities.

The Man. In contrast to the other Socialist writers under examination, Proudhon was neither "born to wealth" nor able to become wealthy later. He was born in Besançon, France (the birthplace of Fourier), the son of a brewer. Forced to go to work at an early age, he later became a largely self-educated man, although he did attend the university at

Besançon. His story is the familiar one of the poverty-stricken student; he had no money for books, and he had to borrow from his classmates. The story is told that Proudhon once came home laden with prizes received for his studies to find the house without food. He began his working career in the printing trade at the age of 19 and advanced to the position of proof-reader. In this position he had an opportunity to learn about theology and study Hebrew, Latin, French, and Greek. A small award made by the university at Besançon made it possible for Proudhon to move to Paris, where he was exposed to various Socialist thinkers of the time. Some of his writings outraged the authorities at Besançon (he dedicated his book *What Is Property?* to them), and he was threatened with the withdrawal of this financial support. An essay entitled *Warning to Proprietors* brought him to trial, but his skill as a witness on his own behalf led to his acquittal. After a brief return to a career in printing in Besançon, Proudhon again settled in Paris, became involved in the publication of a series of revolutionary newspapers, and was subsequently elected to the Chamber of Deputies. While a member of the Chamber, he presented his famous proposal for a one-third tax on interest and rent. He was a strong early critic of Louis Napoleon (the two later became reconciled), and these attacks, in addition to his criticisms of current economic conditions, led to the threat of arrest, from which he escaped by fleeing to Belgium. Discovered while secretly revisiting Paris, he was arrested and imprisoned for three years. While in jail, he continued his writings and married a young working woman. In 1858 he published *Of Justice in the Revolution and the Church,* which contained a violent attack on the church and other institutions. Once again he was forced to flee to Belgium in order to escape reimprisonment. During his enforced exile, he lost many of his supporters by breaking with the revolutionary party of Mazzini and by statements appearing to justify war as a natural or necessary phenomenon. His health deteriorated during this period, and he died a few years after his return to France. His *Confessions of a Revolutionist* contains the essence of his theory of anarchy.

Economic Views. First Proudhon's opposition to Socialism and Communism will be reviewed. No champion of capitalism and Classical economic thought ever launched a more vigorous attack upon all schools of Socialist thought than did Proudhon. Of Fourier he wrote, "Fourier's system is the greatest mystification of our time." Of the character of Socialism he proclaimed, "Socialism is a mere nothing. It never has been and never will be anything." [4] Addressing himself to the Communists, he wrote, "Your presence is a stench in my nostrils and the sight of you disgusts me." [5] Why this attack on those with whom one might have expected Proudhon to be aligned in his disapproval of private property? Part of the violence of Proudhon's attack undoubtedly stemmed from a fear that readers would associate his ideas with these other writers. The trouble with the other critics of capitalism, in Proudhon's view, was that they wished to change things completely, thus losing the good with the bad. Proudhon feared that their programs would merely substitute the tyranny of collective community action for the tyranny of private property, so that the worker would be no more truly free than he was at present. Proudhon's attitude was much like the currently popular definition quoted at the beginning of this chapter: "Capitalism is a system where one man exploits another. Under Communism . . . it is just the opposite." Proudhon was an anarchist who carried the premise of "the less government, the better" to its logical extreme. The goal of society in Proudhon's view was justice, and basic to any system of justice was equality. Even inequalities in wages due to differentials in skill were unjust, since feats of skill were but a form of stored up capital. Obviously the biggest source of inequality, however, was private property. Proudhon never launched any attack on the existence of private property per se, but only on the manner in which it was distributed. Because it was not available to everyone, those who had ownership had the opportunity to acquire special income in the form of interest and rent. If everyone could be given the right to own property, there would be no problem. Property as currently distributed was "theft," but properly shared it could bring freedom. The usual Socialist solution to this problem was communal ownership, but this Proudhon was unwilling to adopt. Men would only be exchanging one form of tyranny for another. Before turning to Proudhon's alternative, however, we must first examine briefly his explanation of value and the manner in which capitalists expropriated a part of it.

VALUE AND CAPITALISTS' INCOME. Proudhon's discussion of value added little or nothing to our understanding of the question. After distinguishing between exchange and use value, Proudhon continued by suggesting that since a single man could not make everything he needed, he had to join in arrangements for a division of labor whereby each worker exchanged his output for that of fellow workers. Those things easy to

[4] Quoted by Charles Gide and Charles Rist, *op. cit.*, p. 296.
[5] *Ibid.*

produce and in abundant supply had low exchange value, while the reverse held true for things which were scarce. Cleared of all the excess verbiage, it became a restatement of the labor theory of value. More important was Proudhon's view of where the capitalist made his profit. As with other Socialists, Proudhon saw productive power resting in labor. But workers were not, as so many critics of the capitalist system had stressed, being paid less than their individual worth. The secret, said Proudhon, lay in the fact that, taken collectively, workers by working together produced more than they could working as separate individuals. The whole was greater than the sum of the parts. Thus the capitalist was able to pay each worker his individual worth and by combining the work of one laborer with that of others the employer could obtain a total product which exceeded the total payments he made to individual workers. Each individual worker was thus paid the full value of his individual contribution, while the capitalist had to pay nothing "for that immense force which results from union and from the harmonious combination of simultaneous efforts. . . ." [6] Note that the result was to make the workers unaware of their exploitation, thereby reducing the pressure for revolt.

THE EXCHANGE BANK. Proudhon's solution for restoring to workers what was rightfully theirs was the organization of voluntary associations of workers who could cooperate in producing and exchanging their output. In order to be successful, these groups must obtain title to capital and property. How was this to be done? The answer provided by Proudhon was the establishment of an exchange bank which would provide loans at little or no cost. Money was deemed the root of all evil, since it was in monetary terms that interest and rent were paid. What prevented workers from obtaining property of their own was the interest charge on borrowed money. Let workers have access to interest-free (or extremely low-cost) loans and they could acquire land, buildings, and machines of their own. Proudhon's theory was predicated on the belief that money was merely a means of exchange and that the bills issued by the bank would be inconvertible into gold and would merely represent a discount of some future sale. The benefits arising from the establishment of such an exchange bank, Proudhon believed, would be wondrous to behold. Since all workers would be able to obtain claim to property, all class distinctions would disappear as capital was made available to everyone, and with the extra returns of property removed, property would become a matter of ownership without any extra benefits of income.

[6] *Ibid.,* p. 295.

In his original formulation, Proudhon had maintained there would be no need for the bank to have any capital. Since the loans were to be made on the basis of immediate or future transactions, Proudhon argued, there was no possibility of loss. When his proposal was put into operation as the "People's Bank" following the 1848 Revolution, it was provided with a capital of 15 million francs. Even thus fortified, the bank proved to be a speedy economic failure, partly because of the imprisonment of its founder. The arrest of Proudhon uncovered one of the major weaknesses of his banking scheme—the bank was only as good as the confidence people had in it. When confidence ebbed and the bank lacked liquid assets to bolster its reputation, it quickly collapsed. There were other reasons for the failure; by stressing the role of money as a means of exchange, Proudhon failed to recognize the other functions of any good money, such as providing a store of value. It is also obvious that Proudhon's explanation of the reaon for the existence of interest was incomplete and failed to take account of the economic function the interest rate provides. Even a socialistic economy may find the interest rate a convenient way of allocating capital.

Summary and Evaluation. It is difficult to tell which of the critics we have examined thus far had the greatest impact upon more recent economics; each in his own way contributed something to the stream of thought.

Proudhon was a curious mixture of opposition to the evils of private property combined with a firm belief in the rights of private property. His goal was justice for all mankind, but except for his Exchange Bank, he proposed very little that was practical to secure this goal. All associations were to be voluntary, and Proudhon saw in Communism an evil as black as the existing situation. Small wonder Marx could find little to admire in Proudhon's writing save his style of expression! Nor can the non-Marxian reader help but wonder whether Proudhon's dream of anarchy and perfect equality were not mutually exclusive. Proudhon's writings had considerable impact upon later thinkers, and perhaps nowhere has this impact been more evident than in the case of Karl Marx. Not that Marx thought highly of Proudhon's work—far from it, and as we shall soon see, he was at some points highly critical. But Marx, in reacting to Proudhon's writing was forced to think through some of his own ideas and to develop further the ideas expressed in the *Manifesto*. Proudhon and Marx had had numerous discussions together while both were in France, and Proudhon had sent Marx a copy of his *Philosophy of Poverty* with a letter saying, "I await the blow of your critical rod." The blow, when it came, proved to be a series of blows constituting a sustained beating, and the two men, who had been drifting apart for some time, ended all bonds of friendship. Proudhon, a mean critic in his own right, as some brief passages quoted earlier have indicated, was repaid in kind by Marx. In reviewing Proudhon's book Marx changed the title from *The Philosophy of Poverty* to *The Poverty of Philosophy,* and set the tone for his critical analysis with the following preface:

M. Proudhon has the misfortune of being singularly misunderstood in Europe. In France he has the right to be a bad economist, because he passes for a good German philosopher. In Germany he has the right to be a bad philosopher, because he passes for one of the greatest of the French economists. We, as both German and economist at the same time, wish to protest against this double error.[7]

All in all, Marx found little to admire in Proudhon's writing save his "bold and vigorous style." Before we begin our appraisal of Marx's writings, however, it is first necessary to skip a few years ahead and some three thousand miles away to look briefly at another writer who, though he read Marx, was little affected in his thinking; the name of this man is Henry George.

HENRY GEORGE (1839–1897)

As the United States became increasingly industrial, some of the same stresses which had racked England and the Continent began to appear in the States as well. Unemployment, business crises, and low wages all became sources of frequent complaint. Henry George was not a lone voice of dissension in an atmosphere of general contentment, but his diagnosis of the problem and his prescription merit his being singled out for special attention. The inclusion of his name among the socialist critics is also somewhat misleading, since he espoused a very special brand of socialist reform. Our justification for so doing lies in the fact that he was a critic of the Classical School as represented by Malthus and Ricardo and that he proposed the confiscation of the return from one type of private property.

[7] Karl Marx, *The Poverty of Philosophy* (Chicago: Charles H. Kerr & Co., n.d.), p. 29.

The Man. Born the second of ten children of middle-class parents, George had a home life markedly different from the other writers we have studied in this chapter. George's father was a Philadelphia publisher of religious books and provided a moral tone in the home which remained a part of the son's thinking throughout his life. Although he was always an avid reader of books, George ended his formal education at the age of 13. Thereafter he led an exciting and varied life, with jobs ranging from deckhand on a ship to journalist, politician, and world-famous author. He experienced both the pangs of abject poverty and the pleasures of moderate wealth. George began his career as journalist and politician in California, and there he acquired the inspiration for many of his economic views. As a journalist, George was a reasonable success, rising from printer to editor of the San Francisco *Times*. As a politician he was less successful; his campaign for a seat in the California State Assembly was lost, due in part to the opposition of the Central Pacific Railroad which resented George's opposition to subsidies it had obtained. In later years, George twice ran for mayor of New York City. The first time he was defeated by what his supporters claimed was not the vote of the people but the counting of that vote by the politicians. A second attempt ended in disaster when George died shortly before election day. Before he died, however, George had become a national and even an international figure. His writings on the problem of Irish land reform won him considerable renown abroad. In addition to his best known work, *Progress and Poverty*, George was the author of *The Science of Political Economy*.

Economic Views. George saw virtually all the evils of industrial society as arising from a single cause—a monopoly of the ownership of land. As society progressed, the stranglehold maintained by the land monopolists grew ever tighter; rent rose to ever-increasing levels while wages and interests were forced to minimum levels. While he was living in California, George had been witness to the feverish land speculations and gigantic land holdings occurring there, thus receiving much empirical evidence in support of this conclusion. Even a superficial glance at George's doctrine will reveal a striking resemblance to Ricardo's analysis of the nature and future of rent. George, however, apparently formulated his first statement, *Our Land and Land Policy*, before he had read much, if anything, in political economy. Later he was delighted to discover that Ricardo's theory of rent lent support to his views. His major work, *Progress and Poverty*, was a further elaboration of the original theme buttressed with the lessons learned (by no means perfectly) from the early masters. The book was an instant success; not only did its message and prescription appeal to those who felt that they were not sharing equitably in the nation's progress, but the lively journalistic style made for easy reading.

Despite George's pleasure in finding Ricardo's position on rent was close to his own, George found many things to criticize in Ricardo's *Principles.* He was particularly opposed to the strong overtones of Malthusian doctrine embedded throughout the work, and to the wages-fund doctrine. About the validity of Malthus' position George said, ". . . when we subject the theory itself to the test of straightforward analysis, it will, I think, be found as utterly untenable as the current theory of wages." [8]

The central criticism of Malthusian doctrine voiced by George was the denial that empirical evidence either during or since Malthus' time gave any support to the theory that the population tended to outstrip means of production. As for the wages-fund doctrine, it was foolish to maintain that a previously accumulated store of capital was necessary to support workers. If anything, the reverse was true; labor was needed to replenish the supply of capital. Let a city like London, rich in capital, be forced to do without its productive workers for only a short time, and it would quickly begin to die.

According to George, the produce of a nation was equal to the sum of rent, interest, and wages. By transposing, a restructured equation could be written whereby interest and wages were equal to the produce minus rent. Since the forces of progress inevitably brought a rise in land rent (because of land's limited supply), most of the economy's gains in production were likely to be absorbed by rising rents. At best, the levels of interest and wages were likely to remain constant, and there was a distinct possibility that they might suffer declines in the face of rising productivity. Wages and interest were determined by what they jointly produced on rent-free land, but the availability of such land grew less and less with time, and rent grew to be a larger and larger proportion of the nation's produce.

The resemblance to Ricardo's earlier analysis is apparent, although some of the details, as well as the proposed solution, were different. While in Ricardo's system, for example, the landlord "misbehaved" by petitioning for the extension of the Corn Laws, in George's picture the landlords were guilty of land speculation, thereby exposing the economy to the business cycle and periodic business crises.

[8] Henry George, *Progress and Poverty* (New York: Modern Library, n.d.), p. 103.

Although Ricardo had deemed rent to be a surplus, he never advocated taxing away all such rent on the ground that it was unjust to single out a single group of individuals for taxation. At this point George dramatically departed from the earlier exponent of rent theory. The solution to the problem of rent as seen by George was a simple one. Enact a confiscatory tax on all rent accruing from the ownership of land. However, improvements on the land, such as buildings, were to remain tax-free. By taxing land rents, land speculation would be ended, the monopolization of land holdings broken, and sufficient revenue could be raised to eliminate all other forms of taxation. This was George's famous single tax proposal; the idea was not new with George, but his forceful manner of presentation has left the idea linked firmly to his name. The notion that all governmental expenses could be financed in this manner was probably more realistic when our federal budget ran at less than two billion, even though present-day supporters of the single tax have argued (correctly) that the current national income accounts grossly understate the total rent both paid and imputed. Even with allowances for substantial understatement, however, it still seems likely that a revenue system so based would prove inadequate. Furthermore, there is much to be said on behalf of a diversity of taxes which hit all groups, and for the benefits of "built-in stabilization" arising from the personal income tax.

Summary and Evaluation. It is important that we reemphasize that George, judged by many of the customary standards, was no Socialist. He opposed the progressive income tax, for example, on the grounds (among others) that it impeded the accumulation of wealth—surely a dubious position for any good Socialist to maintain! Upon the subject of land and the rent derived therefrom, however, George was even more radical in his proposals than many of the writers encountered earlier in this chapter. Both Proudhon and George, for example, agreed that property was theft, but it was George who proposed a virtual nationalization of all land holdings. George's solution of the confiscation of rent assumed that all property was illegally acquired. The rights of property owners who had paid a fair price for their holdings with the expectation of earning an honest return on their investment were ignored by George. It is also ironic that George's book was based on observations of the economic scene in a country where land was far more plentiful than in Europe.

Despite his weaknesses as a political economist, George did have some impact on the thinking of his time, particularly among leaders of the Fabian movement in England, such as George Bernard Shaw and Sidney and

Beatrice Webb. Tolstoy was a devoted follower, and Veblen is reputed to have been impressed during his early years by George's writings. The book *Progress and Poverty* won an enthusiastic audience throughout England, partly because the book's appearance coincided with the emergence of an agricultural recession in that country. A loyal band of followers in the United States continues to propagate the faith even today, and there is still a group which distributes free copies of George's book. For most economists, however, George's views are of only historical interest.

KARL MARX (1818–1883)

"A spectre is haunting Europe—the spectre of Communism." "Working men of all countries, unite! The proletarians have nothing to lose but their chains." Students who remember these exciting words of Marx's and Engel's *Communist Manifesto* will find *Capital* (*Das Kapital*) far duller reading. True, the biting criticism of industrial conditions is still present, as witness Marx's chapters on the employment of women and children, and one can still find sharp criticisms of Marx's opponents—he refers to Bentham as "a leather-mouth pedantic oracle"—but these occasional flashes of excitement are buried in a mass of weighty economic formulas and tortuous logic. In *Capital* we find Marx attempting to meet the capitalist economists on their own ground and prove the folly of their system with their own tools of analysis. Marx is willing and anxious to employ the same abstract and rigorous analysis so dear to Ricardo. As such, all four volumes of Marx's classic attack on capitalism become rugged reading. However, before we attempt to come to grips with its message, as contained in the first three volumes, let us first take a brief look at Marx, the man.

The Man. One of the persistent themes of this book has been (and will continue to be) the thought that the reader is able to have a better understanding of an individual's writing and is better able to appreciate his thinking if something about the man's life is known. Perhaps in no case is this relationship demonstrated more clearly than in the case of Karl Marx.

Marx, the youthful rebel and the adult recluse, has much of his way of life reflected in his writing and economic philosophy. Marx was born in the Rhineland of Germany, the son of a moderately well-to-do German jurist. Even in the nineteenth century, life for Jews in Germany was not without its handicaps, so Marx's father, who had become a Christian, had his son baptized in a Protestant church. Always an intense student, Marx was educated at Bonn and the University of Berlin. He began his academic career with the study of jurisprudence, but soon turned to history and philosophy. His proclivity for antagonizing the supporters of law and order became manifest at an early age, and while still enrolled at the University of Berlin, Marx was expelled for his revolutionary views; he thus set a pattern for his future as a job-seeker—he lost his anticipated position as an instructor of philosophy at Bonn.

At about the time of his first expulsion, Marx married his childhood sweetheart, Jenny von Westphalen, who became his devoted wife, bearing Marx six children. Marx was expelled from Germany because of the critical tone of his newspaper, *Rheinische Zeitung*. He moved to France and continued to be involved in journalism the rest of his life. Most of it won him more fame and notoriety than money, and his career as journalist cannot be judged a financial success, although he did for a time serve as English correspondent for the New York *Tribune*.

Two events of importance occurred while Marx was in France. He first met Friedrich Engels while the latter was visiting Paris on his way home from a trip to Europe, and he began a serious study of the subject of political economy. Marx became so involved in this latter subject that he later gave lectures to small revolutionary groups and wrote his *Critique of Political Economy*, an important step in fashioning his views for the later writing of *Das Kapital*. Thereafter, Marx was successively expelled from France and Belgium, and after returning to France, was given the choice of moving to Brittany or leaving the country entirely. Marx chose this second alternative and moved to England, where he remained, save for brief visits to the Continent, until he died.

In his early years Marx was a fiery young rebel, his intellectual orientation being molded by his study of Hegelian philosophy. Although Marx was never a confirmed follower of Hegel, he did belong in his student days to one of the left-wing splinter groups of Hegel's followers, the "Young Hegelians." Marx was attracted by Hegel both by the rejection of religions inherent in Hegel's concept that man could act as his own god and by the dialectic as an expression of the way history traced out the working of man's mind to the discovery of his destiny. Marx took this concept of the dialectic and shaped it to his own purposes in setting forth his dialectic materialism and the economic interpretation of history. During this period Marx was an active revolutionist, sharing the dangers of police raids and jail with fellow revolutionaries.

When Marx finally fled the Continent completely and settled in England, he became a scholarly recluse who spent much of his time working in the British Museum uncovering the "bricks and mortar" for his economic doctrines. Marx still met with Socialist leaders, but compared to his activities in France and Germany, his life in England was comparatively sedentary, and he confined his revolutionary activities to the writing of tracts and pamphlets. His voice was heard, however, in support of the Irish revolt and against the recognition of the Confederate States of America by the British government. Marx's only real brush with the British police came when he aroused the suspicions of a pawnbroker by attempting to pawn some of his wife's family heirlooms.

Poverty remained a continuous part of Marx's life from his early student days until his death. Some of his bitterness about the moneyed classes can be explained by the fact that he was at times compelled to borrow at rates of interest ranging from 20 to 30 percent. Friedrich Engels, who collaborated with Marx in some of his writings, was also an important source of financial support. However, two of Marx's six children died, probably the victims of poverty and inadequate medical attention.

Marx has suffered at the hands of sympathetic and unsympathetic biographers alike; he has been pictured alternately as a dour, standoffish individual who was a family tyrant and as a joking friend of children who was nicknamed "Daddy Marx" by all of the neighborhood children. The truth probably lies somewhere between these extremes, with aspects of both descriptions appearing from time to time.

The extent of Marx's intellectual indebtedness to Engels is still not fully known. Recently, champions of Engels have laid claim on Engels' behalf for a large portion of the credit (or blame) for the effectiveness of the pieces which the men wrote jointly. It now appears evident that more than merely felicitious phraseology can be attributed to Engels. It also seems likely, however, that in the realm of economic thought, Marx was clearly the superior. Whatever may be the case, our subsequent treatment is generally confined to Marx. Where considered appropriate by the reader, the name of Engels may be included as well.

Communist Manifesto. The most famous product of Marx's and Engel's joint authorship is the *Communist Manifesto.* In this call for revolution, we can find many of the seeds of Marx's later economic reasoning as expressed in *Capital.* For the *Manifesto* is a statement of Communist philosophy, in addition to being a call for action. Here we find one of the clearest statements of the concept of dialectical materialism and an economic interpretation of history. Prior to Marx, much of the writing about change emphasized the role of ideas in inducing it. Even the Socialist critics we have just reviewed emphasized the importance of intellectual activity in stimulating change. Note, for example, the elaborate plans and blueprints each of these reformers devised as a means of moving to a "better" society. It was Marx more than any other writer who centered attention on the role of economic institutions and class differences in producing change.

Indeed, Marx was highly critical of the earlier Socialists on exactly this point, and was scornful of their elaborate blueprints for a future society. In turn, his critics have pointed to this failure by Marx to offer a program for the communist society as evidence of the basic weakness and impractically of Marxian economics. Rather than acknowledge this lack as a weakness, however, Marx viewed the omission as a sign of strength. His version of Socialism was a "scientific Socialism," dependent for its fulfillment not on the mere plans of man but rather on the irresistible flow of history.

In formulating his economic interpretation of history, Marx borrowed heavily from Hegel. Basic to Marx's explanation of history was the concept of the dialectic—each stage in history carrying the seeds of its own destruction embedded within it. Just as the "thesis," feudalism, had been destroyed by its antithesis, the capitalist merchants, so capitalism in turn had its antithesis—the proletariat. Each stage of economic history thus set the stage for the next one. The struggle between the thesis and its antithesis resulted in a synthesis which then became the new thesis. But the process came to an end with the emergence of the final synthesis of Communism. No further development beyond Communism was to be expected, because with the overthrow of capitalism came the liquidation of the bourgeoisie and the end of the class struggle. Prior to Communism, according to Marx's theory, the various stages of production had been characterized by class struggle. Once Communism was achieved, however, all classes but the proletariat would have been eliminated and so historical development written in terms of class struggle would come to an end. More recent students of Communism question whether the class struggle would end even then, and they point to class differentials still existing in Russia. This criticism is predicated on the assumption that the Soviet Union provides a model of Marxian Communism at work—a doubtful assumption at best; Marx elsewhere wrote of Russia as one of the last countries in which Communism was likely to develop. Milovan Djilas' book *The*

New Class is another expression of doubt about the likelihood of ending class differences under Communism—as practiced in Yugoslavia.

In refuting Marx's view of history we need not be satisfied with the conclusion that the class struggle will not end with the emergence of Communism. Equally subject to challenge is Marx's whole view of class loyalties and the propriety of writing history solely in economic terms. It may be true, as the old military adage says, that "an army moves on its stomach," but to apply this to mankind in general is too sweeping a generalization. Men's motives are far more complex than that! Nor do class alignments necessarily form in the manner described by Marx. Identification with any class is more than a matter of owning or not owning the means of production. Even many sociologists and economists who are reluctant to adopt the intricate class strata ranging from upper-upper to lower-lower find Marx's classification too simple. Ironically, repeated surveys of American families have found that most people tend to think of themselves as middle class irrespective of actual income.

A brief description of some of the other salient points in the *Communist Manifesto* should also be made. Although Marx left his followers no definite picture of the Communist state, some evidence as to its expected character may be found in the *Manifesto*. As the economy moved from the intermediate stage of Socialism to full-scale Communism, workers were to contribute "each according to his ability" and receive "each according to his need." Implicit in this forecast was the assumption that the economy would be so productive that no problem of scarcity would be encountered. As we shall see, this ability to produce a bountiful supply of goods and services was one of the contributions capitalism was to make, and it was one of the reasons Marx postulated the need for a fully developed system of capitalism as a necessary precursor to Communism. Marx also saw with the development of Communism the abolition of all capitalistic property and the end of economic classes. The property to be abolished was that which gave men control over other men. Although critics of Marxism have argued that Marx would have ended *all* private ownership, including that of personal possessions and houses, it is quite clear from Marx's writing that this is a cruel distortion. In the same way, Marx has been accused of wishing to end all family relationships and to establish a community of women. In view of Marx's own pursuit of monogamy, this charge might also be dropped. Unfortunately, the early years of the Russian Revolution, with its casual system of postcard divorces, lent credence to the belief that Marx himself advocated such a policy. What Marx actually said was that the capitalist system had already made a mockery of family life and marriage. The association of free love with the ideas of Socialism is not uncommon; Saint-Simon, for example, was also accused of favoring a community of wives. In his case the charges were equally unjustified.

With the establishment of Communism would come the elimination of property for profit and the end to class struggle; as a result of these changes a police power would no longer be needed and so the state would wither away. Another noneconomic change was to be the eradication of religious belief. In the *Manifesto,* Marx's picture of capitalism at the time of its overthrow was virtually identical with the one he painted in *Capital.* Although profit rates were declining, the rich continued to grow even more wealthy, the wealth becoming concentrated in fewer and fewer hands. Meanwhile the middle classes sank into the mass of the proletariat, where conditions grew progressively worse. It was, incidentally, this inevitable decline of the petty bourgeoisie into the proletariat that gave Marx his rationale for working for the proletariat even though he was not born a member of that group. As more and more machinery was introduced, the industrial reserve army of unemployed grew even larger, and business cycles of ever mounting intensity added to their suffering. Eventually the time would be reached when the stage was set for the overthrow. (Note that while the capitalistic economy was an evil, it was a necessary evil—it set the stage for the fulfillment of Communism.) But since the "glorious" day never arrived in the manner prescribed by Marx, it becomes necessary for us to examine more closely his analysis of capitalism and see whether we can find out where he went astray.

CAPITAL. Marx began both his introduction to the *Critique of Political Economy* and to *Capital,* as Ricardo had before him, with a discussion of value, picking up the issue where Ricardo had left off. Marx also presented a labor theory of value, but, in the first volume of *Capital,* at least, one with none of the qualifications and allowances for capital that Ricardo had permitted. Where Ricardo had emphasized labor at the margin as the determining element, Marx wrote in terms of the *socially necessary* labor. Thus, while one worker might be able to produce a commodity in one hour while another worker required three hours, neither person's labor could necessarily be accepted as the standard of value. What was relevant, instead, was the average amount of labor necessary to produce the commodity in question; exceptional instances of ability of a high or low caliber were unimportant. So far so good; Ricardo would have had little with which to quarrel, since he had assumed that the discussion centered around workers of relatively equal ability. Ricardo's major exception (and it is a major one) would be that Marx failed to take account of diminishing returns.

Marx, in setting forth his socially necessary labor theory of value, was led to a consideration of another problem which Ricardo had simply assumed away. If one was going to determine the value of products by the amount of labor contained in them, then it became necessary to find some way to equate labor of different quality and skill. Marx attempted to solve this problem by asserting that all labor could be reduced to a simple homogeneity by granting skilled labor a proportionately greater credit for its contribution to value than its less skilled counterpart. At first glance, this appears to be not unreasonable. Although critics claimed that Marx never demonstrated how this measurement could in fact be achieved—Marx merely declared it was arrived at "by experience"—employers arrive at some such determination regularly when they set differentials between the wages paid skilled and unskilled workers. The problem is not that the equating cannot be achieved through the operation of the market, but rather what the resulting solution does to Marx's labor theory of value. By determining the weight of skill differentials in this manner, Marx became involved in circular reasoning. The value of different types of labor was made dependent upon the value of the products produced and sold on the open market. In order to know the value of the labor, the capitalist must sell his product and so determine its worth. But the value of the product, according to Marx, was set by the value of the labor power involved in its production. Thus the circle became complete and the reader was brought back to where he started. Marx would probably have answered this criticism by saying that the growing industrialization made differences in skill less and less important. As we shall see, one of Marx's major complaints about capitalism was the sense of "job alienation" it produced in workers because of the increasingly routine nature of the work to be performed. Even after accepting this rejoinder of Marx, however, we still must conclude that his theory of value was left incomplete and unsatisfactory.

In pursuing the question of value, we find Marx involved in what at first appears to be an interminable and largely pointless discussion of the fine distinctions between relative and equivalent value. Suppose we have two commodities and want to relate them to each other in value. The relative quantities of each product necessary to produce exchange will depend on the amount of socially necessary labor each contains. If 20 yards of linen may be equated to one coat, then we can identify the 20 yards as the relative value and the coat as the equivalent value. But all one has to do is reverse the positions and the two commodities change relationships —the coat now becomes the relative and the 20 yards of linen the equivalent. Why spend so much time analyzing such an obvious relationship? Marx had followed an even more laborious and tortured analysis in his *Critique* and it had received a poor reception, so why repeat the performance?

We catch a glimpse of the answer when Marx begins his discussion of money as the "universal equivalent." Money is an equivalent for all of the characteristics which serve to make some commodity a good store and measure of value such as its scarcity, durability, and ease of recognition. But something more was involved when money was introduced. When one commodity was exchanged for another, each partner to the exchange benefited equally when commodities of like amounts of socially necessary labor were exchanged. Although the market value in exchange terms of the two commodities was equal, each party might find greater use value from the new commodity obtained during the exchange. The owner of the yards of linen would feel his position improved when he succeeded in trading the linen for a coat, while the previous owner of the coat would be equally satisfied by his new acquisition of linen. In this connection Marx distinguished between use and exchange value, but his analysis constituted no real improvement over the confusions expressed by Smith. To have market value, things must both be useful and contain labor. But of these two requisites, said Marx, the second was the more important. This was because something might be useful, but if it required no effort to obtain it, it would have no value. Air and water were obvious examples. On the other hand Marx, like the members of the Classical School, assumed that there must be a demand for a product; otherwise the labor expended upon it would go to waste.

Marx's relative neglect of utility and use value and his insistence that the exchange value was completely separate from use value is not difficult to understand. The introduction of utility raises the ugly suspicion that value may not be solely a product of labor, and this conclusion was obviously one which Marx was anxious to avoid. No one could disagree with Marx's conclusion that the use value of a coat and the use value of linen were quite different, but to leap from this observation to the conclusion that therefore use and utility played no role in the determination of market value and that only the amount of labor contained could serve as a measure was a jump which many of Marx's readers were unwilling to make. Money, by acting as the universal equivalent, made it easier for the producer to dispose of his own product; he did not have to resort to barter exchange. The resulting "equation" formulated by Marx was $C–M–C$, where after one commodity had been converted into money, this money was used to buy a second product.

Suppose, however, Marx continued, that we consider this from the viewpoint of the capitalist. He starts with a supply of money which he converts into commodities and then sells them again (after their manufacture has been completed) for money. But unlike the crude trade of one commodity of equal exchange value (but of different use value) for another, the capitalist will find no gain from the process unless the quantity of money at the end is greater than it was at the beginning. The previous equation of $C–M–C$ has been converted to $M–C–M'$, and unless M' is greater than M, the capitalist has no reason to enter the market.

SURPLUS VALUE. Marx, however, denied that any surplus leading to a greater quantity of money in the end value emerged from the process of exchange. Rather, it was the value of products as determined by the amounts of socially necessary labor which set exchange. Where, then, was the capitalist to convert his original investment into a larger sum of money? It was at this point that Marx set forth his famous theory that the surplus value was derived from the exploitation of the workers. Before we examine Marx's explanation, let us first look at some possible explanations which he rejected.

Much of Marx's analysis is written in terms of aggregates; his approach was what we could call today a macroeconomic view of the economic system. When the problem was viewed in this fashion, it became impossible for surplus value to emerge from the process of exchange. Not that a particularly astute trader might not be able to gain profits at the expense of others, but his gains would be someone else's loss. The gain of one trader would be canceled by the loss of another, and so no net increment in surplus value would be achieved. The situation Marx wished to explain was the emergence of an excess profit that more than offset trading losses.

Nor did machinery offer any permanent augmentation of surplus value. For reasons soon to be explained, machinery might temporarily improve the earnings of those employers adopting it, while at the same time increasing surplus value in general, but this advantage was merely temporary. Indeed, it was the steadily increasing amount of machinery which was jeopardizing the rate of profits in the capitalist system. Marx argued that a machine could add to the value of a product only that part of the machine's worth which had been lost while producing the new product. Or, as Marx himself put it,

If a spinning machine lasts for 10 years, it is plain that during that working period its total value is gradually transferred to the product of the 10 years. . . . It is thus strikingly clear, that means of production never transfer more value to the product than they themselves lose during the labour-process by the destruction of their own use-value.[9]

What was "strikingly clear" to Marx may not be equally clear to the reader. Why should not the increased efficiency made possible by the machinery reflect itself in greater surplus value for the capitalist? Marx's answer to this query was not completely satisfying. Basically, it rested on the assumption of a fully competitive economy and the necessity of the capitalist to pay the full use-value of the machine. It was only labor-power which could be purchased at a price less than its full use-value. One of the problems of Marx's analysis at this point was that it ignored the role of time and the need for interest as explained by Senior and Mill. Marx did not consider the question of interest until the second volume of his book, and there he merely analyzed it as a "fragment of surplus value."

Marx also denied that either the services of management or the forces of nature ever contributed to surplus value. For the owner who might protest that he had also performed a useful function by supplying managerial talent, Marx had nothing but scorn. "Ask your foreman how valuable your services really are," he advised the capitalist. The capitalist's claim was thus brushed aside without further consideration and dismissed contemptuously as unworthy of analysis. It was as if Marx were treating all capitalists as parasitic absentee owners. Nor did their "abstaining from consumption," so much stressed by Mill and Senior, win the capitalists any recognition in the eyes of Marx. The true abstainers in Marx's system were the workers, who were compelled to "abstain" by not being paid the true worth of their contribution. Marx's treatment of the role of the capitalists at this point differs markedly from the treatment he accorded them elsewhere. It was the capitalists, after all, who provided the fulcrum of economic change by their never-ending search for greater profits. Not the least of the many changes instituted by the capitalists was their introduction of machinery.

RENT AND SURPLUS VALUE. Just as Ricardo had before him, Marx dismissed nature and rent as playing no contributing role in the determination of value. Marx went even further, however, and virtually dismissed it from the subject of political economy. Rent was not a product of differences in fertility or durability of the land. Rent resulted from those same

[9] Karl Marx, *Capital* (New York: Modern Library, n.d)., pp. 226–227.

social relations which permitted the existence of exploitation. Marx saw rent as pools of surplus value which could not be priced away by the market forces of competition. Since rent, like interest, stemmed from the same source—the exploitation of labor—it was an exception and could be properly relegated to a subordinate position while attention was focused on a study of the average rate of profits. Again Marx provided little to substantiate his views, confining himself to the simple assertion that exchange value is simply society's method of recording the amount of labor involved in the production of commodities. Since nature could contribute nothing to value, it stood to reason that it had no part in the formation of surplus value, either.

TRUE SOURCE OF SURPLUS VALUE. If surplus value came from none of the above sources in Marx's judgment, it is not very difficult to guess wherein lay the true Marxian answer. Just as value was a result of the amount of labor bestowed, so, too, did surplus value arise from the employment of labor. How was it possible for the capitalist to extort added value from labor when all of the other sources were closed to him? The forces of competition which had precluded the emergence of surplus value elsewhere in the economy no longer applied. Adam Smith had noted that the bargaining strength of the employers was likely to be far superior to that of the workers. It was this dichotomy in bargaining strength which Marx chose to emphasize. Nominally the worker was free. He could change employers whenever he chose, and he made his contract with the employer for a specified but limited period of time. In short, this was not slave labor which Marx was analyzing. Although free in this technical sense, workers had nothing to bargain with but their labor. Marx took delight in pointing up the irony of a situation where the workers were technically free but still slaves to the economic system. Furthermore, the fact that workers were free served to conceal an important fact. A slave laborer might mistakenly be thought to work solely for the interests of his master. In reality, part of his labor was necessary to earn his own subsistence. The same deception in reverse occurred in the case of free workers. Appearing to labor solely for their own subsistence, they actually devoted a substantial part of their effort to making profits for the capitalists.

Marx rejected Proudhon's thesis that the workers were exploited by capitalists only as a collective group and were therefore unaware of the exploitation. Nevertheless, Marx agreed that the amount of exploitation was concealed from the casual observer by the manner in which the labor market operated. By being "free" to change employers, workers were deluded into thinking that they had some power to improve their position by moving to another factory. Furthermore, the fact that wages varied from time to time gave the impression that, at the worst, exploitation was an occasional occurrence. Marx insisted, however, that even under the best of conditions workers were still exploited and that the good times appeared all too infrequently. The complete dependence of the majority of the workers on the capitalists for their livelihood and the insecurity implicit in that dependence became increasingly pressing when one took cognizance of the reserve industrial army of the unemployed. Faced with the threat of replacement by one of the unemployed anxiously searching for work, the employed workers were unable to reject the miserable wages and working conditions offered them by employers. It was in this way that employers managed to find a way to secure something for less than its true use-value to them. Surplus value was created as soon as workers had earned their subsistence, and Marx accordingly rejected Senior's thesis that profits were earned only during the last hour of the working day.

Like any other commodity, the value of labor power was determined by the amount of labor necessary for its continued production. Marx thus distinguished between the value of labor power, which was dependent on its cost of reproduction, and the value of the labor to the capitalist. Stated as such, Marx provided us with a slightly altered "iron law" of subsistence wages. The amount necessary for subsistence included the cost of rearing and educating the young and varied from society to society and generation to generation. Although a parallel between Marx's variable capital and the wages-fund doctrine can be drawn, Marx's reason why wages remained at the subsistence level was quite different from the explanation advanced by Malthus and Ricardo. Marx, whose own family life was a perfect illustration of the Malthusian principle at work, rejected the Malthusian Law with all its implications. The cause of poverty lay not with the workers themselves, with their tendency to overproduce, but with the capitalist system. Wages were kept at the subsistence level by the intensive competition among workers for the available jobs, but this excessive competition was created not by a tendency of people to have too many children, but by the numbers of workers forced into idleness by the process of technological change. Even the existence of large families was not proof of Malthus' contention. Large families were the fault of the capitalist system, which destroyed the character of the family group. It is interesting to note that this same contempt for Malthus' forebodings has continued to figure in Communist thinking down to the present day. Although there is some evidence that the Chinese Communists have found reason to qualify their views in the past few years, as late as 1960 Chinese leaders were busily denying that there could ever be a problem of overpopulation in China under Communist leadership—this despite the fantastic upsurge in China's population.

MACHINERY. Note also that the introduction of machinery would do nothing to improve wage levels. The increased efficiency resulting from the introduction of the machine did not rebound to the benefit of the working class. One reason we have already explored: Capitalists found no reason for paying higher wages since the number of workers seeking jobs was increased by technological displacement. In addition, the machinery made possible the employment of women and children formerly unemployable because of the heavy nature of the work. Some of the most persuasive chapters in *Capital* revolve around the degrading conditions under which women and children under the age of nine were compelled to work. Not only were women and children available for employment at wages below those necessary for the employment of men—a fact not unfamiliar even to modern-day economists—but their existence in the labor force augmented the supply of labor, again having a depressing effect on wages. Furthermore, machinery reduced levels of skill and made the quality of labor more interchangeable. It was this effect which produced the sense of job alienation among workers previously mentioned. To a great extent Marx undoubtedly owed his views on machinery and the welfare of the workers to the doubts noted earlier as arising in the mind of Ricardo.

Despite the apparent evil wreaked by the capitalist exploiters, it would be a mistake to think that Marx painted them as basically evil monsters. Communist propaganda has repeated this description with such monotonous regularity that the unwary student is apt to read into Marx's critique of capitalism a similar attitude. In many ways the capitalist was in Marx's view more to be pitied then censured, for like the workers, the capitalists were helpless victims of the economic system. Marx did not necessarily view the capitalists as basically good-hearted, well-intentioned men, but as men with weaknesses of character enhanced by the need to exercise their power over workers, a need forced upon them by the inexorable competitive pressures of the capitalist system. Even the capitalist with moral sensibilities and a "social conscience" would be driven to seek the greatest maximum profit possible. To do so was only a matter of self-preservation, and if he failed to exploit every opportunity, he would lose his position of power and wealth and sink down into the mass of the proletariat.

Under capitalism, as Marx foresaw it, wealth would become increasingly concentrated in the hands of a few; the worst enemy of the capitalist was his fellow capitalist, who threatened to swallow up his business and drive him into bankruptcy. Marx's invective sometimes leads the careless reader to assume that Marx was sweeping in his condemnation of all capitalists as free-will doers of evil, but this is a mistake. The Marxian capitalist might well respond to the complaining workers, "It (the capitalistic system) is bigger than both of us."

Let us now attempt to summarize the methods open to capitalists in their efforts to increase the amount of surplus value and then turn to the different types of capital employed. Marx argued that there were two general ways of increasing the total surplus value. Absolute surplus value could be increased by lengthening the working day or by increasing the amount of effort required within the prescribed time; there were obvious physical limitations to this method. The introduction of machinery, by lessening the socially necessary labor time for the production of products, would reduce the costs. This, in turn, would lead to reductions in the subsistence wage, thereby reducing the necessary amount of labor time required for the workers to earn their subsistence. Since employers would maintain the working day at the same length as before, a larger fraction of the working day could be devoted to the earning of surplus value. This increase Marx referred to as relative surplus value.

VARIABLE AND CONSTANT CAPITAL. Because Marx insisted that the only source of surplus value was labor, he argued that surplus value could come only from capital used to employ labor. This capital Marx labeled "variable capital" in distinction to "constant capital," which was used to buy machinery and raw materials. Since surplus value came solely from labor, only that portion devoted to labor's employment could produce a surplus value. The rate of surplus value could be computed by dividing the amount of surplus value by the amount of variable capital or the amount of surplus value by the amount of necessary labor. More important, however, was the fact that the capitalist must compute his rate of profit on the total amount of capital he had invested. In other words, his rate of profit must be figured as a percentage of the variable and constant capital combined. We have seen that the forces of competition drove the capitalist to introduce machinery. If he was the first to find a laborsaving device, then he would be able to produce the product with less than the socially necessary labor time required for the production of the commodity by rivals, and he would thereby enjoy a corresponding competitive advantage. Eventually, of course (and the eventuality would not take too long) other competitors would adopt the new machinery and the value of the product would correspondingly decline as the amount of socially necessary labor was reduced. While temporary advantages might be gained from the introduction of machinery, the long-run effect on the capitalists' rate of profits was more grim. As more and more machinery was introduced, the proportion of constant to variable capital was steadily increased. But we must remember that constant capital was sterile and unable to render the capitalist any long-run profits. Hence in the long run the rate of profit would steadily decrease. This persistent decline in the rate of profit would be interrupted from time to time for reasons soon to be discussed, but before turning to that question we must first consider the problem posed by the preceding analysis. In a famous critique of Marxian economics titled *Karl Marx and the Close of His System,* Eugen Böhm von Bawerk, a member of the Marginal Utility School, detected what he considered to be a fatal flaw in Marx's system. Böhm von Bawerk labeled this flaw "the great contradiction." If surplus value arose only from the employment of labor, with only variable capital capable of earning a return for the capitalist, how was it, asked Böhm-Bawerk, that companies with high proportions of constant to variable capital earned the same rate of return on their capital investments as those firms employing a much larger proportion of variable capital to constant capital? Marx also recognized this discrepancy in the first volume of his book, as is demonstrated in the following passage:

Every one knows that a cotton spinner, who, reckoning the percentage on the whole of his applied capital, employs much constant and little variable capital, does not, on account of this, pocket less profit or surplus-value than a baker, who relatively sets in motion much variable and little constant capital.[10]

Marx stopped there by saying that certain terms had not yet been explained in sufficient detail to resolve the question at that point and promised to return to the issue later. Marx died before the second and third volumes of his work were ready for publication, and there was a delay of several years before the answer was given. Some critics have suggested that Marx stalled the completion of his work because he recognized the danger to his model. Since Marx also postponed the completion of his first volume several times, this may be an unfounded suspicion.

Meanwhile other events served to intensify interest in the question. Supporters of the German Socialist Johann Karl Rodbertus, denounced Marx, claiming that all of the latter's central ideas had been stolen from their leader. Engels, defending his now deceased friend, strenuously denied these charges and challenged the supporters of Rodbertus to solve this problem. No such response was forthcoming, however, and students

[10] *Ibid.,* p. 335.

were forced to wait until the appearance of Marx's third volume for an answer.

The solution when it finally came was neither particularly world-shaking nor convincing. Marx reaffirmed his position as to the source of surplus value, but now fell back on the market forces of supply and demand for an explanation of the manner in which the surplus value was distributed among the capitalists. Marx presented the two tables reproduced here.[11]

Table I

	Capital	Surplus Value	Rate of Profit	Consumed Constant Capital	Value of Commodity	Cost Price
I	80c & 20v	20	20%	50	90	70
II	70c & 30v	30	30%	51	111	81
III	60c & 40v	40	40%	51	131	91
IV	85c & 15v	15	15%	40	70	55
V	95c & 5v	5	5%	10	20	15
Total	390c & 110v	110	110%			
Average	78c & 22v	22	22%			

Table II

Capital	Surplus Value	Value of Commodities	Cost Price	Price of Commodities	Rate of Profit	Difference Between Price and Value
80c & 20v	20	90	70	92	22%	+ 2
70c & 30v	30	111	81	103	22	− 8
60c & 40v	40	131	91	113	22	−18
85c & 15v	15	70	55	77	22	+ 7
95c & 5v	5	20	15	37	22	+17

A few words of explanation seem in order. Marx assumed for purposes of exposition a 100-percent return on the variable capital; the letters *c* and *v* stand for constant and variable capital, respectively. In Table I, the figures for the value of the commodity are obtained by adding together the

[11] Karl Marx, *Capital and Other Writings* (New York: Modern Library, n.d.), p. 55.

amount of constant capital consumed in the process of production (assumed to be different for different products) and the variable capital, plus the surplus value, which at a 100-percent rate is equal to the amount of variable capital used each time. The cost price is the summation of the constant and variable capital consumed. Taking the total surplus value and dividing it equally among the five firms for reasons soon to be discussed, Marx obtained the results contained in Table II. The market price of the commodities is the summation of the cost price, or the amounts of constant and variable capital consumed plus a standard rate of profit. Note that while the surplus value produced in different industries might differ, the rate of profit was made equal by the force of competition. Marx at this point sounded much like Ricardo in his denial that profits could vary appreciably between industries. The result, however, was a more dramatic reformulation of the early theory of value as stated in Volume I than perhaps even Marx himself realized. Whereas products had formerly exchanged in proportion to the average amount of socially necessary labor they contained, now an average rate of profit had also to be considered. Thus socially necessary labor ceased to be the controlling factor. Much of the edifice Marx had so lovingly constructed was therefore placed in jeopardy. If products were exchanged in response to market forces and not in terms of the labor content, the critic had reason to ask, why go to all the bother? If all Marx was arguing was that workers were being exploited, one could agree without resort to such an elaborate and devious explanation. Marx's supporters did their best to defend their master by arguing that this was not an inconsistency at all. Instead, Marx was pictured as recognizing that the capitalist was king in his own factory, with great power to exploit workers and thereby increase the amount of absolute and relative surplus value, while at the same time acknowledging that the capitalist was at the mercy of the economic system.

Even Marx's supporters, however, have been hard pressed to justify another inconsistency in Marx's logic. Marx began his analysis with an acceptance of the perfectly competitive model outlined by the Classical School. His view as to the future of capitalism, however, included a transition toward a model of large business firms with a growing concentration of capital. Any reduction in perfect competition is likely to be accompanied by a lessening of product homogeneity. If we assume the existence of product heterogeneity within a given industry, Marx's explanation of an average rate of product for any industry will be violated, since different firms in the same industry have different organic compositions of capital.

Returning now to a further consideration of the first volume, we find the concluding chapters of the book devoted to a major consideration, the Law of Capital Accumulation. Marx saw the process of capital accumulation developing directly out of his concept of surplus value. What were the capitalists to do with the surplus value their capital earned for them? While part of this surplus might be consumed in riotous living, Marx saw the same process viewed by Ricardo and other Classical writers. The capitalists would reinvest their capital, thus making possible the earning of still more surplus value, which in turn would be reinvested, thereby continuing the process. The irony of the picture thus drawn is clear—the submission of the workers to exploitation made possible the extension of that exploitation on an ever-increasing scale. While the process was certainly not completely painless, workers were unaware of the continuous and ever-mounting exploitation taking place. The comparatively inconspicuous character of mounting capital accumulation was in sharp contrast to its character in early stages. The early phases involved direct and ruthless expropriation in the form of theft and direct seizure of property; it was at this stage that workers were dispossessed and left with nothing but their labor power as a means of supporting themselves. Through this process of expropriation and capital accumulation, workers were separated from their land, their food, and the means of production; the Land Enclosure Acts were typical of the events Marx had in mind.

The process of capital formation did not ultimately benefit the capitalists as much as might, at first glance, be expected. The reason for this rested with the necessity for businessmen to invest more and more of their funds in the form of constant capital from which no surplus was possible. As the amount of constant capital increased, the rate of profit in the economy tended to decrease, since profit came only from variable capital but was computed as a percentage of the total capital invested. If the same proportion went continuously to variable capital, then it would follow that the earnings of workers might be expected to rise. Even such a possibility would not have satisfied Marx's criticism of capitalism, since there would still be a tendency for progress to come to an end as wages encroached increasingly upon profits. The reader should be able to recognize this as being more than faintly reminiscent of Ricardo. Even during the interim period before growth ceased, higher wages would not have lessened Marx's insistence that workers were still being exploited. After all, according to Marx's view, the entire value of the products belonged to the workers. Marx would have regarded the justification for exploitation on the grounds that workers were faring better as an argument akin to asserting that the humane treatment of slaves justified the existence of slavery.

The important fact to remember, however, is that Marx felt that constant capital would increase as a proportion of total capital, thus producing a falling rate of profit.

There were certain offsets to this tendency for the role of profits to fall. Not only might workers be compelled to work longer and harder but the cost of the equipment upon which constant capital was expended might be reduced in cost, thereby (for at least a time) reducing the amount of constant capital invested. Furthermore, the decline in the rate of profit might be interrupted by the variations in the business cycle. In order to have a clear understanding of this relationship, we must first examine Marx's explanation of the business cycle.

THE BUSINESS CYCLE. Marx, like other Socialists, seized upon the business cycle as evidence of the basic fraility of the capitalist system. Unlike other Socialist writers, however, he did not emphasize the maldistribution of income, evil though it was, as a basic cause of the cycle. One has to read all three volumes, and particularly the second volume, to realize this. It is all too easy on the basis of the first volume alone to conclude that Marx, by picturing workers at subsistence wages, was painting a picture where depressions were caused by the inadequacy of purchasing power to sustain continued production. This, however, is an incorrect interpretation. Instead of emphasizing an underconsumption explanation of the business cycle, Marx lay stress on the role of costs and the problem of overproduction.

The distinction between overproduction and underconsumption is sometimes a difficult line to maintain, but in Marx's view the difference was crucial. Marx noted that the downturn in economic conditions frequently came at a time when a rising demand for labor had pushed wages to above their normal subsistence levels. Thus the rising wages, by increasing costs, accentuated rather than helped to avert a downturn in business activity. This observation led Marx to reject the prescription of trade union leaders and other champions of the underconsumption theory. To raise wages might be a desirable goal, but it could never correct the basic inconsistencies of the capitalist system. It was the system, with its tendency to overproduce goods, which accounted for the periodic glut of goods and the necessity of periods of interrupted economic activity when these surpluses could be disposed of. No amount of correction in wage levels could rectify this tendency of the economy to overproduce. Even if unions should have the power to enforce great increases in wage rates—surely a highly dubious assumption in Marx's estimation—the encroachment upon the capitalists' profits would lead them to withdraw their funds, thereby subjecting the economy to depression. In both the *Communist Manifesto* and *Capital,* Marx saw the business cycle increasing in severity as time passed. Despite the more recent experience of the 1930's, following the 1929 crash, there is little evidence in support of this belief, and most economists today who are students of the business cycle doubt whether any such pattern is emerging.

Keeping Marx's explanation of the cause of the business cycle in mind, let us now consider the impact of cylical fluctuations on the rate of profits. Again, first appearances are deceiving. One ordinarily associates declining business conditions with disappearing profits, and indeed, in the short run, this was also the opinion of Marx. Interruptions in business activity would threaten businessmen, and in this manner some of them were forced into bankruptcy and out of the bourgeois class into the ranks of the proletariat. But in the very seeds of this short-run destruction of capital and the short-run fall of profits lay the possibility for the postponement of the reduction in the long-run rate of profits down to the point where no further expansion would take place. One of the results of these periodic collapses was the destruction of much constant capital. With the destruction of part of the constant capital, the stage was again set at a higher plateau then before the depression for a continuation of the process of capital accumulation, with its accompanying long-term downward movement in the rate of profits. Note incidentally the emphasis on the word *rate.* Just as Ricardo had foreseen the possibility that the absolute volume of profits might increase while the rate of profits continued to decline, so also did Marx find no contradiction in these two tendencies.

TAXATION. Marx wrote relatively little on the subject of taxation, but what he did write was in keeping with his view that only the complete overthrow of capitalism and the abolition of the wage system would provide a permanent solution to the existing problems. It is true that in the *Communuist Manifesto* Marx suggested the highly progressive income tax as one of the planks in his platform for the overthrow of the capitalist system. Opponents of the income tax have seized upon this position as evidence of the basic evil of the income tax and have attempted to associate the tax with communist doctrine and proponents of the tax with communism. It is evident from Marx's other writings, however, that he had little faith in the power of taxation to correct the inequities worked by the capitalistic system. The patterns of income distribution were determined by the nature and ownership of the means of production. Central to Marx's thinking was his conviction that the only real solution to the injustices produced by capitalism lay in the overthrow of the capitalist system.

Summary and Evaluation. Marx owed a deep intellectual debt to Smith and Ricardo—although both of these men would have shuddered at the thought of accepting any responsibility for Marx's ideas. Nevertheless, many of Marx's theories can be traced back to these two earlier writers. The idea of a labor theory of value is the most obvious case in point, but several of Marx's basic assumptions were also shared by both Smith and Ricardo. The ideas of pure or perfect competition in commodity markets, a static equilibrium, and the homogeneity of labor are some of the most obvious examples which might be mentioned.

John Maynard Keynes once described Marx's epochal work as " . . . an obsolete economic text book . . . not only scientifically erroneous, but without interest or application for the modern world." In light of the impact of Marxian thinking on events throughout the world, Keynes' critique appears to be unduly slighting. Whatever the merits of Marx's analysis, its appeal to "expropriate the expropriator" had and continues to have wide appeal. No one can seriously deny that the name of Marx has served as a rallying cry for oppressed workers around the world—to deny this would be to deny reality itself. It is true (as many critics of Soviet economic policy have observed) that Communism in Russia is a far cry from the Communism envisioned by Marx himself. Nevertheless, the differences, sharp as they are, do not negate the fact that the basic doctrine preached by Marx has been carried out—abolition of private ownership of the means of production.

Other critics would attempt to minimize the impact of Marx's ideas by pointing out that much of his alleged appeal has been among those who have probably never read even the *Communist Manifesto,* let alone the four-volume *Capital.* Ideas, however, need not be carried by means of the printed word alone, and the fact is that Marx's version of the rationale of Communism caught the imaginations of oppressed workers and won adherents where those of other socialist thinkers failed or, at best, had limited success.

Despite the lengthy and obscure passages in Marx's writing, the diagnosis of the problem and the proposed solutions for it were relatively easy to understand, and the lessons to be drawn were clear and appealing. The message to "expropriate the expropriators" had (and still has) understandable appeal to the oppressed. Like Smith and Ricardo, Marx laid down principles applicable to all countries; unlike Smith and Ricardo, his principles were accepted as having universal application. Marx succeeded in providing a rallying cry for the disaffected while at the same time offering a rigorous theoretical analysis for those more intellectually inclined. In many ways the criticisms which followed were thus inevitably foredoomed to fall on deaf ears, and those hearing the call of Marx remained unshaken in their faith.

As to the quality of Marx's analysis, we have reason to be doubtful. His concentration on labor as the sole source of value, to the exclusion of all other explanations, suffered from the same fatal weaknesses noted previously in connection with the earlier exponents of a labor theory of value. His attempt to reduce labor of varying qualities to a simple homogeneity was never completely satisfying and was never clearly demonstrated; Marx contented himself by saying that it was arrived at "by experience." Even more than Ricardo, Marx was forced to qualify his early description of commodities exchange by the amounts of labor contained therein, when he came to take account of the role of profits.

As a prophet of events to come, Marx must bear the burden of a mixed record, with some smash hits and some striking misses. Perhaps the most notable of the latter was the picture he drew of the increasing misery of the poor combined with an increasing concentration of wealth. Not only has the condition of the working classes failed to sink ever lower, but there has been a steady improvement in the level of real wages in all of the major industrial nations of the world. The question of concentration of economic wealth, in the United States at least, is not a completely settled issue, but it seems perfectly safe to maintain that the present state of concentration falls far below the degree predicted by Marx. Certainly the small business firm has continued to play an important role in the capitalist economic scene. Meanwhile, his forecast about the declining rate of profits still remain to be fulfilled.

On other points, Marx's score has been considerably better. His conclusions about the displacement effects of machinery placed too much emphasis on the long-run aspects to have had validity in the past, but the current threat from automation has led a number of non-Marxian economists to express concern over the future. Whether Marx's position on this question will ultimately be justified still remains to be seen, however. Nor should we overlook Marx's stress on the sense of job alienation experienced by factory workers; the theme has been picked up and emphasized by non-Marxian industrial economists, sociologists, and psychologists. The causes of frustration and discontent among workers has remained an important theme for students in all three disciplines. Finally, although he

overstated the case, Marx's conception of history as interpreted in economic terms set a standard for analysis by succeeding generations of historians and led to the development of the field of economic history.

NIKOLAI LENIN (VLADIMIR ILICH ULYANOV) (1870–1924)

It is no reflection on the importance of Marx's influence on Socialist thinking to point out that much of his message might have been lost without
the further writing and actions of Lenin, the father of the Russian Revolution. Ironically, however, what Lenin did demonstrate was the weakness of
Marx's assumption that all history could be written in economic terms to
the exclusion of intellectual forces. For without the power of Lenin's (or
Marx's) ideas, the tide of history might have ebbed in a quite different
direction.

The Man. Lenin was born in Simbirsk (since renamed Ulyanovsk)
in 1870, three years before the publication of the first volume of Marx's
Capital. He was the son of middle-class parents, but his career in revolution came at an early age. As he was about to graduate from the local
gymnasium in the year 1887, his brother was seized and executed for
plotting to assassinate Czar Alexander III. Thereafter, Lenin's life was a
series of entanglements with the government authorities, ending only with
his return to Russia (from Switzerland) and the overthrow of the Kerensky regime. Shortly after his enrollment at Kazan University, for example,
Lenin was expelled for participation in student political activities. Later
his underground activities in St. Petersburg led to his arrest and intern-
ment in jail for fourteen months. Following this jail sentence, he was
exiled to Siberia (such a sentence was popular even before the Revolution) for a three-year period. Exile in Siberia did not involve prison camp
life, as it did in later years, and while there Lenin married another revolutionary exile named Nadezhda Krupskaya. While still in Siberia, Lenin
completed his first book, *The Development of Capitalism in Russia.*

Upon the completion of his period of exile in Siberia, Lenin decided to
move to Germany, and then Switzerland, where he set up the newspaper
Iskra and continued to develop his Socialistic theories. The early years
away from Russia followed the pattern set earlier while Lenin was still in
Russia, and it reads almost like the life of Marx. He engaged in journalism and had his views circulated clandestinely throughout Russia. Return-

ing briefly to Russia from 1905 to 1907, he organized the Bolshevik Party while he was in St. Petersburg, but he returned again to Western Europe, where he remained until he took his famous sealed-car train ride across Germany and into Russia during World War I. By this time the Czar had already been overthrown and the government was headed by a modified Socialist leader named Alexander Kerensky. Lenin succeeded in producing the overthrow of the Kerensky regime and thereupon signed a separate peace agreement with Germany.

Lenin's Writings. During the period just prior to and during World War I, Lenin wrote some of his most memorable books, including *What Is to Be Done, The State and the Revolution,* and his famous study, *Imperialism.* Any lengthy examination of the first two of these books would take us too far astray from our central theme of the history of economic thought. Essentially these two books were written as textbooks for the Communist revolutionary on how to spur on the coming revolution and what to do thereafter. Basically, Lenin accepted Marx's prediction that the judgment day was near at hand. Unlike some Marxians, however, Lenin was not content to sit back and wait for the tides of history to sweep over the economic system. Rather, he felt that a little proselytizing and forceful help on behalf of the revolution was in order. There followed a remarkably candid assessment of the proper role of the revolutionary in expediting that change.

We shall now devote most of our attention to Lenin's classic study, *Imperialism.* By the time that Lenin was writing, the Communists were faced with the need to explain why two of Marx's predictions had failed to come true. If Marx was wrong in these two instances, might he not be wrong on other points as well? The two areas where Marx's predictions had most widely missed their mark were the lack of class consciouness on the part of the workers of the major industrial nations and the failure of profits to decline rapidly, with the resulting collapse of the capitalist system. The emergence of imperialism as the last stage in the development of capitalism was what Lenin offered as an explanation of why there had been a postponement in the realization of both of these predictions.

IMPERIALISM. Lenin picked up at the point where Marx had ended his first volume. The growth in the concentration of economic power was just as Marx had predicted it, save that it had been carried to an extreme Marx had failed to foresee. Marx had written only fleetingly of colonies (in Chapter 33 of his first volume,) basing his comments primarily on the great student of colonies, E. G. Wakefield. Within the leading industrial nations, Lenin saw developments much as Marx had pictured them; capital had been amassed in the hand of fewer and fewer individuals, the banks played an increasingly controlling role, and the divorce of ownership and management became increasingly apparent. Those readers familiar with *The Modern Corporation and Private Property* by Adolf A. Berle and Gardiner Means will find in Lenin's book an interesting anticipation of their thesis of the mounting separation of ownership and management. With the growth of finance capitalism and large business assets at home, said Lenin, the capitalists now turned to new worlds to conquer abroad. There was thus an outflow of capital to the undeveloped nations of the world. Four major results stemmed from this outflow.

In the first place the export of capital to other lands served to check the tendency for the rate of profit to decline. The pressure on the rate of profit exerted by the mounting proportion of constant capital at home was offset by the opportunities for the fresh exploitation of labor in those countries where the stockpile of capital had still to develop.

The second result was to emphasize the lack of class consciousness in the exploiting nations and the lack of class solidarity around the world. The workers in the colonial powers shared in the benefits reaped from the exploitation of workers in the subservient nations. Thus, since the living standards of the workers in the exploiting nations had improved, they lost their feeling of oppression and were willing to share in the spoils resulting from the exploitation of fellow workers in other lands. The capitalists, by sharing a small portion of the gains, succeeded in quelling worker unrest at home and destroying the bonds of international class solidarity. It is difficult to assess which crime Lenin considered to be the more serious!

Although the end of capitalism had been temporarily postponed by this development, Lenin remained confident that worldwide Communism was still an inevitable part of the future. Monopoly and the increasing concentration of power, both of which Marx had foreseen, were enhanced, Lenin said, by the growth of the power of giant banks and international financiers. But as the colonial powers attempted to dominate more and more foreign lands, their greed would inevitably bring them into conflict with one another. Struggles for control would inevitably lead to war, and a world war would set the stage for the emergence of world Communism.

When one remembers the time when Lenin's *Imperialism* was written, it is easy to see the inspiration for his thinking. World War I in many ways fitted the description sometimes applied to it as a war of the imperialist powers. The attempt by Germany to challenge the dominant position of England and France and acquire an equal world position was quite in keeping with the thesis of Lenin's book. Nor were the growth of finance capitalism and the separation of ownership and management purely figments of Lenin's imagination. Rather, they were a faithful picture of changes transpiring at the time.

The remainder of Lenin's life after his return to Russia is a familiar story to most students of Russian history. After overthrowing the Kerensky regime and establishing the "dictatorship of the proletariat," he successfully warded off the attacks of foreign troops, including English, French, and American. He was less successful in attempts to organize the economy; during his last two years of life, his efforts were handicapped by ill health resulting from an earlier attempt at his assassination. In 1924 he died from the strain of overwork placed on a body weakened by wounds from the attempted assassination. Whether Communism as practiced in Russia might have had a different flavor under his continued leadership has continued to be a matter for endless speculation, but the answer to that question can never be known.

Summary and Evaluation. It would perhaps be wise to close this chapter with a summary statement of the characteristics distinguishing the Marx-Lenin brand of Socialism from that preached by their predecessors, the Utopian Socialists. Out of the multitude of points which might be made, the following three are perhaps the most outstanding. First and foremost was the manner in which the transformation into Socialism was to be effected. Whereas the Utopian Socialists preached reform and the need for active planning, both Marx and Lenin believed that the forces of history were on their side. Lenin, and to a lesser extent Marx, were not unsympathetic to the need for positive action, but both believed in the historical inevitability of the revolution.

Second, whereas the Utopian Socialists saw the problem of profits primarily in terms of a maldistribution of income, with profits made possible by the variety of unethical actions practiced by capitalists and/or the existence of money, Marx and Lenin viewed profits as a basic flaw of the capitalist system; no remedy was possible save the complete abolition of the wage system of employing labor. Whereas the Utopians wrote in terms of moral principles and standards of right and wrong, both Marx and Lenin placed the burden of guilt not on any particular group but on the economic system.

In spite of Marx's and Lenin's condemnation of the economic system rather than the capitalists, their message was generally construed as a statement of hate and conflict. Class was set against class and the proposals for achieving peaceful distribution were abandoned in favor of the overthrow of one class by another. While it would be a mistake to over-emphasize the seeds of violence in Marx's and Lenin's thinking (particularly the former), neither writer shunned violence when he felt it to be necessary. The contrast with the message preached by the Utopian Socialists is too evident to need further comment.

Succeeding generations of Socialist writers have not always followed the lines laid down by Marx and Lenin. In fact, in many instances they have been sharply critical of the ideas of both. Nevertheless, it would be difficult to overestimate the impact these two writers have had on subsequent Socialist literature.

CHAPTER VIII: The German Historical School

The Historical School have discarded abstract deduction, but they cannot write three pages on economic questions, even in the historical style, without general theory, and one can construct no general theory without the use of abstract deduction.

—EUGEN BÖHM VON BAWERK

It would be going against progress and development if we were to place decaying old-fashioned ideas and methods on a par with such as are superior and more fully developed. Neither the strict followers of Adam Smith, nor those of Karl Marx, can lay claim to being considered first-rate nowadays. He who does not strive to be on a level with the present state of research, culture, and method is a teacher of no efficiency.

—GUSTAV SCHMOLLER

Those writers whom we reviewed in Chapter VII emphasized varying points of criticism in their respective analyses of the Classical School. All of them, however, with the possible exception of Henry George, focused their fire on one basic tenet or assumption of Classical thinking. The major error in the thinking of the Classical School lay, in the view of the Socialist writers, in the former's premise that capital was so scarce and tender a flower that it had to be nurtured even if at the expense of human welfare. Although in the heat of the dispute the charge was sometimes made, it was not true that the Classical School consisted of a group of monsters utterly indifferent to human suffering. Rather, they felt that in the short run the supply of labor was so bounteous that individual lives could be sacrificed to the ultimate greater good which would come from assuring capitalists a free hand. The Socialist critics, of course, insisted that considerations of human welfare should and could come first.

The group of writers we are now about to study were critical of a number of the other basic assumptions of Classical thought. Writers of the Historical School questioned the existence of immutable economic principles applicable to all times and to all situations. By the same token, they tended to discard reliance on the deductive method and to emphasize instead the need for vast amounts of historical and statistical research. They were dubious about the effectiveness of the operation of the principle of self-interest and tended to abandon laissez-faire as a guideline to economic policy. Whereas the Classical School had tended to dismiss the study of history of economic thought as largely a waste of time, the Historical School felt that one could best discover the relevance and importance of economic ideas if they were studied in the context of the time and environment in which they evolved. It would not be far wrong to say that the study of the history of economic thought got its beginning from this group.

It is difficult to know where to begin the story of the historical method. After all, Adam Smith made considerable use of historical and statistical material, and numerous other writers also could be cited for their activities in the same direction. We will begin, however, with someone who, while still antedating the German Historical School as usually defined, comes closer to them in time and who was also critical of the Classical School on many of the same grounds as those who followed him. The name of this man is Friedrich List.

FRIEDRICH LIST (1789–1846)

The Man. List was born in Reutlingen, Germany, the son of a well-to-do tanner. While at college he studied the works of the Classical authors. Shortly after graduation he was appointed professor at the University of Tübingen, and he served as a political advisor to the government of Württemburg. His interest in politics and reform led him into serious trouble. While serving in the legislature of Württemburg, the free expression of his views on the need for reform led to a jail sentence. In order to avoid this, he fled abroad and spent a number of years in England, France, Switzerland, and the United States. Harried in both France and Switzerland, List led the life of the perpetual traveler. Before coming to the United States, he returned to Germany, only to be imprisoned, and he managed to gain release only by promising again to leave the country. While in the United States, List became familiar with the views of Alexander Hamilton and others who championed trade protection and denied the universality of Smith's prescription of free trade. Although List met with financial success in the United States (he discovered a coal mine), he longed for Europe and returned to France. Following the death of one of his sons, he reentered Germany. This time he encountered a more hospitable climate of opinion.

During his early days in Germany, List had worked toward an association of businessmen to push for protection, and some progress in this direction had been made during his absence. Upon his return, List took an active role in pressing for a customs union of the German principalities. His first book advocating economic nationalism, entitled *Outlines of American Political Economy,* appeared in 1827, but his statement of the case for nationalism and protection appearing in *The National System of Political Economy* (1841) was the one which won him enduring fame and which represented an early illustration of the technique advanced by the Historical School. Hurt by the numerous criticisms and by the bad treatment he had received both at home and abroad, List was also plagued in later years with poor health and financial reverses; much of his wealth was lost in the American financial panic of 1837. Discouraged and despondent, he committed suicide at the age of 58.

Economic Views. It is manifestly impossible to examine List's writings in any great detail. Instead, we shall note some minor points of disagreement with the Classical School and then focus on his views of economic nationalism and protection and his use of history to justify his program.

List departed from the views of Adam Smith and his followers at a number of points. He denied the threat of overpopulation as stated by Malthus and argued that a country's "capacity for population" expanded with increasing production, thus making possible the maintenance of increased numbers.[1] Unlike Ricardo, List saw no need for any conflict between agricultural and industrial interests; agriculture was aided and strengthened by a healthy industrial sector and the growth of agriculture in turn reinforced the growth of industry. Despite Smith's interest in "the causes of the wealth of nations," List felt that Smith, by emphasizing the question of exchange value, had failed to recognize the crucial issue. The real secret of a nation's wealth lay, in List's opinion, in its factors of production and its ability to use them in such a way as not only to replace wealth currently being destroyed by consumption but to expand it to increased amounts.

Thus far, Smith would have found little with which to disagree, but List's emphasis on the means by which a nation might increase its wealth

[1] Friedrich List, *The National System of Political Economy,* trans. by S. S. Lloyd (London: Longmans, Green and Co., 1928), pp. 103–105.

led List down a quite different path from that pursued by Smith. List accused Smith of "cosmopolitanism." Smith was deemed wrong in arguing that the interests of all nations were alike and that free trade would be equally beneficial to all. In order to achieve full economic development, it might be necessary for a nation to erect tariff barriers to protect its budding home industries. Readers will recognize this as an early statement of the "infant industry" argument still heard today as a justification for trade restrictions. It would be a mistake, however, to categorize List as simply another Mercantilist; several important features distinguished him from this earlier school. Gone was the preoccupation with the maintenance of a favorable balance of trade and the prizing of gold for its own sake. Gone also was the conviction that trade restrictions were everywhere and always a desirable policy for a nation to pursue. Free trade for an advanced commercial nation such as England was, in List's view, proper commercial policy; other nations when they had arrived at a similar stage of development would be wise to adopt a free-trade policy also. List, moreover, recognized that some countries did not have the potentialities for full economic development; in these cases too, a program of trade restrictions might prove to be a detriment rather than an asset. Furthermore, List noted that even where some degree of tariff protection would be helpful to a nation's economic development, care must be exercised to prevent setting the rates at excessively high levels. Industry needed protection, but it also needed the stimulus of foreign competition and when rates were set at too high levels, the impetus to greater efficiency engendered by foreign competition would be lost. List's plea for limited protection for industrial goods rose from the flooding of the German states with British goods after the European market was reopened following the defeat of Napoleon in 1815. Events at the time also played a role in List's unwillingness to extend tariff protection to the sphere of agriculture; he had ample opportunity to observe the detrimental effects England's Corn Laws had had on German exports of agricultural produce.

To support his case for economic nationalism and trade protection, List resorted to the use of historical example. He cited numerous historical illustrations of actions undertaken by various governments which had either aided or hindered the economic development of Spain, France, and other countries. As a part of his historical description of the progress toward full economic development taken by any nation, List maintained that a developing nation went through five distinct stages. Starting with a savage or primitive state, a country moved next to a pastoral and agricultural stage. Some countries, List believed, were doomed to stop at stage two or three, but the more fortunate could move beyond to stages of agriculture and manufacture and finally to the last stage, when a combination of agriculture, manufacture, and commerce was achieved. Although not all countries in List's judgment were capable of attaining the final stages, those nations which did possess the potential (such as Germany) should unquestionably make the effort. In virtually all such cases, there would be a need for action by the state and for the erection of trade barriers.

Summary and Evaluation. Although some writers have included List among the members of the German Historical School, most students have treated him as a forerunner but not an actual part of that school. The justification for this differentiation is not difficult to find. List employed the historical approach as a tool to prove his case for state action; he was not interested primarily in the study of economic history for its own sake. Nevertheless, his writing contains many illustrations of fine historical research and many of the faults he had to find with Adam Smith and his followers were echoed by later writers of the German Historical School. It was as a forerunner of the Historical School rather than as an advisor on economic policy that List had his greatest impact. Even in his homeland, where his writings were most widely disseminated, his advice was seldom taken and his views were scorned by later protectionists, who were (and are) unwilling to concede the eventual arrival of a day when protection would no longer be desirable. List never recognized the possibility that protectionism, once established, would be very difficult to eradicate.

WILHELM GEORG FRIEDRICH ROSCHER
(1817–1894)

Those students who refuse to accord List admission to the Historical School are generally agreed in designating our next writer as the true founder of the school. Even so, it should be noted that Roscher was more sympathetic to the ideals of liberalism as expressed in Classical thought than were later writers of the German School.

The Man. Roscher, who was descended from a family of government officials and judges, was educated at the University of Göttingen, where he received inspiration for the pursuit of the historical method from some of his early professors. After graduation, he remained in the academic environment, accepting a professorship at Göttingen and four years later, in 1848, at Leipzig. Typical of his historical writings were his *Economics Viewed from an Historical Standpoint* and his *History of Economic Thought in Germany*. Although it was these two books which place him as the founder of the Historical School, it was his four-volume *System of Economics* which won him his greatest fame among the members of the general public. Written as a textbook for students and businessmen, it was widely used throughout Germany and was reprinted several times.

Economic Views. The basic weakness in Roscher's approach lay in his inability to decide (or to communicate to his readers the decision, if one was formulated) the use to be made of the study of history. At times, he wrote as if he had no serious quarrel with the deductive method but wished only to buttress the method with empirical historical evidence which Ricardo and other Classicists had neglected. At other times he appeared ready to abandon deductive analysis entirely and rely upon the lessons of historical research as the proper field of study for the economists and as the proper guide for the actions of statesmen. Part of the difficulty lay in the fact that Roscher was basically a liberal at heart and never lost his sense of the need for reform; in cases where reform was felt to be urgently needed, dispassionate historical evidence was not always sufficient.

Roscher was an economic historian in the broadest sense of the word—he was a cultural historian who, in his attempts to put his historical research to practical use, sought for laws dealing with general historical development. Although he set the tone for subsequent historical research, later writers in the school sometimes condemned him as being too quick to make comparisons between different institutions in different times and places before adequate investigation had been completed. Whether or not the criticism is valid is questionable. Granted that later students were to undertake historical studies in far more depth and detail than did Roscher, nevertheless he did make an important start, and hypotheses about the relationship of institutions over time and space are essential as a basis for further research and testing. To leave the implication that Roscher was a superficial scholar would be unfair. When for example, he was commissioned by the Munich Academy of Science to write a history of German economic thought, he included a thousand writers in the study and is reported to have read virtually everything each one had written.

Two other writers, together with Roscher, constitute what is frequently designated as the "older Historical School"; the other two members were

Bruno Hildebrand and Karl Knies. The distinction frequently drawn between the older Historical School and the younger school headed by Schmoller is that the older school emphasized the need for historical research as a means of supplementing and strengthening traditional theory. Roscher and the other members of the older school, it is argued, were less inclined to dismiss Classical theory entirely than to consider that theory had been improperly verified and employed by the Classical writers. Schmoller and later writers are considered to be more sweeping in their rejection of traditional theory and more willing to substitute the study of history as the sole means of arriving at economic truth. Actually, as Schumpeter has pointed out, the distinction is somewhat artificial and difficult to maintain.[2] Some of these difficulties will become apparent as we turn to a brief appraisal of Hildebrand and Knies and then to some of the figures linked to the new school.

BRUNO HILDEBRAND (1812–1878)

The Man. Hildebrand began his academic career by studying theology and later switched to economics and history. A college professor all his life, he began his teaching career at the University of Breslau in 1836 as a lecturer; in 1841 he became a professor at the University of Marburg. In violent disagreement with the government's policies, Hildebrand spent several years in voluntary exile, teaching at the Universities of Zurich and Bern during his stay in Switzerland. In 1861 he returned to Germany and resumed his position in a German university—this time at the University of Jena.

Economic Views. Hildebrand was considerably more determined in his rejection of Classical thought than Roscher had been, and he was at some points sharply critical of Roscher for the latter's willingness to accept the theoretical structure of the Classical School. In his chief work, *The Present and Future National Economy,* Hildebrand denied the existence of natural economic laws. Instead, he emphasized what was to become a familiar theme of the Historical School—the proposition that economic principles varied in accordance with their setting of time and place. In this, his major work, he appeared to accept the notion that there were laws of historical development, and he refined Roscher's five stages

---

2 Joseph Schumpeter, *A History of Economic Analysis* (New York: Oxford University Press, 1954), p. 507.

down to three—the natural economy, the money economy, and the credit economy. Later, however, he seems to have rejected even the possibility of finding laws of historical development. His early claims that the historical method might not only supplement and invigorate Classical theory but eventually replace it were never carried through, as he contented himself with writing fragmentary studies emphasizing the use of statistical methods.

Hildebrand never had a great impact on German economic thought or on economic thinking elsewhere. An economist who supported economics as a moral science and who sought reform, he had little influence on policy. His greatest impact was probably the example set by his firm rejection of Classical thought for Gustav Schmoller and later writers of the Historical School. Even Schmoller, however, tended to dismiss him as a politician who wasted his powers of analysis.

KARL KNIES (1821–1898)

The Man. Like so many members of the Historical School, Knies was a university professor; he served as a professor of government both at the University of Freiburg and the University of Heidelberg, retiring from the latter post in 1890. During the time of his appoinment at Freiburg he served for four years as the university representative to the diet at Baden. Mention should also be made of his elaborate statistical work, some of which has had enduring value.

Economic Views. Knies, who was heavily influenced by his study of Hegel, picked up where Hildebrand had left off. Highly critical of List's five stages of economic development, Knies, nevertheless, was convinced that the study of history would enable the student to detect regularities and consistencies in economic behavior which would be useful in charting policy and meeting current problems. In the book which justifies his inclusion with the Historical School, *Political Economy from the Historical Point of View,* Knies argued that political economy, when properly conceived, was a study of the development of economic thought dealing with alternative policies as they were formulated to meet differing conditions of time and place. Sharply critical of both Roscher and Hildebrand, he argued that they both were too inclined to accept the possibility of discovering certain basic economic "laws" and were thus unable to free themselves sufficiently from the methodology of the Classical School. In his view, insufficient attention had been accorded to the fact that the members of the Classical School had rested their system on a single human motivation —man's pursuit of his own self-interest. Men's motivations, said Knies, were far more numerous and complex than this, however, and any such simplified version was bound to be misleading. Knies suggested that his fellow economic historians should stop asserting the superiority of the historical method, and after having finally freed themselves of all belief in "laws" and universally applicable assumptions, should set about achieving the research which would prove their claims.

In light of this admonition, it is ironic that Knies himself virtually abandoned the historical method in his later work. His subsequent writing, including his book *Gold and Credit,* dealt with the problems of money and credit on a theoretical basis and showed little evidence of any tie with the historical approach. Despite, or perhaps because of, his criticism of Roscher, Knies felt that his own writing had been unfairly ignored by Roscher; such, however, was to be Knies' fate generally. Virtually neglected by all of his contemporaries, Knies' views on the historical approach had little influence until they were picked up by members of the "younger" Historical School. We now turn to this second group.

GUSTAV SCHMOLLER (1838–1917)

The Man. Schmoller is the generally acknowledged leader of the "younger" Historical School. In keeping with the academic orientation of other members of both schools, Schmoller served as a professor of economics at the universities of Halle, Strasbourg, and Berlin. In addition, he has often been called the "maker of professors," in recognition of his efforts to secure academic appointments for his followers and supporters. We will pay scant heed to the work of these other writers; typical of the group was the great pacifist Lujo Brentano (1844–1931), whom students of labor history may remember for his patient tracing of the emergence of modern trade unions from the early craft guilds. Like many of the school, Schmoller was a strong supporter of reform and even entertained socialistic views; he supported reforms in working conditions and social insurance.

Economic Views. In one sense, the "younger" school under Schmoller's leadership can be said to be even more divorced from theory than the previous writers studied in this chapter. Schmoller and his followers turned away from theory to a consideration of practical problems. Economics became but a part of the study of society and economic motivations only one of many forces impinging upon man's actions. Schmoller maintained that a principal fault of the older school was its tendency to draw conclusions too quickly and develop theories on the basis of insufficient historical evidence. At the same time, the "younger" school abandoned one of the key tenets of Knies and Hildebrand, the denial of the existence of economic laws. While perhaps not completely convinced that such laws did exist, Schmoller was inclined to accept the possibility of their existence. What he continued to question was the suitability of the Classical method of deduction as a means for discovering them. Continuous and protracted historical research was offered as a better alternative. Schmoller was also skeptical about finding any laws of human development and rejected as useless a search for a philosophy of history. Nevertheless, like many of the earlier writers utilizing the historical approach, Schmoller saw mankind passing through a series of stages of economic development; his five stages were: village, town, territorial, national, and world. This repeated emphasis on a series of stages in the development of an economy as a part of the Historical School's approach is more than a matter of historical perspective. All of the writers in the Historical School wished to stress that any economy or society was a complicated and interrelated affair, with economics playing an important but by no means dominant role. The simple economic determinism of Marx was denied as the controlling factor in moving mankind from one stage to another. The path had been pointed out for later writers by Schmoller and members of the early school. For example, Schmoller, in his massive two-volume work (called *Outline,* in typical German fashion), not only attempted to respond to Karl Menger's criticisms (see Chapter IX) but covered a wide range of subjects, including the nature and causes of economic progress. Our next two writers, Max Weber and Werner Sombart, dwelt on the process by which capitalism developed, and they substituted religion for economics as a major factor in promoting change.

MAX WEBER (1864–1920)

The Man. Few individuals have had a more distinguished career in the social sciences than Max Weber. Born in Berlin, the son of a wealthy, conservative politician, Weber began his academic career studying jurisprudence and after graduation became a judge in Berlin. His first research on the history of labor in eastern Germany won him a chair of economics at the University of Freiburg. Later he returned to the University of Heidelberg, where he had been trained, and then moved to the University of Munich. Weber won his renown not only in the field of economics but for his studies in sociology, history, and religion. As an author, Weber wrote many books, but we will list only some of his major works. Included among these are *The City, Theory of Social and Economic Organization,* and *The Methodology of the Social Sciences.* Most of these are now available in English translation and a number of them are now in paperback editions; the list is made even more impressive when we remember that Weber suffered from poor health during much of his later life. It is obviously beyond the scope of this book to attempt even to summarize the contents of this impressive array. We will confine ourselves, therefore, to a brief evaluation of the book which won Weber perhaps his most enduring fame. This noted book is *The Protestant Ethic and the Rise of Capitalism.* Weber agreed with the Classical School's picture of man as an individual motivated by self-interest and driving to maximize profits; he defined capitalism as trading for profit and characterized by the existence of a bureaucracy dedicated to making money and a well-disciplined labor force which saw work as a fulfillment of its role in life.

Economic Views. Although all men were judged as being engaged in the pursuit of profit, Weber was primarily interested in the motivation which led the business leaders of the capitalist economies to be so unremitting in this pursuit. Weber applied the historical method to the solution of this question. As he examined the backgrounds of business leaders in Protestant and Catholic countries alike, he detected what he believed to be an important common trait. Virtually all of them were Protestant; not only that, they were a particular brand of Protestant—Calvinists. What lay in the Calvinist philosophy which might prompt this kind of response? Fortunately we can indicate the essence of Weber's answer to this question without becoming involved in subtle theological doctrine. Calvin had preached the doctrine of predestination—a man was either saved or condemned to perdition from the time of his birth. No acts of grace or commission of sins could alter this immutable decision by God. Aimed at the sale of dispensations and the commission of other excesses by the Catholic Church, this doctrine of Calvin was not particularly comforting to his followers. How was anyone to know what his eventual fate would be? While no definite answer was possible, a man might be able to take some comfort by performing well his assigned role in life. Not only did hard work help men to overcome some of their basic anxiety, but worldly success might be construed as some evidence of God's favor and the possibility of ultimate redemption. Even lowly workers, by answering their "calling" and performing well those tasks allotted to them, might receive some assurance of eventual entrance into heaven. Unfortunately, the Calvinist creed was frequently interpreted as meaning that success here on earth was strong evidence of equal success in an afterlife. Failure became, in the eyes of many, something to be despised rather than condoned and comforted. Whereas St. Thomas Aquinas and the Catholic philosophers had preached a doctrine of "just price" and had warned that the securing of excessive profits was a sin, the Calvinist creed saw nothing sinful in the amassing of profits; wealth was a sign of accomplishment, and while the money thus amassed was to be put to the service of the Lord, one did not have to be too squeamish about the method by which it was amassed. Many of the factory owners against whom the socialists had railed were ardent churchgoers who saw no sin in the low wages and miserable working conditions they provided their workers.

Much of Weber's work was of this character—sweeping generalizations drawn from historical research—and his writing has sparked endless controversy. *The Protestant Ethic* has received wide criticism;[3] some of the criticism has been unfair in that it considered this single study in isolation and failed to recognize that Weber never thought of religious values as the sole determining factor shaping change. In his *General Economic History,* for example, he also stressed the role of the state and the development of modern technology. Some critics have denied that the capitalistic drive was any less important in Catholic countries or those with other religious beliefs, citing the early history of the Mediterranean countries or the emergence of Japan as a modern industrial nation. One critic was inclined to accept the connection between religion and economic development but argued that Weber had stressed the wrong religion; this man was another great member of the German Historical School named Werner Sombart.

[3] Douglas C. North has tested the thesis as an explanation of economic development in the United States. See his *The Economic Growth of the United States* (Englewood Cliffs, N.J.: Prentice-Hall, 1961). Students interested in the subject should see R. H. Tawney's *Religion and the Rise of Capitalism: A Historical Study.* (New York: Harcourt, Brace, 1926).

WERNER SOMBART (1863–1941)

The Man. Sombart was the son of a wealthy German farmer who was active in politics as a member of the German Reichstag. He attended the University of Berlin, where he received his doctorate. After a brief period of work for a chamber of commerce, he decided to enter the academic profession but was handicapped by his known admiration for the views of Marx. As a result, he was unable to secure an appointment at the University of Berlin and was forced to accept a post at one of the lesser known universities. He was not appointed to the faculty of the University of Berlin until he was in his mid-fifties. The ideas of Sombart outlined below are found in his two major works, *Modern Capitalism* and *The Jews and Modern Capitalism.* Readers can find a capsule version of the first book in Sombart's famous article on "Capitalism" in the *Encyclopedia of the Social Sciences.*

Economic Views. Sombart depicted capitalism as one of many stages through which mankind has passed, and he subdivided it into three periods—early, high, and late. The early period existed prior to the Industrial Revolution; the peak or high period extended from that era to the time when Sombart was writing, which marked the beginning of the final or late period. During the unfolding of these three stages, capitalism had inflicted many important changes on society; great movements of population took place as techniques of mass production accompanied the development of mass markets. Like Marx, Sombart saw the capitalistic system plagued by the existence of monopoly and business cycles. Sombart saw capitalism passing through various phases, but unlike Marx, he saw no foreseeable end to its existence. As the third period of late capitalism emerged, however, much of its vibrant energy would be lost due to declines in population, decreases in investment opportunities, and a loss by entrepreneurs of their sense of adventure and willingness to undertake daring new projects. Whereas Marx had seen life for the workers becoming steadily worse, Sombart believed that their lot would be made more attractive through the development of cooperatives and the rise of various state controls.

Sombart questioned the existence of a universal drive in all men to improve their condition; they had to be educated to a desire to better themselves. The real drive for economic progress came from a comparatively small handful of men, Jews possessed by a burning desire to make profits —a desire prompted in part by their inability to distinguish themselves in any other way in a society which treated them as an alien minority. Whereas Weber had believed that this drive was manifested among the Calvinists, Sombart assigned responsibility to the Jews. Sombart stressed several bits of evidence in support of this conclusion. He pointed to historical evidence indicating that those cities which the Jews had left declined in economic activity, while those cities to which they migrated suddenly prospered. He argued that many of the financial components of a modern capitalistic system, such as banks, credit, stock markets, and installment selling, were the product of Jewish thinking. Finally, he argued in much the same fashion as Weber had about Calvinism that the spirit of Jewish religion inculcated a drive toward profit-making and business activity.

While Sombart substituted Judaism for Calvinism as the energizing force behind the businessman, he agreed with Weber's thesis that the Protestant doctrine gave workers a sense of fulfillment. It was essential to the development of capitalism that workers be docile and passive; it was this task which Puritanism performed. Calvinist doctrine induced workers to accept their fate peaceably and to bow to the commands of their capitalist employers.

Always a dubious "hero" at best in Sombart's scheme, the Jew became more and more the villain in Sombart's later writings. As his early admiration for Marx faded, Sombart grew increasingly hostile to Socialism. Just as he had seen the Jews as the ones responsible for the development of capitalism, so, too, he believed, were Jews responsible for the spread of Socialism. The sad fact is that Sombart in his later years became a Nazi and the doctrines of racism played an increasingly important role in his writing. Even in the absence of this distasteful development, however, Sombart's thesis of the connection between capitalism and Judaism cannot really be considered proved. The question about Weber's thesis which R. H. Tawney raised in his *Religion and the Rise of Capitalism* can be raised with equal force on Sombart's thesis as well: To what extent was the interrelation between capitalism and religious belief a two-way street, with religious beliefs being shaped by, rather than shaping the character of capitalism?

Werner Sombart was the last of the German Historical School; many scholars argue that the school really came to an end with World War I. If we terminate Sombart's association with the school at that date and ignore the later manifestations of his thinking, we can find much to admire in his work. He used historical technique in the best sense of the term, and in so doing achieved a blend of history and theory of which many other members of the school were never capable. It is unfortunate that his later views on race have necessarily tarnished the reputation of one who otherwise might have been accorded more recognition.

English Counterparts. Thus far, it seems that the Historical School was confined entirely to German economists. Actually that impression is not very far from the truth; the Historical School made little progress in other countries and won only a scattering of followers in France and elsewhere on the Continent. It did have some limited appeal in England, however, and brief note must be taken of two exponents of the historical method in that country, Richard Jones and T. E. Cliffe Leslie.

RICHARD JONES (1790–1855)

As may be inferred from the above dates, Jones can most properly be classed as a forerunner of the Historical School. He did urge use of the historical and statistical method, however, and his criticisms of the Classical School are of a nature which justify his inclusion at this point, even though chronologically speaking he should have been presented earlier.

The Man. Following his education at Cambridge, Jones was appointed a professor of political economy at King's College, London. He remained at this post for only two years, resigning to succeed Malthus at Haileybury College. There he remained until his retirement. The period centering around the change between the two institutions was the most productive era of Jones' writing. The rest of his time he found too occupied with his teaching duties and his position as commissioner of tithes to allow for much new writing. His best-known work is *An Essay on the Distribution of Wealth and on the Sources of Taxation, Part I: Rent.* A more complete version of his economic views is to be found in his *Textbook of Lectures on the Political Economy of Nations,* published three years before his death. A final book, *Literary Remains,* was edited by William Wherrel and published in 1859, four years after his death.

Economic Views. Like many other critics of the Classical School, Jones centered his fire on David Ricardo. Part of Jones' aversion to Ricardo's thinking stemmed from the former's conviction that the Classical School's laws of production were better supported by empirical research than were its laws of distribution. Jones was particularly skeptical of Ricardo's theory of rent. The basic problem with this theory, in Jones' view, was that it rested on the twin assumptions of diminishing returns and variations in fertility. In Jones' view, Malthus and Smith came nearer to the point when they suggested that rent might also be a product of the bounteousness of nature as well as of its niggardliness. Empirical evidence suggested, said Jones, that rents were likely to be the highest in those countries where the level of productive efficiency in agriculture was very high. Thus Ricardo was wrong in thinking his theory was everywhere and at all times applicable.

Jones' conclusions about the nature of rent were substantiated by studies of various economies during different periods of historical development and under varying property arrangements. In all cases, however, the same basic fact held true—rent was made possible because nature yielded to the most primitive tiller of the soil a product which was in excess of his subsistence needs. At the same time, however, land in a particular economy might be so scarce as to make it necessary for the cultivator of even the least fertile tracts to pay a rent. Only "farmer" rents were set by Ricardo's principles; "peasant" rents, which played the larger role in the world scene, were a function of custom rather than competition. This distinction was later picked up and developed by J. S. Mill.

Although he found parts of Malthus' economic reasoning more palatable than Ricardo's, Jones also objected to the more sweeping conclusions of Malthus' population theory. Having rejected the idea that diminishing returns must inevitably govern agricultural output, it is not surprising that he resisted the conclusion that any country would soon run into economic difficulties because of the rising numbers in the population.

Summary and Evaluation. Richard Jones has long remained a minor and little-known figure in the history of economic thought. John Stuart Mill used his work but gave it scanty recognition, while Roscher, without supporting his charge, simply remarked that Jones had not understood Ricardo. As a forerunner of the Historical School, he did not share the aversion of many of the later members of that school to all economic laws of a universal nature, but he questioned most strenuously the laws of distribution as formulated by Ricardo. His insistence that more reliance should be put on inductive methods, and that economists should view the world as it really was, fell on deaf ears.

THOMAS EDWARD CLIFFE LESLIE (1827?–1882)

The Man. Like John Stuart Mill, Leslie began his education under the guidance of his father, who was an able teacher. Eventually, Leslie entered Trinity College in Dublin, where he was a classmate of J. E. Cairnes, whose views on methodology he was later to criticize vigorously. Upon graduation, he moved to London, where he studied law and was called to the English bar. He did not practice his profession, but from 1853 on, he served as professor of jurisprudence and political economy at Queen's College, Belfast. Evidently his duties in this post were not excessive, since he maintained residence in London throughout the appointment.

Economic Views. No major treatise emerged from his pen, unless we include his essays on land reform titled *The Land Reforms of England, Ireland, and the Continent.* Much of his writing effort was devoted to journal articles, most of which were collected in his *Essays in Political Economy* and *Essays in Political and Moral Philosophy.* Unfortunately, during a trip to France, Leslie lost the single copy of a virtually completed manuscript on English economic and legal history.

In keeping with other members of the Historical School, Leslie took sharp exception to the deductive method as constructed by the Classical School. One of his prime targets was Cairnes, whose methodology Leslie claimed to be sterile and divorced from economic and political reality. Leslie prided himself on his break with the Classical economist on other grounds as well. He was sharply critical of Ricardo's assumptions of perfect mobility of factors of production, and he complimented Alfred and Mary Marshall on their realism in analyzing the industrial scene. Again, like other members of the Historical School, Leslie criticized the members of the Classical School (and in particular Ricardo) for their unrealistic presentation of human motivations.

Summary and Evaluation. Leslie's contribution to the history of economic thought is not large; he is best remembered for his criticism and dissent rather than for the positive contributions in his historical and agricultural studies. The *Westminster Review,* perhaps, made the most telling and cogent criticism of Leslie when it suggested that his mind was better for attack than for construction.[4]

[4] "Politico-Economical Heterodoxy: Cliffe Leslie," *Westminster Review,* Vol. XII, p. 222.

An Overall Appraisal. It is difficult to summarize accurately the writing of so numerous and diverse a group of writers as comprised the German Historical School. Not only did they criticize the Classical School, but they were frequently highly critical of each other's writing as well. Certain general areas of agreement can, however, be noted. In addition to their criticism of the methodology of the Classical School, all of the Historical School's followers believed that man's motivations were far more complex than earlier writers had conceived them to be. All of the writers in the Historical School were either skeptical of the very existence of economic laws, or, if they did exist, doubted whether they could be discovered. In addition, most of them were firm believers in the desirability of capitalism, although most of them rejected the laissez-faire version sponsored by the Classical School. They were antagonistic to the ideas of Marx, although they owed some intellectual debt to his use of the historical method. As part of their resistance to Marxism and in their search for a more workable economy, all of them were social and economic reformers. It was by means of reform that the system was to be rendered more operable and satisfying, rather than by its complete overthrow.

Had the writers of the Historical School stopped with their denial of universal and abstract laws of economics and their insistence that such laws must be substantiated with concrete empirical evidence of a given time and place, they would have won much wider support. Unfortunately, they insisted on going beyond this and sought to find in history equally universal and binding "laws." Their stages of history became as inevitable to them as the Classical laws had for the writers they criticized.

Put in perspective, the school becomes but an eddy in the stream of economic thought. Like many eddies, it tended to become stagnant and held back the development of economic theory in Germany for nearly half a century. Nevertheless, the school did make some important contributions. Its emphasis on the need for further historical research has eventually resulted in a firmer acceptance of the value of empirical research and a cessation of the tiring and pointless argument between its supporters and those of the theoretical school; the end result has been a fusion of the two. The impact on later economists can be seen in the growth of institutional economics; we will encounter the views of the members of this school in Chapter XI. Meanwhile, we should note finally that the German Historical School's rejection of a labor theory of value and its emphasis on the importance of use value set the stage for the writers we will meet in the next chapter—the members of the Marginal Utility School.

CHAPTER IX: The Concept of Marginal Utility

Up till about forty years ago [these words were written in 1909] books on the subject of economics were, as a rule, written in fairly plain language. No one of ordinary education could seriously mistake Adam Smith's reasoning; and Mill, except here and there, was reasonably explicit and comprehensible. During the later years of the nineteenth century, however, a different state of things supervened. It began in England with the publication of Jevons' Theory of Political Economy, *followed as it was, shortly afterward by the acclimatization in England of the works of the German writers known as those of the Austrian school. Since this period the science has been every day more and more encumbered with a mass of phraseology. . . .*
—WILLIAM WARRAND CARLILE

. . . economics that leaves out the subjective theory of value is built on air.
—EUGEN BÖHM VON BAWERK

One aspect of the history of economic thought which fascinates many of its students is the pursuit of an economic theory back to the person or persons with whom it originated. For this reason our economic journals abound with articles identifying some hitherto little-known economist as the first Keynesian or the early forerunner of some other modern school of thought. For those who take great relish in "setting the record straight," our next school—the Marginal Utility School—has been a particular source of delight. We have already encountered suggestions of the possible importance of utility in the determination of value from the writers we have reviewed. Adam Smith, it will be remembered, wrestled with the problem of value in use and value in exchange, and confessed an inability to explain the discrepancy between the exchange value of water and diamonds and their use value. Jeremy Bentham, who claimed to "have planted the tree of utility," never developed his principle to a full explanation of value. Although Alfred Marshall, always a devoted admirer of

David Ricardo, professed to find the seeds of the utility theory in Ricardo's distinction between riches and value, Ricardo appears to have denied any such belief when he stated, "Value in use cannot be measured by any known standard; it is differently estimated by different persons." [1]

None of these early writers grasped the importance of the marginal concept, and the first public recognition of the idea had to wait until the 1870's, when the principle of marginal utility was set forth independently by three economists, none of whom appears to have been aware at the time of his first formulation that others were also reaching the same conclusions. The members of this famous trio are William Stanley Jevons, Karl Menger, and Léon Walras. Although acceptance of the marginal utility theory had to wait until the virtually simultaneous "discovery" of these three writers, a number of minor writers had developed parts of the theory some time earlier. A more detailed review would include an appraisal of men such as Cournot, Dupuit, and von Thünen, but we will pass over these names to give recognition to Herman Heinrich Gossen. In the process, we shall also examine the views of the famous Italian economist, Vilfredo Pareto, and the great American economist, John Bates Clark, who was also a member of the school (Clark may have developed part of his thinking on the subject from his days as a student in Austria). Finally, we will note the development of the theory in Scandinavia under the leadership of the Swedish economist, Knut Wicksell.

HERMAN HEINRICH GOSSEN (1810–1858)

Jevons acknowledged Gossen as having anticipated his thinking on most of the major points, although at the time of his original formulation, Jevons was unaware of this man's work.

The Man. Gossen was born in Düren, Germany, the son of a tax collector for the French government. The father later returned to Germany, where he performed similar work for a while before turning to agriculture. Gossen entered the University of Bonn in 1829, but his father felt that two years were sufficient training for the young man to enter government service. Gossen was thus forced to take a government position, despite his strong desire to continue his education. Upon the death of his father, Gossen was happy to abandon this post, and with funds inher-

---

[1] David Ricardo, *The Principles of Political Economy and Taxation,* E. C. K. Gonner, ed. (London: Bell, 1932), p. 420.

ited from his father, became a partner in the insurance business. The venture was not a great success, and Gossen abandoned the business before all his money was lost. In 1853 he contracted typhoid fever, and later he developed tuberculosis. From 1850 to 1854 he did nothing except work on his book. When this project, upon completion, failed to arouse the attention he had hoped, his discouragement and poor health combined to bring an early death at the age of 48.

Economic Views. Judged by the impact his thinking had on his contemporaries, Gossen was a complete failure! His book, *Development of the Laws of Exchange among Men,* published four years before his death, sold only a handful of copies and attracted no attention. The failure, however, was not Gossen's but rather that of his readers (or more properly, his potential readers), who failed to recognize the importance of Gossen's theory. All of the seeds for the later growth of the marginal utility theory were planted by Gossen; if they failed to develop, it was because of the unfriendly environment in which they were planted rather than the quality of the seeds themselves. Not until twenty-five years later, after Jevons and Walras had both called attention to Gossen's theories, was the book reissued and the author accorded some of the attention he so richly deserved.

Gossen's contribution was so striking, despite its early obscurity, because he set forth two laws of consumption. The first was the basic principle of diminishing marginal utility. As successive increments of a commodity were consumed, each additional unit provided less satisfaction than had been enjoyed from the preceding unit. To make his first law realistic, Gossen assumed a comparatively short span of time and illustrated his thesis with homey examples of a man eating successive pieces of bread. On the basis of this first law, Gossen went further and suggested a second law governing consumers in their decisions with respect to varying quantities of different commodities. This second law stated that consumers arranged their expenditures so that the satisfaction derived from the last unit consumed of all commodities was equal. Not only did Gossen express clearly the essence of the marginal utility doctrine, but he also recognized the concept of marginal disutility of labor and suggested that individuals worked until the pain or disutility of additional effort was just matched by the satisfaction or utility obtained from the commodities whose purchase was made possible by the extra income. As we shall soon see, this exposition anticipated in a remarkable fashion the later views of Jevons and members of the Austrian School.

One additional feature of Gossen's analysis appealed to both Jevons and Walras; Gossen chose to treat economics in mathematical terms. In fact, he regarded mathematics as crucial to an understanding of the science. Economics dealt with results brought about by a large number of different factors; it was only possible to analyze the importance of these various factors and the manner in which they intertwined if mathematical concepts were employed. The algebra and calculus so dear to the hearts of Jevons and Walras were accorded equally high rank by Gossen.

WILLIAM STANLEY JEVONS (1835–1882)

Despite this great intellectual achievement, however, it was not Gossen but Jevons, Menger, and Walras who are usually recognized as the founders of the Marginal Utility School. Although all three of them had set forth their views in completed form by 1874, Jevons had outlined his theory in an article some seven years earlier. We will, therefore, begin our study with him and move to a consideration of the other two, at the same time taking note of some of the other figures who contributed to the spread of the doctrine.

The Man. Jevons was a member of a large family headed by a Welsh iron merchant residing in Liverpool. Fascinated with mechanics and science as a young child, Jevons obtained his education at the Mechanics Institute in Liverpool. Although Jevons' family had no academic background, they were deeply interested in intellectual matters; both his father and grandfather wrote pamphlets in the field of political economy and his mother was a poet. Jevons always had a strong sense of family attachment and was reluctant to embark for Australia when an unusually good opportunity presented itself there. His eventual decision to move to Australia and his withdrawal from the University College School in London were prompted in part by a series of financial reverses. Both the grandfather and the father lost their entire fortunes in a financial crisis. Jevons' sojourn in Australia was a lonely one, and he was happy to return to England and pursue his academic career at University College, where he eventually earned his M.A. with a gold medal.

Although the years in Australia were undoubtedly some of the loneliest of Jevons' life, they were by no means wasted. Not only did the money he saved from earnings made while there serve him in good stead upon his return to England—he held no post between 1862 and 1866 and used these savings to support himself and help finance the publication of his pamphlets—but most of his important contributions to political economy were conceived while he was in Australia. His biographer, Keynes, believed that Jevons' main ideas in the subject were all formulated during this period. Certainly Jevons had a feeling that he had achieved a great deal; he wrote his brother: ". . . in the past few months I have fortunately struck out what I have no doubt is *the true Theory of Economy,* so thorough-going and consistent, that I cannot now read other books on the subject without indignation." [2] Jevons was obviously referring to his concept of marginal utility.

Before continuing the biographical sketch of Jevons, we would like to point out that his fame does not lie solely in the realm of political economy. Jevons was a prolific writer, and he wrote a number of important works in the field of logic. Among these were *Pure Logic* and *Studies in Deductive Logic.* In his later years, however, Jevons concentrated increasingly on political economy.

Despite the fact that Jevons served as a university professor for most of his later life, he was never a great success as a lecturer. From 1863 to 1876 he was a member of the faculty at Owens College in Manchester, and for the last ten years of that period was a professor of political economy. In addition, in 1865 he was appointed professor of logic and political economy at Queen's College in Liverpool. Later, for reasons of health and because the new position offered him more time for research, Jevons accepted a similar post at University College in London.

Part of Jevons' failure to become a good professor stemmed from his own sense of inadequacy and his dread of meeting classes. In part, the explanation for this inadequacy may be found in Jevons' reluctance to teach his own ideas. Instead, he confined his lectures largely to teaching the principles set forth by Ricardo and Mill. There can be little question but that Jevons found this task distasteful and largely a waste of time; he once described Ricardo as an "able but wrong-headed man," and Mill as "an equally able and equally wrong-headed" individual.[3] It was therefore a welcome release when Jevons found that his writings provided him with sufficient income so that he no longer needed to teach, and in 1880 he resigned his post at University College in order to devote his time entirely to research.

Although Jevons eventually won much of the recognition he so anx-

[2] W. Stanley Jevons, *Letters and Journals,* Harriet Jevons, ed. (London: Macmillan, 1886), p. 151.

[3] W. Stanley Jevons, in John Maynard Keynes, *Essays in Biography* (New York: Horizon Press, 1951), p. 291.

iously sought, a major portion of his early work, like that of Gossen, went largely·unrecognized. His two early papers setting forth his doctrine of marginal utility went almost completely unnoticed. His first paper on the subject, read in his absence before the British Association, was not included in the published proceedings (it was finally published four years later as a five-page article in the *Statistical Journal*). Another five years passed before the fully developed theory emerged in Jevons' *Theory of Political Economy*. Even this more complete version received rough treatment from the critics. Alfred Marshall professed to find little in it that was new, and Cairnes, although freely confessing himself unable to follow the mathematical reasoning, found this inability to be no disqualification for his judgment that Jevons' analysis was completely wrong. Only Jevons' analysis of *The Coal Question* won broad and instantaneous public acceptance, and, ironically, this was one of the weakest of Jevons' analyses. In later years his work in statistics gained him wider recognition. In 1876 he was awarded an LL.D. by the University of Edinburgh and in 1878 he was elected a fellow of the Royal Society. Part of Jevons' failure to be accorded more attention arose from his own personality—Jevons was a lonely and introspective man whom others may have found difficult to know well. His inadequacies as a teacher meant that he developed no band of student followers to disseminate and popularize his ideas. Finally, his antagonism to the then current views on political economy and his caustic criticisms of Ricardo and Mill, and even of Alfred Marshall, did little to endear him to others. Whatever the cause, the fact remains that Jevons was outside the main circle of current thinking at the time and often unaware of thinking going on at other institutions in England.[4]

Always a devoted husband, Jevons took his wife with him on a visit to Bonhill after his retirement from University College in an attempt to regain his health. The vacation ended in tragedy when Jevons drowned (probably because of a heart attack) one afternoon while enjoying a swim. He died at the age of 47. Keynes has commented that as tragic as the loss was, Jevons had probably already made his major contribution to the field. Certainly his last book, *Principles of Political Economy* edited by Professor Henry Higgins 24 years after Jevons' death, contained no great or startling innovations in thought. In justice to Jevons, however, it should be added that the fragmentary character of this final work leaves the question of the possible value, had it been completed, highly problematic.

[4] *Ibid.*, p. 287.

Economic Views. Before we discuss Jevons' main contribution to economic thought, it is necessary to review briefly some of his lesser known ideas. Jevons wrote his book, *The Coal Question,* in 1865, about seven years after his return from Australia. In contrast to some of his theoretical work, the book won instant attention. John Stuart Mill spoke well of its message, and the publisher's astuteness in sending a copy to the Prime Minister won Jevons an interview with Mr. Gladstone.

The thesis of the study was remarkably parallel to that developed by Malthus. In what Jevons chose to call the *natural law of social growth,* he set forth the thesis that not only did population expand at a geometric rate, but its growth required a similar expansion of things needed to support the growing population. By the way of example, Jevons cited the case of coal. If England was to maintain her industrial rate of growth, production of coal—an item obviously basic to that growth—would have to increase geometrically. Jevons pointed out that "the quantity of coal consumed is really a quantity of two dimensions, the number of the people and the average quantity used by each." [5] With increases in the demand for coal coming from both directions, the supply of coal was likely to prove a serious limitation upon future expansion. Jevons acknowledged that it was unlikely that mankind could build an unlimited supply of ever larger buildings and bridges and ever longer railroad lines, but argued that men could find ". . . new applications of coal . . . of an unlimited character." [6] Like Malthus, Jevons probably overstated his case for purposes of effect, and as in the case of Malthus, some of his dire prophecies have failed to come true. The coal industry in England and the United States has been a sick one in recent years, but certainly not for the reasons advanced by Jevons.

Another aspect of Jevons' work which has continued to tarnish his reputation as an economist is his well-remembered diagnosis of the cause of business cycles. So thoroughly was Jevons rebuffed for this analysis that his extraordinarily fine work as a pioneer in statistical investigation has tended to be forgotten. It was in the course of these statistical investigations that Jevons first became interested in the question of seasonal fluctuations. From here it was an easy step (and one possibly encouraged by his father's and grandfather's losses of their life savings and his own management of savings) to turn to a study of the business cycle. Jevons' theory is

[5] *Ibid.,* p. 261.
[6] *Ibid.*

well known to students of the business cycle—he postulated a causal relationship between solar disturbances or sunspots and variations in business
conditions. Two explanations for this interrelation were deemed possible.
Either the sunspots produced alternating waves of optimism and pessimism in businessmen, thus leading them to overexpand and overinvest,
with a subsequent period of retrenchment and caution to follow, or the
sunspots caused variations in agricultural productivity, which in turn produced repercussions in the industrial sector. Jevons was not unaware of
the weaknesses of the purported relationship between sunspots and business conditions. He once abandoned the notion as foolish, only to return to
it again at a later date. When the time sequence between cycles and agricultural production in Europe proved faulty, he asserted a relationship
between Indian crop production and the resulting changes in England's
economic activity prompted by variations in her trade balance. Few if any
students of the business cycle today give any importance to the sunspot
theory; Jevons, by emphasizing the crucial role of investment was clearly
on proper ground, but his explanation of the cause of that variability
must be rejected.

As was stressed earlier, Jevons' failure to solve the riddle of the business cycle by statistical investigations should not be permitted to dim any
of the luster of his pioneer work in statistics. In this day of modern com-
puters and research assistants, the magnitude of Jevons' accomplishments
are difficult to appreciate fully. It was in his studies of variations in prices
and the value of currency that Jevons perfected the use of the index number. Keynes assigns Jevons the honor of being the "first theoretical economist to survey his material with the prying eyes and fertile, controlled
imagination of the natural scientist." [7] When we consider the vast use of
statistical techniques today, the above tribute becomes even more impressive.

A brief word about some of Jevons' views on other economic subjects is
in order. Although critical of the Classical School at many points, he was,
if anything, even more individualistic in philosophy than they had been.
Trade unions were a menace to the economy, and proposals for social
reform encountered similar opposition. At first reading, he appears to be
more "laissez than really was fair," even by the standards of his times. A
more careful study of his work, however, including his *The State in Relation to Labour*, will show that Jevons was inclined to take rather a pragmatic view and examine each case for government action individually and
judge it on its merits. Only the principle of free trade as applied to the

[7] *Ibid.*, p. 268.

international scene appeared in Jevons' view never to stand in need of qualification.

Jevons found the Classical School's treatment of the theory of value defective in three major respects. He quoted Ricardo against himself to demonstrate that even Ricardo had admitted that the labor theory of value could not be used to explain the value of all commodities. Remember that Ricardo had conceded that the value of certain rare commodities such as paintings and objects of art, which could not be reproduced, had their value determined in some other fashion. Why, asked Jevons, rely on a theory which was admittedly defective by failing to explain the value of *all* commodities? Past labor costs must always be irrelevant, said Jevons, if the demand for a commodity declines; if such was the case it was again logical to ask why we should ever claim that the amount of labor was the sole determining factor. Finally, Jevons felt that the Classical School had been too prone to dismiss the complications arising from the fact that labor was anything but homogeneous. How was it possible to equate labor of widely differing qualities so as to determine value in any meaningful fashion? As we shall see, the disutility of labor had a role to play in Jevons' thinking, but the role was distinctly subordinate, compared to its central position for earlier writers. Far less subject to possible criticism and misinterpretation, in Jevons' view, was his great new discovery —the principle of marginal utility. It was only after Jevons had completed the formulation of his theory that subsequent research revealed to Jevons that he had been anticipated at nearly every point by Gossen!

While it has been important and proper to note the variety and extent of Jevons' other contributions to economics, we must now discuss his central doctrine.

VIEWS ON MARGINAL UTILITY. It did not take long for Jevons to state the essence of his theory. On the very first page of his book *Theory of Political Economy* he stated, "Value depends entirely upon utility." He continued by emphasizing that it was not just utility but marginal utility which was of crucial importance. In Chapter 3 of his book Jevons set forth the core of his utility thesis. Here he developed his argument, using for purposes of illustration a single commodity to demonstrate his theory that the utility of any object possessed two dimensions—the quantity of it available and the intensity of feeling felt for the commodity by a consumer. Typical of his mathematical approach is Fig. 3, which is drawn to show the varying final utilities of additional amounts of food.[8]

[8] W. Stanley Jevons, *Theory of Political Economy* (London: Macmillan, 1871), p. 55.

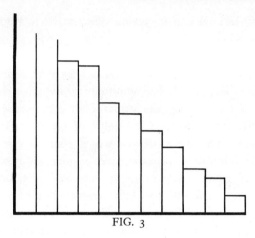

FIG. 3

The absence of a top cap on the first two units of food represents Jevons' belief that the first two units were so essential to a man's continued existence that no upper limit on their final utility could be determined. The utility obtained from each successive unit would, however, be determinable and each bar was drawn shorter than the preceding one in keeping with the principle of diminishing final utility. From this point it was possible, by assuming that one was working with infinitesimal increments of food, to draw a continuous curve looking much like our present-day demand curve. Applying calculus to the changes in amounts and utilities of these small increments, Jevons was able to conclude that "the degree of utility is . . . the differential coefficient of u [the total utility of the commodity] considered as a function of x [the amount of the commodity]." [9]

Thus far Jevons had been dealing only with individual demand as expressed in the final utility derived from varying amounts of a commodity. Jevons began his theory by denying that utility was measurable, but became less convinced of the impossibility as time went along; he toyed with the idea of using money as a measuring rod. One obvious reason for this change of heart was the difficulty of explaining the process of exchange with the use of the utility concept unless some measurability could be achieved. For simliar reasons, a second "impossibility" was altered to the status of "conceivable" when Jevons had to face the question of exchange. Throughout his theory Jevons firmly maintained that interpersonal comparisons of utility were impossible; nevertheless when he moved to the marketplace, he found it necessary to make some.

We will begin our discussion of exchange as seen by Jevons with his conclusions at the end of his chapter on exchange.

[9] *Ibid.*, pp. 60–61.

. . . though labor is never the cause of value, it is in a large proportion of cases the determining circumstance, and in the following way: Value depends solely on the final degree of utility. How can we vary this degree of utility? By having more or less of the commodity to consume. And how shall we get more or less of it? By spending more or less labour in obtaining a supply. . . .[10]

To arrive at this conclusion, Jevons began again with the individual consumer. The consumer attained a state of equilibrium with the assurance of maximum satisfaction achieved by allocating his consumption expenditures in such a manner that the final utilities derived from the commodities consumed were equal. Extending the analysis to two persons, the same principle was found to apply. Exchange would continue to take place until neither person could obtain any advantage from further trading; at this point the final utility of each person would be in proportion to the price. It was here that the question of meaningfulness of the concept in the absence of measurability of utility became apparent.

As Jevons moved to a more complex market, with many individuals involved in trade, the complications grew increasingly grave. In his attempt to convert his final utility theory for individuals into a market explanation of exchange, he devised two rather awkward and unsatisfactory concepts—the "law of indifference" and "trading bodies." [11] By the first of these, Jevons was expressing what has since become known as the principle of perfect competition. Any given commodity, regardless of by whom it was produced, was assumed to be homogeneous in nature. Unable to recognize any appreciable variations in quality, the consumer would be indifferent as to whose product he purchased. It thus stood to reason that only one price for a product could prevail in a market—consumers would be unwilling to pay anything but the price generally prevailing. One of the weaknesses of Jevons' analysis was that he never explained clearly how this one price was determined; instead he tended to take it as given.

By "trading bodies" Jevons meant any collective group of buyers or sellers; the size of the group could vary from one on upward—in effect, any number could play! Jevons then proceeded to apply the principle of exchange he had devised for any two individuals to the exchange in the larger marketplace. The result was a failure to shed any real light on how the competitive market functioned or how prices were determined.

Jevons did recognize that in order for there to be an exchange of goods, first production needed to take place. But what was to determine the

[10] *Ibid.,* pp. 159–160.
[11] *Ibid.,* Chap. 4.

amount of production of any commodity? Jevons responded by attaching to the classical view of labor as a source of pain the principle of increasing marginal disutility. "Labour," Jevons suggested, "will be carried on until the increment of utility from any of the employments just balances the increment of pain." [12] It should be emphasized again that it was in his analysis of the marketplace as we have outlined it above that Jevons came perilously close to abandoning his tenets that interpersonal comparisons of utility were possible. Offsetting this defect, at least in part, was Jevons' discussion of the possibility of a backward-sloping supply curve of labor. The point might be reached, said Jevons, where additional income would call forth not more but less effort on the part of workers who no longer needed additional income and who would shun the disutility of work.

Jevons' explanation of how distribution took place was at best sketchy; his intention to explore this subject more completely in a later book was interrupted by his accidental death. As a result, he did little more than second the Classical School's explanation of rent, and while he came close to a marginal productivity of wages in some passages, the concept always succeeded in eluding him. At times he came perilously near to accepting the wages-fund doctrine. Eventually, however, he managed to reject both the wages-fund and the subsistence theory of wages and to concentrate upon a residual explanation. Wages were what remained of the total product after deductions for rent, interest, and taxes had been made.

When it came to a discussion of capital, Jevons anticipated the Austrian writers to follow. Capital made possible an increase of output by the introduction of more efficient means of production. There was a catch to the employment of these more efficient means, however; the time lapse between the first applications of labor and the availability of the product for ultimate consumption grew increasingly great. It was capital which made this lengthening of the processes of production possible by providing workers with the means of sustaining themselves during the interim. In thus seeing interest as in part the product of the rate of increase of output, Jevons came close to setting forth the marginal productivity theory of distribution. Once again, the concept eluded his grasp, however, and he settled for little more than an abstinence theory decorated with bits of marginal utility theory.

Summary and Evaluation. Jevons built his theory of value on the utility base previously erected by Jeremy Bentham; by stressing the importance of final or marginal utility he considerably advanced the usefulness

12 *Ibid.*, p. 180.

of the concept as a determinant of value and helped set the stage for Alfred Marshall and modern explanations of demand. Although his theory, particularly as it related to the problem of exchange, was crude and awkward, later refinements and polishing revealed that the basic core was sound and well conceived. His statements were cautious and he noted many possible exceptions to his basic theory. The problems of indivisibilities was discussed, where small accretions in amount were impossible, so that buyers and sellers would be far apart in arriving at an equilibrium price, and the possibility of close substitutes distorting the decision-making process of consumers was noted. Jevons also noted that changes in the distribution of income might produce changes in the utility-maximizing effects to be achieved from exchange; greater total utility might be gained from other possible distributions; the current status quo was not necessarily the best of all possible worlds.

Jevons was an interesting blend of empirical researcher, who freely used the historical evidence to substantiate his case, and the economic theorist. In both areas he made important contributions to the discipline; his work with index numbers marked the path for future statisticians, and his theoretical concepts, as strengthened by Walras, Marshall, and others, have served as an important bulwark of modern theory.

CARL MENGER (1840–1921)

Both Jevons and Menger developed the concept of marginal utility (ironically, neither of them ever used the term), but their methods of arriving at this formulation were strikingly different. Whereas Jevons relied heavily upon mathematical techniques and believed that the only hope of making political economy truly scientific lay in extending the use of mathematics, Menger avoided all mathematical terminology. Jevons leaned heavily on the utilitarian and hedonistic psychology in his formulation of a "hedonistic calculus"; Menger was never able to free himself entirely from hedonism but he made a valiant effort in this direction. It should be added that Menger's writing, like Jevons', was seldom dull, and the analysis followed step by step in a logical and orderly fashion. Part of the difference in the approaches of the two men stems perhaps from the backgrounds against which they were reacting. Jevons was well grounded in English Classical thought and had little but contempt for its labor theory of value. Menger, on the other hand, had little or no awareness of English economic thought. At the time of Menger's university training in

Austria, there were few if any Austrian economists. Economics was taught primarily by members of the German Historical School, and it was from the domination of this school rather than from Classical thought that Menger sought to escape.

The Man. Menger was born of German parentage in the province of Galicia, later to become a part of Poland. Here Menger's father, a lawyer by profession, had settled his family on a farm. Menger's childhood was spent in this rural environment until he attended the universities of Vienna and Prague with his two brothers.[13] Upon the completion of his doctorate at the University of Cracow, he became a journalist for a few years and later entered the Austrian Civil Service. Two years after the publication of his *Principles of Economics* in 1871 (which contained the essence of his marginal utility thesis), he received a teaching position at the University of Vienna. Upon his promotion two years later, he resigned his post in the government, and except for occasional short periods of duty, such as the position of tutor to Prince Rudolph when the latter traveled throughout Europe and Great Britain, or as a consulting expert, Menger abandoned government service for an academic career. Judging by reports of former students, Menger was a remarkably effective teacher. Where Jevons had failed to develop a band of followers, Menger was the founder of the Austrian School and had a devoted group of followers. In 1903, Menger resigned his university post to devote his full attention to research and the completion of his writings on value and distribution. His *Principles* had never been revised, and he refused to permit the publication of a second edition without revisions. As so often happens, the pressures of academic work and the diverting of his interest to a study of the Austrian currency problem had prevented the fulfillment of this objective, and Menger hoped to remedy this situation by his resignation. From the time of his retirement at the age of 63 until his death some 18 years later, Menger worked diligently at the task he had set for himself, but his goal was never to be achieved. Failing eyesight hampered his work, and a desire for perfection left him ever dissatisfied with the results. As a consequence, much of his later work was a wasted effort. His son succeeded in salvaging a revised second edition of the *Principles,* but the bulk of the writing by Menger in his final years remained chaotic and fragmentary, and too disjointed to be made useful.

13 Carl Menger never seems to have shared his brothers' and his son's love of mathematics; all three, particularly his son and brother Anton, were noted mathematicians.

Economic Views. Menger's approach to the question of value was devoid of both mathematical paraphernalia and hedonistic psychology; he emphasized the role of utility in the determination of value and was as impatient as Jevons had been with a labor theory of value. The dominant overriding characteristic of any economic good was its scarcity; if consumers could obtain all they wanted of a commodity, its value would decline to zero. Increases in the demand for the product and/or declines in its supply might convert a commodity from a noneconomic commodity to an economic good, but until that happened, the problem of value did not exist. Scarcity was seen as a crucial but not sufficient attribute for determining the value of a product. Menger added four other qualities which defined an economic good. These were: (1) a felt human need—the scarcity of a commodity was obviously irrelevant if it proved to be a medicine for which there was no disease; (2) the ability of the commodity to satisfy the need; (3) consumers' awareness of the commodity's ability to satisfy the need; and (4) the ability of the consumer to utilize the commodity so as to satisfy his need. One of the functions of an economic system was to supply the know-how to make the fulfillment of this last requirement possible.

Men's needs were a complex and interrelated affair and the number of the needs and the complexity of those needs increased as the civilization progressed. Fortunately, as the problem grew increasingly difficult, man's ability to discriminate and make rational economic choices also increased. Economic rationality implied choice, said Menger, and happily, men were becoming increasingly good choosers as time passed. In his discussion of economic goods, Menger wrote of two kinds of goods: those which could be immediately consumed and those which, when combined with others, made possible the production of goods of the first order. We shall shortly examine the value of the second kind, which were subdivided in terms of their proximity to the consumer. Let us first, however, examine the determination of the value of a single consumer commodity and its relationship to other consumer goods.

The essence of the consumer decision-making process resembled that set forth by Jevons and Gossen. Successive amounts of any product added less satisfaction than their predecessors had, and the consumer found the product less attractive as its availability increased. Air, without which man could not live, became valueless because of its superabundance. Furthermore, consumers had different intensities of wants for different kinds of goods. If they became scarce, air or water would become exceedingly valuable; necessities of this nature comprised a higher kind of wants than did luxury items such as tobacco. To illustrate this principle, Menger devised the accompanying table:[14]

I	II	III	IV	V	VI	VII	VIII	IX	X
10	9	8	7	6	5	4	3	2	1
9	8	7	6	5	4	3	2	1	0
8	7	6	5	4	3	2	1	0	
7	6	5	4	3	2	1	0		
6	5	4	3	2	1	0			
5	4	3	2	1	0				
4	3	2	1	0					
3	2	1	0						
2	1	0							
1	0								
0									

The Roman numerals represent the different kinds of wants; I, representing food, was of a higher kind (more essential and thus subject to a greater intensity of need) than IV, such as tobacco. The Arabic numbers under each Roman numeral represented the declining satisfaction to be obtained from additional units of the commodity in question. Thus again was Adam Smith's old paradox of diamonds and water resolved. Although bread represented a higher kind of want (lower Roman number) on the scale of concrete wants, it rated low in value because of its relative abundance. Correspondingly diamonds, which had a low want rating, had a high concrete want because of their scarcity. Reading from the table, it is easy to divine a consumer's decisions; new kinds of wants would be satisfied as the satisfaction gained from additional units of more intense kinds of wants declined. Thus the first unit of income would be spent on I–10, but additional income expenditures would be divided among other kinds of want so that the scale of concrete want satisfaction was equal for the last units of each different kinds of want. More concretely, if we let (as Menger did) I stand for food and IV for tobacco, the consumer would begin the purchase of tobacco with the fourth unit of food.

The use of the numbers is misleading. Menger did not wish to assert the possibility of cardinal utility but only of ordinal utility—it was relative differences in satisfaction obtained of which Menger believed the consumer to be capable. Unfortunately, Menger did not always make this clear, and the process by which the individual consumer arrived at a satisfaction-maximizing equilibrium was not always apparent. The careless

[14] Karl Menger, *Principles of Economics,* trans. by James Dungwall and Bert F. Hoselitz (Glencoe, Ill.: Free Press, 1950), p. 127.

reader guided by the numbers was tempted to equate the fourth unit of food and the first unit of tobacco as providing exactly the same satisfaction.

It is particularly regrettable that Menger left himself open to such misinterpretation, because in several ways his presentation is markedly superior to that of Jevons or indeed that of his own followers. He avoided the use of the rather simple-minded examples of diminishing marginal utility employed by Gossen and Jevons, where the consumer was fed successive units of a good in rapid succession until satiated. Menger postulated instead a situation where the consumer was forced to make choices between food, tobacco, and other goods over a longer span of time, but with the limitation of a restricted budget.

Like Jevons, Menger felt that it was impossible to compare the satisfaction obtained by different individuals. Unlike Jevons, however, and in distinct contrast to his disciples, Böhm von Bawerk and von Wieser, Menger was less prone to relax this assumption to fit the exigencies of his analysis. The satisfactions experienced by the man of wealth were distinctly different from those enjoyed by consumers with low incomes. Menger was not guilty of the more naïve views about the quantification of utility; if anything, he tended to minimize the problem of measurability as an impossible question and thus to gloss over some of the difficulties. By so doing, he ignored the relationship between utility and demand.

Menger did not stop when he had "solved" the problem of the value of final consumer goods, but attempted to apply his solution to those "goods of higher order," [15] which directly satisfied no consumer need. Just because they did not directly satisfy the needs of consumers was no reason to neglect them or to fail to include them as economic goods. From whence did these production goods (the flour and wheat as contrasted to the bread) obtain their value? The answer, said Menger, was simple. One had only to trace back from the final finished product to the components, going into that "good of a first order" to find out the contribution of each of the goods entering into its production. The unit of consumption which would have to be forfeited in the absence of the "higher" good determined the value of that higher good.

DISTRIBUTION. Without realizing it, Menger had made an accurate, if not entirely complete, presentation of the marginal productivity theory of distribution. Menger made little further reference to his division of goods into various ranks, and appeared to be content with the classification and the comments noted above. Again, like Jevons, Menger never seriously

[15] *Ibid.,* p. 165.

entertained the merits of the cost of production theory of value. Perhaps if he had pondered upon this possibility longer, the marginal productivity analysis might have taken clearer shape.

Deeply imbedded in Menger's analysis of distribution was the importance of time. The use of capital to lengthen the period of production and thereby increase productivity—a matter of great importance to Böhm von Bawerk—was clearly recognized by Menger, and the role of the rate of interest in preventing undue applications of capital was also clearly recognized. Menger also recognized the role of entrepreneurial activity—it was the entrepreneur who was responsible for the accurate assigning of factors of production to their most fruitful place. One of the merits of Menger's analysis was that it treated all factors alike. Land and the rent it received were no longer a special case to be explained in a special manner. Rent, wages, and profits all received payment in accordance with their values as determined at the margin.

The brightness of Menger's analysis of distribution did not illuminate all the crevices; murky, obscure points still remained. His analysis would have been greatly strengthened if he had been willing to use diagrams, and his failure to accord recognition to the principle of diminishing returns led to peculiar conclusions about the appropriate amount of factors to be employed when one assumed increasing returns instead.

EXCHANGE. Menger's analysis of the process of exchange was superior to Jevons' in several respects. No reference was made to the awkward concept of "trading bodies," and the assumption of perfect competition was only one of a number of situations in which exchange might occur. Exchange took place not because of any inherent propensity of men to truck and barter as Smith had postulated, but because different individuals valued various commodities differently. Where divergences in subjective value existed, opportunities for mutual gain from trade would exist. Subjective value set the limits in terms of the price and the quantities which would be exchanged. One trader, rich in commodity A, would place a low value on it, and a high value on commodity B, while another trader might find himself in the reverse situation, with a corresponding reversal of subjective valuations. As the first trader gave up amounts of commodity A, its subjective value to him would rise, while the increasing amounts of commodity B would cause a lowering of the value of additional units of B. Other traders would be affected in a corresponding fashion. Exchange would come to an end when ". . . one of the two bargainers has no further quantity of goods which is of less value to him than a quantity of another good at the disposal of the second bargainer who, at the same time, evaluates the two quantities of goods inversely." [16] A situation of monopoly might distort the picture somewhat, but much the same solution would still prevail. Menger suggested that the results in case of monopoly might be indeterminate, and would depend upon the relative bargaining strength of the parties and whether or not the monopolist chose to discriminate among sellers. With these qualifications, the same solution prevailed; the price the monopolist could obtain would be limited by the subjective value placed on the commodity by the most eager marginal buyer. Money was no added complication, whether the situation be one of competition or monopoly. It added another step to the analysis, but its existence not only made the process of exchange simpler than a crude barter arrangement, but eased the problem of quantification of subjective values.

METHODOLOGY. Menger's *Principles* aroused little interest among the members of the German Historical School; his theorizing seemed so unlikely and impossible to them as not to even merit their attention. Menger ignored the old adage of permitting dormant canines to continue their slumbers and launched a vigorous attack on the Historical School's aversion to theory. In his second book, *Studies in the Methods of the Social Sciences and of Political Economy in Particular,* Menger criticized the Historical method for its unwillingness to accord any importance to deductive theorizing. His attack was harsh and biting, and it was answered in kind. Schmoller, the head of the German Historical School, responded in a biting review of Menger's book, and Menger replied in a pamphlet titled *Methodenstreit.* From this point on, the battle grew increasingly warm. Schmoller, as editor of one of the economic journals, rejected an article by Menger and printed instead his letter of rejection. The letter was not exactly a model of politeness, and now the disciples of both masters joined the fray. The dispute continued for nearly a generation, and was partially but not completely ended when Schmoller in his two-volume *Outline* accorded recognition to Menger's analysis and attempted to blend the two approaches. The common-sense solution that there was merit in using both methods in studying the questions of political economy was at last achieved.

Summary and Evaluation. Menger's claims to originality are every bit as impressive as Jevons', and his analysis, despite his lack of mathematical training, was at a number of points markedly superior. His life was that of a scholar, and while not unsympathetic to ideas for social reform, he did little to advance them. Although named a member of the upper

[16] *Ibid.,* p. 187.

chamber of the Austrian Parliament in 1900, for example, he never served actively in this post. Much of his claim to recognition might have been lost by his failure to revise and republish his work if his ideas had not been picked up and popularized by his students and admirers. From this loyal group, who together with Menger constitute the Austrian School, two names stand out—Eugen Böhm von Bawerk and Friedrich von Wieser. Before turning to the third member of the great trilogy of Marginal Utilists, Léon Walras, we will complete the story in Austria by a brief consideration of these two authors and pay our respects to their American proponent of marginalism, John Bates Clark.

FRIEDRICH VON WIESER (1851–1926)

Rarely, if ever, have the lives and economic writings of two economists who were not close relatives been more inextricably intertwined than those of von Wieser and Böhm von Bawerk. Both were born in Austria in the same year, both went to the same Gymnasium, they were classmates at the same university, and both became ardent disciples of Carl Menger, although neither of them was a student in his classes. Both attended a seminar under the direction of Knies and both served as university professors and as government ministers. Von Wieser was a minister of commerce, while Böhm von Bawerk occupied the post of minister of finance. Both made notable contributions to the popularization and dissemination of the doctrine of marginal utility. The bond between the two men was completed by Böhm von Bawerk's marriage to von Wieser's sister. Despite these close ties between the two men, some noteworthy differences in their contributions to the history of economic thought exist, and we will treat the two separately.

The Man. In view of the facts cited in the preceding paragraph, our biographical sketch can be correspondingly abbreviated. Born in Vienna into a family of highly placed civil servants, von Wieser received his academic training at the university in law and economics. Originally he had intended to undertake the study of history, but whether because of events in Austria at the time or because of the stimulus received from reading Spencer and Tolstoy, von Wieser decided current social relationships were more important. In order to understand these, however, von Wieser felt it was necessary to understand the economic relationships, and the key to understanding these was the subject of value. After the completion of a two-year traveling fellowship spent in Knies' class in Heidelberg, von Wieser returned to Austria and served as a fiscal administrator in lower Austria for seven years. For a brief period he was a lecturer at the University of Vienna, and then, upon the recommendation of Menger, was granted a professorship at the University of Prague; there he remained until his return to the University of Vienna in 1903 to fill the chair left vacant by Menger's retirement. Thereafter, his career alternated between service in the government and teaching at his post in Vienna. In later years his research concentrated on the problems of determining the value of money and various issues in public finance. His interest also turned increasingly to problems of sociology, and his last work, published shortly before his death, was a study of the role of elites. His two major works in economics were *Natural Value* and *Social Economics*.

Economic Views. Although all of the writers of this school are frequently included under the label "marginal utility" theorists, it was not until von Wieser's theories appeared that the term was coined. His claim to recognition is far more than simply a matter of nomenclature, however, and von Wieser's concept of alternative or opportunity costs advanced in considerable detail the ideas set forth by Menger and led to frequent references to these ideas as Wieser's Law. Since the concept of "opportunity" cost was so central to von Wieser's thinking, it is appropriate that we begin our examination of his contribution there.

The road to the determination of value was the familiar one well trod by the other economists of this school we have already encountered. The problem remained of how to determine the value or the price paid for the use of the various factors of production. Von Wieser's suggestion was that the price paid to a factor of production was necessitated not by the need to call forth the factor into the market but was the price needed to attract the factor away from some other pursuit. Put in its simplest terms, the alternative cost was the price one had to pay to use the factor for one purpose rather than have it employed elsewhere. The idea strengthened the position of the Marginal Utility School and provided an alternative explanation to the real cost theory as enunciated by the Classical School. Instead of reading forward from cost of production to determine the value of products, von Wieser was suggesting that the correct procedure was to reverse the analysis. Since the value of all commodities was dependent upon marginal utility, the cost of their production was not a decisive factor in the determination of their value. Factors of production would be employed in producing those products which had the greatest marginal utility and for which the best return could be made. The value of a factor in the production of commodity B was determined by the price it could obtain in the production of commodity A, if one assumed that commodity A made the most effective use of the factor. It was competition for the factors of production in their various uses which assured the distribution of factors in such a way as to bring them the same return in every alternative use. Note that with all this elaboration on the value of producer goods it was still the individual consumer with his wants that was the end-all and be-all of the analysis.

Von Wieser's book *Natural Value* is of interest because it represented a bridge between a socioeconomic philosophy, with its emphasis on social forces and a belief in changing stages in economic history, and the individualistic emphasis of the Marginal Utility School. Von Wieser analyzed the problem of value in various stages of history, ranging from the individual or simple economy to the social or group economy and the state and world economy. His book was the only really comprehensive review of economic theory to emerge from the writers of the subjective school.

To begin with, von Wieser had concentrated on value as it was determined in a Communistic society. In an ideal economy free of monopoly, selfishness, and inequalities of wealth and human error, the principle of marginal utility could be applied to the choices of the entire economy as well as to the individual. Since the real world contained all of these imperfections and more, divergences between price and natural value persisted; natural value was no longer the sole determinant of price—the other factors played an important role. Throughout all of these stages, however, the principle of marginal utility still remained operative.

Although the marginal utility theorists are usually interpreted as staunch defenders of the capitalist system, the above analysis led von Wieser to have some doubts. In his view the existence of monopoly and gross inequalities in the distribution of income acted to upset the principle of maximum satisfaction derived from the universal application of the principle of marginal utility. The wants of the "wanton and the glutton" were satisfied instead of those of the "miserable and the poor." [17] The conclusion he left to be drawn, that the marginal utility principle could operate as well under a Socialist as a capitalistic system, was seized upon by later proponents of the efficacy of Socialist planning, such as Oscar Lange.

Von Wieser's treatment of the role of the state was reminiscent of John Stuart Mill's approach; the laws of production were fixed but those of

[17] Friedrich von Hayek on von Wieser in *The Development of Economic Thought*, Henry W. Spiegel, ed. (New York: Wiley, 1952), p. 565.

distribution were subject to considerable interference. Von Wieser was thus no doctrinaire exponent of laissez-faire. The government not only had a role in protecting the weak and performing necessary activities insufficiently profitable for private enterprise to undertake, but for those countries which were in the early stages of their development, the government, by judicious use of state intervention and planning, could greatly increase the process of industrialization.

Summary and Evaluation. Von Wieser's primary contribution to economic thought was in the area of cost and distribution. Although he was a disciple of Menger, he was in many respects an individualist who relied little on the views and contributions of previous writers or of his contemporaries. Friedrich von Hayek reported, for example, in his *Development of Economic Thought,* that it was doubtful whether von Wieser ever discussed his views with his brother-in-law, Böhm von Bawerk.[18] Von Wieser was not always able to avoid the use of interpersonal comparisons of marginal utility; his contrasts between the ideal state where natural value prevailed, on the one hand, and the real world around us, on the other, implicitly assumed the possibility of making such comparisons. Von Wieser was never a major figure in the history of economic thought, and his first book is seldom read today. His *Social Economics* might have had greater success if its appearance had not been overshadowed by the outbreak of World War I.

EUGEN BÖHM VON BAWERK (1851–1914)

Where von Wieser had concentrated on the problems of cost and distribution as explained in marginal utility terms, Böhm von Bawerk's chief contribution lay in the field of capital and interest. In treating these subjects, he dealt extensively with the problem of time and time preference—a subject hitherto virtually completely neglected.

The Man. Böhm von Bawerk was born into a family of civil servants; his father was the vice-governor of Moravia. An early passion for the study of science was diverted into the study of law and economics, but he never lost the scientific thirst for knowledge for the sake of knowledge and tended to set aside moral considerations and value judgments as im-

[18] Friedrich von Wieser, *Natural Value,* trans. by Christian A. Mallock (London: Macmillan, 1893), p. 58.

proper for the study of either law or economics. After graduation, Böhm von Bawerk's career alternated between government service and university teaching. Following a brief period as fiscal administrator of lower Austria, he accepted a post in the Ministry of Finance. His academic career began at the University of Innsbruck, where he was made a full professor at the age of 37. Although he remained there for only a comparatively short time, less than ten years, those years were among the most productive and contented periods of his life; much of his basic theory was formulated during this period and his marriage to von Wieser's sister proved to be a delightful alliance.

In 1889 he resigned from the University of Innsbruck to accept a post in the Ministry of Finance. Here he had the responsibility for working out the great Austrian tax reform, which finally was passed in 1896. During the latter part of this period the lure of academic life led him to accept a special lectureship at the University of Vienna. When the offer of a full professorship came in the last years of his life at this institution, he accepted, and he remained there until his death. Among his best-known books are *The Positive Theory of Capital* and *Karl Marx and the Close of His System.*

Economic Views. As in the case of von Wieser, there is no need to restate the familiar principle of marginal utility as set forth by Menger; Böhm von Bawerk's contribution here was primarily that of popularizer, and the relevant chapters in his *Positive Theory of Capital* contain, even today, one of the clearest statements of that principle. The descriptive term "popularizer" is thus more than appropriate; unfortunately the popularizer did not always exercise the care and precision in his terminology that Menger had displayed.

Böhm von Bawerk's originality lay in his effort to apply the marginal utility theory of value to a clearer explanation of price and to the determination of interest. He was markedly more successful in the second of these two ventures, although his theory of interest is less widely accepted today than formerly. Price, said Böhm von Bawerk, was a social phenomenon resulting from different valuations placed on the same commodity by different buyers and sellers. Obviously, if at least two people did not value a commodity differently in relation to other commodities, no exchange involving that particular commodity would ever take place. Normally this was no problem, and the question was to determine what price a given commodity was able to command. To help resolve this question, Böhm von Bawerk introduced the concept of marginal pairs.[19] These consisted of a buyer just willing to pay the price and a seller just willing to accept the price, and a buyer just unwilling to purchase and a seller barely unable to sell. All other buyers and sellers were simply pawns offsetting each other in the market and therefore irrelevant. As Alfred Marshall later observed, the emphasis on transactions at the margin was valuable, but the stress on the marginal pairs added little to the analysis and placed a false emphasis on the manner in which price was determined.

Böhm von Bawerk's *Positive Theory* had been preceded by a detailed study and criticism of earlier theories of interest; in the second book he attempted to replace these earlier theories with one of his own. Böhm von Bawerk's theory attempted to explain why a rate of interest was necessary in order to induce people to save and from whence the means to pay this interest was to come. The reason was that they valued present consumer goods at a higher rate of marginal utility than they did the consumption of goods taking place at some future date. It was the old story of "a bird in the hand being worth two in the bush," and as such it resembled in some ways the abstinence theory of Nassau Senior. Why did individuals place a premium on present consumption? In part, the answer lay in defects in human nature, said Böhm von Bawerk. Men had faulty imaginations and could not picture the future benefits to be acquired by postponing consumption. But even where they could perceive the nature of the future gains, they were weak-willed and preferred to have their enjoyments at the present moment. This latter motive was reinforced by the undeniable fact that human life is finite and no one can safely count on being here to enjoy tomorrow's pleasures.[20] The possibility that considerable saving might take place in the absence of any reward as people set aside funds for their old age or for their children's education was as alien to Böhm von Bawerk's thought as it had been to Senior's.

There still remained the question of how interest payments were made possible. From what source were the funds forthcoming to make possible the necessary payments? In answering this, Böhm von Bawerk introduced a new term which has remained a part of the economist's vocabulary—the *roundabout means of production*.[21] One of the marks of an advanced economy, said Böhm von Bawerk, was the increasingly circuitous manner in

[19] Eugen Böhm von Bawerk, *The Positive Theory of Capital* (New York: Stechart, 1891), pp. 214–217.

[20] *Ibid.*, pp. 253–259.

[21] *Ibid.*, pp. 17–23.

which commodities were produced and brought to market. There were two important features attached to the use of these indirect means of production. The first was that there was a requirement of greater time between the initial application of effort and the resulting product. As the interrelationship between stages of production grew increasingly complex, with one stage of production superimposed upon another, the period of elapsing time between the initial step and the ultimate consumer purchase became increasingly great. Secondly, the roundabout means of production were more productive and ultimately made possible greater output. It was this increased efficiency and the resulting increase in output which made it possible for borrowed funds to bear an interest rate. This increased output grew at a diminished rate, however, as successive steps in the production were added; each new step increased output less than its immediate predecessor.

Neither the why nor the how of Böhm von Bawerk's theory of interest went unchallenged. Critics denied that there was such a thing as time preference, or, if it did exist, that it was a constant and measurable thing which could be measured by the rate of interest. Similarly, the concept of "roundaboutness" was questioned. It was argued that the concept itself was irritatingly vague and imprecise, with no clear connection between specific inputs and outputs. Böhm von Bawerk's efforts to lend the concept a numerical precision added little to its acceptability. Although it was not a complete explanation, Böhm von Bawerk's theory of interest helped to emphasize the interrelationship between the forces of saving and investment. Whenever, as was normally likely to be the case, savings could be obtained only by the payment of a higher rate of interest, borrowing of capital to elongate the process of production would slow down and so would the pace of economic growth.

Before we leave Böhm von Bawerk, it is only proper that we take brief note of his classic analysis of Marxian economics, for his analysis of the problems of Communism set the stage for his modern-day followers such as von Hayek and von Mises and their opposition to all forms of economic planning. Böhm von Bawerk's distaste for Marx's version of economic theory is not difficult to understand. Not only did it rest on the antiquated labor theory of value, to the neglect of the new and "more scientific" subjective explanation, but it led to an exploitation theory of interest which was completely out of keeping with Böhm von Bawerk's own views as sketched above. Marx had already drawn Böhm von Bawerk's fire in the latter's comprehensive review of existing theories of interest, but with the publication of Marx's third volume of *Das Kapital,* Böhm von Bawerk launched what has been described by one of Böhm von Bawerk's editors as ". . . the best criticism of the Marxian theories of value and surplus value." [22] Böhm von Bawerk detected what he believed to be a glaring inconsistency between the theory of value set forth by Marx in his first volume and the subsequent version appearing in the third volume. The two could not be reconciled, said Böhm von Bawerk, and Marx's attempts to apportion surplus value among various firms so as to assure equality in rates of profit vitiated his theory of surplus value.

Summary and Evaluation. Böhm von Bawerk is remembered as a penetrating but courteous critic of Marx and other earlier views on interest, as well as an original contributor to the field of economic thought. His most important contributions—the role of time and time preference and roundabout means of production—have undergone numerous amendments and qualifications from the form in which Böhm von Bawerk initially stated them, but the ideas continue as a part of our economic thinking.

JOHN BATES CLARK (1847–1938)

The distinguished American economist, John Bates Clark, merits our attention at this point on two counts. First of all, he was almost solely responsible for disseminating and popularizing the concept of marginal utility in the United States. In addition, his well-known controversy with Böhm von Bawerk on the question of capital and the returns to it was one of his major claims to recognition.

The Man. Born in Providence, Rhode Island, John Bates Clark was the son of a small businessman. He began his university training at Brown University but when some of the faculty left, Clark became dissatisfied and transferred to Amherst College. Here his education was interrupted by the poor health of his father, and he was compelled for a time to take over his father's business. Following his return to Amherst, he graduated with high honors, and upon the recommendation of his faculty advisers decided to pursue the study of economics in Europe. He attended the universities at Heidelberg and Zurich and was for a while a student of Knies

---

[22] Franz X. Weiss as quoted by Paul M. Sweezy in the preface to Eugen Böhm von Bawerk's *Karl Marx and the Close of His System* (New York: Augustus Kelley, 1949), p. ix.

and Roscher. Upon his return to the United States, he married and accepted a teaching position at Carleton College. Although he remained there for six years, poor health interfered with his teaching duties and he taught for only four of those years; while there, he had as one of his students Thorstein Veblen, who was later to become one of Clark's severest critics. Thereafter, within the space of a few years, Clark moved to Smith College, where his first major work, *The Philosophy of Wealth*, was written, and then to Amherst and finally to Columbia, where he remained for the rest of his teaching career. Among his other accomplishments were his prime role in the organization of the American Economic Association, service as editor of the *Political Science Quarterly*, and his position as director of the division of economics and history for the Carnegie Endowment for International Peace. This last position was particularly dear to Clark, as he became increasingly impressed with the need to avert war if civilization was to be preserved. Among his better-known works are *The Philosophy of Wealth, The Distribution of Wealth, The Control of Trusts,* and *The Problem of Monopoly.* Not the least of his contributions to the study of economics was his equally famous son, John Maurice Clark.

Economic Views. One of the most striking aspects of Clark's economic thinking was the manner in which it changed through the years. His *Philosophy of Wealth,* evolved from ideas formulated while he was at Amherst, was a collection of widely diverse, sometimes almost contradictory essays, which set forth Clark's belief that the proper approach to the study of economics involved philosophical and ethical considerations, but made only fleeting reference to marginal utility. This early book is little read today, and it is Clark's *Distribution of Wealth* which has won him enduring fame.

Unlike many members of the Marginal Utility School, Clark never disassociated himself entirely from the Classical School. He accepted Ricardo's dictum that the long-run natural price was the cost price, and he subscribed to Mill's market theory of prices as containing many elements of truth. What these theories needed for completeness, in Clark's view, was stress on the importance of consumer demand and the forces which lay behind it.

There were aspects of Classical thought of which Clark was more critical. He denied that men were motivated as completely by the force of self-interest as earlier economists had taught, and he suggested that even in the market men were guided by a sense of what was "right." In his earlier writings, Clark felt that the Classical economists had been too confident of the continued power of competition. Competition, said Clark in his earlier writings, was on the way out, and its disappearance was probably not too bad a thing. Later, however, Clark relied upon competition to make his system operative to an even greater extent than those whom he had previously criticized.

The extent to which Clark independently formulated his views on marginal utility is unknown—he may have become aware of the theory during his period of study in Europe—but most scholars are inclined to award full recognition for an original if somewhat belated contribution. In any case, the version unfolded by Clark in *The Distribution of Wealth* was more than vaguely reminiscent of those writers, beginning with Gossen, who had preceded him. Instead of "marginal" utility, Clark substituted "effective" utility, but the same distinction between total and marginal utility was maintained and value continued to be a result of marginal units. While Clark's message about the importance of utility differed in only a few minor respects from his predecessors, he preached the doctrine to a new audience and was virtually single-handedly responsible for the introduction of marginal utility theory to American audiences. Hitherto in our survey American economists have been conspicuous primarily for their absence; John Bates Clark was not only the first exponent of marginal utility in the United States, but also this country's first economic theorist of major rank. In the explanation of marginal productivity and its application to the theory of distribution, Clark made his lasting and more original contribution.

The nature of marginal productivity and its application to the question of distribution can best be understood with the aid of the simple diagram in Fig. 4 below.[23]

The curve sloping downward from left to right is a demand curve for labor based on the marginal productivity of workers. Its downward slope was predicated on one of Clark's basic assumptions—the law of diminishing returns. $\frac{AD}{DC}$ constituted the supply of labor available in the economy and BD the marginal product of the last worker hired. Clearly the wage of the last worker could be no more than the value of his output, and since all workers were assumed to be of equal ability and hence of equal value to employers, the average wage for all workers would be at this same level. Note that in addition to assuming equal ability among workers,

[23] John Bates Clark, *The Distribution of Wealth* (New York: Macmillan, 1899), Chap. 21.

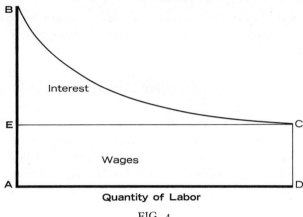

FIG. 4

Clark also assumed an absence of occupational specialization, so that there could be free interchangeability between employers and jobs; perfect mobility of labor and capital was a basic assumption of Clark's system.

It might seem at first glance that the area *CEB* was nothing more than the surplus value of which Marx wrote so scathingly. As a matter of fact, Clark's interest in the question of distribution stemmed in large part from his interest in ethics and social policy and the question of the justice of existing patterns of distribution. It is ironic that Clark's theory was converted into an apology for the status quo and a justification of the current pattern of distribution. The area *CEB,* according to Clark, was no unearned surplus value kept out of labor's rightful share, but a return to capital in the form of interest for the contribution it made to production.

To understand how this excess could emerge, we must take account of two more of Clark's assumptions. The first of these was that the stock of capital was constant (a part of his static model to which we will turn later) and that his stock could be redistributed as needed to accommodate varying supplies of labor. As more laborers were employed, the amount of capital available per worker was correspondingly reduced. The decline in the marginal productivity of labor as additional workers were employed was due to this accompanying decline in the amount of capital per worker, and thus no exploitation was involved. As we have noted, it was Clark's deep interest in questions of justice that had led him to examine the ethics of distribution. His belief had always been that a just society would assure just wages, and his marginal productivity theory was able to satisfy him as to the correctness of this premise. Clark's defense of the status quo was adopted by later writers and broadened into a major argument against the demands by unions for higher wages. One of the obvious lessons of

Clark's theory (which he also drew) was that wages could only be increased if marginal productivity could be raised or the supply of labor reduced. The heroic and unrealistic assumptions of free mobility of labor and capital, and of perfect competition, were forgotten or ignored. Clark, who had started with a desire to discover whether current distribution was ethically correct, ended by "proving" that the existing situation was the best of all possible ones. Little wonder that union leaders took the position, "With a friend like this, who needs enemies?" Nevertheless, the marginal productivity theory contains an important kernel of truth. Assuming, as Clark did, conditions of full employment and free mobility of capital and labor, so that workers are actually paid their marginal productivity and constant price levels, the theory demonstrates that wages above the market level can only result in unemployment.

The reader may have been struck by the limitation of returns to only two forms—wages and interest. Whatever happened to rent and profits? In the case of rent, the answer was an easy one. The Classical economists had treated land as a special factor made different by its absolute scarcity and its variations in quality. Clark argued that land was no special form of capital. In a stationary economy land was no more limited in supply than other forms of capital. Furthermore, the second characteristic of land—its variations in quality—was, Clark said, equally true of other forms of capital. Rent elements were present in the return to all impersonal factors of production, and they could even be extended to wages, if the assumption of equal ability were to be removed.

The absence of profits resulted from Clark's assumption of a stationary economy. His description of such an economy, as distinguished from one that was dynamic, was an early version of that drawn in our first chapter. The static economy involved no change in population or supply of capital, fixed techniques of production and forms of industrial organization and unchanging consumer tastes. These dynamic features, with the changes they produced in the economy, gave birth to profits. The function of the entrepreneur was to seek out these opportunities and gain profits. In the absence of these dynamic changes, however, profits through the force of competition were reduced to zero, so that all that remained as a return to capital was in the form of interest. The idea that profits emerged from dynamic change and the uncertainties resulting therefrom was picked up and elaborated upon by one of Clark's followers, Frank H. Knight, in his book *Risk, Uncertainty and Profit*.

We come now to Clark's famous controversy with Böhm von Bawerk over the determination of interest. Clark agreed with Böhm von Bawerk as to the reasons why interest was a necessary payment, and he endorsed the time-preference explanation as to the why of interest. It was to Böhm von Bawerk's answer to the question of how this payment was made possible that Clark took exception. He substituted his marginal productivity theory for Böhm von Bawerk's roundabout means of production (with interest paid from the resulting increases in output). Just as wages were determined by the marginal productivity of labor, so interest was determined by the marginal productivity of capital. The dispute was complicated by Clark's distinction between capital and capital goods and his accurate insistence that Böhm von Bawerk had confined his analysis to concrete capital goods. The distinction was crucial in Clark's view, since capital in the abstract sense in which economists viewed it was more than simply a collection of material goods of production. Whereas the addition of an extra laborer increased the quantity but not the quality of the labor supply, augmentation or diminution in the supply of capital meant an alteration in its entire character. Thus it was important to talk about the added productivity of additional capital in terms of supplies of capital, not capital goods.

Clark's version of marginal productivity analysis had many critics. We have already noted that union leaders took exception to his position that the existing distribution of income was equitable. Clark's warnings to labor (and business) not to "rock the boat" provided little assurances to these leaders. Although Clark repeatedly spoke of the need for dynamic analysis, he never adequately pursued the issue, and his confinement largely to a static analysis subjected him to charges of being too unrealistic. His distinction between capital and capital goods was also criticized on the grounds that he pushed his analysis too far by arguing that capital goods were ephemeral while the stock of capital was permanent. The obvious point was made that the supply of capital was not permanent by itself but depended upon the process of production for its permanence. Finally, he was criticized for concentrating upon diminishing returns to the exclusion of increasing returns; the latter, Clark said, could occur only in a dynamic economy.

Although Clark confined much of his analysis to a static situation, and perfect competition, he was well aware that the real world was not this perfect, and as the titles of some of his books indicate, he was, particularly in his early years of writing, preoccupied with the problem of monopoly. Competition, Clark had said, was declining and could be relied upon less and less. What was to take its place? Clark was not altogether sure. One possibility was the evolution of a more cooperative society, where men would forego exorbitant profits in the interests of the entire economy. Such a possibility was far more appealing to Clark than some form of government arbitration; Clark was buoyed in this hope by his conviction that the Classical economists had mistakenly pictured man as dominated solely by economic motivations; men were, in Clark's view, endowed with higher motives as well. In some ways, Clark's discussion harked back to the days of the guilds and St. Thomas Aquinas' concept of a just price. As his son, John Maurice Clark, has pointed out,[24] Clark's concern over monopoly became less pronounced as time went on; his alarms preceded the furor of the antitrust acts and seem to have subsided as the general public grew increasingly concerned.

Even in the early years, when Clark was most pessimistic about the future of competition, he never was tempted to entertain the possibility of socialism as an alternative; the ethics of private property was accepted by Clark without question. Like many of the adherents to the Marginal Utility School, Clark was a determined opponent of Marxism. Böhm von Bawerk, whose own analysis of the Marxian system we have already noted, complimented Clark on his ability to turn the tables on Marx and use Marx's own analytical tools against him, in the same fashion that Marx had attempted to meet the capitalist economists on their own ground.

Clark's own vision of the future remained somewhat murky. In the last chapters of his *Distribution of Wealth,* he attempted to outline some of the implications of moving to a dynamic analysis. Although the completed picture would emerge, Clark warned, only with the work of future generations of economists, Clark was now confident that the future was a rosy one, where the forces of dynamic change would produce an alignment between the natural laws of distribution and a system of distribution that was morally and ethically proper.

Summary and Evaluation. Alfred Marshall once referred to Clark as one of the three or four major theoretical economists of the early twentieth century. This judgment may be overly generous, but certainly Clark was one of the leaders of the era and the first theorist of major importance in the United States. Clark undoubtedly acquired his views of ethical values and the concept of society as an organic structure during his period of study with Knies and Roscher. The tone of moral earnestness remained an integral part of his economic philosophy, although colored by his own

[24] John Maurice Clark on his father in Henry William Spiegel, ed., *The Development of Economic Thought* (New York: Wiley, 1952), pp. 593–612.

ethical valuations. Other aspects of his economic thinking went through a much more drastic change, but the causes for these changes remain unknown.

It was his attempt to investigate the ethics of existing patterns of distribution that led him to his chief contribution to economic thought—the concept of marginal productivity. His formulation of marginal utility, although apparently achieved independently, made no notable changes from the concept as formulated by earlier writers. We have mentioned some of the criticisms of his marginal productivity analysis. His views on marginal utility made him a target for attacks by his most famous student, Thorstein Veblen. Clark's pleas to labor and business to find a way of reconciling their divergent interests were developed later by his son, John Maurice Clark.

MARIE ESPRIT LÉON WALRAS (1834–1910)

We shall now turn to the third of the three economists credited with originating marginal utility—Léon Walras. If we were to devote a chapter to the mathematical economists, Walras would surely play a leading role in that chapter, for it was he, as much as or more than any other individual, who established the use of mathematical techniques in economic analysis. Partly because of his mathematical predisposition and partly because his writing, even when devoid of mathematical symbols, was seldom easy to read, Walras, like Jevons, had difficulty winning any recognition from his contemporaries. In the preface to his *Elements of Pure Political Economy,* Walras apologized by saying that the awkward phrasing was made necessary by the inherent nature of the subject matter. Walras was not the first or last writer to seek extenuation in this fashion, and his rationale seems no more appropriate than it was for others.

Even if Walras' French had been crystal clear, however, it is doubtful whether he would have been accorded more recognition by his contemporaries. Although the names of a few illustrious exceptions can be cited, the general state of French economic thinking had improved little from the days of the Physiocrats. Walras' mathematical approach and theory of marginal utility fell on deaf ears.

The Man. Born the son of the economist Auguste Walras, Léon Walras turned to the study of economics only after careers in engineering and journalism showed little promise. Walras studied to be a mining engineer, but withdrew from engineering school to embark on a career as a free-lance journalist. His early attempts as a novelist won no more favor among French audiences than his later economic writings did. For the next twelve years Walras followed a varied career as journalist, lecturer, and editor, without winning great success in any of these fields. During this period, his interest in economics was by no means entirely lacking; he became an ardent proponent of agrarian reform and even dallied with socialist doctrines. A virtual failure in France, Walras won recognition after his appointment to a professorship at the University of Lausanne in Switzerland in 1870. His classic work, *Elements of Pure Political Economy,* was published in 1874 and thereafter his fame was assured. He remained at Lausanne for 22 years until his retirement in 1892.

Economic Views. Although we will do no more than scan Walras' version of marginal utility (or what he chose to call *rareté*), in order to avoid undue repetition, it is important to remember that Walras deserves just as much recognition as one of the originators of the concept as Jevons and Menger did. His analysis, stripped of its mathematical terminology, reduced itself to the same principles of hedonism and individualism employed by Jevons and Menger. The price of consumer goods was determined in the market by the process of exchange. In elaborating upon this process, Walras coined the expression *prix crié,* or the price announced by the auctioneer. Buyers and sellers came to the market in order to maximize their *raretés* and made their decisions to buy or not to buy in response to the price quoted by the auctioneer. If the price quoted was too high, excess quantities of supply would appear, and the auctioneer would thus learn to lower the announced price. The process by which equilibrium was achieved was left disturbingly vague. Were any sales consummated before the equilibrium price had been achieved or did all the buyers hold off until the equilibrium price was announced? If the first hypothesis was true, what effects did these early transactions have on the final equilibrium price? If the alternative assumption was made, how could one analyze and forecast this consumer action? Walras never resolved these questions and confined himself to a description of the process by which the market would, in the event that the initial announced price was too high (so that quantities supplied exceeded the quantities demanded) or too low (so that the quantities demanded exceeded the quantities supplied), eventually work itself to the equilibrium position. At this point, the ratio of the *raretés* of commodities would equal the ratio of their prices.

The prices of producer goods, or those Menger had referred to as being

of a "higher order," were determined in much the same fashion. After
consumers had determined the prices of consumer goods, producers were
able to judge the amount they could pay for the various factors of production. The same process of bidding was repeated, with each producer limited
in his bids by the market price of the goods he produced and by a fixed
determination of the proportions of the various factors of production
which could be utilized. This assumption of what is technically known as
"fixed coefficients of production" prevented Walras from developing a
full-blown marginal productivity theory of production. The failure is
made all the more regrettable because the possibility of changing proportions did not entirely escape Walras' attention, and in later editions of his
book he noted that this assumption of constancy was merely an approximation and was quite likely subject to qualification. Consumers and businessmen entered both markets; consumers entered the factor market
when they offered their services for sale—they were then on the supply
side. They entered the commodity market when they were on the demand
side as potential buyers. The relative positions of the businessmen were
correspondingly reversed.

Walras presented two types of equations for the consideration of his
readers. The first dealt with the dependence of the quantities of supply and
demand by individuals upon a system of market prices. At this point, he
pursued the traditional hedonistic line of thinking and placed great emphasis upon the individualistic and subjective explanation of value in con-
tradistinction to the cost of production and labor theory of value. His
second set of equations expressed the equality of demand and supply in
particular markets, and here Walras made his second major contribution
—the one which won him the most enduring fame—the concept of general equilibrium.

The principle of marginal utility need not necessarily be attached to the
concept of general equilibrium, but Walras was of the contrary opinion
and felt that the two were inextricably linked. Walras laid down two
premises for the determination of the position of equilibrium; the first of
these was the assumption of perfect competition and the second was laissez-faire. A brief discussion of Walras' system is sketched below for those
who are mathematically inclined.[25] It perhaps suffices to note here that

[25] Equilibrium in the Walrasian system required: (1) that for each trader the
marginal rate of substitution between any two goods be equal to their rate of exchange
in the market; (2) the purchasing power represented by the goods which each trader
brought to the market had to be just exhausted by the final selection of goods of each—
that is, each trader had to take as much as he could; and (3) the total amount of each

Walras began by assuming one commodity which could serve as a *numer-aire* (or money) for the measurement of the prices of all other commodities. For a total of R commodities, $R - 1$ equations are needed, and for N individuals, $N(R - 1)$ equations. With as many equations as unknowns,

---

good taken from the market by all traders equaled the total amount brought to the market—that is, supply equaled demand.

The System

1. R commodities
2. N individuals

Let:

Sy/x = marginal rate of substitution of Y for x

aUx = marginal utility of x to individual a

Px/y = price of x in terms of y

(1) $aSy/x = Px/y$

$$Px/y = \frac{Px}{Py}$$

$$aSy/x = \frac{aUx}{aUy} \therefore \frac{Px}{Py} = \frac{aUx}{aUy} \text{ or } \frac{aUx}{Px} = \frac{aUy}{Py}$$

Generalizing,

$$\frac{aUx}{Px} = \frac{aUy}{Py} = \frac{aUz}{Pz} \cdots = \frac{aU}{P}$$

For each individual a, the marginal utility of a dollar's worth of each commodity must be the same as for any other good. For R commodities, there are $(R - 1)$ independent equations for each individual and $N(R - 1)$ equations for N individuals.

(2) Let aQx = amount of x bought by individual a, which is the excess of the amount he consumed over the amount he started with:

$$aQxPx + aQyPy + \ldots aQP = 0$$

(The sum of the value of the goods bought less the value of those sold must equal zero. A single equation for each consumer or N altogether can be written.)

(3) $aQxPx + bQxPx + \ldots + nQxPx = 0$

(The sum of the value of purchases of commodity x by all consumers less the value of sales of x by all sellers must equal zero. There was one equation for each commodity, or R altogether.)

To Solve the System:

(1) Combining equations 2 and 3, we obtain $N + R$ equations. But one equation can be derived from these, so that we have only $N + R - 1$ independent equations.

(2) Combining these with equation 1, we obtain $N(R - 1) + (N + R - 1) = NR + R - 1$ total equations.

(3) To solve these $NR + R - 1$ equations, we have to determine the amounts of each of R commodities bought or sold by N individuals—NR quantities and $(R - 1)$ prices. There were $R - 1$ and not R prices to be determined, since the price of one commodity can be fixed arbitrarily because it is the ratio of prices that was important, not absolute prices.

Number of equations = $NR + R - 1$ (from 2)

Number of quantities = $NR + R - 1$ (from 3)

and since the number of equations equalled the number of unknowns, a solution of the system existed.

it thus became a mathematical possibility, by the process of solving simultaneous equations, to arrive at a determinate solution for equilibrium. The accomplishment was of greater theoretical interest than of practical utility. Earlier, Cournot, the mathematical economist, had denied that a solution to a general equilibrium situation was possible; Walras succeeded in conquering some of the mathematical difficulties, but the task of gathering and solving the almost infinite number of equations has remained unsolved. Walras' solution has remained a solution "in principle" and lacking in empirical content.

Walras considered the situation of general equilibrium to be a situation of maximum satisfaction as seen from the viewpoint of society as a whole. Since certain institutional barriers prevented the economy from arriving at equilibrium, it followed that desirable policy would be to seek their elimination. Obviously, since Walras' solution was predicated on the assumption of perfect competition, monopoly was a clear violation and needed to be eliminated whenever it existed. We have noted earlier that Walras was an ardent proponent of land reform. At certain times he sounded like Henry George at his best, and he was equally vigorous in his denouncement of the "unearned increment" rent arising from the process of economic growth. More important, however, was the fact that the current structure of land ownership impeded the free mobility of labor and hence made impossible the attainment of general equilibrium. It becomes apparent from the preceding sentences that Walras was not as laissez-faire-oriented as some of his economic writings would lead us to believe. Nor did Walras stop here; he supported John Stuart Mill's conclusion (without ever acknowledging the fact) that the laws of production were immutable, while those of distribution were subject to the dictates of society. Walras, for example, supported compulsory education as a means of making the general public wiser consumers, and he advocated a shortening of the work week.

Walras' discussion of money and interest is quite brief. His treatment of money was routine and added nothing to our store of knowledge, while his treatment of capital and the returns to it was marred by his assumption that new capital was always being added to the economy. Otherwise Walras' capital market worked much as his other markets; on one side were the savers who in effect spent part of their income on capital goods rather than consumer goods, while on the other were businessmen who produced capital instead of consumer goods. The price set (the interest rate) was the result of interaction between these two groups. Although Walras' model provided an explanation for the interest rate in new capital markets, it was by Walras' own treatment inapplicable to a stationary economy. As J. R. Hicks has pointed out, this flaw was not fatal and could have been easily remedied, but Walras never saw the need to make the required amendments.[26]

Summary and Evaluation. Of Walras' two major contributions—the concepts of marginal utility and general equilibrium—the latter has earned him greater fame. Walras was neglected for a long time by his contemporaries; his treatment at the hands of present-day critics has varied widely from Schumpeter's judgment that "so far as pure theory is concerned, Walras is . . . the greatest of all economists"[27] to others who have belittled Walras' general equilibrium equations as having little practical relevance. Some of our more mathematically inclined economists have even taken exception to the quality of Walras' mathematical presentations and observed that it is quite understandable why Walras flunked some of his early examinations. Walras would probably not have been unduly concerned about this charge, even if proven true, since he thought of himself as first an economist and only second as a mathematician. Mathematics was a way of analyzing and discarding some principles, while precisely stating other basic principles. Although ignored for a long time, Walras, unlike Jevons, did eventually win a band of supporters and admirers who polished and refined his work. We will consider the work of one of these in our next chapter when we discuss Alfred Marshall, but at this point we must pay respects to Vilfredo Pareto, the economist who immediately succeeded to the post at the University of Lausanne held so long by Walras.

VILFREDO PARETO (1848–1923)

The Man. Vilfredo Pareto was born the son of an Italian nobleman who professed the politics of Mazzini, and of a French mother. He spent the first years of his life in Paris, the city where he was born. Pareto went to Italy at the age of ten and later to the University of Turin to study to be an engineer. He had a successful career in this field and later became president of an Italian iron company. His training as an engineer provided

[26] J. R. Hicks in his evaluation of Walras in *Econometrics* (October, 1934), reprinted in Henry William Spiegel, ed. *The Development of Economic Thought* (New York: Wiley, 1952), p. 590.

[27] Joseph Schumpeter, *History of Economic Analysis* (New York: Oxford, 1954), p. 827.

him with a command of mathematics which was beneficial to him when in his forties he began a study of economics. Pareto received his post at the University of Lausanne in 1893 upon the recommendation of Walras, who had been much impressed with Pareto's demonstrated mathematical ability. He remained at Lausanne until his retirement in 1906. Although Pareto freely acknowledged Walras' inspiration in his own views on utility and general equilibrium, the social philosophy of the two men was markedly different and the two were personally quite antagonistic. Pareto was skeptical of all proposals for social reform, and his well-known law on income distribution is symptomatic of this attitude. In later years, Pareto became increasingly interested in sociology and worked out an analysis of the circulation of elites. After World War I, the internal chaos in Italy led him to flirt with the idea of Fascism and the need for a strong leader, but he never became a full-fledged Fascist and insisted until his death upon the right of citizens to free speech. Among his most notable economic works are *Heart of Political Economy* (1896–1897) and *Manual of Political Economy* (1906).

Economic Views. For a person who participated in the construction of economic theory for only a comparatively brief period of time, Pareto changed his views during that period most remarkably. His first book, *Heart of Political Economy,* was closely patterned after the writings of Walras. While he made some amendments and improvements on Walras' work, these were perhaps more than matched by offsetting weaknesses. Although he followed much the same path of utility pursued by others, Pareto saw marginal utility as a function of all commodities and not of a single commodity, as some of his predecessors including Walras had maintained. Furthermore, he was already expressing some uneasiness about the possibility of measuring it with any precision. His abandonment of the fixed coefficients of production formulated by Walras was an important step forward, but one to which Walras, although never taking it himself, had pointed the way. Furthermore, Pareto's statement about the possibility of varying the factors was expressed in such a complicated and obscure fashion that it was difficult to uncover the significance of his message. His equations of general equilibrium were those of Walras with minor modifications, but Pareto argued that these equations could and should be substantiated with empirical evidence. The magnitude of the task did not appear to concern him at this point, although in later years he became more skeptical about the realization of this goal.

Pareto found little inspiration in Walras' treatment of money and capital. As Hicks has suggested, one way of describing his attitude is a simple "ignoring." [28] Pareto never developed any great ideas about money and capital either; perhaps his most important contribution was his denial that there was a constant marginal utility of money—an assumption which figured prominently in writings of Alfred Marshall (see Chapter X).

Two other aspects of his early book deserve brief comment. Pareto took a dim view of society's being able to achieve much lasting progress; history was a repetition of recurring scenes and events. Where progress did occur, its form was in the nature of growing freedom from state regulation and intervention. At this point, as at many others, Pareto was championing the principle of laissez-faire. His insistence on this issue may have been the basis for Schumpeter's observation that "he helped to create . . . the impression that marginal utility was just a wicked trick with which to thwart reformers." [29] In keeping with this opposition to government intervention was what has since come to be known as Pareto's Law of Distribution. This "law," as explained by Pareto, argued that throughout history down to the present moment the pattern of income distribution had remained fixed and unchanging. The conclusion to be drawn was that public policy could have little effect on the character of the distribution and Walras was wrong in agreeing with Mill that the laws of distribution were readily subject to the whims of the society. Improvements in the distribution of income, Pareto maintained, could only be achieved by increasing the general level of production.

Pareto's "law" underwent bitter criticism from those who felt that his case was based on insufficient evidence. Critics objected when Pareto stated that the distribution of income was solely a function of ability and that the distribution of ability was the same at all times and places. While the scientific character of Pareto's "law" has thus been subject to serious challenge, it remains true that his basic premise that redistribution of income is difficult to achieve has proved to be by no means wide of the mark. His position at this point is in sharp contrast with his later views as outlined below.

While Pareto never completely disassociated himself from the utility concept, his later writing shows a marked move in that direction. His other major contribution to economic thought is the concept of indifference curves. The rejection of cardinal (measurable) utility did not originate with Pareto. Irving Fisher first stated precisely why economists should abandon cardinal utility, and F. Y. Edgeworth first introduced the

[28] Hicks in Spiegel, *op. cit.,* p. 589.
[29] Joseph Schumpeter, *Ten Great Economists* (New York: Oxford, 1951), p. 116.

indifference curve to the world. (We will discuss both of these economists in Chapter X.) Unlike Edgeworth, however, who began with the premise of cardinal total utility and then deduced indifference curves therefrom, Pareto took the indifference curve as his point of departure and from it arrived at the determination of equilibrium. For those students unfamiliar with the idea of indifference curves, no explanation which can be encompassed within the confines of the brief space available would be adequate, while those who have already met them need no introduction. It suffices to note that the idea was to present a map of consumer preferences as to various combinations of two commodities. When greater amounts of both were possible, the consumer was able to move to a higher indifference curve showing these increased combinations. No absolute differentials between curves were assumed, but presumably the consumer could tell that he was better off on a higher than a lower curve, even though the absolute amount of the improvement remained indeterminate. By postulating changes in price or income, the response of the consumer could be determined, and the distinction between increases in the purchase of a commodity arising from the substitution of it for other commodities and the increase in consumption arising from a sense of having greater income from the lower price could be mapped. Pareto argued that the indifference curve approach could have not only theoretical but practical significance, and that the curves could be derived from empirical observation without any reliance on the utility concept. Both economists and consumers have remained indifferent to this suggestion, and no successful empirical investigation has been achieved.

Pareto reversed his position about state action at this point. If his formulation of indifference curves was to be accepted, with its accompanying abandonment of cardinal utility and the possibility of interpersonal comparisons, the case against state welfare programs would seem to be all the more complete. How could one justify government intervention when the amount of benefit to be derived at best could be only an approximation, with no existing means of aggregating social welfare? The temptation to follow this line of reasoning must have been great for a supporter of laissez-faire such as Pareto, and at points he almost seems about to yield to the temptation. In the end, however, he concluded that this was no scientific basis for a choice between a system of private property and one of socialism. If the state could raise the position of some of its citizens without damaging the position of others, its actions might be desirable.

Summary and Evaluation. Although Pareto belongs to the Lausanne School as developed by Walras, the follower was as instrumental in winning disciples to the school as his predecessor. This was true despite the fact that neither was widely accepted and both still remain little read or recognized by English-speaking students of economics. As in the case of Walras, Pareto's fate at the hands of his critics has been a mixed one. Some, such as A. A. Young, the British economist, have charged him with achieving only "arid generalizations"; others like Giovanni Demaria, the Italian economist, have been excessively generous in their praise. His work on indifference curves and his formulation of the law of distribution of income are the contributions for which he is best remembered.

JOHN GUSTAV KNUT WICKSELL (1851–1926)

Our final figure to be introduced in this chapter provides a glimpse of the "Stockholm" or "Scandinavian" school of economics. In addition to Wicksell, the school has included such well-known economists as Gustav Cassel, a contemporary of Wicksell, and more recent representatives such as Gunnar Myrdal and Ragnar Frisch.

The Man. Knut Wicksell was born in Stockholm and studied at the University of Upsala, where he became interested in a wide range of subjects, including languages, literature, philosophy, and mathematics. Following his graduation, he did postgraduate work in mathematics and physics. As time went by, however, Wicksell's interest turned more and more to the social and economic problems of the day and the need for reform. This interest in social reform prompted him, as it did von Wieser, to undertake the study of economics. Beginning at the age of 34, Wicksell spent the next five years studying economics in England, France, Germany, and Austria. His study in these countries was particularly important in formulating his views on marginal utility and his theories of capital, and the work of Böhm von Bawerk played a major role in sparking Wicksell's own economic writing.

Wicksell was handicapped in his career as an economist both by his comparatively late start and by his reputation among the conservatives of Sweden as a radical reformer. Wicksell's views on the problem of population and his recommendations in the form of birth control were particularly irritating to his fellow citizens, and his views on the ways to deal with prostitution and alcoholism, and his support of universal suffrage, also aroused opposition. Nor did his championship of progressive taxation enhance his image among his opponents. As a consequence, Wicksell was 48 before he was appointed assistant professor. Two years later, in 1901, he sought a position as full professor at Lund. His rival for this post was Gustav Cassel, but when opposition to Wicksell's appointment arose on the basis of his radical ideas, Cassel withdrew his application, leaving the field open for Wicksell. Here he remained until his retirement in 1916, except for a two-month period when he was jailed for a satirical commentary on church doctrine. The last ten years of his life were spent at his home on the outskirts of Stockholm, where he continued to commune with his fellow economists. His chief works were *Interest and Prices* and *Lectures on Political Economy*.

Economic Views. Wicksell, of necessity, came as late to the concept of marginal utility as he had to the subject of economics, and he cannot be counted as one of the great pioneers in the topic of consumer choice. Since Wicksell was one of the latecomers who formulated views on the concept of marginal utility, he was also late to avoid many of the pitfalls and misconceptions embedded in the thinking of earlier exponents of marginal utility theory. Wicksell's treatment of marginal utility is chiefly noted for the clarity of its exposition and the realistic fashion in which it took account of the numerous imperfections contained in the theory. All of the various weaknesses we have noted earlier in this chapter were recognized by Wicksell, including the problem of measuring interpersonal differences, the discontinuities in consumer purchases, and the fact that consumers were not guided by a simple hedonistic principle but acted on the basis of a variety of motives.

Wicksell is best known for his work in monetary theory, his discussion of the market and "natural" rate of interest, and the role of interest rates in promoting stability in the economy. His interests in this direction led him to a study of the business cycle and the conclusion that stability could not be assured through the operation of the market forces. If the market could not assure stability by itself, said Wicksell, it was only logical to turn to the central government and particularly to the central bank for guidance. In the course of his discussion of business cycles, Wicksell devoted some attention to the relationship between aggregate savings and investment, thus in part setting the stage for the later Keynesian analysis. However, Wicksell, unlike Keynes, placed primary emphasis upon monetary maladjustment as the cause of business cycles and devoted only secondary attention to possible imbalances in other factors.

Summary and Evaluation. Much of Wicksell's analysis lies outside the scope of this book, let alone this chapter; his work belongs more properly with a discussion of other monetary theorists' views of the business cycle. His contribution to marginal utility theory was primarily one of refinement and clarification and its dissemination to another sector of the world.

An Overall Appraisal. Although we have already assembled an impressive array of economists, the list of those who might be included under the heading of marginal utility is by no means exhausted. We will discuss Marshall, Edgeworth, and Fisher in Chapter X. Others, such as Philip H. Wickstead (1844–1927), the great English popularizer of the marginal utility concept, must be passed over for lack of space. Even without proceeding further, however, it should already be evident from the writers examined in this chapter that the members of the Marginal Utility School varied widely in their interpretation and application of their central doctrine. Some accepted a strict hedonistic basis for their theory, while others rejected the hedonistic base almost entirely. Differences also arose as to the measurability of utility. Despite this diversity, however, all of the economists met in this chapter were bound by the conviction that an individualistic and subjective approach to value was preferable to the semiempirical cost-of-production theory of value. One of the intriguing but still unresolved questions in the history of economic thought is why the Marginal Utility School was so late in its development. Emil Kauder, the German-born economist, has suggested two possible explanations for this "retardation." [30] Perhaps the one most widely accepted is the strength of the Ricardian influence and its impact on later theorists, to the exclusion of any rival theories. Kauder also suggests that the labor theory of value had attached to it Calvinist overtones (about the value of labor) that made it particularly palatable. Although it is difficult to accept these suggestions as the complete explanation or to formulate more acceptable hypotheses for the relative slow acceptance of the theory, it is probably true that the increased popularity of the marginal utility theory toward the end of the nineteenth century was enhanced immeasurably by the re-

[30] Emil Kauder, "The Retarded Acceptance of the Marginal Utility Theory," *The Quarterly Journal of Economics* (November, 1953), pp. 564–575.

jection by many economists of the use to which Marx had put the labor theory of value and the accompanying desire to seek an alternative explanation.

The value of the marginal utility theory to modern economic thought has been questioned, both as to its scientific accuracy and as to the extent to which it added anything important. Modern psychology suggests that the cruder forms of utility theory based on hedonistic principles were in error. Readers of the economic journals have witnessed in the past two or three decades a series of articles alternating between upholding and rejecting the principle of cardinal utility. Modern demand theorists such as J. R. Hicks have continued their efforts to refurbish their theory by pursuing the Walrasian proposal for employing indifference curves. Some of the author's more mathematically inclined friends state that some of the mathematical economists have sought to give mathematical precision to cardinal utility. Some later economists, such as Herbert Davenport, have turned their backs on psychology in response to this denial; few have dared to remove the building block of hedonism for fear that the entire edifice of value theory would collapse. Obviously the story is by no means completed, and much additional work remains to be done. The fact that these earlier economists provided us with so much material upon which to ponder is no small tribute in itself. Of the three chief architects of marginal utility, Walras with the aid of Pareto went farthest beyond the marginal utility theory per se to develop the concept of general equilibrium. Their general equilibrium approach stands in sharp contrast to the concept of equilibrium as devised in Chapter X by our next writer, Alfred Marshall.

CHAPTER X: Alfred Marshall and the Neoclassical System

> *The chief fault in English economists at the beginning of the century was not that they ignored history and statistics, but that they regarded man as so to speak a constant quantity, and gave themselves little trouble to study his variations.*
>
> —ALFRED MARSHALL

ALFRED MARSHALL (1842–1924)

Few books on the history of economic thought do justice to the work of Alfred Marshall. Frequently he is relegated to a few pages or included among other writers of the Marginal Utility School, and in one notable case he was omitted entirely. The disrespect thus displayed is not intentional and few economists would question the greatness of his contribution. The inadequacy of treatment afforded Marshall's work can be explained on several counts. He is difficult to categorize. Not only was he a Marginalist, but much more! [1] His major book is long (nearly 900 pages) and is difficult to summarize briefly. Many of his contributions are of not only historical but contemporary value, and the reader is impressed by how much of it serves as a basis for intermediate texts on price theory; his *Principles of Economics* is still widely used in many universities as a part of an advanced principles course. Few students, even in the elementary course of economics, have failed to hear about the Marshallian "scissors" of supply and demand.

As our discussion proceeds, it will be evident that he can be distinguished from the other members of the Marginal Utility School at a number of points. Even at this early stage, we should stress one prime differ-

---

[1] In a sense the same could be said for many of the Marginalists encountered in Chapter IX, and Marginalism was only one part of the thinking of many of the economists encountered there. Marshall, however, developed a more complete economic system; it would not be too much to say that Marshall wrote what was in all probability the last great treatise in economics.

ence. Whereas most of the other members of the Marginal Utility School dramatized their differences with the Classical School, Marshall was a firm believer in the continuity of change—his title page bore the inscription, *Natura non facit saltum* (Nature does not make leaps), and he applied this to his economic theory. He found much to admire in the writings of David Ricardo and John Stuart Mill and purported to find passages in their writing demonstrating that they were not unaware of the importance of utility and demand. Like Adam Smith's *Wealth of Nations,* Alfred Marshall's *Principles* was a very large book and took a long time in preparation. One estimate is that it was the product of twenty years of labor. Unlike Smith's, Marshall's book went through repeated revised editions. We will have occasion to comment on these numerous editions and the message they contained after we take a brief look at Alfred Marshall himself.

The Man. If Alfred Marshall's father had had his way, the world would have been deprived of a great economist. The father was a cashier in the Bank of England; he possessed strict religious convictions and wished his son to study for the ministry. However, when a scholarship at St. John's College, Oxford, was offered to the younger Marshall on the condition that he study for the ministry, he rejected it because of his love of mathematics. Although a loan from his uncle made the study of mathematics possible and Marshall became a good mathematician as a result, his concern over ethical issues and the problems of social reform led Marshall to study economics rather than to follow his early training as a mathematician. No one should conclude from this, however, that Marshall was a failure as a mathematician; he was second wrangler (a placement in the first-class mathematical tripos at Cambridge) in 1865. Immediately after this success, he was elected to a fellowship, and with money he earned from tutoring, he started to repay his uncle's loan.

While tutoring at Clifton College, Marshall came in contact with the economist Henry Sidgwick (1838–1900). Sidgwick, who followed in the Mill tradition, had begun his student career in the fields of theology and moral philosophy, and it was his views on social ethics which attracted Marshall's attention. This interest in moral questions replaced Marshall's original plan for further studies in physics, and he became a student of Sidgwick in moral science. In 1868, Marshall was appointed to a special lectureship in moral science at St. John's College.

While at St. John's, Marshall worked with Sidgwick and Fawcett toward the formation of political economy as a distinct discipline. When he married one of his former students, Mary Paley, in 1877, he was forced to give up his fellowship because marriage was deemed an improper part of a fellow's life. He moved to Bristol to accept the position of first principal of the University College and professor of political economy. Four years later he resigned this position because he found it uncongenial and perhaps in part because of concern about his health. Although Marshall lived to be 82, he verged on hypochondria and always pictured his condition to be much worse than it actually was. In order to restore his health, Marshall spent a period relaxing in Italy. The death of Arnold Toynbee and the removal of the ban on married fellows led him to accept a post as fellow and special lecturer at Oxford in 1883. Henry Fawcett died two years later and Marshall was invited to return to Cambridge to fill the chair of professor of political economy; here Marshall remained until his retirement in 1908.

Schumpeter has compared Marshall with Newton in his reluctance to publish and his critical attitude toward his own work. Throughout much of the period above, Marshall was busy formulating his own views on political economy and he began intensive work on his *Principles* in 1881, but it was not published until 1890. Meanwhile, much of the luster and originality of his work had been skimmed away as his former students published papers based on ideas developed while attending Marshall's classes. Marshall continued a painstaking revision of this work throughout much of his later life, shifting relevant passages from one chapter to another or removing them to an appendix. (Some wag has suggested that the result was that Marshall's chief work eventually suffered a severe case of appendicitis.) In the view of one Marshall scholar, the opportunity costs involved were high and the net product small, and he has suggested that after the third edition, the changes were unimportant and that the work lost its spark and verve.[2]

An earlier study by Marshall entitled *The Economics of Industry,* with his wife as co-author, appeared in print at a considerably earlier date, but it is known that the idea had been originally conceived by his wife and the suspicion remains that a considerable portion of the credit for its completion rests with Mrs. Marshall.

During his years at Cambridge, Marshall gave about forty-five lectures a year, but his greatest impact on students came from the daily gatherings in his home each afternoon. Here in informal discussions he bred a long list of distinguished economists, including A. C. Pigou and John Maynard

---

[2] C. W. Guilleband, "The Variorum Edition of Alfred Marshall's *Principles of Economics,*" *The Economic Journal* (December 1961), pp. 677–690.

Keynes. His efforts in the classroom were somewhat less distinguished; his lectures tended to be disjointed and rambling and no complete set of notes based on them was ever compiled.

Marshall supported a number of outside causes during his years at Cambridge. For example, in 1890 he was founder of the Royal Economic Society. In light of our previous emphasis on Jevons' work in statistics, it is only fair to note that Marshall's abilities as a mathematician served to make Marshall a good statistician also. He was the originator of the chain index number, and in his *Principles* he constantly made references to the possibilities and difficulties of statistical verification. Like John Stuart Mill before him, Marshall was generally accepted in England as *the* economist of his day and he was frequently called upon to testify before and serve with various government committees. Unlike Mill, however, who had championed the cause of women, Marshall took a dim view of women as scholars and worked against their being granted degrees at Cambridge. His position was a strange one in view of the fact that his wife was a former student and an economist in her own right, plus the fact that he himself had lectured at Newnham College (for women). Evidently he harked back to his father's views; the latter had once written a book entitled *Man's Right and Women's Duties*!

Marshall never gave up the study of economics, even after his retirement from Cambridge. Unlike the earlier treatises on political economy, Marshall's *Principles* gave only fragmentary attention to the problems of international trade, taxation, and government finance. In his later years, Marshall attempted to fill the second omission by writing another book. One of the saddest pictures in the history of economic thought is the efforts of Marshall to accomplish this goal and his inability to do so because of advanced years.[3] A mark of his humility and his love for economics is found in the following quotation: "The more I study economics the smaller appears the knowledge I have of it . . . and now at the end of half a century, I am conscious of more ignorance of it than I was at the beginning."[4]

---

[3] Marshall's total literary output, however, was impressive. In addition to his *Principles*, his major works included *Industry and Trade*, *Economics of Industry*, and his *Official Papers*. Work on many of these continued until the last years of Marshall's life.

[4] Joseph Schumpeter, *Ten Great Economists* (New York: Oxford University Press, 1951), p. 109.

Economic Views. Marshall's *Principles of Economics,* like Smith's *Wealth of Nations,* deals extensively with various problems of wealth and distribution. One is impressed immediately by the unexpected ease in reading. Keynes was quite correct in suggesting that Marshall let his readers off much too easily! [5] The difficult parts of the analysis tend to be buried in the footnotes or relegated to an appendix. Although he never achieved his goal, Marshall's book was written to be read by the intelligent layman and he had hopes that it would be a popular book. As a result, Marshall the mathematician makes few appearances throughout the main text.

Marshall's failure to apply his mathematical skills was a matter of conviction as well as a desire for popularity. In Marshall's judgment, mathematics was a tool for the better understanding of economics, but he felt that it should be kept within bounds. "The chief use of pure mathematics in economic questions seems to be in helping a person to write down quickly, shortly, and exactly, some of his thoughts for his own use. . . ." [6] Evidently Marshall felt his ability to think as easily in mathematical terms as in English was not shared by others and that mathematical expressions could be clearly presented in nonmathematical language.

The third aspect of Marshall's *Principles* likely to impress the reader coming to it for the first time is the familiarity of much of the material. While in part this reaction is a reflection of the exposure of the student to a good course in economic principles, part of the fault lies with Marshall. We have already noted his delay in publication, so that much of his thunder had already become a familiar rumble. The comparatively small amount of interest aroused by Jevons in England assured Marshall of an enthusiastic reception for his book at home, but economists on the Continent took a more jaundiced view and tended to view Marshall as a latecomer to the theories of marginal utility and marginal productivity. In addition, the simplicity of presentation and the relegation of the more difficult analyses to footnotes and appendices concealed much of the originality.

A fourth characteristic of the *Principles* (and Marshall's work in general) is its gentleness when dealing with the views of others. Repeatedly Marshall managed to find some saving grace in another's conflicting views and he was constantly seeking to resolve these views. Rarely did

[5] John Maynard Keynes, *Essays in Biography* (New York: Horizon Press, 1951), pp. 191–192.
[6] *Ibid.,* p. 159.

Marshall enter into disputes with other economists. He was sensitive to the criticism of others and was badly hurt by the aspersions cast upon his originality. Because of this sensitiveness about his own writing, he was reluctant to criticize the work of others; for this reason Marshall wrote very few book reviews.

It would be pointless to attempt to cover all of the material reviewed by Marshall in his *Principles* and other writings, even in summary form; the best we can hope to do is highlight some of his major contributions. We will begin as we did with Adam Smith by examining the kind of economic man Marshall was picturing. Marshall's view of man's character changed somewhat through successive editions of his *Principles*. The first edition, for example, pictured men pretty much as hedonists acting in the straightforward manner expected of "good" hedonists. In later editions, however, men's motives became more complex and Marshall saw little hope of predicting the actions of individual men. Despite the fact that men frequently acted in irrational and unpredictable ways, however, all hope for a scientific study of men's economic behavior was not lost; there were two saving graces: Men were most rational in that part of their lives dealing with economic behavior. Furthermore, said Marshall, there was safety in numbers. While the actions of a single consumer might be unpredictable, the actions of larger groups could be more easily discerned. The economist was also blessed by having a reliable measuring rod— money—as a gauge of men's desires. By the ways men chose to spend or earn their money, Marshall declared, one could judge the power of the various motives acting upon them.

Despite Marshall's apparent later willingness to discard hedonism, one is left with the impression that he never completely abandoned the economic man. Most of the people about whom he wrote were solid, middle-class citizens who were both prudent in their decision-making and rational in their decisions. The fact that he agreed with Jeremy Bentham in declaring men also to be creatures of habit did not upset his belief in their rationality as consumers. While many purchasing decisions were made out of habit, the habit itself rested on rational choice in the beginning. The possibility that the economic scene might change so frequently as to require constant reevaluations appeared not to bother Marshall. Nor did the apparent conflict between his picture of men as profit-maximizing individuals and their tendency to display a sense of "economic chivalry" concern Marshall any more than it had Smith.

Marshall's economic man was every bit as industrious and hardworking as Adam Smith's had been. Marshall firmly rejected the backward-sloping supply curve of labor as being applicable only to slothful and backward races and thus quite clearly not to Englishmen!

If it is correct to charge Adam Smith with being an eclectic, the same accusation can be leveled at Marshall with even greater force. Many students of Marshall have ignored the great impact that the German Historical School had upon him. Marshall had a strong sense of history, as the quotation at the start of this chapter shows, and his book *Industry and Trade* was primarily a blend of empirical study with historical perspective. One of Marshall's great contributions to economic thought was to tie more clearly together theoretical reasoning and historical research.

VALUE. The central issue in economics for Marshall, however, as it was for so many other economists, was the problem of value. Here, too, his debt to earlier writers was heavy. Even if we credit him with being unaware of the work of Jevons and the marginal utility theorists on the Continent at the time he was formulating his own version, his acknowledged debt to Cournot and von Thunen was great. His debt to the members of the Classical School is even more obvious. But, although Marshall was not the first to analyze the relationships in the marketplace between demand and supply, it is with his name that the relationship is most frequently associated. Ricardo and Mill both had made reference to the market forces of supply and demand, but it is evident that they used neither term in a schedule sense and that both of them concentrated on supply and the cost of production lying behind it as the ultimate determinant of value. Nor had the contributions of Cournot and some of the Continental proponents of marginal utility, with their more concise versions of demand and supply curves, made much impression on English economists.

Marshall's discussion of elasticity of demand, for example, was anticipated by Cournot, but Marshall developed the concept far more completely than Cournot had; Marshall's analysis of elasticity and the reason for the demand curves' negative slope should be familiar to all students who have passed through a modern principles course; their impact at the time was considerably more significant. We will not dwell on these familiar aspects of Marshall's theory of demand and supply; instead we will confine our analysis to two points: his mention of Robert Giffen's Paradox and the concept of consumer surplus.

The first we can deal with relatively briefly. The possibility was raised by Marshall, and attributed by him to the thinking of Robert Giffen (1837–1910), a British civil servant[7] who was supposed to have suggested

---

[7] Giffen was primarily a statistician. In addition to serving in the British government, he was assistant editor of *The Economic* and for fifteen years was editor of the

that not all commodities necessarily had the typical demand curve sloping downward from left to right. If a commodity played a sufficiently important role in the consumption patterns of low-income families and if it was markedly less expensive than its closest possible substitutes, a rise in the price of this essential and low-cost item would produce an increase in the quantity demanded instead of the normal expected reduction. The rise in price led to the substitution of the commodity for other commodities instead of the substitution of other commodities for it. Marshall made little use of this theoretical nicety and was probably wrong in sharing any credit with Giffen; with the emergence of indifference curve analysis, the question has received further analysis.

The second question—that of consumer surplus—deserves more attention, since Marshall saw practical applications possible. The term "consumer surplus" is based on the principle of diminishing marginal utility and is the result of the fact that consumers may pay less for additional quantities than they would be willing to pay for the first units of a consumed commodity. The point can be made clearer by an examination of Fig. 5.

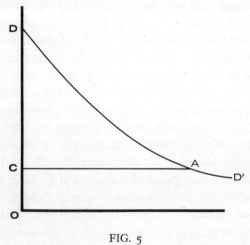

FIG. 5

Note that the consumer would have been willing to pay a high price for the first item if he had had to do so. Instead he paid no more for the first than for the last item purchased, where the price paid, *C*, just matched

---

Royal Statistical Society Journal. Professor Stigler has raised serious doubts whether Giffen ever suggested such a possibility. See George Stigler, "Note on Giffen Paradox," *Journal of Political Economy* (April, 1947), pp. 152–156.

the satisfaction yielded. The difference between the actual cost of the first item and the price the consumer would have been willing to pay represented the amount of consumer surplus obtained from the purchase of the first unit. Similar reasoning could be applied to additional units, and when the results were aggregated, the total consumer surplus achieved could be represented by the triangle *ABC*. We will turn to Marshall's attempts to derive policy implication from this concept shortly, but first we must examine the forces lying behind the supply curve.

Again, Marshall's presentation should be familiar to students previously exposed to a course in the basic principles of economics. Marshall employed somewhat different terms than those used today—variable costs were called "prime" and fixed were referred to as "supplementary," but the roles they played were exactly as they are today, with the *MC* curve serving as the firm's supply curve. From the cost structure for a typical individual firm, Marshall moved to the picture of costs for industries with the now familiar situations of increasing, decreasing, and constant cost industries. Having developed the distinction between increasing and decreasing cost industries, Marshall was then prepared to make a policy suggestion based on his principle of consumer surplus. Suppose, said Marshall, that the government imposed a tax on an increasing cost industry and then used the proceeds to subsidize production in a decreasing cost situation. What would be the result? His answer was that it would be possible to provide an increase in total consumer surplus. That consumer surplus lost from the tax imposed where there was increasing cost was more than made up by the consumer surplus gained from the added output made possible by subsidies to the decreasing cost industry. An examination of Figs. 6 and 7 reveals the reason for this. Before becoming entangled in the geometry of the solution, however, we should take note immediately of an interesting implication of this analysis which set Marshall off from previous supporters of the capitalist system. If it were to be granted that Marshall was correct in his analysis, it would follow that the system of perfect competition was not always able, by itself, to assure the maximization of consumer satisfaction and would leave the door open for government intervention in the pricing system.

Note that in Fig. 6, the result of the tax is to reduce the quantity demanded, thereby reducing the quantity supplied. But with a reduction in the quantity supplied comes lowered costs; thus, part of the burden of the tax can be borne by the producers. Of the reduction in consumer surplus occasioned by the tax, only the area *aka* is not offset by compensating tax revenues, and when this revenue is applied to the subsidization of a de-

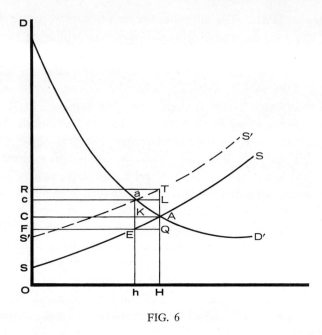

FIG. 6

creasing cost industry, as in Fig. 7, the resulting gain in total consumer surplus is appreciable.

Much of the later discussions of the gains from marginal cost pricing and the justifications for free bridges and other public utility services has been based on this concept of consumer surplus as set forth by Marshall. The theory has been subject to serious attack on several counts, however. One obvious point is the propriety of aggregating individual consumer surpluses. If the same individuals do not make use of the products of both industries (and to the same extent), some consumers may benefit while others may suffer. If a bridge is kept toll-free as a result of a tax imposed elsewhere in the economy, and a particular consumer never uses that bridge but does purchase the taxed commodity, then the consumer's subsidizing another person, and who is to say that the increase in consumer surplus accorded that person is more important than the loss experienced by that consumer? The old problem of interpersonal comparisons that was raised with the earlier marginal utility theorists again makes its appearance.

Closely allied with this first criticism is a reservation about one of the assumptions Marshall made when formulating the consumer surplus concept; Marshall assumed a constant marginal utility of money. This means he assumed that the value of money in relation to other commodi-

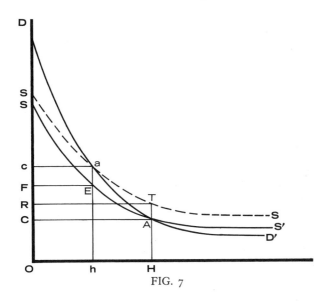

FIG. 7

ties remained the same whether it was the first or last unit spent and irrespective of how much money (or income) the individual consumer possessed. It will be remembered that Walras had warned that the assumption was unrealistic and inappropriate for the real world. Unless money can be assumed to have a constant marginal utility, however, its usefulness as a tool of measurement is seriously compromised. Marshall sought to meet this difficulty and retain the assumption of constant marginal utility of money by specifying sufficiently small quantities of a relatively inexpensive commodity so that any changes in the marginal utility of money taking place would be so microscopic as to be safely ignored.

As to other possible objections to the whole idea of consumer surplus, Marshall was even less cognizant. Do demand curves always intersect the vertical axis, and if not, how can one measure it in even theoretical terms? Do consumers really think in this way on items which they consume continuously? If not, can one speak of a surplus in any meaningful sense? These and similar questions apparently never bothered Marshall.

Most, if not all, economists would agree that if they had to use one word to sum up Marshall's system that word would be equilibrium. But the equilibrium in which Marshall was interested was quite different from that conceived by Walras and Pareto. In the first place, Marshall's system was set forth with a minimum of mathematical analysis; a minimal grasp of simple geometry is all that is required of the reader, although some familiarity with calculus brings a more complete understanding. More important, perhaps, is the fact that Marshall was writing in terms of a partial equilibrium solution. Instead of seeking a simultaneous solution for all markets, all commodities, and all prices, he focused attention on a given commodity produced by the average firm in an industry small enough to leave the rest of the economy unaffected by the change in output; price and output were determined by boundaries prescribed by the *ceteris paribus* assumption. Analysis was confined to a particular product, with the resulting changes produced by shifts in demand and supply duly recorded but with the prices of other commodities assumed at the moment to remain unchanged. This permitted Marshall to dissect the response of consumers to changes in price with greater precision and in a way that was more easily understood by businessmen and consumers alike.

An important part of the Marshallian "scissors" was the role assigned to time. In the very short-run or market situation, the supply was made perfectly inelastic. Under these circumstances, price was set by the level of demand. Marshall assumed a situation where there was no storage and the supply had to be disposed of during the course of the market day. If the demand remained high for a protracted period, some increase in the quantity supplied would be forthcoming as prime costs were increased. Men might work overtime or additional numbers could be employed. Should the demand continue high, long-run appropriate expansions in supply could be made by firms already in the industry through the adjustment of their supplementary costs, so that the size for already established firms was increased while new firms would be attracted to the industry. An American economist, Jacob Viner, later developed this long-run analysis further, with the appropriate diagrams, but the original impetus for this now familiar analysis was Marshall's.[8] To complete the picture, Marshall postulated a fourth situation where long-run adjustments were made in response to changing technology.

While Marshall denied that either blade of his "scissors" was more important in determining value, it is evident that the supply blade played an increasingly important role over a period of time, and in the long run, value, as explained by Marshall, came close to the cost of production explanation advanced by the Classical School. Marshall's thinking in this direction may have been influenced not only by his respect for these earlier theorists but also by the conviction that the task of investigating costs and the supply side of the market was more easily achieved than similar

[8] Jacob Viner, "Cost Curves and Supply Curves," reprinted in *Readings in Economic Analysis,* ed. Richard V. Clemence (Cambridge: Addison–Wesley, 1950).

investigations on the demand side. Marshall repeatedly warned his readers about the difficulties of measuring consumer demand.

Partly for reasons of ease of presentation and partly because he believed it to be largely true, Marshall couched much of his discussion in terms of perfect competition. The demand curve for the individual firm was a horizontal line representing perfect elasticity, and consumers continued to play a dominant role in price determination. Marshall was well aware, however, that the real world did not always function in the manner his model postulated. There were two possible exceptions—businessmen might have enough control over prices to resist cutting prices when demand declined or firms might increase in size. The first of these, in Marshall's judgment, was more likely to be a problem than the second.

Businessmen might refrain from cutting prices in the face of falling demand because of what Marshall called a "fear of spoiling the market." He never made clear what he meant by this cryptic phrase and left the problem of interpretation and elaboration to later students. Marshall's major suggestion was the possibility that businessmen might fear offending and antagonizing rivals. If so, as the English economist Professor Hague has pointed out,[9] this suggests that Marshall had in mind a market sufficiently small in the number of sellers so as to have everyone easily identifiable. The implications of this for competition will be discussed in Chapter XII. Whatever the phrase might be interpreted to mean, the central point was clear—businessmen might possess sufficient market power so as to be able to exert some control over prices. Note also that to the extent that businessmen exert this power, the concept of marginal costs as a factor in pricing and output is correspondingly rendered inadequate.

Marshall also recognized that there were forces acting to increase the size of firms; these forces were of two kinds, internal economies and external economies. Internal economies referred to those coming from within the firm in response to increasing size, such matters as the economies of mass purchasing, mass advertising, and the greater efficiencies associated with large-scale production. Adam Smith's division of labor was again at work! External economies, on the other hand, referred to those external to the individual firm and materializing as a result of expansion by the relevant industry or from economies experienced by supplying industries. It was thus quite possible that the external economies of one firm might be the result of internal economies elsewhere.

[9] D. C. Hague, "Alfred Marshall and the Competitive Firm," *The Economic Journal* (December, 1958), p. 677.

By the same token, it was perfectly possible for a firm to experience both internal and external diseconomies. These internal and external diseconomies, in Marshall's judgment, prevented the problem of monopoly from growing to serious proportions. We have made reference to the average or typical firm in Marshall's analysis several times. Actually Marshall had a different term, which he introduced in his third edition, to connote the way in which firms were kept from expanding beyond normal proprotions; the term he employed was "representative firm." When Marshall introduced this term, he drew by way of analogy on the trees in the forest. Some trees (firms) were young and just beginning to grow, while other trees had reached full maturity and were already beginning to decay. But the representative tree (or firm) was the one just at the stage of early maturity—healthy, vigorous, and typical of the average tree (firm) in the forest (business world). As the representative firm grew older, its days of expansion would come to an end and it would begin to decay just like the older trees in the forest. The analogy was an appealing one, but it overlooked some important differences between trees and business concerns.

Why, for example, should a business firm, after a period of time, not only cease to grow but also experience decline? In part, Marshall's answer was based on the belief that a business firm's health was inextricably tied to the health of its founder or some other single individual. When that man died, the moving force of the firm would be lost. Although in *Industry and Trade* Marshall took greater note of the importance of the joint stock company, its significance was never recognized in his *Principles*. There Marshall continued to write as if a company's life expectancy was not much greater than its founder's.

Marshall did not rely entirely on the mortality of men to curb the excessive growth of business firms; there were other forces at work as well. One saving grace was his belief that internal economies were relatively widespread and rarely so exceptional as to give any one firm a competitive advantage. Furthermore, markets were sufficiently imperfect that it was difficult for the efficient firm to extend its operations beyond certain limits, so that room would always be left for newcomers to carve out their own little niche. At the same time, the ability of newcomers to get started was furthered by the existence of plentiful capital at reasonable rates of interest. Finally, businessmen were precluded from acting toward each other in too ruthless a competitive fashion by the existence of a sense of "economic chivalry." Incidentally, this sense of "chivalry" served also as a protection to consumers.

Modern corporate finance suggests that Marshall was wrong on several counts. First, the modern corporation or stock company need not falter with the death of its founder. For example, the Ford Motor Company has continued to prosper long after Henry Ford ceased "driving" it. Nor are exceptional cases of internal economies as infrequent in appearance as Marshall would lead us to believe. As for Marshall's implication that there was a ready supply of capital for the new infant business concern, similar doubts might be expressed.

Marshall's interjection of the possibility that businessmen might be motivated by a sense of "economic chivalry" was a forerunner of the present-day position, taken by Adolf A. Berle[10] and other economists, that the modern corporation has a conscience and that its managers fail to exercise the market power at their disposal because of a feeling of social responsibility toward workers, consumers, and the entire economy. Whether one can take comfort in this reassurance is a matter of individual preference. What does seem strange is that Marshall, who had built up an elaborate system of analysis to explain the operations of the market, should fall back on this argument. Perhaps the best explanation for this seeming inconsistency lies in Marshall's determination to "prove" that the economic order was efficient enough in both the short and long run.

Marshall had begun his long period analysis of the adjustments in the market as early as 1870 in order to solve the dilemma posed by Cournot as to the determination of equilibrium under conditions of decreasing marginal costs. Cournot had concluded that a decreasing MC curve might be incompatible with a competitive model, but Marshall refused to accept this solution because of his belief in the competitive nature of the economy. Marshall's answer was to devise an equilibrium for the industry without insisting that it also hold for the individual firm. Marshall never devoted his analytical powers to the question of how this might be achieved, and he limited himself to the observation that his description accorded well with the situation as it really existed. Marshall's intuitive solution persisted for a long time, and it was not until late in the 1920's that it became subject to serious question.[11]

One final point is in order before we leave Marshall's discussion of partial equilibrium. Although Marshall believed in the principle of "the survival of the fittest," he did not consider it necessarily true that the best results were thereby achieved. The benefits obtained from a given act of exchange did not assure equal benefits to both parties to the exchange.

[10] A. A. Berle, *Power Without Property* (New York: Harcourt, Brace, 1959), and *The Twentieth Century Capitalist Revolution* (New York: Harcourt, Brace, 1954).

[11] See the discussion of Piero Sraffa in Chapter XII.

Marshall used, by way of illustration, the sale of lace handkerchiefs. The suppliers of the handkerchiefs might have worked for hours, straining their eyes in the process, to earn a few coins which the rich buyer would scarcely miss as he made the purchase. The pleasure and satisfaction in obtaining the handkerchief came nowhere near the pain and effort involved in its creation. Thus the marginal satisfactions and dissatisfactions of the two parties to the transactions could not be compared. All that could be certain, Marshall added, was that the seller and the purchaser had equated the respective gains and losses to themselves from the transaction. Painful as the effort of making the handkerchief had been, the money thus obtained made it worth the effort, while as little as the handkerchief might add to the satisfaction of the buyer, it was still worth the money he spent for it. The assumption of constant marginal utility of money implicit in his statement of consumer surplus no longer existed.

DISTRIBUTION. Before we begin a detailed analysis of Marshall's treatment of distribution, a few general comments should be made. There is a striking difference between Marshall's treatment and that of members of the Classical School, such as Mill and Ricardo. With Marshall, as with other marginal theorists, distribution ceased to be a matter of a division between classes. The issue was no longer one of how much went to the capitalists, how much to the workers and how much to the landlord, but rather how much was apportioned to various factors of production. Gone also was the early preoccupation with the Malthusian doctrine. While Marshall was aware of the possibility that excessive gains in population might result from rising levels of wages and might create problems, he was quite calm about the possible danger. Higher wages and improved living standards were as likely to reduce as raise the birth rate. Furthermore, improved means of transportation and the gains in productivity stemming from technological developments in industry would be more than enough to offset the diminishing returns taking place in agriculture. With the elimination of the class struggle explanation of distribution, this factor in Marshall's view now became more complex and less easily explained. As a result, the treatment accorded to distribution was expanded; Marshall devoted nearly a quarter of his book to the problem.

WAGES. Marshall thought it appropriate to begin his analysis of distribution with the topic of wages, since wages were most subject to other than simple economic considerations. ". . . human beings are not brought up to their work on the same principles as a machine, a horse or a slave." If they were, Marshall continued, ". . . there would be very little difference between the distribution and exchange side of value. . . ." [12]

Despite this qualification, wages were set in the same fashion as the return to other factors of production: "Every agent of production, land machinery . . . labor . . . tends to be applied in production as far as it profitably can be." [13] "Wages tend to equal the net product of labour. . . ." [14] Where the forces of competition were sufficiently great (true for virtually all cases), and where the mobility of labor was sufficiently large (less likely to be true), wages tended to settle at the level indicated by marginal productivity. The manner in which this was attained was similar to that sketched by John Bates Clark, and it need not be mentioned here. It suffices to point out that in the course of his two early chapters on distribution, Marshall employed two analogies which have remained a part of the economic literature: his "marginal shepherd" (that shepherd just worth employing), and his comparison of the decision about the employment of various factors of production to the interdependence of a group of balls lying in a bowl. The use of each factor depended not only on its own price and productivity but on the prices and productivity of all other factors as well. As in the case of the determination of value, the combination of demand and supply and the forces lying behind them was the answer. Unlike the Austrian economists, Marshall never assumed that the total supply of factors of production was fixed.

Marshall was at his empirical best when discussing the earnings of labor. The market did not function in even close-to-perfect fashion. Workers tended to be immobile both in the geographical and occupational senses of the word. Love of home or familiar surroundings, or attachment to a particular line of work might induce workers to remain where they were despite the opportunity to make more money elsewhere. While such cases were frequently found, however, Marshall still felt there was considerable labor mobility in the economy. Workers, particularly unskilled laborers, were often at a competitive disadvantage and unable to protect themselves from the superior bargaining position of employers. In many ways the analysis was more than faintly reminiscent of Adam Smith's. The resemblance held in the long-run period as well. Marshall might be described as a cautiously optimistic Malthusian. Wages had risen and "standards of comfort" might rise more, making possible further increases. One must not forget, however, Marshall cautioned, that the working

[12] Alfred Marshall, *Principles of Economics* (London: Macmillan, 1946), p. 504.
[13] *Ibid.*, p. 521.
[14] *Ibid.*, p. 532.

classes were not always prudent and that overexpansion in numbers might occur.

INTEREST AND PROFITS. The *net* rate of interest (after allowance for variations in the degree of security involved) was again a matter of supply and demand. Individuals were reluctant to supply funds for the same reasons advanced by economists from Smith on—their reluctance to save in the absence of a reward. Marshall replaced Senior's term "abstinence" with "waiting," but the theory was the same despite the change in terminology. The demand for capital came from businessmen who were able to put it to productive use. The amount of interest they were willing to pay was dependent upon the marginal yield forthcoming from its application. Marshall felt that the quantity of money was unlikely to affect the rate of interest. Money simply raised the general level of prices, and since people wanted control over a certain quantity of goods, their response would be to hold more money aside in the form of cash. This last was a part of Marshall's famous quantity theory of money, to which we will turn shortly.

In Marshall's discussion of profits the role of the businessman stood in such striking contrast to the picture drawn by Marx that a brief quotation is in order to provide the reader with the flavor of Marshall's views: "it is probable that those businessmen who have pioneered new paths have often conferred on society benefits out of all proportion to their own gains, even though they have died millionaires." [15] Other equally flattering passages might be quoted as evidence of Marshall's admiration for English businessmen; the tone is different not only from that of Marx, but from that drawn by Adam Smith also. The stage was thus set for a full justification for the existence of profits, as management was raised virtually to the status of another factor of production.

Marshall denied that there was any general law which governed the average rate of profits. He also denied that they were purely a payment for risk borne, "as some American economists allege," and again emphasized the important role played by the creative actions of management. While rates of profit might for these reasons vary widely from trade to trade, each trade had a "fair" rate of profit. Firms failing to make this "fair" rate would soon be forced out of business, while those who made more would soon find their excess reduced by the force of competition.

Marshall never squarely faced the issue of generally declining rates of profit as set forth by Mill and Marx, but he hinted that profit rates might be declining because the risks of trade were "on the whole diminishing

[15] *Ibid.*, p. 598.

rather than increasing." [16] His suggestion that some trades were becoming less challenging and more suitable for joint stock companies was an interesting anticipation of the views of Joseph Schumpeter.

As to whether or not profits entered into the determination of price, Marshall distinguished between the short and the long run. While short-run profits were not a part of price but arose as a kind of surplus made possible by excess demand, in the long run profits must be included as a part of the cost of production since, without them, continued production would not be worthwhile.

RENT AND QUASI-RENT. True rent, or the return to land, was also included in Marshall's application of the principle of supply and demand. The basic difference between land and other factors of production was the obvious one that the supply of land in an old country could not be expanded to meet increases in demand. As to the exact amount of rent any particular piece of land could bear, the answer was found in the principle of diminishing returns and variations in fertility, along the line previously sketched by Ricardo and others.

Between the regular returns on invested capital and the return to land in the form of rent stood a kind of hybrid return called quasi-rent. Long-term investments which could not be immediately duplicated might earn excessive returns for considerable periods, while additions to their supply were being made. In the short run their supply was limited, just as in the case of land, and part of the return to them was analagous to a rent. Unlike land, however, in the long run new supplies could be brought to market and the quasi-rent eradicated. The term was not reserved for capital goods alone; skills which required a long period of training might also yield a quasi-rent, should the demand justify it.

BUSINESS CYCLES AND THE QUANTITY THEORY OF MONEY. Neither of these topics received any attention in Marshall's *Principles,* although both played an important role in his thinking and writing. It is clear that in Marshall's judgment the primary cause of the business cycle was the mismanagement of money and credit. Basic to his explanation of the cycle was the critical role played by the rate of interest in encouraging and discouraging borrowing. The resulting short-run variations in prices were the principal means of spreading the cycle throughout the economy. Changing prices had two effects—they disturbed the allocation of resources, because a generally rising price level meant that some prices rose more rapidly than others, thus leading to diversions in production plans, and second, the expectation of further price changes led to changes in

---

[16] *Ibid.,* p. 621.

plans by both consumers and businessmen. Unemployment was not a basic source of concern to Marshall, although he clearly recognized its evils. One sharp point of contrast between Marshall and Marx is in their attitudes toward technological change, unemployment, and business cycles. While Marx saw the three tightly linked to each other, Marshall viewed technological change as a boon rather than a curse for mankind. He was willing to concede that the displacement problems for older and skilled workers might, on some occasions, be severe, but his analysis led him to more cheerful conclusions than those held by Karl Marx.

Marshall's version of the business cycle is chiefly notable for its view of the cycle as an exceptional occurrence. The normal situation was one of equilibrium, and each cycle, caused by some particular set of circumstances, was a movement away from that norm. Once those disrupting influences were removed, there would be a return by the economy to the equilibrium position.

Marshall applied the quantity theory of money to long-term changes in prices which were unconnected with the business cycle. But with the growth of Keynesian economics and the national income approach, the quantity theory of money has come to play a much smaller role in the principles of economics course than formerly was true; frequently it is now relegated to an appendix of the chapter on monetary policy. This comparative neglect in modern economics obscures the important role played by the quantity theory of money in the past, and it is proper that we sketch briefly the essence of the argument here.

The belief that there was some relationship between the quantity of money in circulation and the general level of prices can be traced back to Ricardo, who blamed the Bank of England's issuance of excessive money for the depreciation of the currency; some version of this theory was generally accepted by most of the economists who followed. Marshall's contribution was to refine the theory and to supply an equation to describe the relationship. Sometimes referred to as the Cambridge equation, it read as follows: $n = yk$ where n stood for the number of monetary units, y for the level of money income, and $k,$ the constant, for the amount of goods and services over which consumers wanted to hold command. We will postpone our criticisms of the quantity theory of money until we have had an opportunity later to examine a second version set forth by Irving Fisher. Even at this point, however, it is quite evident that the interjection of the $k,$ while providing a more complete picture of the relationship between money and prices, has no significant bearing on that relationship as long as k can be assumed to remain constant. Remove the assumption of constancy of k, however, and the direct relation between n and y is lost.

INTERNATIONAL TRADE. Surprisingly, in a book devoted to an examination of the problems of value and distribution, Marshall's *Principles* was singularly devoid of references to international trade. Nevertheless, a considerable amount of attention was given by Marshall to the topic elsewhere in his writings.

Marshall's contribution in this area was mainly a polishing and refining of the views set forth by J. S. Mill. He constructed a geometrical model that clarified and made more precise the gains from trade. In general, Marshall's position on tariffs was much like that of Smith—the gains to the protected individual companies were more than offset by the resulting misallocation of resources, with a concomitant lowered efficiency of output for the entire economy. Marshall, though usually included as a free trader for this reason, was more willing to relax some of the rigidities of that opposition to proposals for trade restrictions which was characteristic of the position of many earlier exponents of free trade. Here, again, the similarity to Smith's position is apparent.

Given his endorsement of the quantity theory of money, it was natural that Marshall should recognize the purchasing power parity theory as a basis for the establishment of exchange rates. It will be remembered that this theory stated that the rate of exchange between any two currencies should be based on the comparative purchasing power held by the two currencies over a given market basket of goods. Although Marshall made note of this relationship, it remained for later economists to develop the theory more completely.

Summary and Evaluation. Marshall, unlike virtually all of the other marginal utility theorists we have previously studied, made no open break with the Classical School. He attempted to put the writings of Mill and Ricardo into mathematical terms, while at the same time grafting onto their theories an expanded role for demand. Like Mill, he wanted to join theory and policy. Although he deemed some of the claims of the German Historical School to be too sweeping, he believed that the historical approach had much to contribute and was himself a devoted collector of facts.

We have already made the assertion that the word "equilibrium" has been irrevocably linked with Marshall's name. An equally accurate word to describe Marshall's economics is "cautious." Marshall was cautious both as a reformer and as a formulator of economic theories. Because of the caution he displayed in presenting his system, and his use of innumerable qualifications and reservations, it is more difficult to criticize his views than those of some of his predecessors. Some of the breadth and comprehensiveness of Marshall's approach stemmed from the fact that, like Adam Smith, he was an eclectic. Even more than his predecessors, Marshall took the various contributions and wove them into a comprehensive and comprehensible system. Well aware of the general equilibrium solution, he nevertheless chose to concentrate on partial equilibrium, and his work along these lines clarified and elaborated various aspects of the theory into a meaningful whole. He was also well aware of the importance of a dynamic approach, and he attempted to introduce dynamic aspects into his system wherever possible. It was his ambition to develop a complete dynamic model at a later date, but he never achieved this goal. Although his failure to do so has sometimes been the basis for criticism of his work, Marshall, by concentrating primarily on a static model, was able to work out solutions for many of the ambiguities previously plaguing static models.

While there is much that has become dated in Marshall's analysis, there is also much that remains fresh and continues to be a basis for current economic thought. His joining of the forces of supply and demand with his exploration of the forces lying behind them and the nature of the interrelationship through time was sufficient to earn him a major place in the history of economic thought. It is therefore all the more regrettable that Marshall spent so much of his later years polishing and revising his *Principles* rather than applying himself to new problems.

The remaining four writers in this chapter are included here because they were influenced by Marshall either as critics or disciples. We will begin with F. Y. Edgeworth, a contemporary of Marshall's and one with whom he frequently exchanged views.

FRANCIS YSIDRO EDGEWORTH (1845–1926)

If it can be said that Marshall concealed his abilities as a mathematician extraordinarily well when writing his *Principles,* the remark hardly can be applied to any of Edgeworth's writings. James Bonar, in his memoir honoring Edgeworth, used the same words against the latter as Edgeworth used against Walras: Edgeworth displayed, said Bonar, "the exuberance of algebraic foliage." [17]

[17] James Bonar, "Memories of F. Y. Edgeworth," *Economic Journal* (December, 1926), p. 651.

The Man. Edgeworth was the brilliant fifth son of a sixth son of a family of Irish writers and poets. Educated at home by tutors until he entered Trinity College in Dublin, he acquired considerable familiarity with the classics, a familiarity which was evident later throughout his writings. He also attended Oxford and was an outstanding student at both universities. In 1877, he was admitted to the bar, but he never practiced law. Instead he adopted an academic career, beginning as a lecturer in logic and then becoming a professor of political economy at King's College in London. In 1891 he went to Oxford as Drummond professor of political economy, following the retirement of the economist, Thorold Rogers. There Edgeworth remained until his own retirement in 1922. Retirement from academic life, however, did not end his career as a practicing economist. Edgeworth continued to write and take an active part in professional organizations.

During his career he held many posts of distinction in those organizations. He was president of the Economics Section of the British Association, a vice-president of the Royal Economic Society, president of the Royal Statistical Society, and a fellow of the British Academy. From 1891 on, he gave a great deal of his time to *The Economic Journal* serving as its first editor and afterward as chairman of the editorial board and still later as coeditor.

Edgeworth produced only three small volumes, and fairly early in his career: *New and Old Methods of Ethics, Mathematical Psychics,* and *Metretike.* The second of these contained much of the core of his writing on mathematical economics. A substantial part of his work, however, is to be found in the numerous journal articles he wrote on probability and statistical theory and economics. Edgeworth collected 34 papers and 75 reviews (a marked contrast from Marshall in this latter figure), a year before he died, and published them in the three-volume series, *Papers Relating to Political Economy.*

Economic Views. Edgeworth gave as the reason for never writing a treatise that large-scale enterprises such as treatises and marriage never appealed to him. Although he succeeded in avoiding both, his contribution to economics was considerable. Edgeworth's three books (the first was little more than a pamphlet, dealt chiefly with the problems of according numerical precision to Utilitarian concepts. The first was a weird combination of Greek quotations and abstract mathematics, until, as Keynes has pointed out, the reader could hardly tell ". . . whether it is a line of

Homer or a mathematical abstraction which is in course of integration." [18]

In his second book, *Mathematical Psychics,* Edgeworth continued his appraisal of the applicability of mathematical symbols. He concluded that cardinal measurements of utility were impossible but that this did not negate the whole principle. It was enough for the consumer to know that he was better off with one combination of goods than with another; there was no need to be able to tell precisely how much better off he was. Having reached this conclusion, it was logical for Edgeworth to seek some way of analyzing ordinal comparisons of utility. The answer he supplied was the introduction of indifference curves; Edgeworth and Pareto share honors for this innovation. Edgeworth had precedence in time, although Pareto's were somewhat superior in formulation. The second part of Edgeworth's *Psychics* dealt with his famous (or infamous) contract curves. Edgeworth attempted to solve the problem largely evaded by Marshall, of the effect on ultimate equilibrium of purchases made by eager buyers before the equilibrium price in the market had been established. Marshall had avoided the issue by assuming that such purchases were few in number and small enough in price (thus leaving the marginal utility of money unchanged) to have no significant effect upon the location of the ultimate equilibrium position.

Edgeworth's solution was to juxtapose the two traders' indifference curves and derive a contract curve through their points of tangency. The result was a considerable range of indeterminancy, and to reach equilibrium in a multiperson market, sales were assumed to be subject to renegotiation or "recontract." Once equilibrium had been achieved, all earlier orders changed accordingly. This exposition reveals Edgeworth at his best and his worst. The theory is ingenious and demonstrates Edgeworth's ability to theorize in an abstract fashion. The only difficulty was that it bore little relevance to factual performance in the marketplace. Whatever reservations we might have about Marshall's solution, clearly he was the better observer of the real business world about him. The charge of lack of realism can be leveled at Edgeworth's other work as well; as Keynes has remarked, Edgeworth had a propensity for skating on thin ice. This fault was confounded by a certain carelessness in presentation. Possessing a sharp eye for the faults of others, he seems to have been unable to cast an equally sharp eye on his own work. His mathematics was rendered even more difficult for his readers by misprints of the symbols.

This failure is rendered all the more significant by the goal which Edgeworth set for himself. He wanted to attach mathematical precision to

[18] Keynes, *op. cit.,* p. 225.

the issues of ethics and sought to find a means of measuring utility, probability of evidence, statistics, equilibrium, and value. "Numbers," wrote Keynes, "constitute . . . Edgeworth's life work." [19] Considering the impressive work he did with those numbers, it is unfortunate that the right numbers were not always used or that they symbolized a world which did not exist.

· TAXATION. Any evaluation of the approximately fifty papers written by Edgeworth on probability and the "law of error" is much too lengthy to be discussed here, but it should be noted that Edgeworth spent almost as much if not more of his effort applying his mathematical techniques to probability and statistics as he had to economics. However, we will, at this point, devote a few words to Edgeworth's views on tax problems.

Edgeworth brought his Utilitarian predisposition to bear when discussing equity in taxation; he was a strong advocate of progressive taxation and worked out the various sacrifice theories of taxation in detail. His support for progression in taxation was tempered by three considerations: (1) his agreement with Marshall that everyone who voted should help support the government; (2) his belief that Utilitarianism could be expressed only in terms of the greatest amount of total happiness without any allowance for the numbers involved; and (3) his aversion to Socialism. Edgeworth also made notable contributions to our understanding of tax incidence. Various taxes were cited by way of illustration, but for the most part he analyzed the problem under varying conditions, such as competition, immobility of capital and labor, and increasing costs.

Summary and Evaluation. Most critics agree that Marshall was a more able mathematician than Edgeworth, but that because of his reluctance to employ mathematics in much of his economic writing, in effect he left that field to Edgeworth. This is mentioned not to belittle Edgeworth's talents as a mathematician, for they were considerable, but only to emphasize the stature of Alfred Marshall. Like Marshall, Edgeworth combined an interest in ethics and social problems with a love of mathematics, but whereas Marshall chose to emphasize the first, Edgeworth placed more emphasis on the second, earning enduring fame as a pioneer in mathematical economics. It was Edgeworth who gave the word "measurement" new significance in economics.

We will now turn to Irving Fisher, an American economist who possessed an equally impressive mathematical skill, and postpone a consideration of Edgeworth's views on monopoly until Chapter XII.

[19] *Ibid.*, p. 231.

IRVING FISHER (1867–1947)

Fisher, like Edgeworth, disowned the notion of cardinal utility and was even more insistent about the impropriety of identifying demand theory with hedonism. As was the case with many of those who attempted to blend marginal utility with mathematical techniques, much of his early work went largely unacknowledged.

The Man. Fisher was born in Saugerties, New York, the son of a Congregational minister. He attended Yale, where he received his A.B in 1888 and his Ph.D. three years later. In 1890 he had become a tutor in mathematics at Yale. His contact with William Graham Sumner, the distinguished professor of economics and ardent exponent of laissez-faire, turned his interest from pure mathematics to its application to economics. His dissertation entitled "Mathematical Investigation in the Theory of Value and Price" set the tone for much of his later work in economics. From 1890 until his retirement in 1935, Fisher was a member of the Yale faculty. While on sabbatical leaves, he also taught at the universities of California, Southern California, and London, as well as the Geneva School of International Studies. Most of his teaching was confined to those subjects in which he was doing research, where he was able to use some of his graduate students as assistants. In addition, Fisher served as a director of a number of American corporations, including the Remington Rand Corporation.

Fisher has frequently been accused of being a health crank and a food faddist, and the charge is not without foundation. In addition, he was a strong supporter of the Prohibition movement. While some of his "fads" were out of keeping with his general level of economic sophistication, his preoccupation with health is more easily understood when one remembers that his father had died of tuberculosis and that Fisher himself had suffered from the disease as a young man, although later he fully recovered. However, his death at the age of 80 suggests that his preoccupation with his health was somewhat overdone.

Economic Views. Space does not permit a detailed review of Fisher's contribution to value theory. To say that his work in the field paralleled Pareto's and Edgeworth's is somewhat misleading, for Fisher was a forerunner of Pareto and Edgeworth in denying the validity of cardinal utility and in providing the basis for indifference curves, although he never fully developed the latter idea. His thoughts on the subject were quite original, but they are no longer new to us.

Fisher made many other contributions; his primary interest was in the question of the purchasing power of currency. He approached the problem from three different directions. His first approach was to seek a means of measuring the changes in purchasing power of currency. In his efforts to do so, he developed what has been called "the ideal index"—a blending of two previously constructed indices by Hermann Paasch and Étienne Laspeyre, the statisticians. His second approach was to seek some explanation for variations in the value of money. This led him to formulate a second version of the quantity equation of money. Fisher's equation read as follows: $MV = PT$, where M was the quantity of money in circulation, V the velocity or rate of turnover of that money, P the general level of prices, and T the total number of transactions. Although Fisher had added another variable to the Cambridge equation, the result was the same; it was still possible to move from the equation to a statement of the quantity theory of money. V was the inverse of Marshall's k; the amount of goods over which consumers desired to have control was reflected in the velocity of money. T, or the total number of transactions, did not appear in Marshall's equation, but given the assumption of full employment, it remained a constant; as a constant it had no bearing on the relationship between M and P.

Numerous criticism arose over the usefulness of the new equation. It was argued that the statement was a truism and as such gave no guide as to existing relationships or appropriate policy to be followed. Other critics argued that the relationship between M and P was actually the reverse of that indicated by the equation; it was changes in P that called forth additional amounts of money, not necessarily changes in M that affected P. The most crucial question, however, was the validity of the asserted stability of V and T. If these two were not assumed to be constant, any exact relationship between M and P was impossible to determine. What, then, were the justifications for assuming them to be constant, and how valid were these justifications? Fisher and his supporters argued that the velocity of money remained constant because, among other reasons, it was a function of the state of transportation and communication of a country and of the pattern of wage payments. Obviously the velocity of money would be lower in an economy where everyone was paid on a monthly rather than a weekly basis; the shorter the time between periods of payment, the higher would be the velocity. But all of these factors changed only very slowly over time, and therefore it was accurate, declared Fisher, to assume that they and the velocity which they determined remained constant in the short run. The constancy of T was even easier to justify. Operating on the assumption of a norm of full employment, it became impossible to alter T in the short run. All factors were assumed to be utilized completely, so that no further increases in output were possible. As Keynes and other critics have pointed out, neither of these conditions necessarily hold even in the short run. The velocity of money has been found to vary with the phases of the business cycle, increasing during periods of upswing (perhaps in anticipation of further rises in prices) and decreasing during downturns, when businessmen and consumers alike are more cautious in their spending habits. It has become even more apparent in recent decades that the assumption of full employment is not always fulfilled.

Having diagnosed the problem at least to his own satisfaction, Fisher undertook the third approach—seeking a means of stabilizing the currency. Actually, Fisher proposed not one, but six different means of achieving that goal. We cannot examine these "remedies" in any detail, but they ranged from proposals familiar to current students of economics as to the use of open-market operations by the Federal Reserve, to the regulation demanding 100-percent reserves for commercial banks. Limitations on profits and the establishment of reserves for bonds and the use of scrip money were also among Fisher's proposals. The proposal that was dearest to his heart was his suggestion for a "compensated" dollar. This was one in which the gold content of the dollar would be made to vary according to changes in the index number of prices. By this means Fisher hoped to achieve a dollar which represented a fixed quantity of purchasing power instead of a fixed quantity of gold, and thereby avoid the unfortunate results when borrowers and lenders tried to protect themselves through changes in the rate of interest.

Summary and Evaluation. Our emphasis upon Fisher's contributions as a monetary theorist have led us to minimize his work as a mathematical economist. It is only proper, therefore, that we point out that he was one of the first economists, not only in America but in the entire world, to emphasize the tie between statistics and theory; thus he became one of the first econometricians. Even in our treatment of his monetary theories, we have not given him all the credit due him. No mention has been made of his "impatience" theory of interest, which was really much more than a new name for abstinence and which involved anticipations of Keynes' marginal efficiency of capital. Some idea of the added space needed to do justice to Fisher's writing can be seen in the titles of his six books: *Mathematical Investigations, Appreciation and Interest, Capital and Income, The Theory of Interest, The Purchasing Power of Money,* and *Booms and Depressions.* The excellence of the scholarship is evident throughout all these works. Only one blemish marred Fisher's scholarly output. The same zeal which he displayed as a health faddist was evident in his enthusiasm for a stable currency, and he organized a Stable Money League to exert pressure on Congress. His conviction as to the correctness of his position and the lengths to which he was willing to go in order to defend it opened him to the criticism that he sometimes jeopardized the scientific character of his work by losing his objectivity.

JOHN ATKINSON HOBSON (1858–1940)

Whereas Irving Fisher was a reformer in the sense that he wished to remodel monetary theory so it would be better able to explain and surmount the problem of the business cycle, John Hobson was mainly interested in social welfare and the problems of distribution. He took his lead partly in response to the economics of Alfred Marshall but more from the teachings of Arnold Toynbee and John Ruskin. A brief résumé of his views is included here not because of his importance as a theorist—his lack of formal training in economics precluded this—but because his writings, although directed to a popular audience, did have considerable impact upon professional economists and because they illustrate another ramification of Marshall's economics—the interest in social welfare.

The Man. Hobson was born in Derby, England of middle-class parents, and was educated at Oxford in the classics. Upon receiving his degree, Hobson took up a career of teaching the classics in a number of public high schools, but he soon decided that this was unsuitable and decided to apply for a university post in economics. He never achieved this goal, however, partly because of his own lack of training in the subject, partly because there was an adequate supply of alternative candidates, and partly because his economic views were (particularly after his early books) considered heretical and unsound. As a result, he spent much of his life as a lecturer (he was an excellent public speaker) and as a writer. From 1906 to 1922 he served on the staff of *The Nation.* Hobson was a prolific writer. Among his better-known works are *Evolution of Modern*

Capitalism, The Industrial System, Work and Wealth, The Economics of Distribution, The Economics of Unemployment and his autobiography, *Confessions of an Economic Heretic;* in all, nearly forty books came from his pen.

Economic Views. Hobson is perhaps best remembered today as an underconsumptionist. We will examine more closely his diagnosis of the problems caused by savings in their relationship to the business cycle and unemployment when we review Keynes in Chapter XIII. The necessary point to be made at this time is that Hobson's views on savings were tied in with his views on distribution. He was not primarily an economic theorist and he relied heavily upon the work of Mill, Marshall, and others to see him over the difficult spots. Nowhere is Hobson's debt to Marshall more evident than in the former's discussion of distribution. Hobson's book on the economics of distribution virtually presupposes a thorough acquaintance by the reader with the writings of Marshall. The conclusions drawn by Hobson in the field of reform went beyond those envisioned by the cautious Marshall, and Hobson's use, and sometimes misuse, of Marshall's economics accounts for the frequent attacks made on Hobson's writing by some of Marshall's students.

A basic postulate made by Hobson was that the economy tended to save too much. Why did this happen? Hobson's answer can be summarized as an assertion that the distribution of income was so unequal that the wealthy received excessive amounts of money and saved them for lack of anything better to do with them.

Hobson saw distribution, whether in the form of wages, interest, or rent, as a payment to the various factors of production. These payments were necessary both for the maintenance of the factors and the assurance of their continued growth. But, said Hobson, all three factors, including labor at times, but more regularly land and capital, were likely to be overpaid, because of actual or contrived scarcities. These excess payments served no useful service to the economy. In fact, the reverse was true; surpluses led to excessive savings and were the source of much of the discontent in the society.

Of the three returns, labor was the one least likely to get even the amount needed for maintenance and growth. Higher wages would almost inevitably lead to increased efficiency and productivity, but increases in wages were won all too infrequently because of the weakness of the forces of competition. The bargaining strength of the capitalists was too great, with the result that surpluses continued to mount in the hands of the capitalists. These surpluses accounted for the excess of savings in the economy and the inability of businessmen to sell all their products. Basic to all of Hobson's concern about distribution was his rejection of a belief in "free" competition sufficient to ensure a satisfactory operation of the market.

From here the step to an analysis of the nature of imperialism was an easy one. If excessive savings with no outlets for investment existed at home, and if businessmen were unable to find an adequate market for their products in the domestic arena, the logical step was to seek markets in other countries. The governments of the various industrial nations were seen as being coaxed into seeking colonies abroad, with the inevitable results. Note that Hobson's study, *Imperialism,* was published in 1902 (following his experiences in the Boer War), and that it set the stage for the later work of Lenin by the same title.

Hobson had a solution for all of these difficulties—a more equitable distribution of income. How was this to be achieved? Hobson held out little hope of labor unions being able to achieve the desired goal; history had demonstrated that while their intentions were good, the success of unions was small, particularly in the case of the workers with the lowest incomes, who most urgently needed assistence. Hobson relied instead upon state action as the best remedy. While government regulation of monopolies and even the operation of public utilities played a part in Hobson's thinking at this point, he was most interested in the use of taxes. By taxing those surpluses in excess of what was needed for maintenance and growth, excess savings would be eliminated, a sufficient market created at home, and the motives for imperialism eliminated.

Summary and Evaluation. Hobson is frequently included among the Socialist critics, and in many ways this designation is not too wide of the mark. We have already seen that his book *Imperialism* anticipated Lenin's at several points, and Lenin commented favorably on some of Hobson's other writings. Hobson's discussion of the neglect of human suffering and pain when computing the cost of commodities was also reminiscent of Socialist writers. Nevertheless, Hobson is more properly classified as a middle-class bourgeois critic of capitalism who had little taste for Marxian philosophy. Banking, insurance, and the basic public utilities were deemed by Hobson to be proper spheres for government operation, but he had no desire to see all of the economy run by the state. In his autobiography, Hobson conceded that his book on imperialism had been too much dominated by a belief in the economic determination of history. Although a popularizer and unversed in the finer points of economic theory, he attempted to apply those principles he had learned to the issue of social reform. In so doing, he earned a minor but enduring place in the history of economic thought.

ARTHUR CECIL PIGOU (1877–1959)

John Hobson came to an appreciation of Marshall's economics the hard way. He was educated at the wrong university (Oxford instead of Cambridge) and never had an opportunity for direct contact with the master. Pigou, on the other hand, was a natural to follow in the Marshallian tradition; he was a student in Marshall's classes and Marshall was his dissertation adviser, and upon the master's retirement, Pigou succeeded to the chair held by Marshall for so many years.

The Man. Pigou was born in England, the son of an army officer. He was educated at Cambridge, where, next to John Maynard Keynes, he was perhaps Marshall's most distinguished student. Like Alfred Marshall, Pigou came to economics by way of mathematics, and in the beginning of his studies was primarily interested in the more lofty theoretical aspects of the subject. At Marshall's insistence, however, Pigou wrote his doctoral dissertation on the more mundane topic, "Industrial Disputes—Their Causes and Consequences." This lesson in the importance of realism and empirical research remained with Pigou throughout his career.

Pigou was so highly regarded by Marshall and the authorities at Cambridge that when Marshall retired in 1908 the young Pigou—then only 31—was asked to occupy the vacated chair. There followed an illustrious career in teaching, writing and government service. Like Marshall, Pigou was frequently called as an expert to serve upon or to testify before various governmental committees. Pigou taught at Cambridge University until his retirement in 1943; the remaining years of his life were spent in continued writing and research. Among his best-known works are his *Wealth and Welfare,* parts of which served as the basis for some of his later writings, *The Economics of Welfare* and *The Theory of Unemployment.*

Economic Views. Much of Pigou's economics was patterned consciously after the man whom he so greatly admired—Alfred Marshall. The spirit of reform which we noted as one of Marshall's chief characteristics was very much in evidence in Pigou, but Pigou's concern over social welfare, unlike that of Hobson, was tempered with the cautiousness and conservatism that had marked Marshall's approach. What chiefly differentiated Pigou from Marshall was the former's more complete willingness to embrace the Utilitarian philosophy of Jeremy Bentham and his more exclusive preoccupation with the problem of welfare.

In embracing the Utilitarian philosophy, Pigou attempted to counter the two charges most frequently leveled against previous attempts to utilize it for practical policy implementation—the difficulties of measuring utility and the impossibility of making interpersonal comparisons of utility. As a solution to the first difficulty, Pigou adopted the same reasoning advanced by Marshall. He was concerned with economic welfare, said Pigou, and fortunately the economist had a measuring rod for the computation of economic welfare; that rod was money. By the ways people spent and worked for their money, the economist was able to measure the satisfactions and disutilities involved.

Pigou believed strongly in the principle of diminishing marginal utility of income, and was convinced that frequently a redistribution of income would result in raising the aggregate welfare of the economy. "Any transference of income from a relatively rich man to a relatively poor man of similar temperament, since it enables more intense wants to be satisfied at the expense of less intense wants, must increase the aggregate sum of satisfaction." [20]

The key qualification in the above statement, of course, is the words "of similar temperament." If the man of wealth is better able to enjoy his money than the poor man is, any redistribution of income might result in a deterioration of society's total welfare rather than its enchancement. Pigou, however, denied that the capabilities for enjoyment differed widely between members of the same society. Furthermore, even where such differences did exist, they would be narrowed with time after a redistribution of income had taken place. The time of adjustment might be a protracted one lasting possibly into another generation, but the important thing to remember was that the tastes of the poor were not permanently stunted by their condition of poverty. Nurtured by an increased flow of liquid funds, their tastes were as capable of expansion into full bloom as those of the rich.

The steps toward redistribution had to be taken very carefully, however, and it was here that Pigou displayed the results of his close association with Marshall. Pigou shared none of Hobson's concern about the possibil-

[20] Arthur C. Pigou, *The Economics of Welfare* (London: Macmillan, 1924), p. 78.

ity of stifling the economy by oversaving. Rather, he was a firm believer in the traditional economist's conviction that savings were all channeled automatically into investment. It was this conviction that later led Pigou to dissent sharply with his colleague and former student, John Maynard Keynes.

Since savings were not a drain upon the economy but a prerequisite for continuing the economic growth of the economy, Pigou ruled out as dangerous many of the usual means for redistributing income. Accepting the implications of time preference and abstinence theories of the interest rate at full face value, Pigou was much concerned that the government do nothing to tip the scales further in the direction of people satisfying their current wants in favor of future satisfactions. This reluctance to endanger thrift led Pigou to condemn any tax which might constitute a threat to savings, including in his list such taxes as property, estate, and progressive income taxes. So great was Pigou's concern about the possible damage to savings that at times he wrote as if any government action which encouraged people to prize the present over the future was a threat to the welfare of the economy.

Pigou also saw other complications in a program of income redistribution fostered by state action. A redistribution of income might endanger the incentive for investment and thus further hamper economic growth. The possibility that the redistribution might benefit unduly the idle and lazy also had to be recognized. At points, Pigou sounded like Malthus in his denunciation of the operation of the Poor Laws. With all of these possible dangers in view, it was little wonder that Pigou was cautious in his recommendations for state action.

Nevertheless, Pigou took a long step away from the traditional position of laissez-faire. In his view, the free market did not always assure the best possible results, and the state could play a creative role in improving the general welfare. The general welfare, said Pigou, was more than a summation of all the individual welfares, and one could not be certain of obtaining the greatest total general welfare by permitting each individual to attempt to maximize his personal position. Pigou accepted the Utilitarian premise that every individual sought to maximize his own individual satisfactions, but denied that the economy always functioned in such a way as to assure that the costs (or benefits) of production were always properly allocated so as to ensure their proper distribution or the maximizing of total welfare. In order to explain how resources were diverted away from their ideal use, Pigou developed two new terms: the marginal private net product (*MPNP*) and the marginal social net product (*MSNP*). Balancing each of these, respectively, were the marginal private costs and marginal social costs. Whereas the marginal private cost and the marginal private net product accrued to the individual producer from the production and sale of a given commodity, the social costs and products were the costs and gains borne or acquired by society. The problem was that the private costs might be less than the resulting social costs which fell on society. The opportunities for differences were not difficult to uncover. The smoke from the factory chimney that dirtied the housewife's laundry, or the effect upon property values from the improper location of the factory, were costs not paid for by the individual producer but borne by society. Numerous similar instances where modern industry does not pay the full cost of its production to society have been enumerated in Karl Kapp's book, *The Social Costs of Industry.*[21]

Pigou also had harsh words to say about the damage to the nation's moral standards resulting from the sale of alcoholic beverages and the hiring of women by employers seeking to capitalize on a cheap source of labor. The damage to the society in the form of weakened family ties resulting from this latter policy might be far greater than the gains for the employers. Advertising also came in for its share of criticism; some advertising was useful in providing the consumer with needed information, but most of it reduced rather than increased the social net product. All of these conflicts between private and social products, in Pigou's opinion, provided ample opportunity for intervention by the state.

The message contained in the foregoing examples can be summarized by saying that the output of the economy was maximized when private net product and social net product were equal, and costs were best allocated when marginal private cost equaled marginal social cost. One other major source of divergence between the two still needs to be expressed; the influence of Marshall's thinking at this point will be obvious. Marginal private net product and marginal social net product, said Pigou, were most likely to be equal when increasing costs prevailed. The situation, however, was quite different, given decreasing costs. In such cases, the firm was unlikely to push its output to the amount which society was capable of utilizing, at the costs of production involved. The solution Pigou proposed was much the same as Marshall had offered before him— a system of taxes and subsidies to insure expansions of output by those

[21] Karl W. Kapp, *The Social Cost of Private Enterprise* (Cambridge: Harvard University Press, 1956).

industries experiencing increasing returns. Pigou, however, was willing to go beyond Marshall's solution and consider the possibility of strict government regulation or even government operation of such industries.

Pigou also saw a role for the state in directly fostering improvements in the conditions of labor. There was a tendency of men to work longer hours than were good for them, and the state could improve conditions by regulating hours. Unlike Hobson, Pigou saw considerable opportunity for labor unions to improve the situation for workers and achieve redistribution of income through collective bargaining. It was only proper, therefore, that the state do nothing to hinder the development of unions.

Although we have been emphasizing those differences between private and social net product which were at the expense of society, it should be noted that Pigou recognized that the reverse might also hold true. Most such cases were variations on Marshall's "external economies"; Pigou offered scientific research as a good example. Not only did research spread knowledge to competing firms, thus reducing their costs as well as those of the innovating firms, but the resulting gains to society in the form of lower costs and better products were equally great. Where Marshall had discussed such gains under the heading of "consumer surplus," however, Pigou shied away from the term, feeling that it was misleading in that it provided no means of measuring the gains and losses resulting from variations of very small amounts of output in different industries.

Keynes used Pigou as his primary target in attacking Classical and Neoclassical views on employment and equilibrium. After taking brief note of Pigou's position here, we will return to the question again when we examine Keynes in Chapter XIII.

Although the comment is sometimes heard that Keynes selected a straw man in choosing to focus his attack upon Pigou, there was much in Pigou's position to justify Keynes' choice of his former teacher as representative of the theorists whom he (Keynes) wished to attack. Pigou was one of the early students of the business cycle, but he never was convinced that the economic system would fail to return to conditions of full employment if it were permitted to operate without institutional interferences. (However, some of his confidence on this point was shaken by Keynes.) Both in his writing and in testimony before Parliamentary committees, Pigou expressed the belief that full employment could be restored by cutting wages. Pigou also expressed great confidence in the power of the Central Bank to assure stability by its employment of open market operations and an appropriate discount policy.

Summary and Evaluation. Pigou developed the social reform aspects of Marshall's economics in a fashion much closer to the spirit of Marshall's philosophy than was true for Hobson. Although Pigou's belief that the goal of mankind was not wealth but "welfare" set the tone for the numerous welfare economists who followed, his predication of his system upon the basis of Bentham's version of Utilitarianism considerably reduced his acceptability for many twentieth-century readers. His loyalty to his teacher led him on one hand to champion the redistribution of income and on the other to worry lest any penalizing of property might jeopardize savings. Since property was then, and continues to be, the major cause for the unequal distribution of income, the two positions were difficult to maintain. Later writers have attempted to rehabilitate Pigou's weaknesses by removing his assumptions that utility was measurable and was capable of interpersonal comparison. By being less concerned about preserving savings, they have also been less compelled to face the contradiction described above that was forced upon Pigou.

For those economists who found the welfare overtones of Alfred Marshall's cautious suggestions for reform distasteful, the welfare economists who followed his lead have been an even more bitter dose to swallow! All of the expected complaints about the fallacy of economists trying to set goals for society and make value judgments have been repeated. Welfare economists have in turn rejected as pointless attempts to formulate instruments of policy without having reached at least tentative agreement of what the goals are to be. Some clearing of the air might be achieved if the welfare economists offered a more definite meaning for the word welfare and made clear precisely whose welfare they had in mind. Neither Hobson nor Pigou (both of whom set welfare as their goal) ever clearly defined the term, and other welfare economists have been equally negligent in this respect.

CHAPTER XI: Three American Institutionalists

America, which has produced the most finished and tenacious brand of business civilization, has also produced the most finished and tenacious criticism of it. That is the core meaning of Thorstein Veblen's work. It was a body of work bounded on both sides by the image of economic power.

—MAX LERNER

Our orthodox economists have a most inadequate conception of psychology—and economics also, for that matter. They write as if the economist's only concern with psychology lies in the problem of motive.

—WESLEY MITCHELL

Economics is a branch of social Philosophy.

—JOHN R. COMMONS

The acknowledged founder of the American Institutional School is Thorstein Veblen, and it seems quite clear that he received part of the inspiration for his ideas from the German Historical School. It is not surprising, therefore, that we can detect many points of similarity between the two schools. Both groups expressed a strong skepticism about traditional and marginal utility economic theory. Both schools were dubious of finding final and enduring principles which could be applied to all places and all times; both schools were convinced that times changed and that economic theories must change with them. Most significant of the changes taking place over time was the evolving character of the institutions which shaped men's patterns of behavior.

Because eternal principles were impossible to discover in the opinion of most members of both schools, great emphasis was placed on the use of empirical research and the inductive method, with a corresponding minimization or dismissal of the deductive method. The proper procedure was first to collect all the facts and then devise an explanation based on the facts, rather than erecting a model before all the parts (facts) were available. Wesley Mitchell's approach to the study of the business cycle was representative of this approach. Since the assemblage of facts can prove to be an endless task, the problem still remained as to when conclusions could be safely drawn—a problem neither school was able to solve completely.

We can, however, overdo the comparison of similarities between the German Historical and American Institutional School; the latter had a distinct flavor and approach of its own, and the three economists whom we have selected as representative of the institutionalist were no mere parrots of an earlier doctrine but three of America's most original economic theorists. It is only appropriate, therefore, that we also explore briefly some of the things which distinguish their approach from that of the German school.

Unlike the members of the Historical School, the Institutional School saw less to be gained from the intensive study of history. History was not important in itself, but only as a means of studying changing institutions. As a result, the institutionalists tended to place more emphasis on contemporary changes. Even Veblen, who wrote of a "savage period" spanning some ten to twelve thousand years in time from the Neolithic Age to the Middle Ages, devoted a small fraction of his writing to those early periods and was interested primarily in their anthropological aspects.

Although the Institutionalists derive their name from their study of institutions, it is difficult to define what they meant by the term. What is certain is that they placed more stress upon the role of institutions than had the German Historical School, and saw institutions evolving through history in a Darwinian rather than a Hegelian manner. Because of differences in the approach of the three writers to be examined in this chapter, the term institution can best be defined in the broadest sense of the word to include not just organizations such as corporations, unions, courts, and other branches of government, but the patterns of habit, custom, and thought as expressed in group behavior. Defined as such, the term comes very close to what the anthropologist means when he speaks of a people's "culture."

If anything, the Institutionalists were even more willing than the German Historical School to go beyond the customary definition of the boundaries of economics and to extend their analysis into areas traditionally reserved for the political scientist, the sociologist, or the anthropologist; this tendency was particularly characteristic of Veblen and Commons.

In varying degrees, all three of the Institutionalists we are about to study were reformers, and their dissatisfaction with the way the current economic scene appeared aroused them to biting criticism (Veblen) or to efforts to improve the situation through corrective legislation (Commons). Unlike the Socialist critics we have previously studied, however, the Institutionalists, with the exception of Veblen, saw no need to overthrow capitalism, and even Veblen was unwilling to support state control of the economy. Laissez-faire and a complete reliance upon the market would no longer suffice, however; the problems of the business cycle and business monopolies were becoming too great for that. Both the German Historical and the Institutional School had social reformers in their membership, but the Institutionalists were willing to espouse a more drastic and complete set of reforms.

It might be noted by way of a final contrast between the two schools that the American Institutional School was less nationalistic in orientation than the German Historical School—the American state had been an accomplished fact for over a century—and that the Institutionalists tended to be more liberal and democratic in their views.

THORSTEIN BUNDE VEBLEN (1857–1929)

The Institutional School began with the writings of one of the most brilliant and peculiar individuals ever to grace the economics scene. Judged by the usual American criterion of success, Veblen was in most ways a failure. He was always in financial difficulties (partly of his own making), and despite the publication of eleven books, he never became a full professor. At the University of Chicago he started at the lowly salary of $500 and was still an instructor when many of his classmates were already at senior ranks. He did not become an assistant professor until he was in his forties.

The Man. Veblen was born in Wisconsin. He was the son of Scandinavian immigrants in a family of twelve children, and spent his early years on a Minnesota farm. Little is known of these early years, but Veblen's life as a pioneer in pioneer country must have been a difficult one. Encouraged by a father who sought college educations for all his children, Veblen's rural heritage did not interfere with his pursuit of learning. At the age of 17 he entered Carleton Academy, and three years later was admitted to the college, where he was a student of John Bates Clark. Upon graduation, he taught briefly at a private Norwegian school and then undertook graduate study at Johns Hopkins University, where he studied economics with Richard T. Ely. His failure to obtain a fellowship at Hopkins and his dissatisfaction with the university led him to move to Yale, where he received a Ph.D. in philosophy. The first of a series of reverses in Veblen's life now took place; despite his degree, Veblen was unable to secure a teaching position, probably because his agnosticism made him unacceptable at a time when philosophers were supposed to have religious overtones. For the lack of anything better to do, and because of poor health resulting from an attack of malerial fever while at Yale, Veblen returned to the family farm in Minnesota, where he spent the next years in intellectual isolation. Little of importance occurred during this period in Veblen's life, save that in 1888 he married a former classmate at Carleton; most of his time was occupied in wide and apparently aimless reading.

In 1891, Veblen attempted to venture again into the academic field. He applied to Cornell, where he impressed Professor J. Laurence Laughlin, then head of the economics department, who aided Veblen in securing a teaching fellowship. When Laughlin moved to Chicago the following year, he invited Veblen to accompany him, and Veblen did; Veblen remained at the latter university until 1906—his longest period of time at any one university.

While at Chicago, Veblen displayed many of the strengths and weaknesses which were to characterize his entire life. His encyclopedic knowledge and interest in a wide variety of subjects was demonstrated by his command of Norse literature and his expertise in Cretan and Icelandic archaeology. During this period he wrote many articles and book reviews, and completed his first and best-known book, *The Theory of the Leisure Class*.[1] He also rendered a creditable performance as editor of the *Journal of Political Economy*. Unfortunately, he also displayed at Chicago his weaknesses as a teacher. Most of his classes were conducted in a dull monotone and he displayed little interest in the students who ventured into his courses. Already in evidence was his contempt for the customary social amenities and his inability to get along with his colleagues. Undoubtedly, these deficiencies explain why it took him eight years to become an assistant professor, even though he possessed his doctorate at the time of his employment. Eventually, one of several affairs with women led to a dis-

---

[1] A long list of books was to follow. In addition to those included among the recommended reading, mention should be made of *Absentee Ownership and Business Enterprise*, *Imperial Germany and the Industrial Revolution*, and *The Economics of Higher Education*.

pute with his wife and he was forced to leave Chicago. In 1906 he moved
to Stanford, where the same handicaps, including his well-known attrac-
tion to women (even when they were already married to other men),
compelled him to shift five years later to the University of Missouri. There
he was aided by Herbert Davenport, a former student and now a well-
known price theorist in his own right. For some years, until the time of
Veblen's second marriage, he lived in the cellar of Davenport's home.
Veblen was no greater success as a teacher at this institution (although he
lasted nearly ten years), and eventually he went to the New School for
Social Research, where another former student and friend was on the faculty—Wesley Clair Mitchell. This proved to be Veblen's final teaching
position; the last few years of his life were spent in virtual seclusion in
California, where he was financially supported, in part, by another of his
former students.

In between the teaching positions at Missouri and the New School, he
worked briefly in Washington for the Food Administration in 1918 and
for another brief period as editor of the journal, *The Dial.* One of his
acquaintances relates the following story which is indicative of Veblen's
outlook on life: Several economists who, along with Veblen, had just lost
their government positions, were sitting at a restaurant table discussing
their plight when Veblen walked in. One of the party asked Veblen how
he felt about being fired, and Veblen replied, "When you have sucked as
many lemons as I have, you grow accustomed to the taste." Perhaps it was
this bitterness which led Veblen to reject curtly the proffer of the presi-
dency of the American Economic Association in 1924 when Paul Douglas
(later a senator from Illinois) persuaded his colleagues to make the offer.

Economic Views. In addition to the usual difficulties encountered
when attempting to compress the ideas of someone like Veblen, who
wrote so widely on so many subjects, Veblen's writings impose an additional handicap. When is Veblen to be taken seriously and interpreted at
face value and when is he quietly poking fun, not only at his subject but at
his audience as well? We will begin our analysis where it is most certain
that Veblen was in deadly earnest—his criticism of Classical and marginal utility value theory. So complete was his rejection of earlier theories
of value that at times he appeared to confuse the two schools and write as
if the Classical theorists could also be interpreted as proponents of marginal utility.

Veblen based his case against earlier theories of value on four major
criticisms. First of all, he denied that men were as rational as marginal

utility theory implied; men did not act as rational economic individuals but rather as creatures of habit and custom. The role of habit in shaping men's actions played an important part in Veblen's system. Closely connected with his rejection of the assumption of rationality was Veblen's equally firm dismissal of hedonism.

> The hedonistic conception of man is that of a lightning calculator of pleasure and pain, who oscillates like a homogeneous globule of desire of happiness under the impulse of stimuli that shift him about the area. He has neither antecedent nor consequent. . . . Spiritually, the hedonistic man is not a prime mover. He is not the seat of a process of living, except in the sense that he is subject to a series of permutations enforced upon him by the circumstances external and alien to him.[2]

Veblen's third reason for rejecting early theories of value was based on his belief that work was enjoyable and played an important part in men's lives. Work was, therefore, not a pain, and it was fallacious to measure value in terms of the amount of work contained in a commodity. Veblen even went so far as to assert that one of the basic "instincts" motivating men was an "instinct of workmanship." This "instinct," like custom and habit, played an important part in Veblen's thinking, and we shall return to a discussion of these factors when we review his analysis of capitalism.

We should add here, however, that the "instinct of workmanship" was, according to Veblen, but one of forces motivating mankind. The others were custom, habit, the "parental bent," instinct for pugnacity and the propensity to "idle curiosity." Veblen included under "parental bent" all those acts of a nonmonetary and unselfish character which men performed on behalf of the group of which they felt themselves a part. "Idle curiosity" was what drove men forward to make new discoveries; in the process they became more familiar with the nature of science and less dependent upon magic and superstition as ways to combat the unknown. Men had a desire to learn, and it was this desire rather than necessity that was "the mother of invention." To explore these instincts in any detail would take us too far from the central purpose of this book, but it should be noted that by stressing these three motivations to the exclusion of others, Veblen was just as guilty of presenting only part of the story as those economists whom he criticized.

Veblen's last (but by no means least) basis for rejecting Classical value theory and the concept of marginal utility was the fact that their expo-

---

[2] Thorstein Veblen, *The Place of Science in Modern Civilization and Other Essays* (New York: B. W. Hubsch, 1919), pp. 73–74.

nents had considered only a static state. Nothing, in Veblen's judgment, could be further from the way in which the real world operated. Analysis which was confined to the static state was limited to a single stage of development and ignored the possibility that in other circumstances hedonism would be inapplicable. Imagine, said Veblen, trying to apply hedonism to the activities of the Aleutian Islanders. The fact that nothing could be further from the intentions of the earlier economists was no excuse; it only compounded the error. In Veblen's view, the primary error of the Marginal theorists lay not so much in the fact that they had come up with the wrong answers to their questions, but that the questions which they asked were wrong. Other economists, who confined themselves to a static approach and analyzed prices and distribution in terms of pleasure and pain, missed the fact that men were motivated more significantly by various instincts and propensities. The really important questions to be studied, therefore, were how these instincts were formulated by the institutional environment and what forces produced changes in these institutions. Properly studied, economics should become "an evolutionary science." [3] A failure to recognize the evolutionary character of economics, in Veblen's judgment, reduced its study to little more than a defense of private property and the status quo.

Not only did most other economists ask the wrong questions and thus produce meaningless answers, according to Veblen, but they were also guilty of presuming to advise others of appropriate actions. Nothing could be more wrong, in Veblen's professed view. The proper role for the economist was one of the detached observer; he might be amused at peoples' foibles but he should never venture to suggest corrective actions. The economist who displayed any traces of partisanship was no true scientist. Even the later German Historical School, in which Veblen found so much to admire, was sometimes guilty of this sin, according to Veblen.[4] However it is hard to interpret Veblen's writing as other than that of someone who hoped to achieve reform. His attacks on the preconceptions of the Classical School make no sense except as an attempt to reform economic theorizing. It seems likely that despite his apparent playfulness Veblen intended to be taken more seriously than he frequently was—by friends and foes alike. If one accepts Professor Max Lerner's interpretation (as seems quite appropriate) that Veblen believed men were basically good [5]

[3] *Ibid.*, pp. 56–58.

[4] See Veblen's review of Schmoller's economics in *The Quarterly Journal of Economics* (November, 1901), pp. 68–93.

[5] See Max Lerner's critique in his preface to *The Portable Veblen*, Max Lerner, ed. (New York: Viking, 1948), p. 42.

but that the institutions they had developed led them in improper directions, it seems logical to conclude that Veblen hoped by his writing to change some of these institutions.

CRITIQUE OF CAPITALISM. Veblen's playfulness and his assessment of the current economic scene came quickly to light in his first and undoubtedly best-known book, *The Theory of the Leisure Class*. Veblen's protestations that he was but an impartial disinterested observer made his sardonic irony all the more biting. His addiction to sarcasm and cutting criticism made him appear to be making judgments even if none was intended. Veblen saw the social and economic structure as headed by a group whose chief claim to fame lay in their ability to live handsomely without any need to work. Not only did they not work, but they flaunted their ability to escape such exertion by various kinds of conspicuous leisure. The acquisition of a classical education and useless bits of information (such as Icelandic archaeology?) could be offered as evidence that the possessor could afford the time necessary for their acquisition. One of the most challenging problems, therefore, facing the leisure class was demonstrating their financial superiority, and another favorite means of accomplishing this was what Veblen called "conspicuous consumption."

"Conspicuous consumption" could take various forms, including dress, servants, and the customary pleasures usually reserved to the wealthy. Women were a highly satisfactory means for men to display their station in life. And few women could help but agree with Veblen's prescription of the means by which the husband (by dressing his wife extravagantly and permitting her to be free of work) could achieve recognition from society. The cream of the jest, however, lay in the fact that conspicuous consumption became a way of life for all the members of the society as the process of "pecuniary emulation" assured a process of "keeping up with the Joneses" on a grand scale. The impersonal character of everyday life made it imperative that consumers rely on minor items such as clothing as a means of proclaiming their station in life; Veblen's point has been reemphasized in recent years by Vance Packard's *The Status Seekers*. In Veblen we have an analysis of the factors motivating consumers quite different from that postulated by the Marginal Utility School.

One of the major motifs of the *Leisure Class* was wastefulness, and concern over this problem continued to dominate Veblen's later books. In his *The Theory of Business Enterprise* and *Absentee Ownership and Business Enterprise,* Veblen pictured a sharp contrast between the forces of technology and business interests. Technology made possible expanded output and greater abundance, but it was prevented from achieving this goal by "business sabotage." Veblen denied that business interests were dedicated to increasing efficiency; in fact, the exact opposite was true; businessmen were afraid of efficiency and did everything within their power to slow its pace. Why did this happen? The entire story requires some time to tell, but the final answer was simple—efficiency endangered business profits and businesses were interested not in producing larger amounts of more serviceable goods but in maximizing profits.

The second major figure in the Institutional School, and a warm friend and admirer of Veblen's—Wesley Mitchell—has suggested that Veblen came to this conclusion because of his belief that money played a greater role in economic affairs than that assigned to it by the Classical economists.[6] According to Mitchell, Veblen saw money not as a mere convenience in the process of exchange, but as an important end in itself. Thus Marx was right when he converted the equation $C–M–C$ to $M–C–M'$.[7] The making of money became a part of the culture and a means of securing recognition; its possession was the magic key for entrance into the leisure class.

The old "instinct of workmanship," with its accompanying pride in craftsmanship and the desire to produce material goods, was subverted by absentee owners, driving for monetary gains, into a program of restricted output, the production of shoddy goods, and various other monopolistic practices. When expansion in output corresponded with the opportunities for greater profits, it was possible for the economy to have its cake and eat it too, but too often the two objectives were in conflict, and when this occurred, the result was inevitable. Output was sacrificed on the altar of profits.

Most of the ills plaguing the capitalistic system were the fault of the businessmen. The small firm owned and operated by its founder was squeezed out, leaving the scene to the trusts and monopolies. The tendency noted by Adam Smith over a century earlier for businessmen to form conspiracies was seconded by Veblen, who, in looking at the scene about him, felt that the efforts to eliminate competition had been all too successful. "It is very doubtful if there are any successful business ventures within the range of the modern industries from which the monopoly element is wholly absent."[8] The reason for this irresistible pressure toward monop-

[6] Wesley C. Mitchell, ed., *What Veblen Taught* (New York: Viking, 1936), reprinted in Henry W. Spiegel, ed., *The Development of Economic Thought* (New York: John Wiley, 1952), pp. 397–398.

[7] See Chapter VII on Marx.

[8] Veblen, *The Theory of Business Enterprise* (New York: Scribners, 1935), p. 54.

oly, as set forth by Veblen, was reminiscent of Marx. Technology outran the markets for the goods produced and businessmen sought combinations in order to protect their profits. Unemployment and business cycles were frequent by-products of the quest for profits. When business activity declined, the bears on Wall Street would reap the benefits.

BUSINESS CYCLES. Veblen not only recognized the existence of business cycles and made them an integral part of his view of capitalism, but also he had to devise an explanation for their existence. According to him, the root of the problem was the overexpansion of credit. When business prospects appeared favorable, businessmen were eager to borrow money and were willing to continue doing so as long as their earnings exceeded the rate of interest. But as borrowing continued, three things happened: The rate of interest began to rise, expected increases in earnings failed to materialize, and the discrepancy between earning power and capitalization of the property, based on expected earnings, became excessive in terms of the real earning power of the assets. Veblen was unclear as to precisely when the turning point would come, but presumably at some point one or more businessmen would become aware of the discrepancy and attempt to liquidate their holdings. The edifice collapsed swiftly, much like a house of cards, as other businesses underwent forced liquidations, with the elimination of small business occurring much in the manner pictured by Marx.

Recovery would occur when a sufficient amount of liquidation had taken place. But Veblen was extremely pessimistic about the future; he saw the downturns as becoming increasingly severe and protracted. Speculation and easy credit were the most likely means of promoting temporary recoveries, but these were likely to worsen things eventually.

Veblen's emphasis upon the overexpansion of credit as an explanation of the business cycle was in anticipation of some of the more modern monetary explanations, but it differed from the latter in one important respect. Veblen was unwilling to concede any creative role to credit when viewed in the aggregate. The benefits a businessman achieved through the use of credit were dissipated when competitors also made use of it. The creative role credit might play in enabling a businessman to organize his plant more efficiently or to employ unutilized factors of production in his plant won no recognition from Veblen. If criticized on this point, however, Veblen would probably have responded that the critic was only revealing his orientation toward a capitalistic system; with other types of economies, credit would have no constructive role to play.

The prospects of worsening depressions and the continued sabotage of progress by businessmen in search of profits made Veblen very pessimistic about the future. At times he seems to have given way to complete despair, declaring that perhaps the best hope for the future lay with the Russians. The depth of the sense of hopelessness displayed by this remark becomes more apparent when it is remembered that he was never a Socialist (although frequently sympathetic to Socialist ideals) and found much of Marx's theory confusing if not downright misleading.

At other times, Veblen suggested that the day might come when the military would assume a position of dominance. Throughout much of his writing, there was the suggestion that certain activities such as the military preceded the industrial order and were a part of men's thinking from early times. As business expanded on an international scale, the resulting conflicts between the businessmen of different nations inevitably involved the use of the military, with the possibility that society might revert back to an earlier stage of complete totalitarianism.

One less grim possibility suggested itself. The battle between the business interests and the technological order might be resolved in favor of the latter if the engineers grew sufficiently impatient with the bonds imposed upon their creative efforts by business and seized power for themselves. In his *The Engineers and the Price System* Veblen predicted that the day might come when the engineers and skilled workmen would seize the means of production and use them to the best interest of society. The gains in output thus achieved would be sizable; Veblen estimated that ouput could be almost doubled if it were freed from the hampering restrictions imposed upon it by businessmen.

Let us digress at this point to note Veblen's views on the transmission of technological information to other countries. Veblen believed that the country which was a late starter might, once development had begun, be able to progress at a much more rapid pace than had been true for those countries which were pioneers. As examples of his point, he cited the cases of Germany and Japan. Why was this likely to be true? Because, said Veblen, the imitating country did not take along with the technology those institutions which had hampered the progress of the forerunner nations. Veblen would have been the first to admit that the adopting nation might have institutions of its own which might slow its progress, and that his theory could not be applied without qualification to all underdeveloped nations.

One can find sizable traces of the farm boy in Veblen's attitudes toward business and his aversion to waste; there is a kind of country-lad suspicion of the ways of high finance and the big city. By the same token,

Veblen's awe of technological science and his warm admiration for the wonders of the machine may also in part be attributed to his rural background.

The role of the machine was crucial in Veblen's thinking. The largest single segment of men's time was spent at work, and it was natural that conditions of work should shape men's habits and way of life. Unlike the Socialist critics, however, Veblen saw no necessary evils resulting from the use of machinery. It was the abuse, not the use of machinery that was the problem, and the abuse lay in failing to use it in the most productive manner possible.

Veblen conceded that the machine might change workers' lives in some undesirable ways. Home ownership and the possession of many personal belongings might be limited because of the greater mobility necessitated by the introduction and use of machines. Veblen completely rejected, however, the notion that the machine acted to brutalize men's work. Much of the loss of pride in workmanship came before the advent of the machine, when men began to produce things for money and when the numbers in the market reduced the ability to identify a worker with his products. As for the machine and the changes it involved, Veblen remained confident that men's intelligence would enable them to adjust to the changing conditions of work occasioned by machinery with little difficulty. Even more important than the material progress made possible by the machine, in Veblen's view, was the way in which it matured men's thinking, leading them to abandon magic and superstition for a scientific approach to problems.

Summary and Evaluation. It would be impossible to award Veblen anything but the highest honors for originality and brilliance. His loneliness and his unwillingness to follow the familiar paths marked out by earlier economists led him to novel approaches to the question of what was important for economists to study. In an early article on the role of the Jew as an intellectual,[9] Veblen suggested that the Jew's position in society as an outsider permitted him to analyze the situation in a detached and impersonal way, freed from many of the conventions binding other members of the society. Much of Veblen's analysis with respect to the Jew could be applied to Veblen himself; he was a stranger almost from another world, who considered himself (not always correctly) as divorced from

[9] Veblen, "The Intellectual Preeminence of Jews in Modern Europe," in *Essays in Our Changing Order* (New York: Viking, 1934).

the conventions and mores of the society in which he lived. And some of his strongest attacks were launched against men like Clark and Davenport, who had aided his career.

Much of Veblen's work reads as fresh today as it did forty to fifty years ago, when it was written. Students today can still enjoy discussing whether "conspicuous consumption" plays as large a role in our economy as Veblen suggested or whether "pecuniary emulation" remains an important part of the American way of life.

Some of Veblen's points were more clearly subject to rejection, even at the time he wrote them. His various "instincts," including the "instinct of workmanship," were as questionable in the eyes of students of psychology as the hedonism which he so firmly rejected. Attempts to salvage Veblen's views by substituting the word "propensity" for "instinct" have not been altogether successful in this writer's estimation.

Veblen's acid attacks on traditional theory and his attempt to divert economic inquiry along different channels make interesting reading. His somewhat pompous style and his love of big words sometimes make for laborious reading. The author remembers one passage from Veblen which he read in his college days, when in a long paragraph the only words he understood without the aid of a dictionary were the connectives! Veblen's savage wit and his piercing analysis, however, removed the danger of boredom. His critique failed to accomplish his purpose. This was not because of any lack of readability of his message—much of it is as easily or more easily followed than those he sought to displace[10]—but because most contempoary economists remained convinced that the questions earlier economists had asked were the correct ones, and that the answers, if not correct, were at least more relevant and nearer the truth than those offered by Veblen. His thinking has not been without impact upon later economists, but the main stream of economic thought has remained undiverted.

The contrast in the impact made by Veblen and another famous critic of capitalism, Karl Marx, is also striking; Veblen never won an enduring band of disciples such as those who followed Marx. The gospel according to Veblen kindled no burning flames among a group of ardent followers as that of Marx had among his disciples. When we compare the central ideas of the two men, it is not difficult to see why. Whereas Marx had preached a message of exploitation, class struggle, revolution, and an eventual utopia, Veblen's message held far less appeal. His central theme was wastefulness and the conflict between the making of goods and the making of money. Veblen made no appeal along class lines (save his

[10] Max Lerner, *op. cit.,* pp. 43–47.

condemnation of businessmen) and saw little hope for an uprising of the workers. His doubts on this score were based on two beliefs: (1) that increasing misery on the part of men only reduced their will to resist subjugation; and (2) that even the lowliest workers were imbued with the capitalistic ethic, with its values of "conspicuous consumption" and "pecuniary emulation." At the end, Veblen expressed little hope that his beloved engineers would rescue society. Where Marx was irritatingly vague about the future society, because he felt it unnecessary to provide details since it would inevitably come to pass, Veblen was equally vague about the future, but for a different reason. Whereas Marx's picture of history had a Hegelian flavor, Veblen was distinctly Darwinian in outlook. Institutions would continue to evolve, perhaps for the betterment of mankind as the process of natural selection took place, but there was no way to tell the precise character of this change. Because Veblen provided no standards of welfare for his readers, he left them with no way to measure progress or any indication in which direction progress should be made. Whatever influence Veblen did exert among his followers was to a large extent swallowed up in the 1930's with the emergence of the Keynesian philosophy.

WESLEY CLAIR MITCHELL (1874–1948)

Of the two remaining economists to be studied in this chapter, Mitchell was the younger and should in terms of strict chronological order be placed at the end of the chapter. His ties with Veblen were considerably closer than those of Commons, however, and for this reason he is the next figure to pass in review. Ironically, some students of the history of economic thought will remember him best for something he never wrote! Two of his students took a verbatim shorthand record of his lectures on the history of economic thought and these notes have been published and preserved for future generations of students of economics.[11] Mitchell, who had contemplated and started such a book, never completed the project.

The Man. Wesley Mitchell was the second of seven children. As in the case of Veblen, Mitchell's early years were spent on a farm, near Rushville, Illinois. His father was a doctor who had served in the Union Army during the Civil War. Bad health led his father to settle the family

[11] *Lecture Notes on Types of Economic Theory* (New York: Augustus Kelley, 1949).

on a farm, where they lived in straitened financial circumstances. Despite these difficulties, Mitchell's mother encouraged him to go to college, and he enrolled in the opening class at the University of Chicago in 1891. Upon the completion of his undergraduate studies, Mitchell became a graduate student in economics at the same university and was awarded a traveling scholarship, which he spent in Germany and Austria. Not finding German and Austrian economics to his taste, Mitchell returned to Chicago the following year and was granted his Ph.D. *summa cum laude* in 1899. Three intellectual figures deserve particular mention for their role in shaping Mitchell's intellectual views: Professor Laughlin, who had taken Veblen with him when he left Cornell, imparted to Mitchell early in his academic career a skepticism about the value of marginal utility, and it was Laughlin who guided Mitchell in his choice of his Ph.D. topic. Impressed with Veblen's original mind when he studied under him, Mitchell came to know and appreciate Veblen's originality even more when the former returned to Chicago as a faculty member. Mitchell was also profoundly influenced by his exposure to the pragmatic philosophy of John Dewey.

For a brief period after receiving his Ph.D., Mitchell took a position with the the Census Bureau in Washington, but this first tour of duty in government service was of comparatively brief duration, as were subsequent ones. In 1900 he accepted a teaching position at the University of Chicago. After three years on the faculty at Chicago, Mitchell followed one of his former teachers to the University of California. While at California, Mitchell met Lucy Sprague, then the dean of women, and in 1912 they were married. That same year Mitchell moved to New York in order to be near Wall Street and the heart of the money economy. The following year he joined the faculty at Columbia University as a replacement for John Bates Clark, who was about to retire; there he remained until his death except for a brief period at the New School immediately after World War II. He returned to Columbia in 1922, upon the urging of his colleagues there.

In contrast to Veblen, Mitchell's frequent shifts between academic institutions should be regarded as the mark of a highly gifted teacher rather than of someone unable to present his ideas clearly. Mitchell found in academic life exactly what he wanted, and although it was the research opportunities which he found most appealing, all reports suggest that he was an excellent teacher as well. Mitchell was for brief periods an editorial writer for a Chicago newspaper and an executive for the Red Cross, but he quickly abandoned each of these to return to the life of an academician.

In addition to the contributions to economic thought summarized below, three other notable aspects of Mitchell's work deserve brief mention. When he was offered the position of president of the American Economic Association, he accepted the opportunity willingly instead of rejecting it as Veblen had. Numerous other tokens of recognition were bestowed upon him by his colleagues: he was president of the American Statistical Association, the Econometric Society and the American Association for the Advancement of Science. In addition, he was the recipient of honorary degrees from the University of Paris and numerous universities in the United States.

Mitchell was one of the founders and for many years the director of the National Bureau of Economic Research. The Bureau has continued until the present day as an important organization for furthering economic research—much of this research along the lines laid out earlier by Mitchell. We should not overlook Mitchell's work with index numbers; his monograph, written in 1915 for the Bureau of Labor Statistics and entitled *The Making and Use of Index Numbers,* has remained a classic and has undergone numerous reprintings.

Much of Mitchell's life was devoted to the study of the business cycle. Of a large number of books dealing with this problem, two of his best remembered are *Business Cycles: The Problem and its Setting,* and *Measuring Business Cycles* (coauthored with A. F. Burns). Some of his most provocative essays dealing with various aspects of institutional economics are contained in the delightful collection titled *The Backward Art of Spending Money.*

Economic Views. In view of Mitchell's close relationship with Veblen, it is not surprising that he shared with Veblen the latter's belief in the importance of institutions in the formulation of economic theory. But Mitchell's brand of institutionalism was quite different from Veblen's; a comparison of the ideas of the two men makes a convenient point to launch our discussion of Mitchell. The most striking difference between the two approaches, and Mitchell's primary contribution to Institutionalism, was his emphasis on the importance of empirical, particularly statistical research. One can find scattered references in Veblen's writing acknowledging the importance of empirical research, but his use of empirical evidence was much like that of men such as Clark whom he criticized; empirical evidence was used by Veblen to fortify a previously formulated theory. Another part of the difference in the approach of the two men arose from Mitchell's concentration on the problem of the business cycle and his belief that theorizing about cycles in the absence of abundant empirical evidence was fruitless. These were not the only differences. One should never forget that Veblen received his Ph.D. in philosophy and all his life maintained a philosophical attitude toward the institutions which he observed. Although Mitchell was not devoid of philosophical perspective, his approach of empirical realism was quite different from that displayed by Veblen. No reader of Veblen's writings would ever question that Veblen was a theorist, whereas Mitchell concealed his theoretical framework so well that the careless reader is led to the conclusion that no such framework exists. This, of course, is a mistake, but one in which Mitchell must share at least part of the blame. Theory played a part in Mitchell's work, although he never developed a complete framework in the style of Alfred Marshall or other earlier writers. No treatise flowed from Mitchell's pen, and most of his work was in the form of a series of monographs. Typical of Mitchell's failure to make his theoretical framework explicit was his failure to make clear what institutions he considered to be important; money received ample attention, but other institutions remained murky and unidentified.

Variations in the approaches of Mitchell and Veblen also resulted from marked differences in the personalities of the two men. Mitchell was not the lonely and embittered critic Veblen had been. Instead, Mitchell resembled Alfred Marshall in his unwillingness to be harsh in his evaluation of the work of others, although his disagreement with it might be even more substantial than Marshall's had been. Nor did Mitchell share Veblen's pessimism. His treatment of the business cycle exemplifies this optimism. Although he saw cycles as an inherent feature of the capitalistic system, he was doubtful that they grew increasingly severe and was confident that there were always forces lurking in the background to assure an eventual recovery.

Despite these differences between the economics of the two men, there are many similarities justifying their inclusion in the same school. In the first place, Mitchell found many of the same grounds for disagreement with earlier theorists that Veblen had emphasized. Mitchell was opposed to Marginalism and denied that the consumer was as rational and well-informed as marginal utility implied. What, in fact, most distinguished the household consumer from the businessman was the former's ineptitude in handling his money—a point Mitchell summed up in the title of one of his essays, "The Backward Art of Spending Money." Earlier economic theories were further weakened, in Mitchell's view, by their failure to be evolutionary in character. Mitchell joined Veblen in a rejection of the philosophy of laissez-faire and stressed the point that acceptance of the doctrine led economists to be blind advocates of a particular system. Mitchell placed considerable reliance on national planning as a cure for social evils in his denial that laissez-faire produced the best of all possible worlds. Again Mitchell's optimism can be seen; when planning was done on a national scale, much could be accomplished to improve conditions. Mitchell was less sanguine about the success of attempted reforms at lower levels of government or by private groups, although in private life he was often a party to such attempts.

A final note of similarity in the approach to economics by the two men should be made. Veblen's desire to expand economics to include work in allied social sciences was shared by Mitchell, who thoroughly approved of an interdisciplinary approach. One of Mitchell's first steps after assuming teaching duties at the University of California was to inaugurate a course in primitive cultures linking economics with anthropology. Mitchell, however, never identified his thinking with any particular school of psychological theory. Dissatisfied with the crude hedonistic psychology of earlier economists, he was apparently unwilling also to follow Veblen's lead in adopting an "instincts" approach. Accurate as Mitchell's criticisms of other economists' psychological preconceptions may have been, he offered nothing positive in their place.

THE BUSINESS CYCLE. No résumé of Mitchell's economics could possibly be considered complete without reference to his studies of the business cycle which have made his name well known to economists all over the world. Since our treatment of theories of business cycles in this book has been relatively brief, it is difficult to emphasize the marked change in approach to the problem exhibited by Mitchell. Although recognition of the importance of the business cycle came comparatively late in the history of economic thought, once it had been brought to economists' attention, they hastened to rectify their earlier neglect. The result was the emergence of a vast number of theories, each alleging to diagnose *the* cause of the business cycle. When Mitchell undertook his studies, there were almost as many explanations of the business cycle as there were cycles to be explained.

Mitchell arrived at his eventual approach to the problem gradually. We have noted in our discussion of Veblen that Mitchell commended Veblen for the latter's recognition that money played a far more important role in shaping men's thinking than earlier writers had thought. It was natural for Mitchell to stress this aspect of Veblen's economics, for Mitchell was interested in the role of money from the beginning of his study of economics. His Ph.D. dissertation dealt with the role of greenbacks in the Civil War, and since its publication in book form, has remained a standard reference on the subject. Given his preoccupation with money, it was natural that Mitchell should explore the quantity theory of money. After considerable investigation, Mitchell concluded in one of his first articles ever published that the quantity theory would always remain inconclusive as far as empirical evidence was concerned. In later years Mitchell somewhat modified his original position about the validity of the quantity theory,[12] but he was never convinced that it would serve as a tool for analyzing the business cycle. The principal defect in the quantity theory when used for this purpose was that there were time lags between the left and right sides of the equation; payments (the MV side) were mostly made in response to transactions (T) agreed upon at some earlier date at prices (P) which in all probability were set at an even earlier date.

From this early interest in money and variations in prices, it was a logical step to the study of business cycles. The exact impetus for Mitchell's pursuit of the business cycle is uncertain, but he was probably encouraged to move in this direction by his belief that the study of economics needed more empirical research (and the area of business cycles was a particularly fertile field for such research). Another important consideration may have been the mounting concern over the business cycle in the United States following the panic of 1907 coming on the heels of previous similar disturbances. Although Mitchell avoided basing his research on any preconceived theories about the business cycle, two general points served as a basis for his departure from earlier views. First was his belief that the business cycle and the fluctuations resulting therefrom were the normal state of affairs. This was a marked departure from Marshall's view, which had maintained that the normal situation was equilibrium and had regarded each departure from that norm as an exception due to special circumstances. Second, Mitchell accepted Veblen's view that there was a conflict between the interests of businessmen and the technological order, and he believed that cycles were caused by variation in rates of profits and businessmen's attempt to secure greater profits.

Aside from these, however, Mitchell's theoretical preconceptions about

[12] Wesley Mitchell, "The Real Issues in the Quantity Theory Controversy," *Journal of Political Economy*, (June, 1904), pp. 403–408.

the cycle were few. Mitchell's colleague and friend, Professor Arthur F. Burns, has suggested that Mitchell took "existing explanations [of the business cycle] as guides to research, rather than as objects of research." [13] While Mitchell suggested some of the same theories about causes of cycles as those advanced by other students of the cycle, Mitchell's theories were advanced only after long and painstaking research leading to the accumulation of mountains of statistical data. Mitchell's insistence on painstaking research cannot be overstressed. He strongly believed that it was only through such diligent effort that economics could be made into a cumulative science where the work of one scholar could be safely built on that of his predecessors. Even the work of accepted scholars was reworked by Mitchell when, as in the case of Fisher's estimates of deposit currency, additional information became available. The result was not only a staggering quantity of statistical information about the business cycle, but information of a quality that has remained valuable through the years that have followed.

Because of this mass of statistical material and because Mitchell couched his conclusions in such tentative terms, with innumerable reservations and qualifications, it is difficult to present a concise, definite statement of his theories of the business cycle. What is perhaps most clear is that Mitchell rejected exogenous factors as explanations of the business cycle; there was no reason for such fortuitous events to occur in such a way as to produce the regularities occurring in the past.

Among the endogenous factors singled out by Mitchell for special attention were changes in price levels. Even while emphasizing rising costs as a factor in choking off continuing expansion as a tentative hypothesis, however, he was reluctant to embrace any single explanation as a primary cause. Furthermore, business cycles, like other features of the economy, were an evolutionary process, with the result that the causes might change over a period of time. Much of Mitchell's analysis remains fresh, but where it has become outdated, its outmoded character is in itself a fulfillment of Mitchell's analysis.

Summary and Evaluation. While Mitchell's views on economics were somewhat different from those of his teacher, Thorstein Veblen, there was more than enough similarity in the approach of the two men to justify fully the inclusion of Mitchell as an Institutionalist. This is true even though he never fully developed a statement of what he included under

---

[13] Arthur F. Burns, *Wesley Clair Mitchell: The Economic Scientist* (New York: National Bureau, 1952), p. 39.

the heading of institutions. Primarily, Mitchell's exhaustive study of business cycles, marked as it was by the Institutional approach, rather than his views on Institutionalism per se, accounts for his lasting fame. He was one of the leading economists of the early twentieth century, and Professor Burns is quite correct in asserting about Mitchell's book *Business Cycles* that "No other work between Marshall's *Principles* and Keynes' *General Theory* has had as big an influence on the economic thought of the Western World." [14]

JOHN ROGERS COMMONS (1862–1944)

Thorstein Veblen disclaimed all efforts at social reform and denounced them as unscientific; Wesley Mitchell was willing to support reform in economic theory and social and economic institutions alike, but felt that these could be best achieved by national planning. We now turn to John Commons, the third great member of the Institutional School. He was an incessant reformer who worked actively—not only in his writings, but in his daily activities—to effect reforms.

The Man. There are few economists who have throughout their lifetime had to work harder for recognition and who have suffered more setbacks and personal misfortunes than those experienced by John Commons. Anyone questioning the validity of this generalization has only to read Commons' autobiography, *Myself,* written ten years before his death.

In many respects, Commons' early childhood parallels that of Veblen and Mitchell. He was born in the Midwest (in Ohio), and his father was a farmer who loved the practice of "horse-trading." Unfortunately, the father's skill as a trader did not always match his love of the process and the family labored under difficult financial circumstances. Commons' education was made possible by his mother's willingness to run a boarding-house to send him and two other children to preparatory school and college.

One of his father's early trades resulted in the ownership of a newspaper, and here Commons learned typesetting—an activity at which he worked full-time during his college days at Oberlin in order to supplement the family's income. Commons did not graduate from Oberlin until 1888, when he was 26. Plagued with a weak stomach and a nervous temperament, the combination of full-time work and studies proved too

[14] *Ibid.,* p. 23.

much, and in 1885 Commons suffered the first of a series of nervous breakdowns. He experienced some academic difficulties at Oberlin occasioned by his health. Nevertheless, one of his professors at Oberlin encouraged him to go to graduate school at Johns Hopkins. Again financial problems arose, but he managed to borrow money from two of the trustees of Oberlin—a loan which Commons took fourteen years to repay. As Commons has wryly remarked, "I never could get rid of debts. I finally made debts, instead of liberty, a foundation of Institutional Economics." [15]

The final blow to Commons' educational aspirations at Hopkins came when he flunked an examination in history, thus eliminating all possibility of a fellowship to support his work there for a third year. As a result Commons never obtained his Ph.D., although in later life he was granted honorary degrees from Oberlin, Lake Forest, and Wisconsin.

Commons' early attempts to find a career in the teaching profession met with little success. The lack of the Ph.D. was a handicap in and of itself, but almost as important was Commons' reputation as a radical thinker plus his deficiencies as a teacher, the combination of which led to a series of short-term appointments. Even after his teaching had improved, the other handicaps continued to plague him. Typical of his experiences was his dismissal from Syracuse University because his views on Sunday baseball offended some of the trustees (Commons opposed paid Sunday admissions but favored the playing of the game on the Sabbath as a source of recreation for workingmen). Earlier he had worked for brief periods at Wesleyan University, in Connecticut, and at Oberlin and Indiana University, but not until Syracuse did many students consider his dismissal a loss to the college in question.

Commons found a home when he went to the University of Wisconsin in 1904, remaining there until his retirement in 1933. While at Wisconsin, Commons won a loyal band of followers among his students and was instrumental in formulating much of the reform legislation which came to light during the reign of Robert M. LaFollette as governor of Wisconsin. As a result of the cooperation between the two men, Wisconsin was a pioneer in workmen's compensation and unemployment insurance as well as in the regulation of public utilities.

Commons had a rare understanding of the problems of other men and a sympathy and desire to help them that was perhaps born of his own adversities. In addition to the health and financial problems previously mentioned, he experienced enough other difficulties to keep a soap opera broadcast running for years! At the time when his autobiography was

15 John R. Commons, *Myself* (New York: Macmillan, 1934), p. 42.

written, only one child of the six he sired was still alive; four had died in infancy and his oldest son had run away from home (after distinguished service in World War I) while suffering from a persecution complex. His wife died sixteen years before Commons, and his last fifteen years were spent in his home, where poor health prevented his working for more than a brief period each day. This inability to work for protracted periods must have been a great trial in itself for anyone as active as Commons had been in earlier life.

Among his better-known publications are his *Institutional Economics* and *Legal Foundation of Capitalism.* In addition, he wrote extensively in the field of labor relations and was one of the editors of a ten-volume study entitled *Documentary History of American Industrial Society,* and a four-volume *History of Labor in the United States.* As these and his other writings make abundantly clear, few professors have been more generous in acknowledging the assistance of their students.

Economic Views. We shall divide our examination of Commons' writings into two parts: his differences with the Classical School and his positive contributions. In describing his departure from Classical thinking, Commons suggested that he changed the foundations of economics from abundance, sin, and holding for one's self to scarcity, collective action, and withholding from others. Where did these substitutions lead Commons in his separation from the earlier economists? The answer to this question provides part of the justification for including Commons among the Institutionalists; many of his points of dissent were the same as those made by Mitchell and Veblen. Commons felt that men were not as rational as Classical and Neoclassical thought had postulated, and while he acknowledged that self-interest did play a role in men's actions, Commons stressed the importance of habit and custom. Custom, for Commons, was less a matter of heredity than it was a means for men to provide security for themselves. Men, instead of responding entirely to the forces of pleasure and pain, usually chose from a list of alternatives with which they were faced. Commons also felt that earlier economists had misused history, either by failing to provide their abstractions with any historical context, or by using history as a means of testing already existing theories rather than as a basis for formulating new ones. Commons was convinced that the Classical and Neoclassical economists had been overly anxious to retain the tractability of their assumptions, with a resulting loss of realism. It might be better, said Commons, to use history and empirical research to reconstruct economic theory rather than merely to attempt to patch it up.

Although he pronounced Ricardo to be free of the error, Commons considered that many of the economists who followed Ricardo were guilty of confusing productive power and bargaining power. The result was that many economists wrote in such a way as to show a gain to the economy when a businessman succeeded in buying at a low price and selling at a high one. Productive power was exhibited when men took command of the resources provided by nature to increase the supply of goods, while bargaining power resulted from the control exercised by a few men over the scarcities of nature or the supply of labor. Any resulting benefits accrued only to the few in a position of power rather than to the society at large.

Despite the fact that Commons was regarded as a radical by many of his contemporaries, he was no supporter of Marx and found much to criticize in the latter's doctrines. Commons denied, for example, that the Marxian version of the class structure could be applied to the United States and questioned whether workers had a clear sense of class identification. Furthermore, despite the many criticisms Commons had to make about capitalism, he never advocated its overthrow. He had doubts about the efficacy of any alternative system, and the conviction that "labor cannot manage" played an important part in his thinking.

In another criticism of Classical economics, he stressed a point little noted by either Veblen or Mitchell. The proper study of economics, said Commons, involved three types of transactions. Of the three, earlier economists had confined their study to those transactions occurring in the market. But, said Commons, the other two were also of great importance, and the study of economics was incomplete without their inclusion. The two transactions neglected by previous economists were (1) managerial transactions involving transactions between supervisors and those they supervised, and (2) rationing transactions involving such things as the determination of dividends by the boards of directors of business corporations.

Much of Commons' positive contribution to economic thought was devoted to an exploration of these latter two types of transactions and the role institutions played in their completion. Where the resulting market situations proved undesirable from a societal viewpoint, Commons did not hesitate to recommend state action. He denied that the setting of a "reasonable" price was an impossible goal and argued that while individuals might differ among themselves as to what constituted "reasonable," it was still possible to work out a standard through collective action that would be perfectly reasonable and valid. What was unreasonable was permitting the price to rise to whatever level the market would bear.

Commons defined institutions as "collective action in control of individual action." We can best make Commons' meaning clear if we use the role of labor unions as an illustration. As the process of technology grew increasingly great and as the operation of the market became increasingly complex, the forces of competition came to bear more and more onerously upon workers. The capitalists in their attempts to meet competition were driven to exercise their command over workers to hold down wages and increase the pace of work. It was the collective force of the unions as an institution which controlled this abuse and helped "take labor out of competition." Commons likened the position of unions in the contemporary scene to that of the merchants in England at the time of the beginnings of mercantile capitalism. Essential to the success of the merchant in the latter case was the role of the courts in their willingness to recognize the demands of the merchants and to broaden judicial interpretation of the law accordingly. Commons saw in the existing position of the courts a corresponding shift with respect to unions and welcomed this as another illustration of the changing evolution of economic institutions. The role of the judges as intellectuals should be noted. While it was the pressure from institutions such as unions which initiated the change, it was the willingness of the judges to adapt to these pressures, criticize them, and at some points modify them that prevented the pressure from emerging in a violent eruption. By his stress on the persistence of these struggles in the economy, Commons made the conflict of interests rather than the harmony of interests the starting point for his version of institutional economics.

Summary and Evaluation. Much of Commons' analysis of the role of institutions arose from the observations he and his students made as they studied the working of the economic world about them. Commons was a devotee of field work par excellence. From his contacts with the legal profession made while helping to draft legislation for Governor La-Follette, Commons acquired much of the basis for his *Legal Foundations of Capitalism,* and his work on public utility legislation led him to his idea of the "rationing transaction." In view of his interest in the role of unions in the economy, it is not surprising that Commons made the conflict of interest rather than the harmony of interest the center of his economics. He sought means by which those conflicts evolving out of private property might be resolved, and he emphasized the need for men to cooperate harmoniously. To achieve this goal, Commons suggested a development of institutions which could, through collective action, restrain excessive power in the hands of individuals. He denied that "reasonable" prices or wages were impossible to determine when arrived at in a collective manner. Commons was at his best when he was "digging up" historical and empirical evidence. His weakness lay in his emphasis upon empirical rather than theoretical work and the resulting lack of useful generalization. Although in his own time Commons was criticized by many as a radical with impractical ideas, today much of the legislative reform he sponsored is accepted as commonplace.

CHAPTER XII: Monopolistic vs. Imperfect Competition

> There are some mistaken notions in the general field of monopolistic and "imperfect" competition. The most mistaken notion of all is that the two are merely two different names for the same thing.
> —EDWARD HASTINGS CHAMBERLIN

> Since the 1930's when the rival doctrines of imperfect and monopolistic competition were in their heyday, economists have increasingly reverted to the use of the concept of perfect competition as their standard model of analysis.
> —GEORGE STIGLER

As our preceding chapters have made abundantly clear, few of the earlier economists included monopoly, with its concomitant impact upon prices and output, in their economics. Adam Smith had recognized that businessmen would seek to band together to control prices whenever the situation permitted, but clung to the belief that the situation rarely would present itself. Monopolies, when they existed for any protracted period of time, were the responsibility of faulty government action, which fostered them instead of discouraging their existence. Without the protective security afforded by government intervention, monopolies would, in Smith's opinion, rapidly collapse under the impact of competition, leaving the consumer in full command of the situation. Later economists were equally prone to classify monopoly as a special situation unlikely to have much significance in the general market, or to dismiss the issue of monopoly completely.

The earliest exception to the general bypassing of the question (and a lone and solitary exception it was for many decades) can be found in the writing of the French mathematical economist, Antoine Augustin Cournot. In 1838 he had devised a determinate solution for the situation of duopoly, or two sellers, and showed how his solution could be extended to include more than two sellers. His solution can be best made clear with the aid of the diagram shown in Fig. 8.[1]

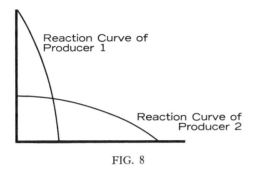

FIG. 8

The two reaction curves plot the output of each of the two producers when each assumes that the adjustments made by his rival to his own change is a final one. Each time one person moves, the other seeks to maximize his profit by producing and selling that amount which will give him the largest total profit. Equilibrium occurs at the point where the two reaction curves intersect; here both duopolists would sell equal quantities and each would maximize his profits. Starting with one seller maximizing his profit when he was alone in the field, appropriate adjustments in output would be made by each seller in response to changes in his rival's output. Each adjustment was made to produce maximum profits, on the assumption that no further changes in the rival's output would be forthcoming. When changes in output did take place, neither seller ever learned by it, with the result that the "game" continued until the indicated equilibrium was reached.

To say that Cournot's model went uncriticized for a number of years is only to point out that it also went unread. His book was not reviewed until forty years after publication. When economists generally began to take note of Cournot's work, one of the first criticisms voiced was on his assumption that each seller repeatedly took the other's output as given. When this assumption is removed, a variety of other solutions to the case of duopoly can be constructed. Edgeworth, for example, in his paper entitled "The Pure Theory of Monopoly," written in 1897, assumed that each seller would accept his rival's price as given, and he arrived at an indeter-

[1] Augustin Cournot, *Researches into the Mathematical Principles of the Theory of Wealth,* trans. by Nathaniel Bacon (New York: Macmillan, 1927), p. 82.

minate solution where prices oscillated continuously up and down. Fig. 9 will help to make Edgeworth's "solution" clearer.[2]

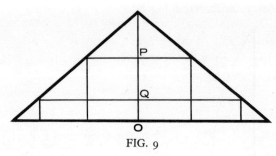

FIG. 9

OP represented the price which would be set if the two sellers colluded or if there was only one seller in the market. When seller *A* set the price at that level, however, seller *B* found it advantageous to shade his price slightly on the assumption that seller *A* would keep his price fixed. When he failed to do so, a series of price reductions took place until price *Q* was reached. At this point no further reductions were forthcoming because each seller had reached the point of maximum output. But now one of the sellers found that he could increase his profits by slightly raising his price, and so the two sellers chased each other back up to price *OP,* where the whole process once again reversed itself. Here, also, the result of indefinite oscillation was based on a key assumption—this time the assumption that each seller continued to take his rival's price as determined and unchanging. Edgeworth's sellers were as insensitive to experience as Cournot's had been previously. Like Cournot also, Edgeworth saw no difficulties in adding to the number playing the game—in the Edgeworth solution, the result was to shrink the range of indeterminacy.

It is important to emphasize again that the analyses of Edgeworth and Cournot received little attention from their fellow economists. Even the critics of capitalism, including Marx, centered their fire on deficiencies in the way in which the competitive model performed rather than denying its existence. Nor did the members of the Marginal School make more than casual reference to monopoly as an interesting but not particularly important aberrant.

The stage was thus set for Alfred Marshall to make a dramatic innovation in economic thought, but he too for the most part muffed the opportunity. It is true that one can find scattered references throughout Mar-

[2] F. Y. Edgeworth, "The Pure Theory of Monopoly," *Papers Relating to Political Economy,* Volume I (London: Macmillan, 1925), 118–120.

shall's writing as evidence of his recognition of monopoly. He noted the existence of demand curves for particular commodities, and his discussion of "spoiling the market" demonstrated an awareness of the market power exerted by many firms. On the whole, however, Marshall's analysis has a distinct flavor of perfect competition. In many ways, Marshall was more reminiscent of Smith than were many of Marshall's contemporaries; it was Marshall, after all, who emphasized the perfectly elastic demand curve, and his exposition of the representative form was in part an effort to solve the problems posed by Cournot's analysis. So powerful was Marshall's influence on the economic theorists of his time that no serious challenge to the doctrine of perfect competition was presented until the Italian-born economist Piero Sraffa (1898–), who migrated to England and studied at Cambridge under Marshall, wrote his now famous article in the December, 1926 issue of the *Economic Journal,* entitled "The Laws of Returns Under Competitive Conditions." It was only a 15-page article, but it marked a new landmark in economic thought. Sraffa's point of departure was the observation that the Classical economists had in their concern over diminishing returns neglected the fact that a firm might instead experience increasing returns or decreasing costs as it expanded its operations. If such were the case, an important conclusion could be drawn; decreasing costs, whether they stemmed from internal economies or the spreading of overhead costs, were incompatible with the assumption of perfect competition. Continued expansion because of resulting economies would inevitably result in the existence of firms able to affect price and total output by their production decisions. Sraffa saw the real world as one quite different from that pictured by the model of perfect competition, but he did not fall into the opposite error of thinking solely in terms of pure monopoly. Long before the firm had pushed its expansion to the point where all rivals were eliminated, it would run into a deterrent in the form of the negatively sloped demand curve. It was the fact that additional sales could be achieved only by lowering the price at which the product was to be sold, rather than any lack of additional increasing returns, which prevented the firm from continued expansion. The result was that many markets which looked highly competitive on the surface actually contained important monopoly elements. Individual producers found themselves with special markets reserved for their products because consumers were not perfectly indifferent between one seller and another; a consumer might even be willing to pay a higher price knowingly in order to do business with a certain firm. Many firms, therefore, possessed considerable leeway in setting their prices. Although neither Chamberlin's nor Robinson's study appeared for several years, the stage was now set for a full-blown theory of monopolistic (imperfect) competition. When it came, it arrived in two versions appearing almost simultaneously.

EDWARD HASTINGS CHAMBERLIN (1899–   )

Chamberlin's book, *The Theory of Monopolistic Competition* was one of those rare instances where a Ph.D. dissertation had a profound impact upon the discipline in which it was written. The dissertation, completed in the late 1920's, was revised and published in 1933.

The Man. Professor Chamberlin was born in La Conner, Washington, and attended the University of Iowa, where he received his B.S. in 1920. Two years later he obtained an M.A. at the University of Michigan, thereafter transferring to Harvard, where he earned a second M.A. in 1924 and his Ph.D. in 1927. Most of his teaching career has been spent at Harvard, although he did teach for a brief period at the University of Michigan and has had visiting appointments at the universities of Paris and Copenhagen. During World War II, he served with the O.S.S. Among his professional activities have been his ten years of service as editor of *The Quarterly Journal of Economics* (1948–1958) and a term as vice-president of the American Economic Association in 1943. In addition to *The Theory of Monopolistic Competition,* Chamberlin has written several other books dealing with various aspects of value theory and the problem of labor union power.

Economic Views. Chamberlin's book on monopolistic competition can best be described as an attempt to fuse the theories of monopoly and perfect competition. According to Chamberlin, there were elements of monopoly in almost every market situation regardless of how competitive it might appear to be at first glance. In fact, competitors might make use of these monopoly elements in their competition. Even when the number of sellers was large, they might still be able to distinguish themselves in customers' minds, thus acquiring a certain amount of freedom in pricing. Chamberlin adopted the point raised by Sraffa on negatively sloped demand curves and emphasized the resulting impact on the marginal revenue curve. How did sellers achieve a negatively sloped demand curve? The answer lay in the many ways by which a seller could differentiate his product, ranging all the way from trade names and advertising to the use of a pretty girl as sales clerk. In order for these techniques to be successful, we also have to assume that the consumer acts on the basis of this differentiating process and does not remain indifferent between sellers.

Beginning with the assumption that the methods of differentiation were costless, Chamberlin compared the results obtained under pure and monopolistic competition. Where competition was insufficient to lower the demand curve to a position of tangency with the total cost curve, the picture resembled that for any monopoly. High prices and excess profits existed, and they might continue for an indefinite period. The situation, as pictured in Fig. 10, is one of oligopoly, where the number of firms was

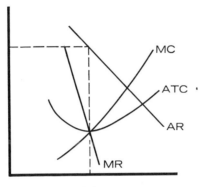

FIG. 10

small but rigorous competition might still exist; whether or not it did, depended upon the attitude taken by management. Perhaps the more interesting and different situation, however, was when competition was sufficiently great in terms of the number of firms to ensure tangency of the demand curve with the total cost curve, but with sufficient monopolistic elements still existing so as to retain the demand curve's negative slope. Figs. 11 and 12 show the differing results, given the alternative situations of pure and monopolistic competition. Note that in Figure 12, under conditions of monopolistic competition, even though the firm was making no excess profits (the tangency between the demand curve and the total cost curve means it is just breaking even) it was still forced to operate at a position of less than peak efficiency and to charge a higher price than would be true under pure competition. The reason for this is not difficult to find; it rests with the tilted demand curve. With a sloping demand curve, it is impossible for the demand curve to be tangent to the total cost curve at the latter's minimum point. The steeper the slope of the demand curve, the higher up on the left-hand portion of the cost curve will be

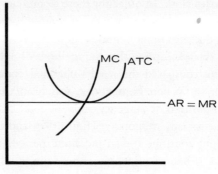

FIG. 11

the position of tangency. With higher costs and lowered output, a higher price to the customer is inevitable.

The picture changed slightly when Chamberlin introduced selling costs. The price might be still higher because of the necessity of covering the additional selling costs and the expansion in demand occasioned by the

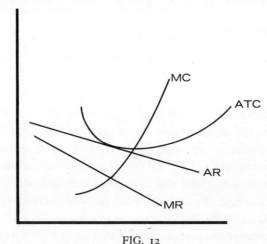

FIG. 12

advertising, but this was uncertain and depended on the assumptions made about changes in the elasticity of demand. Output would increase, as compared with a situation of monopolistic competition without selling costs. It was still deemed likely, however, that output would be inferior, when compared to a purely competitive model.[3]

[3] Edward Hastings Chamberlin, *The Theory of Monopolistic Competition* (Cambridge: Harvard University Press, 1947), chap. 7.

Summary and Evaluation. Part of our evaluation will have to wait until we have had an opportunity to examine Professor Joan Robinson's version, but we should take note here of some of the reactions produced by Chamberlin's theory. A number of writers, including John Maurice Clark, have criticized Chamberlin's conclusions about the excess capacity resulting from monopolistic competition and the corresponding advantages of pure competition in the way of larger, more efficient levels of output and lower prices; they have argued that much of Chamberlin's analysis is based on doubtful geometry. Without demand curves drawn to be as inelastic as Chamberlin made them, many of the dire aspects of the monopolistically competitive picture were removed. It is particularly questionable whether the demand curves would retain the same slope irrespective of the number of sellers involved. Other critics have suggested that Chamberlin did not develop the process of management decisions sufficiently and that he left in question whether or not businessmen know who their rivals are. Doubts have also been expressed that a situation where the monopolistic competitor's average revenue curve lies tangent to his average total cost curve at the indicated level of output may be treated as one where he is just breaking even. A similar case of tangency in the case of pure or perfect competition can be described as breaking even because there is included in the average total cost curve what is thought to be a "normal" profit for that industry. But where firms succeed in differentiating their products and carving out small segments of the market for their own, the question can be raised whether it is possible to speak of a "normal" profit for such a monopolistic competitor in any meaningful sense of the word.

It is not completely a fair attack upon Chamberlin to charge that his analysis is incomplete. Many firms and market situations cannot be fitted into the categories of oligopoly, monopolistic competition, or pure competition as described by Chamberlin. It was Chamberlin's (and Robinson's) analysis, however, which prompted much of the later investigation into the economics of various industries on both an empirical and theoretical basis. Chamberlin must share credit for the growing interest in industrial organization with the empirical research of such scholars as A. A. Berle Jr., Gardiner Means, and others; part of the honors accorded to Chamberlin must also be accorded to our next writer, Joan Robinson.

JOAN VIOLET ROBINSON (1903–   )

Whereas Professor Chamberlin's contributions to economic theory have been limited almost entirely to the field of monopolistic competition, Joan Robinson has written on a wide variety of subjects ranging from monopolistic competition and price theory to Keynesian macroeconomics. She has been a sympathetic critic of Marxism and was an early interpreter of Keynesian economics; many refinements in both theories have been occasioned by her writings. She is without question the world's leading woman economic theorist. We will bypass much of her original work in the various fields indicated above to concentrate on one of her most significant contributions, the theory of imperfect competition.

The Woman. Joan Robinson was the daughter of Major General Maurice and was educated at St. Paul's Girls School in London and later at Girton College at Cambridge. She passed her economic tripos in 1925 and the following year married the distinguished British economist E. A. G. Robinson. Since 1949 she has served as a reader in economics at Cambridge and in 1958 became a fellow of the British Academy. Among her better-known writings are: *The Economics of Imperfect Competition, Essays in the Theory of Employment, Introduction to the Theory of Employment, Essay on Marxian Economics, The Accumulation of Capital,* and *Economic Philosophy.* In addition, several books containing her collected essays on economic growth and various problems of economic theory have also appeared.

Economic Views. A substantial part of Professor Chamberlin's subsequent writing has been devoted to an effort to get economists to recognize the differences in approach between his and Professor Robinson's work. His limited success in this effort can be attributed partly to the intellectual laziness of some economists, but more to the substantial similarities in treatment of the problem contained in the two books.

Professor Chamberlin has suggested by way of differentiating the two versions that even the inception of interest in the subject sprang from different roots. Whereas his own interest began with an early study of railroad rates—an article on the subject was rejected by the journal of which he was later to become editor[4]—Mrs. Robinson's study resulted

---

[4] Edward Hastings Chamberlin, "The Origin and Early Development of Monopolistic Competition Theory," *The Quarterly Journal of Economics* (November, 1961), pp. 515–543.

from the attacks launched on Alfred Marshall's competitive solution by Sraffa and others. Robinson's work, therefore, can be best described, as she has stated, as an edifice erected "on the foundations laid by Marshall and by Professor Pigou." [5]

The crucial difference seen by Chamberlin was the failure of Robinson to recognize that most modern business was a blending of elements of competition and monopoly. In treating the two as being mutually exclusive, Robinson was judged by Chamberlin to be following in the old tradition of Marshall and Mill and failing to come to grips with the business world as it actually existed. Not the least of the resulting errors was Robinson's failure to accord proper attention to the importance of the differentiated product.

It is impossible to enumerate all of the other differences existing between Professor Chamberlin's and Professor Robinson's approaches. Instead, we will concentrate on three major distinctions in the problems examined.

After a comparison of pricing under situations of perfect competition and monopoly, Robinson tackled an issue largely ignored by Chamberlin —the case of the discriminating monopolist. If a monopolist were able to separate his market into distinct parts, how might he determine his most profitable price and output so as best to maximize his gains? Her answer can be best understood if we reproduce one of her diagrams, shown here in Fig. 13.

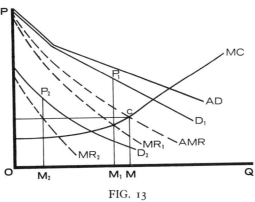

FIG. 13

D_1 and D_2 are, respectively, the demand curves for a monopolist's product in two separate markets, with MR_1 and MR_2 their accompanying

[5] Joan Robinson, *The Economics of Imperfect Competition* (London: Macmillan, 1946), p. v.

marginal revenue curves. The *AD* or aggregate demand curve is the total demand for the product, and is the sum of D_1 and D_2. To maximize his position, the monopolist equates his *MC* curve with his *AMR* or aggregate marginal revenue curve relevant to his *AD*. This gives him the level of total output, and reading across, he can determine what part of that total output should be in market *A* and what part in market *B*. Once the outputs in a market have been determined, it only remains to read up to the appropriate demand curve for that market to determine what price should be charged. Whether output would be greater or less under a discriminating monopolist than in a case of pure monopoly depends on the comparative elasticities and concavities of the two market demand curves. Note that the diagram explicitly assumes that marginal costs remain the same, even when the market is divided. Without this assumption, a determinate solution would be much more difficult to achieve.

Professor Robinson also introduced the concept of monopsony—the situation analogous to monopoly but on the buyer's side. Just as a firm which was sufficiently large or able to differentiate its product was able to have some control over the price it charged, so might a firm which had some control over the factors it purchased be able to affect the price it paid by varying the amounts it purchased. The supply curve for any factor of production thus could no longer be considered perfectly elastic. Instead, there now existed a marginal cost and an average cost curve. The firm maximized its use of the factor by hiring up to the point where the marginal cost of the factor equaled its marginal productivity, and then paid the price indicated by the supply curve as being necessary to bring forth that quantity of the factor in question. An examination of Fig. 14 will make the explanation clearer.[6]

The firm hired quantity *ON*, determined by the intersection of the *MC* and the *D* (or demand curve for the factor) at *Z*. Price was then set at *NP*, or the relevant point on the *AC* or supply curve. Neither the problem of the discriminating monopolist nor of monopsony received much attention in Chamberlin's book.

Another important distinction between the first editions of Chamberlin's and Robinson's works was the exploration by the latter of the implications to productivity theory of the separation of the marginal revenue and average revenue curves. For purposes of illustration, Robinson used the factor of labor; the result was to introduce a new theory of exploitation of labor. Because the employers' demand curve was no longer the simple marginal physical productivity of labor multiplied by a constant

[6] *Ibid.*, p. 220.

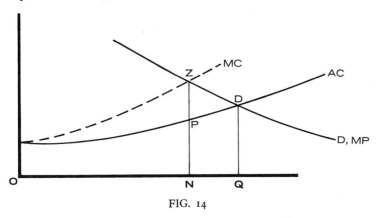

FIG. 14

marginal revenue (inherent in the assumption of a perfectly elastic demand curve for the product), but multiplied instead by a marginal revenue that declined as output and sales increased, the laborers were no longer paid their full marginal physical product as postulated by Marshall. It was thus possible for workers to be exploited in two directions: (1) from the power implicit in monopsony, whereby fewer workers might be employed than under perfect competition, even with a lower wage rate prevailing; and (2) from the failure to pay workers their full marginal physical productivity.

Chamberlin, who had not originally included any discussion of the implications of his theory to marginal productivity and distribution, did so in later editions. There he denied that the exploitation of labor was any more pronounced than it was for any other factor. All factors were similarly "exploited," Chamberlin asserted, since it was impossible under conditions of impure competition for any of them to be paid their full marginal physical productivity.

An Overall Appraisal. A more complete review of the writings on monopolistic competition can be reserved more appropriately for books on contemporary thought, and it is perhaps too soon to give a definitive appraisal of monopolist theory's significance in the development of economic thought. Certainly it is safe to say, even at this point, that the exploration of the question in theoretical terms was long overdue. Elements of imperfection and monopoly were a part of the competitive scene long before economists paid more than passing attention to the implications of these elements for theoretical models.

Once enunciated, the theories won rapid and wide support for a variety of reasons. Part of the support arose from the dissatisfaction of economists with the theories of the market as hitherto formulated. Other economists were quick to recognize the powerful tool marginal revenue provided for analyzing a variety of market situations. Some support for the new theory also emerged from those writers critical of the operation of capitalism.

Some of the same features which made the theories of monopolistic or imperfect competition appealing to many economists have led to their rejection by others. Some view them as an attack on the operation of the market system and fear their use as a justification for government intervention. This group is probably quite right in its suspicions, although this fact does not constitute a condemnation of the theory's validity. Adam Smith's consumer frequently comes closer to being a faithful servant than a dominating king, and the new theory raises additional doubts about the advisability of pursuing a policy of laissez-faire.

Other economists have tended to reject the new theory because the picture as now painted becomes much more complicated and difficult to analyze. The basic decisions to be rendered by businessmen are infinitely more complicated than they were with the model of perfect competition. Under perfect competition with standardized products and perfectly elastic demand curves and with price a known quantity, the businessman had only to decide whether or not he could produce profitably the product in question at the price given to him by the market. Now, with the new theory, the businessman was accorded not only some discretion as to the price he would charge, but also some freedom as to the quality of the product to be sold. Nor was that all! Not only was he free to build a better mouse trap, but by various promotional gimmicks such as advertising he could pass the old mouse trap off as a new and revolutionary device designed to trap unwary mice and consumers alike. Life also became more complicated for the consumer, who now was assumed to act not only on the basis of price and quality but under the influence of a variety of other pressures as well. Consumer choice became an increasingly laborious and difficult task; the only wonder was that consumers performed the duty as well as they did!

What also made monopolistic competition theory distasteful to some economists was that the more complex decisions for businessmen and consumers alike, sketched above, brought corresponding difficulties for the economist attempting to describe the situation. A Pandora's box of troublesome issues had been opened. Under the inspiration of Chamberlin's and Robinson's theories a wealth of literature on various aspects of monopolistic competition has arisen.[7] Models of price leadership, discrimi-

[7] See, for example, the bibliographies compiled by Professor Chamberlin in *The*

nating monopolists, base point pricing systems, and quality competition have arisen in rapid order. The implications of monopolistic and imperfect competition have not been overlooked by social scientists working in fields closely allied to economics. The effects upon society of big business have received as much if not more attention than some of the economic implications. Economists also have found themselves, along with the courts, immersed in the issues of the relationships between bigness and efficiency and the extent to which control of the former is likely to jeopardize the latter. Again, much of this is perhaps more appropriately left for a book dealing with modern theory, but we should note that more recently attempts have been made (without great success) to apply game theory to the solution of various market situations. The work of Oskar Morganstern has been particularly important in this connection.

Despite the previously noted qualifications, it seems safe to say that only a minority of economists share Professor Stigler's views about the relative uselessness of this new theory. Both Chamberlin's and Robinson's versions, despite the differences emphasized by Professor Chamberlin, have two great points in common. Both emphasized a continuation of the traditional analysis, i.e., finding a means of determining market equilibrium, and both produced a theoretical innovation for achieving this analysis that was quite as revolutionary to micro theory as the achievement of our next economist, John Maynard Keynes, performed for macro theory.

Quarterly Journal of Economics (August, 1948), pp. 629–638; and (November, 1956), pp. 613–643.

CHAPTER XIII: The Economics of Capitalism

The difficulty lies not in the new ideas, but in escaping from the old ones, which ramify, for those brought up as most of us have been, into every corner of our minds.
—JOHN MAYNARD KEYNES

There is seldom anything truly new under the sun in economic policy, where the allegedly new generally turns out to be the discard of a prior century in flimsy disguise.
—MILTON FRIEDMAN

The last economists we are to study, in this chapter, are of widely varying economic philosophies. All shared two common traits; they were giants in the history of economic thought, leaving behind them a wealth of new insights into economic problems, and they were concerned about the future of capitalism.

While each of these three men left an indelible imprint in the field, Keynes was the most provocative contributor and won the greatest number of supporters.

JOHN MAYNARD KEYNES (1883–1946)

One of the marks of any great book is the storm of controversy it arouses and the further research which it provokes. Judged on both of these counts, Keynes' *General Theory of Employment, Interest, and Money* thus far has been the major economic work of the twentieth century. It would take this entire chapter (and probably much more) merely to list all of the comments in the form of books and articles elicited by Keynes' views. Someone once suggested that after a theory has crept into the introductory textbooks, its future, whether for better or worse, is assured. Keynes' contribution, which has been described at times as "The

Keynesian Revolution" or "The New Economics," has cleared that hurdle. A reader can get some idea of the magnitude of Keynes' impact by comparing any widely used economics principles text of today with a text used less than thirty years ago. The most noticeable difference is the introduction of national income analysis, mainly the responsibility of Keynes.

The Man. Keynes' formidable intellectual abilities were furthered by his family background and his intellectual training. He was born into a distinguished family; his father was John Neville Keynes, the well-known logician and political economist, and his mother was the mayor of Cambridge. Educated at Eton and King's College, Cambridge, Keynes was a student of Alfred Marshall and A. C. Pigou; the latter bore the brunt of Keynes' later attacks as the main contemporary representative of the neo-Classical School. Upon the completion of his studies at Cambridge, Keynes worked briefly in the India Office, where he acquired the background for his first book, entitled *Indian Currency and Finance,* published five years later. Between the time he quit the India Office and the appearance of his first book, Keynes had returned to Cambridge, this time as a member of the faculty, and in 1911 he assumed the position of editor of the *Economic Journal,* the official publication of the British Economic Association.

Keynes' first recognition from the general public came at the end of World War I. During the war he had entered government service, this time with the Treasury, and at the end of the war he was appointed as a technical expert at the Versailles Conference on reparations. Convinced that the reparations imposed upon Germany by the Allied leaders were unreasonable and would produce Germany's economic collapse, Keynes wrote a biting criticism of Woodrow Wilson and the other Allied leaders, entitled *The Economic Consequences of the Peace.* Some critics of Keynes' *General Theory* have referred to this later book and the repercussions it produced as "The Economic Consequences of John Maynard Keynes!" [1] Never one to mince words when he felt someone to be in error, Keynes was the author of a slashing attack both on the personalities and the economics of the chief participants at the Versailles Conference. While time has shown Keynes' fears about the inability of Germany to assume the debt burden to be correct, it may also be true that Keynes' attack contributed to Wilson's failures at home and the reversion of American foreign policy to isolation.

---

[1] The list of Keynes' critics is long. Among the best known are such names as Milton Friedman, David McCord Wright, W. H. Hutt, and the French economist Jacques Rueff.

Keynes returned to university teaching after World War I, but at the same time he branched out into other activities. The charge often made by businessmen that the academic economist knows nothing of the *real* world of business cannot be leveled properly against Keynes. He accepted the chairmanship of a life insurance company and for years was bursar for King's College. Both institutions thrived under Keynes' financial management. Some early attempts at speculation in his own behalf were failures, but at the time of his death Keynes had amassed a fortune of around $2,000,000.

Keynes was a well-rounded individual in the best sense of the term. In college he was not only a brilliant student but active in extracurricular activities ranging from sports to debate. His training in the latter served him in good stead, both in the classroom and in his frequent disagreements with fellow economists while he was in government service, as well as when he was out of it. There was little of an intellectual nature that did not interest Keynes at some period of his life. Like Alfred Marshall, he began his academic studies with an interest in mathematics, but again, like Marshall, the interest flagged in later years. In neither case did the decline in interest reduce capabilities, and Keynes remained an able mathematician throughout his life. His taste in reading was quite diversified, ranging from Newton to Plato to Shakespeare. He had a deep interest in music and art and he became a member of one of the most distinguished groups of artists, painters, writers, and musicians of the time, a group which came to be referred to as the Bloomsbury Group. Keynes did not marry until he was 42, and when he did, he chose as his wife a member of the performing arts—Lydia Lopokova, a ballerina. The choice proved to be a happy one and she served both as a gay companion and as his nurse and protector when the occasion demanded.

Keynes seems to have excelled at whatever he undertook. This sweeping generalization applies to all his activities, but we will stress only three of them: his skillful teaching, his service to his government, and his economic writings.

As is so often the case, Keynes became less and less involved with teaching as he grew more famous. In the early years when he had served as a tutor, he had been eager to take on additional students in order to earn extra money. In later years, however, he lectured only infrequently and he tutored only a select group of the best students. Infrequent as they were, however, his lectures were always brilliant and he exercised great influence through the Political Economy Club at Cambridge. At the club, students presenting seminar papers found their work subjected to a ruthless vivisection at the hands of Keynes and his colleagues.

Keynes had a second career in government beginning in World War II and continuing until the time of his death. Few economists have been as influential in shaping the financial decisions of their government. He was a constant adviser to the British Treasury and offered invaluable advice on the financing of both World Wars, including his famous little book written at the start of World War II entitled *How to Pay for the War.* Like his teacher, Alfred Marshall, Keynes was repeatedly called upon for expert testimony before various government investigating committees. His final great achievement was his participation in the Bretton Woods Conference in 1944, and his work there aided in the establishment of the International Monetary Fund and the World Bank.

Keynes left us with even more tangible evidence of his brilliance in his writings. Seymour Harris, the distinguished Harvard economist, has given us a figure of 806 different items which emerged from Keynes' pen, including 10 books, 6 pamphlets, and 78 articles in various professional journals or anthologies.[2] Keynes, also was a frequent contributor to the more popular magazines and was a regular writer of letters to the editor of the London *Times.* Besides the two previously-mentioned volumes, Keynes' best-known books include *A Tract on Monetary Reform, A Treatise on Money,* and *The General Theory of Employment, Interest and Money.*

No one can deny the impressiveness of this list of achievements. One can only wonder what more might have been forthcoming if Keynes had not suffered poor health and had not died at the age of 63. From the time he was a young boy, Keynes found it necessary to pace himself, and when he failed to do so, found himself ill and thus forced into bed. In 1937 he suffered a serious heart attack, which further limited his activities, and the eventual complete failure of his heart resulted in his death. During these difficult years, Keynes' wife was invaluable in protecting him from the undue pressures from a world seeking his aid and advice.

Many students of Keynes and many of those who read his works have found it interesting to speculate how his thoughts might have turned had he lived longer. Keynes' willingness to change his views and alter his thinking in response to new ideas and changing situations has been a basis for criticism by his detractors, while his admirers have found this trait to be evidence of a flexible mind. Whichever position is taken is a matter of

[2] Seymour E. Harris, *John Maynard Keynes: Economist and Policy Maker* (New York: Charles Scribner's Sons, 1955), p. 36.

personal choice, but it is evident from a brief review of his writings that Keynes did alter his views considerably through the years, but one can also find seeds of Keynes' later views in the earlier writings. It is important that we concentrate on Keynes' major opus, which overshadowed his other writings, but it is only appropriate that we begin our study of Keynes' writing by taking brief note of earlier books before turning to a more detailed appraisal of his most important work.

Earlier Economic Writings. A common feature of all of Keynes' early books was their concentration on the formulation of policy, particularly with reference to the management of money and the problems emerging from the operation of the gold standard. Suggestions of this kind can be found in his first book, *Indian Currency and Finance,* but Keynes first clearly demonstrated his interest in public policy in his *Tract on Monetary Reform.*[3] In this book, Keynes used the Cambridge quantity theory of money as an explicative device to show the way to assure the stability of business activity. Although the quantity-of-money equation had a familiar Marshallian ring, the policy decisions Keynes built upon it were a far cry from Marshall. All his life, Keynes remained a determined opponent of monetary and fiscal policies which were tied to the gold standard; his *Tract on Monetary Reform* was no exception to this opposition. In his attack on the gold standard, he recommended the employment of a managed currency by a monetary authority with greatly increased freedom of action.

Keynes' next major work, *Treatise on Money,* forms a bridge between the *Tract* and his *General Theory.* It was a difficult book, much too long, and it never received as much attention as it deserved, partly because by the time it appeared (1930) reports were already being heard that Keynes was working on a new and dramatically different concept. Unlike his *Economic Consequences of the Peace,* the *Treatise* was not written for the general public; the language was difficult, at points relieved only by Keynes' skill with the English language, filled as it was with new terms and complicated analysis. His fundamental equations were difficult enough for the professional economist to digest, let alone the lay reader.

Many of the terms were defined in a way markedly different from the way they subsequently appeared in the *General Theory;* savings and investment were defined so that the economy was in equilibrium only when they were equal, and disturbances arose whenever inequalities emerged. As in earlier theory, the interest rate was determined by the interaction of

[3] J. M. Keynes, *Tract on Monetary Reform* (New York: Harcourt Brace, 1923).

the two forces of savings and investment, and much of Keynes' analysis was directed to how savings and investment could be kept equal so that the market and national rates of interest would be equal. In some ways, this was a clearer presentation than that given in the *General Theory*, and it avoided the endless difficulties which later arose when Keynes defined savings and investment so that they were at all times equal in amount. Aside from some additional recommendations about appropriate policy which anticipated his later work, the *Treatise* today is primarily of historical interest, containing as it does some fine descriptions of various financial markets and institutions. If the casual reader found Keynes' *Treatise* a bit too difficult, his reaction to the *General Theory* was utter despair! Keynes openly declared that his book was intended for his fellow professional economists, and there is much evidence to support Professor Paul Samuelson's candid confession that not many of them fully understood it when it first appeared in print.[4] There is even indication that Keynes himself did not fully appreciate all the implications of his master work. In order for us to understand the revolutionary character of Keynes' message, it is necessary to sketch briefly the prevailing views about the business cycle and those of the small group who dissented therefrom.

The first of these tasks we can perform very quickly. We have seen in earlier chapters that the economists we have studied, with a few exceptions such as Marx, accepted the concept of Say's Law. In their view, there could never be generalized overproduction, for in the process of producing goods, the purchasing power to buy those goods was also created. Early economists had paid scant attention to the business cycle, but once they admitted its existence, they proceeded to treat it as a temporary deviation away from the normal equilibrium position of full employment. There were automatic sources of recovery built into the economy which assured that any period of unemployment and depression would be temporary in nature. One likely cause of unemployment was the tendency of wages to rise above the level of productivity associated with full utilization of available manpower. A sure remedy for unemployment, therefore, was the reduction of wages to the point where labor again became a "good buy"; as employers hired more workers in response to the lowered wage, full employment would again be assured.

Only a handful of economists chose to quarrel with this generally accepted truth, and they were relegated to the underground of the economic

[4] Paul A. Samuelson, Chapter XIII, *The New Economics,* ed. Seymour Harris (New York: Knopf, 1948), p. 146.

world and subjected to professional scorn by most economists. Keynes himself has sometimes been referred to as a "slick" Underconsumptionist, and it is therefore necessary that we outline briefly the views of the Underconsumption theorists so that we may compare them with Keynes' position. We can only touch briefly on the views of this school. A standard text on theories of the business cycle should be consulted for a more complete treatment.

Some form of the underconsumption arguments was put forward by three of the economists we have already studied—Malthus, Marx, and Hobson—and there were a number of lesser-known writers, including Major Douglas, W. T. Foster, and W. Catchings, who limited their economic writings to the business cycle and its causes. Members of the Underconsumption School differed among themselves as to the reason for underconsumption, but many of them followed Hobson in emphasizing that inequalities in the distribution of income led to excessive savings on the part of the rich. These savings, if held idle, obviously would constitute a drag on the economy in the form of goods produced for which there would be no demand. Even if savings were put back into investment, the result would be merely to increase the supply of goods, thus ultimately leading to a still greater oversupply of goods and an eventual worsening of the situation. There were many flaws in the Underconsumptionists' argument; perhaps the most serious of these was their failure to account for the resumption of economic activity once the economy had become depressed. If the economy consistently tended to consume less than was produced, what accounted for the frequent and protracted periods of prosperity?

With the emergence of the 1930's, the telling force of this criticism lost some of its power. By the time Keynes' *General Theory* appeared in 1937, Great Britain had already been experiencing nearly a decade of depression, and the United States, after the spectacular stock market crash of 1929, had undergone the worst and most prolonged depression in its history. Between a fourth and a third of the labor force remained unemployed, and repeated forecasts of an imminent recovery proved each time to be based on false optimism. A sharp recovery in the early 1930's in the United States was halted by an even more precipitous collapse in 1937. Not until after the United States became involved in World War II did its economy return to a condition of full employment. Little wonder that economists became more receptive to the thought that capitalism based on a system of laissez-faire was slowing down and no longer able to function properly by itself.

Keynes' Views. Many sources of inspiration for further thinking and research have come from the *General Theory,* but without question the central theme was, as the title implies, the question of employment and the relationship of interest and money to it. Keynes appears to give two different versions of the interrelationships involved. One followed the line pursued in his earlier books that much (and perhaps enough) could be accomplished with forthright monetary management to overcome the problem of unemployment. The second version was more pessimistic, raising doubts about the ability of the capitalistic economy to ever regain full employment, in the absence of extensive governmental intervention, for more than very brief periods of time. This more pessimistic viewpoint was later developed by Alvin Hansen into the concept of secular stagnation. In developing both versions, Keynes offered his readers a formidable new set of analytical tools and a new perspective of the economic scene. We will begin our review of these new terms with an examination of the one that linked him to the earlier underconsumptionists—his consumption function.

Keynes postulated a basic psychological law: As income increased, so did consumption, but not to the same extent. Thus, as national income grew greater, so did the amount saved increase. Keynes offered no empirical evidence in support of this tendency, but reasoned that what was apparently true for individuals in their patterns of consumption and saving would also be true for aggregates of individuals as well. Although Keynes gave his readers no diagrammatic representation, his interpreters have furnished us with the now familiar picture of the consumption function shown in Fig. 15.

An obvious conclusion to be drawn from Fig. 15 is that as the level of income becomes larger and larger, more and more savings will appear,

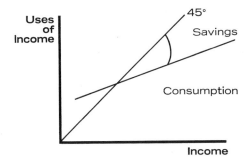

FIG. 15

as shown by the gap between the consumption curve and the 45° line. Many of the earlier Underconsumptionists would have been satisfied with this display of the potentialities of the economy for excess savings as evidence of the inability of the economy to buy back all of the goods it produced. Keynes' analysis was far more sophisticated than this, however. Nor did he fall into the elementary trap of arguing that if the savings were invested they would merely create more goods for consumption at a later time. The problem as Keynes saw it was that these savings, for reasons soon to be explored, might fail to reenter the income stream as investment. When the volume of current savings was not matched by a counterflow of investment, income shrank until the excess savings were eliminated. Before proceeding to that line of analysis, however, we need to say something more about the consumption function.

From the consumption function, Keynes derived a variety of other terms, such as average propensity to consume, marginal propensity to consume, and the multiplier. The first two are self-descriptive. Average propensity to consume, or C/Y, was the amount of a given level of income spent on consumption goods while marginal propensity to consume $\Delta C/\Delta Y$ was that proportion of an extra dollar of income spent on consumption. Thus, with an income of $100, of which the population spent $90, the average propensity to consume would be 90 percent. If the income rose by an additional $10 to $110, and $8 of the additional $10 were spent, the marginal propensity to consume would be $\frac{4}{5}$ or 80 percent.

The concept of the multiplier was not original with Keynes, but had been discovered by a colleague, R. F. Kahn; Keynes, however, fitted it into a total theory of the relationships between savings and investment. The multiplier was based on the concept of the marginal propensity to consume. If new *net* spending took place somewhere in the economy, the result would be not just one round of spending terminating with the first transactions, but the setting into motion of a series of subsequent transactions as well. Suppose that the marginal propensity to consume was one half, meaning that consumers spent one half of every additional dollar they received above their normal income. If business invested or consumers spent new money in the sum of $10, the recipient of the additional money would spend half that amount or $5; the next party receiving the extra $5 would in turn spend half of that and so on until the respending was dissipated to virtually nothing. When that had happened, however, the total resulting spending was not just the original $5 but the sum of all the rounds of additional spending as well, with the result that total income would have increased by $10. The size of the multiplier depended upon the size of the marginal propensity to consume, and the exact size could be determined by the equation

$$m \text{ (multiplier)} = \frac{1}{1 - MPC} \text{ or } \frac{1}{MPS}$$

The emphasis upon the words *new* and *net* spending is important. The consumption function, as conceived by Keynes, was a passive element responding to changes in the level of national income. Consumer expenditures which occurred in accordance with the average propensity to consume generated no new secondary rounds of spending. The point is not an unimportant one. Keynes wrote as if the propensity to consume was highly stable, both in the short and long run. Many of his early supporters were equally convinced that this was true. One result was that after World War II many economists were gloomy about the chances of the United States maintaining full employment after the conversion to peacetime production. Henry Wallace's *Sixty Million Jobs* was deemed an overly heroic goal. One factor that made the achievement of that goal easier than many had imagined, however, was that the consumption function shifted upward sharply at the end of the war. A desire for consumer goods stifled by wartime needs was strengthened by the backlog of savings in the form of savings bonds and bank accounts; although the consumption function has proved to be unstable in the short run, the variations are counter to Keynes' original theory; he expected changes in investment to call the tune.

Another aspect of the multiplier which Keynes left unclear was the time period necessary for the completion of the multiple process. For purposes of simplicity in his analysis, Keynes treated the process as an instantaneous one, which quite clearly in real life cannot be. One of the subsequent bits of empirical research sparked by Keynes' writing has been the attempt to determine the time required for the completion of the multiple effects.

Keynes' conception of the consumption function led him to one of his many disagreements with the Classical and Neoclassical writers. It was quite possible, said Keynes, that workers would be unable to encourage employers to hire them no matter how low the wage they were willing to accept; he described such a situation as one of "involuntary unemployment," and distinguished it from "voluntary unemployment." The latter occurred when the workers, rather than accept a reduction in wages, were willing to accept unemployment, whereas "involuntary unemployment" emerged when workers were unable to find employment no matter how low a level of wages they were willing to accept.

Earlier writers, in stressing the efficacy of wage cuts as a solution to unemployment, had emphasized that the reduction in costs thus made possible would place employers in a better competitive position. What was true for the individual employer or a few employers was, however, not true for the aggregate economy. When all workers accepted reductions in their wages, the result was to reduce the general level of purchasing power and thus the demand for businessmen's products. With a decline in the demand for their products, employers would find less reason to hire workers, and so the demand for labor would experience a further decline. The movement along the demand curve for labor resulting from a shift in the supply of labor to the right would be offset by a downward shift to the left in the demand for labor. Fig. 16 presents a graphic picture of the change Keynes had in mind.

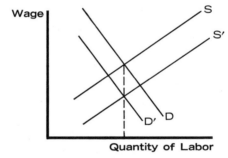

FIG. 16

Professor Pigou, Keynes' former teacher, attempted to salvage the neoclassical position by arguing that if only wages and prices were sufficiently flexible, the restoration of an equilibrium as envisioned by the neoclassicists would come true. In attempting to defend this position, Pigou finally used a variation of Keynes' consumption function. If wages and prices were permitted to fall during periods of depression without any obstacles interjected by labor unions or other institutions, Pigou argued, a point would be reached where recovery would occur. Why? Because, said Pigou, using the old Cambridge quantity theory, people attempt to hold command over a certain quantity of goods. As prices continued to fall, the savings already accumulated would become increasingly valuable until a point was reached where they could command all the goods consumers wished without any further accretions in savings. At that point, consumers would reenter the market with renewed vigor and the downturn would be halted. Although some economists have attempted to continue their defense of flexible wage rates as a path to full employment, most of them, including Pigou himself, have conceded that Keynes' doubts about the efficacy of wage flexibility have won the day. Even if one grants the theoretical validity of Pigou's solution, the extent to which wages and prices would have to be flexible is unimaginable in these days of giant corporations, large labor unions, and agricultural price supports.

Keynes saw only two ways that wage reductions might lead to expansions in the volume of employment—the impact on the volume of foreign trade, and the effect on the rate of interest. The first of these is easily explained and needs little attention, since Keynes assumed a closed economy in much of his analysis. Given a situation where trade with other countries was permitted, however, reductions in wage rates which resulted in lower prices would encourage the sale of exports to other countries. The resulting expansion in output would produce obvious favorable effects on the volume of employment. The relationship Keynes saw between reductions in wages and the rate of interest is more complex, and its explanation will have to wait until we have had an opportunity to examine another of his basic tools—his explanation for the rate of interest, which he called the liquidity preference.

Keynes regarded the loanable funds doctrine set forth by Marshall, which made the rate of interest dependent on the intersection of the demand and supply schedules for savings, unsatisfactory, because the intersections varied with the level of the income. As national income rose, said Keynes, the supply of savings would shift to the right, thus producing a new equilibrium. The result was that with the loanable funds doctrine it was impossible to know the rate of interest without knowing the level of national income. Since the level of income was dependent upon the rate of interest, it was impossible to tell the rate of interest without first knowing the level of income. The result was therefore indeterminate, with the rate of interest and the level of income dependent upon each other.[5]

As an alternative to the loanable funds approach, Keynes proposed to rely solely on the supply side for an explanation of the role of interest, and to ask why people held money in the form of idle cash hoards. We have already seen that Keynes linked the act of saving out of current income (nonconsumption) to the level of income. The problem left to be solved was why people or institutions chose to hold their resources in the form of

[5] Professor Hansen has pointed out that the same problem applies to the determination of the liquidity preference. Alvin Hansen, "Classical Loanable-Fund, and Keynesian Interest Theories," *The Quarterly Journal of Economics,* (August, 1951), pp. 429–432.

idle cash hoards rather than making them available to others. Keynes provided three answers to this question. Men hoarded for precautionary reasons—"saving for a rainy day" in case of accident, sickness, or other act of God. Second, a certain amount of money was held idle in anticipation of transactions to take place in the immediate future; business firms and individual customers alike needed some pocket money for their day-to-day forays into the marketplace. The most important reason for seeking liquidity, however, according to Keynes, was the speculative motive. The reasoning behind this third motivation is somewhat more complex. It can be elucidated if we consider the diagram illustrated in Fig. 17.

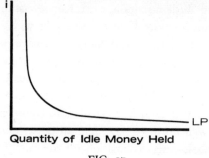

Quantity of Idle Money Held

FIG. 17

In Fig. 17, the interest rate is located on the vertical axis, and the amounts of idle cash held in hoards are on the horizontal axis. Note that at high rates of interest, relatively small amounts of cash would be held idle, but that as the interest rate declines, the amounts of idle money held would increase greatly until, at the bottom, the liquidity preference curve becomes virtually parallel to the horizontal axis. This shows a willingness by savers to absorb unlimited amounts of money into cash hoards at the prevailing rate of interest. It is easy to see why the willingness to hold idle cash would decline when the interest rate was high, since the loss of interest would become increasingly expensive as the rate of interest rose. The same explanation would work in reverse when the rate of interest was low; the individual would forfeit little by holding idle cash. Furthermore —and this was central to Keynes' speculative explanation—a person would prefer to hold cash when the interest rate was low in the hopes that the rate of interest would soon rise. If the saver offered his money at the then prevailing low rate of interest and his expectations of a subsequent rise in the interest rate should materialize, the capital value of the security he had purchased would be correspondingly reduced through the process of capitalization. This means that the capital value of long-term capital securities bearing a low rate of interest would decline in market value when the interest rate on newly issued securities rose.[6] Since, when the interest rate became low, savers deemed further declines in the rate unlikely, they had everything to gain and little to lose by continuing to hold their assets in a liquid form.

Therefore the rate of interest was, according to Keynes, the price business borrowers had to pay to get savers to part with liquidity. If the price (interest rate) which savers demanded for giving up their liquidity was greater than businessmen could afford to pay in light of their current profit expectations, then the circular flow concept predicated by Say's Law was in danger of being broken. Funds might be held out of the income stream for protracted periods of time or until their absence reduced the size of the income so that they in turn were diminished.

We are now in a position to understand Keynes' other qualification to his generalization that flexible wages would do little to stimulate recovery during a business downturn. If, said Keynes, the lowered wage bill necessitated a lower total amount of money to be held in a liquid form for that purpose (the transaction's motive), the result might be a lowered liquidity preference, thus making possible a lower rate of interest. Although Keynes acknowledged this possibility, he concluded that if this was the only gain from flexible wages, the end could be achieved more efficiently through a proper application of monetary policy. Sufficient courage on the part of the monetary authorities would produce the same result with none of the agonies and disruptions to the economy produced when wages were forced downward.

Note the implications of Keynes' theory for the quantity theory of money as set out by both Fisher and Marshall. The V (velocity of circulation) and the k were no longer constant, but varied with the various phases of the business cycle. The precise relationship between the quantity of money and the general level of prices was thus destroyed.

There have been numerous attempts to reconcile the liquidity preference theory of interest with the loanable funds doctrine. By concentrating on the supply side of savings when discussing the rate of interest, Keynes glossed over the demand for capital and treated it as if it were of no

[6] Those who have forgotten their capitalization arithmetic can refresh themselves with the following example. Suppose that a long-term security bearing a fixed return of $2 a year was purchased for $100, thus in effect yielding a 2-percent return. Should the market rate of interest subsequently rise to 4 percent so that new $100 securities yielded a return of $4, anyone wishing to dispose of his old bond yielding $2 income would have to accept a sufficient reduction in market price to bring its return to 4 percent. For a very long-term investment, the market price would be virtually halved.

consequence. When he came to a discussion of the motivations for investment, however, the demand for capital was reintroduced through the back
door, so to speak. With a consideration of the demand side reintroduced,
the difference between the two approaches became considerably less. Liquidity preference could be incorporated into the loanable funds doctrine
as a factor on the supply side of savings, thus improving its usefulness
without completely destroying it. Interest rate theory still remains somewhat murky even today, and economists differ among themselves as to the
extent to which the liquidity preference can be satisfactorily grafted onto
the earlier theory. Equally puzzling to many readers of the *General Theory*
is why Keynes devoted so much of his time to developing the liquidity
preference concept in view of his belief that the volume of investment
might prove to be insufficient to match the volume of savings generated at
full employment, no matter how low a rate of interest might prevail.

MARGINAL EFFICIENCY OF CAPITAL. Another new tool introduced
by Keynes was the *marginal efficiency of capital* (*mec*). The term
is less forbidding than it appears at first glance. The marginal efficiency of
capital is the same as another term used previously, the marginal productivity of capital, but with emphasis placed on the *expected* yields from
additional amounts of invested capital. Keynes felt that the Neoclassical
economists had been too inclined to confine their analysis to a situation
where businessmen acted solely in terms of the current yield on capital
investment. Such a static approach was, in Keynes' view, highly unrealistic. What was needed was a recognition that "the expectation of the future
influences the present." [7] In computing the marginal efficiency of capital
one had to total the expected yearly yields over the life of the capital
investment after allowing for depreciation and other costs. A process of
capitalization of annual returns would give us

$$R_1 + R_2 + R_3 \ldots + \ldots R_N.$$

If we let i stand for the market rate of interest and S the value of the
capital good, we could set up the following equation:

$$S = \frac{R_1}{1+i} + \frac{R_2}{(1+i)^2} + \frac{R_3}{(1+i)^3} + \cdots \frac{R_N}{(1+i)^N}$$

As long as S was greater than the replacement cost of the capital good, the
businessman would find it worthwhile to continue to invest. To determine
the rate of expected returns in the future, all that was necessary was to

---

[7] J. M. Keynes, *The General Theory of Employment, Interest, and Money* (New
York: Harcourt, Brace, 1936), p. 145.

substitute the *mec* for *i* in the above equation and then solve for the unknown *mec*.

Note that expected earnings from a capital good now became a function not only of the actual costs in terms of rate of interest and other expenses, but also of businessmen's expectations. Prospects in terms of actual earnings might be good, but if businessmen did not think so, the volume of investment would remain small. At this point, Keynes stressed the generally low state of investors' knowledge about the future as, for lack of better guides, they tended to project the current situation into the future and to rely upon the judgment of their businessmen—a variation on the theme of the blind leading the blind!

Keynes' treatment of the marginal efficiency of capital was not always clear; sometimes he wrote as if he regarded it as a single point which remained unchanged irrespective of additional amounts of capital invested. More often, he seems to have viewed it as a schedule and we shall discuss it in the same manner. Figs. 18 and 19 illustrate two possible shapes of the marginal efficiency of capital.

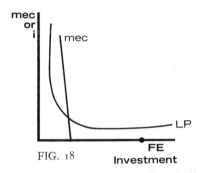

FIG. 18

Important differences in one's appraisal of the future of capitalism emerge, depending upon which of the two *mec* schedules is selected. If one considers the curve in Fig. 19, the future becomes much brighter than if the curve in Fig. 18 is adopted as the more typical; the reason for this is not difficult to understand. With a more elastic *mec*, the opportunities for expanded investment become almost unlimited, assuming that the interest rate can be maintained at sufficiently low levels. With the *mec* curve shown in Fig. 19, however, the volume of investment is likely to be inadequate, irrespective of the rate of interest. The point can be made even more obvious if we designate point *FE* as the level of investment needed to obtain full employment. Given the first *mec* schedule, there is no way for the amount of investment needed for full employment to be achieved, even if the interest rate should fall to zero.

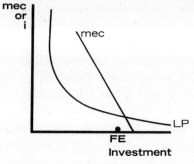

FIG. 19

The point made earlier about the significance of the liquidity preference explanation of the interest rate is now more easily understood. If the marginal efficiency of capital is assumed to be highly inelastic, the question of the interest rate becomes largely an academic one.

Thus far, we have primarily discussed the long-term marginal efficiency of capital. Short-run changes in the marginal efficiency of capital also played an important role in Keynes' thinking and had a leading role in his explanation of the business cycle. We shall discuss the short-run changes below, but a composite picture of the various tools supplied by Keynes should first be obtained. Although the consumption function played a central part in Keynes' thinking, investment was the main factor. Investment, as interpreted by Keynes, was almost exclusively autonomous investment, dependent upon outside factors such as population growth and new technology rather than (as in the case of induced investment) upon consumption and the level of national income. Therefore, investment set the other dependent variables of income and consumption into motion; through the multiplier it produced multiple effects upon the level of national income. Consumption was the passive, dependent variable which responded to changes in the level of national income. As the level of national income rose, the level of consumption also rose, but not to the same extent, leaving increasing amounts which went into savings. Unless the economy was able to generate a sufficient volume of investment to match these savings, businessmen would find themselves paying out (consumption plus savings) more than they got back (consumption plus investment) with the result that they would contract their operations. A decline in business spending would cause a decline in national income, which in turn would produce the necessary decline in the amount of current savings. The above would have been less difficult to follow and Keynes' message would have been more readily understood if he had not chosen to muddy the waters by defining the relationships between *I, C, S,* and *Y* by the following equations:

$$Y = C + I$$

$$Y = C + S$$

By transposing these equations, both *I* and *S* became equal to *Y*—*C* and things equal to the same thing are equal to each other. By defining *I* and *S* so that they were always equal, Keynes obscured the functional manner by which they became equal in the more meaningful sense of the word. It is quite true that in one sense *S* and *I* always remain equal in amount, not, as some critics have alleged, because Keynes made the two equal in a purely definitional sense (as one could make black equal white by defining them both as equaling gray), but for a more fundamental reason. We can see what Keynes meant if we employ a very simple numerical illustration. Suppose that national income totaled $100, with $80 spent on consumption and $20 saved, and a corresponding amount of $20 invested. For the sake of simplicity, an absence of government activity is assumed. If consumers now decided to consume only $75 and save $25, businessmen would find their sales reduced by $5 and they would have an unexpected $5 of stock remaining. Since inventories are also a part of business investment, investment would have risen by an additional $5; savings and investment would remain equal in amount, but at the higher figure of $25.

Although the volumes of investment and savings are technically equal in amount, they are not in equilibrium. Businessmen do not wish to hold an additional $5 of inventories and will attempt to dispose of them by cutting their current levels of production. When this happens, a process described earlier takes place—national income falls, consumption declines, and so do savings, and savings and investment once again are equal and in equilibrium, but at a lower level of income. The lower level of income will inevitably be one of less than full employment, but the position is one of equilibrium and nothing in the economy assures restoration back to the original level of full employment. This latter relationship in Keynes' system was the important one, and by failing to explain that it was equality in equilibrium that was important, Keynes created a vast amount of needless confusion for his readers.

Nor did Keynes offer any diagrammatic representations to assist his readers in following his reasons. The familiar *C* + *I* diagrams, where *I* is added to the *C* curve shown in Fig. 15 and equilibrium found at the point where *C* + *I* crossed the 45° line, is a product of his popularizers. The

message of effective demand and its frequent ineffectiveness is still much
the same even though the analysis has been simplified considerably. It is
important to remember, however, that there have been many modifications and improvements made on the original text as written by Keynes,
and one can sympathize with the beginning economics student who in-
quired how much of the material on national income analysis was a direct
product of Keynes' thinking and how much was the result of Keynes'
followers, including the author of the text.

SECULAR STAGNATION. It is interesting, for example, to trace the role
of secular stagnation through successive editions of one of the most popular economic principles texts. In the first edition, the idea that the capitalistic economy might be doomed to almost perpetual recession and
unemployment was accorded several pages. In more recent editions no
mention of the idea can be found. Although the idea of secular stagnation should be attributed to Professor Alvin Hansen[8] (1887–   ), now
retired but for many years one of Harvard's most distinguished economists
and the best-known Keynesian in the United States, the seeds of the idea
can be found in Keynes' *General Theory*.

The concept of secular stagnation was formally presented by Professor
Hansen in his presidential address before the American Economic Association in December, 1938. Professor Hansen argued before that distinguished body of economists that there were three major bases for business
investment: population growth, new frontiers, and technological change.
Hansen maintained that each of these three forces had either experienced
declines in their rate of growth or had been otherwise altered so that they
no longer provided sufficient outlets for investment funds. The relation
between population growth and business expansion is not difficult to see,
and our Department of Commerce was, at least until 1963, sending out
mail stamped with the current U.S. population and the words, "More People, More Jobs." The argument was (and continues to be) that larger
families ensure the population's consumption of more of its dollar income
in order to support the nonworking children. This greater consumer demand, in turn, reflects itself in greater business sales, which in turn en-

[8] A few words by way of a biographical sketch seem most appropriate at this point.
Hansen was born in Viborg, South Dakota and did his graduate work at the University
of Wisconsin. Following a few years as a high school principal and superintendent, he
taught at Brown University and the University of Wisconsin before moving to the University of Minnesota, where he remained from 1919 to 1937. In 1937 he was appointed a Littauer Professor at Harvard, where he remained until his retirement. Among
his better-known works are *Economic Policy and Full Employment, Monetary Theory
and Policy, Business Cycles and National Income* and *A Guide to Keynes*.

courage more investment. Viewing the situation as it appeared in the 1930's, Hansen saw a decline in the rate of population expansion. Similarly, the settlement of the West and the discovery of most of the nation's major resources was alleged to have had depressing effects on business investment, as these outlets dwindled in importance.

Hansen's argument about the changing nature of technology was not so much that it was declining, but that its rate of expansion was insufficient to provide an offset from the closed opportunities for investment resulting from the decline taking place in the other two forces. Furthermore, said Hansen, much of current technology was capital-saving in nature, in the sense that it made unnecessary other forms of investment which required greater capital and more extensive utilization of labor than the new innovations replacing them. A good illustration of his point would be the development of the airplane, which made the construction of extensive railroad mileage unnecessary in places such as Alaska. Hansen's forecasts were not completely pessimistic. Just as John Stuart Mill had seen the stationary state as an opportunity to cultivate the finer things of life, Hansen also saw in the increasing scope of government a way to alleviate many social and economic ills.

It is an indication of the general gloom and pessimism of the time that Hansen's extension of Keynes' position aroused little opposition among fellow economists. The secular stagnation thesis was widely accepted as a reasonably accurate forecast of the future of capitalism. Not until sometime later did George Terborgh's critique titled *The Bogey of Economic Maturity* raise serious doubts about the validity of Hansen's thesis. There were many subsequent exchanges between Hansen and Terborgh, but we shall only sketch briefly the nature of Terborgh's criticism. As to the impact of the retardation in the rate of population growth and the disappearance of the frontier, Terborgh asked why, if these were significant factors, the impact had not been felt at a much earlier date in our history. After all, he reasoned, the rate of population increase had been slowing down since the end of the Civil War, and if population growth had an important effect on the rate of investment, its slowing pace should have made itself felt decades earlier. A similar argument was made with respect to the disappearance of the frontier. It, too, had disappeared from the American scene considerably before the onset of the Great Depression of the 1930's. Terborgh also expressed doubts as to whether the frontier had really accounted for as much investment as Hansen's thesis had suggested; greater sums were expended on the more settled eastern seaboard, suggesting that the West still held great promise as an outlet for future investment. Nor did Terborgh find much to support in Hansen's third argument about the changing nature of investment. If the great outlets of investment of the past had left the scene, their place could be filled by the tremendous number of new smaller investment opportunities which would provide sufficient stimulus to keep the economy operating at levels of full employment.

Economists have become increasingly skeptical about the more pessimistic phases of Keynes' doctrines, and a belief in the inevitability of the secular stagnation (at least for the reasons advanced by Keynes) has grown less and less prevalent. Keynes himself appears to have grown less pessimistic in later years, but, of course, he never lived to witness the great postwar boom. Hansen's recent position also has been somewhat more optimistic; he has suggested that the failure of his grimmer predictions to come true can be explained by the fact that the government has taken corrective action along the lines recommended by him. The increasing share of national income accounted for by the activity of the various levels of government has been advanced by Hansen as a reason why the danger of stagnation has been forstalled. He has warned that the danger would still be considerable if the government should revert to its pre-1930's activities. Evidence that Hansen has not completely abandoned the stagnation thesis can be found in his more recent writings about the slow pace of America's economic growth.

THE BUSINESS CYCLE. Although some of the pessimism of Keynes' message has dissipated through the years, it is important to remember that this pessimism was an early part of Keynes' message in the *General Theory*. One of his major points was the tendency of the economy to seek an equilibrium and the strong possibility that the equilibrium would be at less than full employment. His explanation of the business cycle was confined to a single chapter, and perhaps symptomatically entitled "A Note on the Trade Cycle."

Keynes' explanation of the occurrence of the cycle was in keeping with those of many other theorists who had stressed the variability of investment. The cause for variations in the level of investment, in Keynes' view, was changes in the marginal efficiency of capital. The trade cycle, said Keynes, was ". . . mainly due to the way in which the marginal efficiency of capital fluctuates." [9] The question to be determined was why the marginal efficiency of capital fluctuated and why it fluctuated in a cyclical fashion. The answer to the first question was a two-part one. Changing

9 Keynes, *op. cit.*, p. 313.

stocks of capital in proportion to other factors of production would yield changing yields on the capital; this was the marginal productivity theory of capital as developed by Clark, Marshall, and others. But the marginal efficiency of capital also involved entrepreneurs' expectations, and these might waver between optimism and pessimism, either with or without justification in terms of actual yields currently being achieved.

Keynes saw no reason why fluctuations in the marginal efficiency of capital had to be cyclical in character. He was faced, however, with a sizable amount of historical data assembled by Mitchell and others which showed that in the past cyclical variations had occurred, and if the marginal efficiency of capital was to serve as a cause for these cycles, its fluctuations must also be cyclical. Keynes, therefore, suggested several tentative reasons for the cyclical character of the *mec* in the past. The marginal efficiency of capital collapsed at the peak of the cycle, said Keynes, because the rising stocks of capital accumulated through the earlier stages of the cycle and because the rise in costs experienced during the same period led to a situation where "doubts suddenly arise concerning the reliability of the prospective yield." [10]

These same doubts produced a sharp increase in liquidity preference, and this, by forcing upward the rate of interest, only worsened the situation. The collapse in the *mec*, however, preceded the increase in the liquidity preference, rather than the other way around. Hoarding became increasingly severe during the crisis stage and then became less extreme as recovery began to take place. Thus the lower rate of interest encouraged expansion during the upturn, just as it had fostered contraction during the downturn.

Keynes' treatment of the consumption function over the range of the business cycle was less certain. He was inclined to believe that it acted as a restraining influence on the swings of the cycle. Keynes was convinced that the consumption function tended to flatten out as the cycle progressed because of the tendency of consumption to lag behind changes in income. The point is only suggested in the *General Theory*, and it has remained for later writers to develop the nature of the short-run consumption function. Keynes' failure to distinguish clearly between the long and short run with respect to the consumption function is all the more regrettable because of the importance that changes in the consumption function have upon the multiplier. If Keynes was correct in his belief that the *CC* curve flattened out as prosperity resumed, then the resulting change in the mar-

[10] *Ibid.*, p. 317.

ginal propensity to consume would produce a sharp reduction in the multiplier. As the following passage makes clear, Keynes was convinced that
this change was more than just a possibility.

The marginal propensity to consume is not constant for all levels of employment, and it is probable that there will be, as a rule, a tendency for it to
diminish as employment increases. . . .[11]

The result, of course, would be to impose still another drag on the expanding economy, tending to pull the economy back toward a position of equilibrium of less than full employment.

Some of Keynes' pessimism about the business cycle is made evident in
his suggestions for appropriate credit policy. Keynes warned against any
efforts to choke off what appeared to be unduly vigorous rallies. Such
rallies were too hard to come by to risk destroying one prematurely. His
unwillingness to adopt vigorous monetary controls to check upswings exposed him to criticism from those economists more concerned about preserving the purchasing power of money. These critics have accused
Keynes, not without merit, of being biased in favor of inflation. Although
his later writings demonstrate that Keynes was too good an economist not
to be aware of the dangers of inflation and that he was quite able to
prescribe measures to hold it in check, it is also quite clear that throughout
the *General Theory* Keynes was too concerned about the danger of unemployment ever to be willing to come to grips with the inflationary implications of consistently maintaining full employment. It was not so much
that Keynes chose inflation as the lesser of two evils, but rather that he
refused to consider the possible conflict.

Now that we have sketched the central theme of Keynes' work, we are
in a better position to judge to what extent Keynes was presenting a re-
hash of ideas frequently advanced in the past and to what extent some
books evaluating Keynes' views have been properly descriptive in their
titles, *The New Economics* and *The Keynesian Revolution.*[12]

As is so frequently the case with what first appears to be a completely
new idea, one can find many anticipations of parts of Keynes' writings in
the economic thoughts of his predecessors. Keynes, himself, was aware of
this and acknowledged some of these earlier views. We will confine our
comments to a comparision between Keynes' theory and that of two of his
forerunners; first, Malthus, for whom Keynes expressed great admiration,

[11] *Ibid.,* p. 120.

[12] Seymour Harris, *op. cit.* Also, Lawrence R. Klein, *The Keynesian Revolution*
(New York: Macmillan, 1949).

and second, Wicksell, of whose work Keynes seems largely to have been ignorant.

We have noted in Chapter IV that Malthus had considerable doubts about the validity of Say's Law, and a closer examination reveals other points of similarity between the views of Malthus and Keynes. Malthus was also concerned about the paradox of thrift, in which the more people attempted to save, the less realized saving was possible, and suggestions of a propensity-to-consume concept can also be found in Malthus' writings, with references to the effect of public debt and the distribution of income upon it.

Malthus' position, however, resembled more closely that of other Underconsumptionists previously referred to than to Keynes, and it is mainly the Underconsumption overtones in Keynes' analysis that produced the resemblance. Actually, Malthus' and Keynes' diagnosis of the relationship between savings and investment was quite different. The problem, as Malthus saw it, was that if the rich did not spend their money on needless luxuries but instead saved their money, the result would be that the funds saved would flow into investment. The problem was not as Keynes saw it—the difficulty of assuring the flow of savings into investment channels —but as Malthus saw it, the funds flowing into investment would make possible the production of goods far beyond the capacity of the economy to consume them. Excessive capital accumulation would lead inevitably to a declining rate of profit and a condition of stagnation.

Malthus' treatment of the end result—stagnation—was closer to Keynes' view than the stationary economy envisioned by most of the Classical economists, beginning with Smith. Although secular stagnation and the stationary state both sound an ominous note to our ears, the two concepts were quite different in character. To Ricardo and other believers in the eventual coming of the stationary state, this final stage in capitalism was not one of unemployment and depression but simply a cessation of economic growth. Ricardo's solution to the problem of oversavings was quite simple: When investment was no longer profitable, savings would cease. Neither Keynes nor Malthus felt this was true, and Keynes in particular took great pains to emphasize that the people who saved were not the same as those who invested and that there was no way of assuring that the amounts people intended to save would be matched by the amounts people wanted to invest. It seems quite evident from the above discussion that parts of Keynes' analysis were anticipated by Malthus, but that Malthus' structure was far from complete and led him to quite different conclusions as to the nature of the problem.

Keynes' employment of aggregates and the relationships between savings and investment were anticipated on the Continent by Knut Wicksell. Wicksell also denied that savings were channeled automatically into investment, as predicated by Say's Law. Although much of Wicksell's analysis revolved around the role of interest in stabilizing output and price levels, he also went beyond the simple credit disturbances employed by Marshall and other English economists (including Pigou) to explain the existence of the cycle; Wicksell, instead, sought for more fundamental causes for disparities in the volumes of savings and investment. Wicksell was interested in the total spending power of the economy. When consumers spent all of the money they received, Say's Law was fulfilled. Nor did savings necessarily upset Say's Law, as long as they were returned to the economy in the form of investment. But situations might arise when all the funds being saved might not be reinvested, and then Say's Law became inoperative and unemployment would develop. The resemblance to Keynes' version is readily apparent. In addition, one can also find in Wicksell's writings hints of the marginal efficiency of capital and even of the multiplier. While Wicksell's contribution should receive more attention than it has, particularly from English and American economists, in the author's judgment it was not only the barrier of language which prevented his work from having the powerful impact achieved by Keynes, but the fact that Wicksell achieved only a partial construction of the model.

Considering the complicated nature of Keynes' theory and the frequently abstruse fashion in which he presented it, the miracle is the tremendous amount of discussion, shocked agitation, and staunch approval it has won. Few books, even when couched in less complex terms, have won more ardent supporters or fierce attackers than has the *General Theory*. Whatever Keynes' intellectual debt to predecessors may have been, it was Keynes and his book which have remained the center of controversy. Keynes, the millionaire, the English lord, and an avowed foe of Marx and Communism, has probably produced as many if not more chills up and down the spines of conservatives than those caused by Marx! One widely read book, William Buckley's *God, Man and Yale*, even went so far as to compile a list warning against all the known colleges using a popular text in the principles of economics which was favorable to the Keynesian viewpoint. The designation of Keynesian economics as "revolutionary" thus has another meaning, aside from its implications for previous economic thought. We will now deal with some of the aspects of Keynes' thought which aroused all of this criticism from economists and the general public alike.

Among the greatest sources of dispute about Keynes' economics were the policy conclusions to which it led. At an earlier period in his career, Keynes had written a pamphlet titled *The End of Laissez-Faire;* the need for its abandonment (in Keynes' judgment) became even more evident in the years that followed. When a private sector of the economy was unable to generate sufficient investment to offset the volume of savings occurring at levels of income assuring full employment, it was only proper for the government to step in and fill the gap. A multiplier effect could be generated by government as well as by private business spending. Although the policy implications are an important part of the *General Theory,* they cannot accurately be said to have originated with Keynes' book. Keynes had earlier made similar recommendations to the British government, nor did the idea of supplementing private spending with government spending originate with Keynes. The early years of the New Deal in the United States launched a program of deficit spending considerably before the *General Theory* appeared in print.[13] Although Keynes did not originate the idea, his theoretical apparatus strengthened and has continued to lend a theoretical support for what was in large part a pragmatic solution born out of desperation. Economists, like most other people, are uneasy when they support a policy without being able to provide a theoretical justification for that policy. Keynes, once he was understood, provided such a theoretical basis, and many economists embraced it as much for that reason as for any other.

All those economists and members of the general public who feared the increasing role played by the national government in public affairs, however, saw (and continue to see) Keynes' book as a justification for further encroachment of the government on the private sector. This fear has been coupled with an equally great fear of the inflationary repercussions of Keynesian policies. Many of these same groups also have expressed concern over the mounting burden of debt. These issues are much too involved for this book, but it seems fair to say that Keynes did little to calm the fright of the critics. He and his followers saw little to fear in a rising debt; provided national income continued to grow, it might even have favorable repercussions on the propensity to consume, as individuals felt wealthier.

[13] Keynes had written earlier pieces, including a famous letter to the *New York Times* supporting public works programs and deficit spending.

Nor did Keynes ever face up to the implications for private ownership of socializing investment. It is an easy step from an advocacy of government spending to the support of some government ownership in order to provide outlets for the government spending.[14] This is not to say that the two must inevitably go together, but only that Keynes left the door open to such interpretation. To accuse Keynes of inspiring inflationary pressure seems much more of an overstatement. Periods of inflationary pressure existed long before Keynes wrote, and not always for different reasons. In all fairness, Keynes must be interpreted in the context of the times in which he wrote. If he appeared unconcerned about inflation, his indifference to it was no more blatant at the time than the undue fears expressed about its imminent outbreak by various monetary authorities, including our Federal Reserve. This fear was prevalent at a time when the United States still had nearly a quarter of the labor force unemployed.

Keynes' formulation of the consumption function also lent itself to proposals for redistributing income. Various social reformers had seized earlier upon the concept of diminishing marginal utility of income as a justification for imposing steeply progressive income taxes. As the principle of marginal utility came under increasingly heavy attack, supporters of progressive taxation sought other grounds for its justification. Little wonder that these advocates of progressive taxation seized happily on Keynes' consumption function. If the rich tended to consume a smaller amount of their income than did the poor, the consumption function for the economy could be raised, thus stimulating the entire economy, by taking money away from the upper income groups and returning it to those with low incomes. It requires little imagination to determine which groups found this aspect of Keynesian thinking most distasteful! Recent empirical research has somewhat diminished the theoretical support for this policy; studies made by the National Bureau of Economic Research and others suggest that the marginal propensity of the upper and lower groups to consume differs remarkably little. Hence, little stimulus to the consumption function is to be gained from redistributing income. Although some of the sting of this particular policy implication has thus been removed, critics have continued to use the program of redistributing income as another illustration of where Keynes was wrong.

One of Keynes' most startling concepts was his attack on the value of thrift. For the many economists to whom thrift had been second only to

---

[14] The British Labor Party, immediately after World War II, used this argument in support of their programs for nationalization.

cleanliness in its proximity to eternal truth, Keynes' warning that thrift might be a private virtue but a public vice was a difficult one to accept. For a long time, savings had been the means by which the economy made a better tomorrow possible; thus it was difficult to conceive of savings making a tomorrow that was less attractive. Little wonder that some economists and businessmen saw Keynes as no more than another Underconsumptionist in academic robes.

Keynes also met opposition in his argument that cutting wage rates would do little to restore full employment. Many economists and businessmen alike had found labor unions, with their pressure to make wages less flexible downward, a convenient whipping boy in explaining the delays involved in restoring the economy to a condition of full employment. Keynes, by stressing that more fundamental adjustments were needed to promote recovery than simply slashing wages, threatened the destruction of a widely held explanation which laid the responsibility for a failure to recover from depression not on the economic system itself but on labor unions, one of the institutions permitted to grow up in it.

Many economists also found the position taken by Keynes on the question of free trade in his *General Theory* more than a little disturbing. Keynes undertook a limited defense of the Mercantilists. The men of this school, said Keynes, were not simply interested in the quantity of gold secured from a favorable balance of trade, but also in the expansive effects on the health of the economy produced by such a favorable balance. Since trade was a laborsaving device, some stimulation to industrial activity could be achieved by using various protective devices. The chapter was brief and Keynes never pushed the analysis very far. As his subsequent work at the Bretton Woods Conference suggests, Keynes never became a champion of trade restrictions, and in fact worked hard to secure a larger volume of world trade. Nevertheless, so firmly was the gospel of free trade implanted in the thinking of most economists all over the world that any questioning of this gospel was certain to be treated as the rankest form of heresy.

All of these points of disagreement between Keynes and earlier writers were based on the fundamental point that the private sector of the economy might be unable to generate sufficient effective demand by itself to assure full employment. Private investment might consistently run below the levels necessary to offset the volume of savings produced at a level of full employment. Keynes did not see much prospect of stimulating the consumption function. He has often been accused of overlooking the power of Madison Avenue, with its elaborate advertising campaigns. However, he believed that the consumption function was largely geared to the level of national income. Furthermore, he doubted whether the conspicuous consumption of which Veblen spoke was sufficient to bolster consumption habits substantially. If anything, the consuming public just was not wasteful enough! Both positions—the view that the outlets for investment were limited and that people could not be encouraged to spend more of their incomes—were highly distasteful to many businessmen and economists.

There is another aspect of Keynes' theory which was "revolutionary" in the sense that it sparked a new line of economic thinking, but which did not arouse the antagonism created by the "new" aspects just presented. This refers to Keynes' emphasis on the role of expectations in economic affairs. Prior to Keynes, the subject had received relatively little attention; since then, however, it has become an important area for economists to explore.[15]

Summary and Evaluation. Over a quarter of a century has gone by since Keynes wrote the *General Theory,* and endless criticisms, qualifications, and extensions of Keynes' thinking have occurred. As one who is reasonably conversant with much of this literature, the author can only add how frequently he is impressed to discover, upon reexamining the *General Theory,* that Keynes had at least partially anticipated the point in question, and to find how well his theory has stood up under meticulous study and evaluation.

This does not indicate that Keynes was always right. He was quite clearly wrong, for example, in thinking that money wages almost always proceeded in a direction opposite from real wages, and his formulation of the consumption function led many of his followers to believe that it was far more stable in the short run than it actually is. Later writers have also been correct in stressing that the ties of consumption to the level of national income are not as tight as Keynes suggested. The effect of the stock of past savings, the interest rate, and anticipations of the trend of future prices are some of the more important other variables shaping the nature of the consumption function. Furthermore, while the use of aggregates has provided us with many fresh insights into the operation of the economy,

[15] Expectation theory has become an important part of modern economic theory. See Albert G. Hart, Chapter 31, *The New Economics,* Seymour E. Harris, ed. (New York: Alfred Knopf, 1948).

there is also the danger of not being able to see the trees for the forest. Possible maladjustments in the economy tend to be slurred over as reliance upon government spending for all downturns in business activity is prescribed.

In many important ways, Keynes remained true to his Classical heritage. He accepted much of the microanalysis with little question, and, despite his references to the importance of expectations, most of his analysis was confined to a static model. Although it has been suggested that Keynes' analysis would have been strengthened if he had incorporated into his system the concept of monopolistic competition, it has always seemed to the author that it was Chamberlin and not Keynes who suffered from having the two books appear so close together. Part of the strength of Keynes' contribution lay in his accepting the micromodel much as it had been postulated by the Neoclassical writers, and demonstrating how its operation might prove faulty at points. While Chamberlin's analysis was theoretically independent of Keynes', much of the originality of Chamberlin's contribution was for many years obscured by the furor provoked by the *General Theory.* Even though Keynes never divorced himself completely from the Neoclassical tradition, the differences between him and his predecessors were great enough to startle economists all around the world. Some of Keynes' claims to have advanced economic theory greatly were overstated. For example, his liquidity preference explanation of the interest rate and some of his other ideas had been more fully anticipated than he was aware of or willing to acknowledge. Nevertheless, his writing did prompt a drastic change in economic thinking, and his view of the system was a fresh and novel one. Although anticipated at points by earlier writers, Keynes put together into a meaningful whole the consumption function, the marginal efficiency of capital, the liquidity preference, and the multiplier. Is it wrong to suggest that the mark of a great theorist is not so much a matter of being the first to conceive an idea as being the first to present it in a way which wins it wide attention?

JOHN MAURICE CLARK (1884–1963)

Hailed by many of his colleagues as the dean of American economists, and by businessmen as the number one economist in the country, John Maurice Clark left an indelible mark on the course of economic thought throughout the world. His interests in economics were broad and his approach eclectic. His range of writings was so extensive that it would embarrass anyone to attempt to provide a capsule version, and our sketch will only attempt to touch the highlights.

The Man. Clark was one half of one of the most famous father-son teams in economics; we have previously noted that his father John Bates Clark, was a distinguished economist in his own right. The younger Clark was born in New York City, and like his father, attended Amherst College. After completing his undergraduate studies with honors, Clark took his graduate degree at Columbia University, where he eventually occupied the post previously held by his father. Although students found him to be a delightful individual outside of the classroom (he regularly attended the students' economics club meetings—one of the few faculty members to do so), his performance in the classroom left much to be desired. The contrast between his rambling classroom lectures and the acute clarity of his writings was startling.

Clark's competence as a professional economist and writer won him worldwide fame, and the number of honors accorded him was impressive. In 1952, he was the first recipient of the highest honor the American Economic Association can bestow, the Francis A. Walker Prize. Seventeen years earlier, he had served as president of that same association and was designated at other times as an honorary president of the International Economic Association and a fellow in the Econometric Society. The latter had its more humorous aspects, since Clark was never a devotee of the more esoteric exercises in mathematical ingenuity. Students in his classes will remember his somewhat wistful remark, "I am sure that the mathematical economists have discovered a great deal. I only wish they would tell us what it is." After Clark's retirement from Columbia in 1956, he continued his writing and lecturing until his death. Among his better-known books are *Studies in the Economics of Overhead Costs, Strategic Factors in Business Cycles, Preface to Social Economics, Alternative to Serfdom,* and *Guideposts in Time of Change.*

Economic Views. In view of our previous caveat about the breadth of Clark's writing, it seems best to divide our examination into three major parts: his approach to the problem of business cycles, his views on the problem of monopoly, and his diagnosis of the social problems of society, with some of his suggestions for remedying the latter. The reader who has studied the discussion of John Bates Clark will find it profitable to compare for himself the differences in approaches of the father and son. As a start, the reader should know that the younger Clark went much further in developing a dynamic analysis for viewing the various questions he wished to examine than his father had.

THE BUSINESS CYCLE. One of Clark's contributions to the study of the business cycle was the principle of acceleration. The acceleration principle was offered as an explanation of two characteristics of the business cycle that previously had defied solution: (1) why fluctuations in investment in capital goods were so sharp and abrupt; and (2) why the cycle sometimes turned downward when consumption was at an all-time record and perhaps still increasing.

As an answer to these questions, Clark postulated a fixed relationship between levels of consumption and the amount of necessary investment. The accompanying table will help to make the relationship clearer.

Period	Consumption	Capital Stock	Net Investment	Gross Investment
1	$80	40	0	$ 4
2	88	48	8	12
3	88	48	0	4+

A word or two about the assumptions involved is necessary before we can apply the table to developing an answer to the preceding two questions. A total capital stock of $40 is assumed to exist in Period 1, consisting of 10 machines, each costing $4, with one machine wearing out each year and necessitating a gross investment of $40. The $40 stock of capital makes possible an output of $80 of consumer goods—the amount in demand at the first period.

Now note what happens in Period 2, when the demand for consumer goods rises by 20 percent to $88. Net investment rises from zero to $8 and gross investment from $4 to $12. A 20-percent increase in consumer demand has produced a threefold expansion in gross investment. In Period 3, where we assume that consumer demand remains at the $88 figure, there is a resulting collapse of gross investment back to its previous level of $4. The figures, of course, are purely hypothetical; the same point could be made with other figures, providing that the same relationships were maintained. What is crucial are the assumptions made about the relationships between consumer and capital goods. In the first place, the response in the output of capital goods, as a result of changes in the level of consumer demand, assumes that there is no other possibility of increasing output. In other words there is full employment of available resources, with no possibility of expanding output through overtime or other means.

The magnitude of the change in investment would also be reduced if businessmen were assumed to hold sufficiently large inventories so that they could, by reducing these stockpiles, meet consumer demand without being forced to add to their productive capacity. Whether or not they would choose to do so would depend upon their forecasts as to the strength of the upturn in consumer demand and the extent to which they had been previously concerned about excessive stockpiles of goods. Despite these reservations, the acceleraton principle has remained an important part of business cycle theory, and its importance has been increased by the work of Professor Paul Samuelson in constructing a mathematical model showing the interrelationship between the acceleration principle and the Keynesian multiplier.[16]

In many important respects, Clark can be counted among the forerunners of Keynesian thought. Although he never launched a full-scale attack on Say's Law in the style of Keynes, Clark did have serious reservations about whether the level of productive activity was consistently large enough to assure full employment. Clark expressed doubts about the ability of the free market to maintain stability by itself, and he was hopeful that action by the state might be more successful. One can also find in Clark's writing anticipations of the consumption function and the marginal efficiency of capital.

MONOPOLY AND BIG BUSINESS. Clark was considerably less worried about the threat of monopoly to the operation of the economy than many of his fellow economists. Clark argued that the invidious comparison drawn between perfect and monopolistic competition was the result of making the demand curves for monopolistic competition far more inelastic than they actually were. He doubted whether the degree of inelasticity between the two brands of competition was markedly different, particularly if one allowed for the adjustments in consumer demand sure to take place with the passage of time. Clark also doubted whether the various methods of product differentiation did much to influence consumer choice greatly or to increase costs of production.

Clark felt that the earlier models of perfect or pure competition were unrealistic in the current world, but suggested that we should not become dismayed by the fact that they did not exist. As a substitute, Clark proposed that economists concern themselves more over the question of whether or not the existing amount of competition was "workable." The standard of "workability" could, Clark suggested, provide a standard for

[16] Paul A. Samuelson, "Interactions Between the Multiplier Analysis and the Principle of Accleration," *The Review of Economic Statistics* (May, 1939), pp. 75–78.

performance to economists and lawyers alike. Instead of attempting to attain the impossible, it would be better to ask ourselves whether the results currently being achieved were adequate to meet the needs of the economy. Clark's own answer to this question was yes.

Clark's pragmatic approach to the problem of monopoly was based in part on his conviction that what businessmen sought in their drives for monopoly positions was security. Security was an important goal in the businessman's life, but it was difficult to achieve, given a fiercely competitive system. When one firm cut its prices and attempted to undermine its rivals' market position, the result was likely to be upsetting to the economy. Without the security that comes with some measure of monopoly, the businessmen were likely to act in ways that would be damaging to each other as well as to the economy. In one of his early books, *The Economics of Overhead Costs,* Clark had pointed out that costs which were variable from the point of view of the individual firm were overhead or fixed costs from the viewpoint of society. An individual employer could reduce his costs by cutting wages, for example, but since wages were the basis for subsistence of a majority of the population, wages in some form must continue to be paid if people were to continue to live. Clark's conclusion, that labor would be better off if it was also made an overhead cost by the institution of guaranteed annual wage plans, was drawn up many decades before the drive by American labor unions for such benefits. Without such protection, said Clark, excessive competition might produce disturbing fluctuations throughout the economy.

Clark defended his position that other economists were too concerned about monopoly on three major points. First, there was his implicit if not explicit belief that businessmen were well-intentioned, with a strong sense of social responsibility. The second was Clark's conviction that the basic problem in the society today, and the thing which most people, including businessmen, sought, was not production but security. The thought that production no longer had the central role to play, as it did in the time of Adam Smith, was an interesting forerunner of Professor Galbraith's *The Affluent Society.* Finally, on the basis of these two previous assumptions, Clark argued that it was possible to bring the various groups in the society to a point where they would respond to the pressure of social control.

SOCIAL CONTROL OF THE ECONOMY. Clark felt that too many economists clung to outmoded theories and preconceptions about how the economy should work. At the same time, he was not blind to the many faults in the operation of the American economy. Clark, however, was even more concerned about the danger of collectivism, and he tried to construct a solution whereby the various power blocs could accommodate to each other's interests without damaging the economy.

It is important to note at this point that Clark was not worried solely about big business. Powerful labor unions had come to play an increasingly important role in the economy since Clark had written his *Economics of Overhead Costs,* and Clark saw dangers in this growth to the stability of the economy. In some ways, Clark found more cause for alarm from big unions than from big business. The problem was that unions had achieved a bargaining strength which permitted them to gain wages in excess of the increases in productivity. The result could only be inflation or unemployment. To avoid these twin dilemmas, Clark recommended that wages in general should rise no more rapidly than the gains in productivity; in some cases, wages would rise less than productivity, and in these instances prices should fall, while in other industries the rise in wages would be greater than the gain in productivity, necessitating price increases. The total price level would remain unchanged, however. Clark was willing for the state to provide guidance as to appropriate changes in wages in the short run, but he hoped that in the long run the two parties —labor and management—could resolve the question through free collective bargaining. As a step in this direction, Clark urged the pursuit of more reliable gauges of productivity increases. The traditional marginal productivity theory so dear to his father and other economists of the past was, Clark warned, defective in many respects. Unless the two parties succeeded in finding ways to accommodate to each other, the result was almost inevitably state interference and the possibility of totalitarian control.

Conventional economic theory all too frequently appealed to what Clark regarded as the least desirable traits in men. Perhaps more might be achieved by assuming that men were basically well intentioned and willing to acknowledge the rights of others. Clark's proposal for an *Alternative to Serfdom,* therefore, was the formation of voluntary associations; all members of society should enter into a kind of voluntary social contract in which they would plead not only their own special interests but come to recognize the interests of others. By this means, a harmony of interests could be restored and the chaotic conflict which was threatening to envelop the economy would be resolved.

Summary and Evaluation. The brief sketch provided above of some of Clark's major ideas reveals the breadth of his thinking. Somewhat like the Institutionalists, he went beyond the boundaries usually prescribed for the economists, and in many ways he was, in his later years, a social philosopher. Certainly there was never any hesitancy on Clark's part to offer value judgments whenever he felt they were needed. For this reason, some economists will find his ventures into the realms of pure theory more satisfying than his prescriptions for a new tomorrow. One can admire his pioneer work in the study of business cycles and the many ways in which he anticipated Keynes, or his warning to economists not to be unduly concerned about the effect of big business on the economy, or his caveat about the applicability of marginal productivity theory to the problem of determining wages, without accepting his views on social balance.

Perhaps Clark was too generous in his estimate of human character. His belief that businessmen meant well and should be freed from some of the tyranny of competition came dangerously close to accepting power in the hands of those who had never been voted that power, so long as they exercised it wisely. His belief that men's character was malleable and could be shaped so that a group of harmoniously cooperative associations could be formed and made to function also seems quite optimistic. While some economists may find this kind of thinking difficult to digest, Clark's challenge to devise something better has been left unanswered.

JOSEPH ALOIS SCHUMPETER (1883–1950)

Although Schumpeter never founded a school or won a devoted set of followers in the sense that Keynes did, few economists would deny that Schumpeter was one of the great economists of the first half of the twentieth century. Born the same year as Keynes, Schumpeter never accepted the Keynesian philosophy, although his own forecasts about the future of capitalism were in many respects even more pessimistic than those of Keynes.

The Man. Schumpeter was born in Triesch, Moravia (now a part of Czechoslovakia); he was the only child in his family. His father, a textile manufacturer, died when Schumpeter was four. His mother remarried an Austrian army general some years later and Schumpeter was reared as a member of the aristocracy in pre-World War I Vienna. After eight years at the exclusive Theresianum, a school for the sons of the Austrian aristocracy, Schumpeter went to the University of Vienna, where he had among his teachers two leaders of the Austrian school—Fredrich von Wieser and Eugen Böhm von Bawerk. After his graduation from the University, Schumpeter married and went to Egypt, where he practiced law for two years. Neither venture proved to be a success. His marriage was not formally dissolved until 13 years later, but for all practical purposes it had ended much earlier. His work in Egypt was terminated when he contracted Malta fever. In the meantime he had completed his first formal book on economic theory, *Nature and Principal Content of Theoretical Economics,* and upon his return to Europe, he was awarded a professorship in economics at the University of Czernowitz. In 1911, Böhm-Bawerk secured a position for him at the University of Graz, and in 1913 Schumpeter paid his first visit to the United States, when he was appointed an Austrian exchange professor at Columbia University. Upon his return home, Europe was plunged into World War I, and Schumpeter worked to get Austria out of it by negotiating for a separate peace. Immediately after the war, he became the finance minister for the Austrian Republic. His appointment lasted less than a year because of his disagreements with the socialists who headed the government. Schumpeter next entered the world of private finance, where he served for a brief period as president of a Vienna bank. This position ended disastrously when, for reasons not of Schumpeter's making, the bank failed in 1924. Schumpeter lost his own private fortune in the bank's collapse and went heavily into debt; rather than escape his financial obligations through bankruptcy proceedings, he spent the next ten years repaying his creditors from the proceeds of his writing and teaching. To add to his many misfortunes, his second wife died in childbirth a little over a year after they were married.

Schumpeter moved to the University of Bonn upon his return to academic life, and there he remained until two visiting appointments to Harvard in the late 1920's led to a professorship at Harvard in 1932. There Schumpeter found his permanent home; his students found him to be a kindly, sympathetic, but not always inspiring teacher who was never too busy to discuss a student's problem. His personal life at last became a happy one, as he found in 1937 another mate—Elizabeth Boody—who provided him with companionship and new home life.

Schumpeter was the recipient of many tokens of recognition from his fellow economists. He was president of the Econometric Society from 1937 to 1941, an organization of which he was one of the founders. In 1948 he was named president of the American Economic Association, and just before his death he had been chosen to serve as the first president of the International Economic Association. His numerous articles and books have assured him of a distinguished position in any history of economic thought. Among his best-known books are *The Theory of Economic Development,* his two-volume *Business Cycles,* and *Capitalism, Socialism, and Democracy.* His *History of Economic Analysis* was unfinished at the time of his death, but thanks to Mrs. Schumpeter, who was also an economist, it was finally published. Despite certain obvious inadequacies in organization which make it difficult to use, it remains a giant among studies of economic thought and will serve as a guide to students of the subject for many years to come. A collection of his biographical sketches of famous economists with appraisals of their economic systems, written over a span of forty years, was published under the title *Ten Great Economists* shortly after his death.

Economic Views. Schumpeter found the inspiration for his views of the economic system in the writings of Léon Walras. He was greatly impressed with the Walrasian equations of general equilibrium as a basis for explaining the interrelationships between prices and for imputing returns to the various factors of production. What Walras lacked was the element of dynamic change, and this deficiency Schumpeter attempted to supply in his *Theory of Economic Development* and in his later books and articles.

Schumpeter began with a circular flow, stationary economy, where all earnings accrued to either land or labor, since in Schumpeter's stationary state both profits and interest were stipulated to be zero. This notion that interest would be zero, when the stationary state was assumed, led Schumpeter into numerous controversies with other economists, including his former teacher, Böhm-Bawerk. Schumpeter argued that interest payments were made possible only by the existence of profits, and when the latter disappeared in the absence of dynamic change, so would interest. Most economists have agreed with Böhm-Bawerk, who argued that interest was an independent economic payment, which was necessary irrespective of the institutional system in existence. Schumpeter weakened his case more by denying that interest had any place in a socialist economy. As Böhm-Bawerk pointed out in response to Schumpeter's contention, interest could serve an important service as an accounting device even in a completely socialistic economy. Recent attempts at socialistic planning have borne Böhm-Bawerk out, and most, if not all Socialist writers would agree on this point with that old foe of Socialism.

In many respects the whole question was somewhat of an academic one. Schumpeter would easily have conceded the point and still maintained his position that in the present-day capitalistic economy it was dynamic change and the forces of economic development that accounted most significantly for the existence of interest payments. The heart of Schumpeter's analysis was this process of change and the dynamic consequences it produced; the controversy over the zero rate of interest only served to distract economists from his central message.

Although Schumpeter wrote at considerable length on the subject of monopoly, he treated his static state as if pure competition still reigned supreme and monopoly profits were nonexistent. Since there were no profits to be made in the stationary economy, it behooved the businessman who wanted to make profits to introduce some element of change into the system, such as new products, new methods of production, or the acquisition of new positions in the market. Two groups supplied the drive for these necessary changes—the entrepreneurs and the innovators. For Schumpeter, the two were virtually synonymous and he contrasted them with the inventor. While the latter was important, it was the entrepreneur who brought the invention to market and capitalized on its uses. An important part of Schumpeter's system was his belief that these individuals who promoted change were relatively few in number. The typical businessman was conservative and willing to rest on traditional ways of doing things, until he was shaken out of his lethargy by the actions of the few. The manner in which these daring few found the necessary funds to undertake their new ideas and the resulting impact upon the economy brings us to an examination of Schumpeter's theory of the business cycle.

BUSINESS CYCLES. Schumpeter's definition of capitalism included the usual features of private ownership and private decision-making, but also emphasized the importance of a private banking system. The capital available to the entrepreneur for his proposed changes could not come from savings emerging from the circular flow of the static state, since Schumpeter believed these were inadequate for the task involved. The banks and the credit they provided the entrepreneurs made the fulfillment of the entrepreneurs' plans possible.

Earlier economists, including Böhm-Bawerk, had seen the process of capital accumulation and economic progress as a gradual but steady process. Schumpeter's analysis constituted a sharp break from this earlier view; he saw the business cycle as an integral and inevitable part of the process of economic growth and feared that the elimination of the cycle would bring with it a corresponding cessation of growth. The reason was that innovations did not come continuously but in waves or clusters. Schumpeter argued that each great new innovation set the stage for a flood of "imitators," who scurried down the path hewed out by the original entrepreneur. The less venturesome businessmen were attracted by the great profits made by the leader and by the general air of business confidence inspired by the existence of business prosperity. The initial upward thrust was therefore reinforced by a second upsurge as the flood of "imitators" swarmed into the market, aided by further extensions of bank credit.

Eventually the boom came to an end, cut off by forces of its own making. The expanded business activity resulted in rising prices and costs, while the new products and techniques brought losses to those firms which had not made the transition. The result was a period of contraction where businesses held back from further investment, thereby leading to deflation. Eventually, however, the deflation would come to an end, a position of static equilibrium would be restored, and the stage would be set for a new upsurge based on another innovation.

Several characteristics of the Schumpeterian business cycle provide an interesting contrast with the explanations provided by other writers. His theory was not basically one of financial crises, although the banks played an important role in providing the necessary credit for the expansion phase; instead, the basic explanation lay in the process of innovation and the entrepreneurs' role in exploiting those innovations. Similarly, costs which played an important role in choking off the boom played only a minor role in the upturn. At points, Schumpeter acknowledged that unemployment and lower costs might help foster an upturn, but since he preferred to begin each wave of innovations at a position of static equilibrium, the importance of reductions in costs was minimized.

Schumpeter's most extensive treatment of business cycles came in his two-volume study by that title. In this study Schumpeter provided extensive empirical evidence designed to fit his explanation of the business cycle to the pattern of cycles which had occurred in the past. The suspicion was left that Schumpeter was too tempted to try to fit his empirical evidence to his theory instead of permitting the theory to develop from the facts. Whether or not this suspicion was groundless, it seems safe to conclude that, much as Schumpeter emphasized empirical research, he was far more willing than Wesley Mitchell had been to generalize and formulate theories about cycles before all of the evidence was available.

Schumpeter did not share Keynes' view of the economic system. Savings were too small when the economy was in the position of static equilibrium to constitute a problem, and Schumpeter doubted whether the driving force of new innovations would ever be exhausted. Absent also from Schumpeter's model were any considerations of the problem of diminishing returns, which had played such an important role in the thinking of Ricardo and those economists who had followed his leadership.

Nevertheless, Schumpeter did see an eventual slowing down in the process of economic growth, and somewhat like Marx, saw capitalism germinating the seeds of its own destruction. The dialectical process of Marx was not present, however. Rather, the seeds of destruction lay not in the proletariat but in the inimical (to capitalism) forces of the intellectuals and more particularly of the state. Both groups launched attacks on the businessman just as he was beginning to lose some of his spark and verve. How the weakening of the entrepreneurial spirit transpired, with the resulting loss of impetus to the economy, deserves a few words of explanation and comment.

Schumpeter argued that, as time went by, the process of production became increasingly routine. More and more decisions came to be made by collective agreement formulated by boards of directors with no one assuming full individual responsibility. The result, said Schumpeter, was that much of the challenge and excitement that had stimulated the entrepreneur in the past would be lost. At the same time that these sturdy individuals most willing to champion the cause of capitalism were suffering a deterioration in health, attacks were being launched against them which threatened to topple the system at an even earlier date. The capitalistic system produced a civilization whose intellectual leaders were antithetical to the system. Because businessmen were generally politically inept, control of the government would pass increasingly into the hands of those forces antagonistic to the capitalistic system. The result would be—and in Schumpeter's view, already was—a multiplying variety of government policies such as progressive tax plans which would further impede investment. Like Ricardo, Schumpeter never set a definite date when this expected change would take place and the further expansion of the capitalistic system would cease; Schumpeter displayed varying degrees of pessimism throughout his writings. It is quite evident in all his writing, however, that despite a passionate devotion to the cause of capitalism, Schumpeter saw the "march to Socalism" as only a matter of time.

VIEWS ON KEYNES. Schumpeter was strongly anti-Keynesian in his economic outlook, and it is worthwhile to explore possible explanations for this antagonism. Perhaps the most important reason for this was that Schumpeter regarded Keynes as one of those intellectual critics of capitalism who by their efforts to reform the system were actually destroying it. No clearer evidence of Keynes' weakening of capitalism could be found, in Schumpeter's view, than in the Keynesian attacks on savings. Schumpeter also feared that the governmental interference advocated by Keynes would continue to grow whether or not the need for it persisted. As the role of government continued to expand, the opportunities for private investment would be correspondingly reduced, and thus much of the creative force that had made capitalism so successful in the past would be abolished. Schumpeter was also worried about the inflationary implications of the Keynesian doctrine and foresaw correctly that it would be easier to get legislative bodies to lower taxes and increase government spending in periods of depression than it would be to persuade them to raise taxes and reduce spending in periods of boom. The spectacle of the 1950's, when some of our leading economists were preaching the merits of a 2- to 3-percent annual rate of inflation as a means of assuring full employment and continued economic growth, would have provided Schumpeter with a grim satisfaction as to the accuracy of his forecasts.

There are other reasons why Schumpeter may have found the Keynesian philosophy distasteful. Educated in the Austrian School by Böhm-Bawerk, Schumpeter never embraced the reform implications of marginal utility adopted by Marginal theorists from other countries. Schumpeter, unlike Keynes, was no reformer, and he was suspicious of all those who would use their economics to foster reform.

Schumpeter adopted the long-run view of which Keynes was so contemptuous; he believed that the process of economic growth would solve many of the problems created by unequal income. He had great faith in the power of the capitalistic system to provide an abundant society for all its members, if only given enough time. In his *Capitalism, Socialism, and Democracy,* Schumpeter estimated that, within a fifty-year period, the American economy would be able to double the output per capita. If this estimate was correct, Schumpeter added, the dreams of even the most wild-eyed reformers could be fulfilled without any tampering with the capitalistic system in the form of income redistribution or other measures.

There were also aspects of Keynesian economics, aside from the policy implications, to which Schumpeter took exception. In the Ricardian tradition, Schumpeter argued that people saved in order to invest. If investment opportunities should disappear, much savings would also disappear. Schumpeter thus found no basis for the gloomier aspects of Keynes' views and rejected completely the possiblity of secular stagnation in the sense that Hansen had employed the term.

Professor Samuelson, in an evaluation of Keynes' contribution, has written of the wonders of having been born before the 1930's, but not too long before, so that he could obtain a full appreciation of the magnitude of Keynes' contribution.[17] Having developed his own economic system and overall view of economics at a considerably earlier date, it may be that

17 Harris, *op. cit.,* p. 145.

Schumpeter was already too fixed in his views to accept the full measure of Keynes' contribution. In all fairness, it should also be noted that Keynes took even less notice of Schumpeter's work; Schumpeter's attitude toward Keynes was one of antagonism, while Keynes' treatment of Schumpeter was mainly one of neglect.

Despite the antagonism Schumpeter displayed to Keynes' theory, it would be wrong to conclude that Schumpeter was also opposed to the macroeconomic approach. Thanks to his training on the European continent, Schumpeter came to the macroeconomic approach considerably earlier than many of his American and English colleagues. The lack of a consumption function and a multiplier were what most differentiated Schumpeter, in his macro approach, from the Keynesian system. Much of Schumpeter's innovation explanation of the business cycle could be incorporated easily into Keynes' marginal efficiency of capital, and both Keynes' and Schumpeter's theories of interest would have been strengthened by a blending of the two.

MONOPOLY AND BIG BUSINESS. Not unexpectedly, Schumpeter was opposed to most of the attempts of the government to regulate big business and control monopoly actions. In his *Theory of Economic Development,* Schumpeter assumed a condition of near perfect competition, and while he came to recognize the existence of monopolistic competition and even wrote extensively about the various forms of product differentiation emphasized by Chamberlin, Schumpeter's final conclusion was much the same as that held by Clark. All of the various means of differentiating products did little to lessen the elasticity of the demand curve for the product, and price and output remained much as they had been under conditions of perfect competition.

Schumpeter's conclusion that his fellow economists had greatly overstated the problem of big business rested on a number of additional points. Three lines of defense for the existence of big business were drawn up by Schumpeter, in addition to the argument noted in the preceding paragraph: (1) Big business deserved its extraordinary gains; (2) Its contribution to the health of the economy was considerable; and (3) True positions of monopoly, even when they existed, were of short duration because of the process of economic change which constantly undermined such monopoly positions.

Perhaps because of his aristocratic background, Schumpeter was inclined to accept the idea that society was headed by a small group of the elite. The members of this group, by their superior abilities and constructive action, rose to the top, and the rewards they reaped were richly deserved. Such was the case with respect to the leaders of big business, who were, for the most part, in Schumpeter's judgment, properly placed in positions of authority, and who earned the high incomes which they and their business firms received. We have already noted the great confidence Schumpeter displayed in the ability of the capitalistic system to expand output; this increase in production was made possible in large part by the big business concerns and the men who directed them.

Other economists, in Schumpeter's view, were in danger of forgetting the benefits to the economy accruing from the large firms' research facilities and the degree of stability which big business imparted to the economy. Particularly during the 1930's, with the Temporary National Economic Committee investigations and other research into big business pricing, there were charges heard from many economists that big business' control over prices produced an inflexibility in the price system that made the problem of employment worse. Business was accused of holding prices rigid in the face of declining demand and permitting output (and hence employment) to be the variable. Schumpeter's response was to argue that the oscillations in the business cycle would be much wider and more destructive if industrial prices were permitted to fluctuate as widely as agricultural prices did. Instead of condemning big business for fostering price inflexibilities, Schumpeter observed, economists should thank it for providing price stability!

The final line of defense in Schumpeter's position was by no means his least important one. Schumpeter argued that many economists were unduly concerned about the problem of monopoly because they limited their analysis to a static approach. When dynamic factors were permitted to enter, the picture changed greatly. Whatever monopoly positions might from time to time be established, they were constantly being endangered by the process of "creative destruction." New technology, new products, new firms, ?nd new industries were constantly encroaching upon those firms currently in a dominant position. Any monopoly position, Schumpeter proclaimed, could be retained for only a brief time as these dynamic forces uprooted the old business firms to make room for the new.

OTHER ASPECTS OF SCHUMPETER'S CONTRIBUTION. Although the above sketch contains Schumpeter's analysis of the operation of the workings of the capitalistic system, the heart of his contribution, brief mention should be made also of the techniques employed by Schumpeter in his analysis. Like Marshall and Keynes, he began with a great enthusiasm (but considerably less talent) for the role of mathematics in rendering economic theory more precise, but as the years passed, his interest also dwindled and he made little use of the new mathematical models in perfecting his own system. Instead, he came to rely increasingly on historical research as the best guide to the economist in helping him to formulate his ideas. Schumpeter had always regarded mathematics, statistics, and history as the three indispensable tools of the economic investigator, but as the years went by, Schumpeter promoted the last of these three to primary position. Schumpeter also found other social sciences of importance to the economist trying to understand the workings of the economy; the scope of his interest was broad, and few economists have been as widely read in their own and allied fields.

Summary and Evaluation. Trained by members of the Austrian School, Schumpeter's own economics showed as many departures from the teachings of his former professors as it did adherence to them. The subject of value held little interest for Schumpeter, and he dissented vigorously from the theory of interest set forth by Böhm-Bawerk, while his own preoccupation with the dynamic aspects of the economy was shared by few of the Austrian School. Traces of their influence, however, can be found in Schumpeter's aversion to reform, and the roundabout means of production as set forth by Böhm-Bawerk provided a basis for Schumpeter's theory of economic growth. Satisfaction with the Walrasian equations permitted Schumpeter to move beyond them to a dynamic analysis that Walras spoke about but never provided.

As to the validity of Schumpeter's system, in many respects his analysis departed sharply from those of his colleagues. He was and remains in many ways strictly a minority of one; economists found his ideas interesting and challenging, but unconvincing. Some of his major ideas were lost in the controversy over details; his postulation of a zero rate of interest in the static economy is a good example. His analysis of the role of innovation lost some of its appeal to many economists because of his belief in the eventual collapse of the capitalistic system. It is highly questionable whether businessmen of today are finding less challenge in the business world than they did formerly or that any slowing down of growth can be expected from such a loss. It is at least debatable whether or not the end of laissez-faire and the growing role of government has not done as much to strengthen capitalism as it has to destroy it. Schumpeter's avowed opposition to Keynesian economics and his unwillingness to reconstruct his own theory in the light of the Keynesian contribution did not win him wide approval at a time when virtually all economists were to some degree Keynesians.

The result was that Schumpeter never developed a Schumpeterian School under his leadership. He remained a "lone wolf" in economics—respected and honored for his intellectual prowess, but not followed. Schumpeter was well aware of this failure and tried to claim it as a part of his deliberate policy when he said in a farewell address to his students at the University of Bonn, "I have never tried to bring about a Schumpeter school. There is none and it ought not to exist. . . . Economics is not a philosophy but a science. Hence there should be no 'schools' in our field." [18]

[18] Quoted by Gottfried Heberler in *Schumpeter: Social Scientist,* Seymour E. Harris, ed. (Cambridge: Harvard University Press, 1951), p. 47.

CHAPTER XIV: The Present Generation of Economists

> *Economists today generally wish to avoid the simple labeling by "schools," and prefer instead to deal with problems of research as they arise, drawing wherever necessary upon the contributions from many different approaches.*
> —ROLLO HANDY
> AND PAUL KURTZ

With three or four major exceptions, all of the members of our cast of economists are no longer alive. One reason for this is the obvious greater ease of presenting ideas that have been fully developed, analyzed, and digested by the members of the economic profession. Parenthetically, there is also less possibility of a writer's rising up to protest misinterpretation of his ideas, but this advantage is reduced by the fact that one of his followers would be likely to hasten to correct any such errors on behalf of the master. A more important reason, however, is the large number of economists who would have to be included if our review should proceed much beyond the point where it ended in the previous chapter. While not subject to a strict interpretation of the Malthusian Law, the growth in the number of economists in the past thirty years has come close to fulfilling that law. The number of economists from the past who have already been slighted in this book has not been small, and even so, we have found it necessary to include numerous figures under a single heading (e.g., in the chapter on marginal utility) instead of treating each one in a separate chapter. Fifty years from now it may be possible to pick out the four or five figures from the current period whose contributions have added the most to economic thought. While it would be possible to nominate two or three possible candidates at this point, it requires a far braver man than this author to include even those few alongside the great names who have gone before.

It is only fair, however, that we attempt an answer to the questions of whether or not all the economic theorizing that has gone before has added anything to our understanding and whether there is any more general agreement among economists than there was fifty or one hundred years ago. Have the variety of theories and the accumulation of facts helped to clarify problems, or were we better off, at some earlier date, when less was known and therefore there was less about which to disagree?

Some years ago Professor Galbraith gave a series of lectures at Rutgers University, which was later published under the title *Economics and the Art of Controversy*. His central theme was that many of the great economic issues of the past which formerly divided liberal and conservative economists had now been settled. Despite Galbraith's attempts to rectify this deplorable condition by interjecting his concepts of countervailing power and the affluent society into the scene, there is something to be said for Galbraith's earlier contention. There is a core of economic principles upon which virtually all economists would agree, and even two such unlikely candidates for comparison as Milton Friedman and Alvin Hansen could find in the field of economic theory much upon which both could agree.

There are a number of reasons why the boundaries of disagreement have been narrowed through the years. The growth of statistical data, particularly in the United States, where it was made possible by the work of various government agencies and the National Bureau of Economic Research, has been phenomenal. The expansion of "scientific" knowledge has not been confined to the natural sciences alone! There is less and less excuse today for the armchair theorist of the type personified by David Ricardo. The old adage that "a little learning is a dangerous thing" is as applicable to the field of economics as elsewhere. The growth of mathematical techniques has provided a precision (sometimes, alas, a spurious precision) to points about which most economists were already in agreement in any case. At the same time, a wealth of information from the allied social sciences has become available to the economist. In particular, great efforts have been made to make economists more literate in psychology.

In the final analysis, however, there still remain a number of important areas where economists continue to disagree, and there seems little reason to expect that such differences will not continue to arise. Someone has suggested that only an economist could become agitated over the issue of cardinal utility, but such issues, of doubtful validity to the layman, probably will remain subjects for disagreement in the professional journals. What is more important, some of the bases for disagreement noted in Chapter I are likely to grow in importance. Economists today play a

greater and greater role outside the academic halls of learning, and their
formulation of policy decisions will continue to furnish fodder for disagreements. Even after all of the facts have been collected, their interpretation will still remain subject to question.

Not only are such disagreements inevitable as the cast of economists
and the economic stage both change, but the results thereby produced are
healthy both for the system and for the discipline. From the many disputes
of the past we have garnered the economic truth we hold today, and hopefully future truths will emerge from the current disagreements among
economists. Despite the occasional assurances from the author's economics
students, to the contrary, he has serious doubts whether all of the economic problems have been solved!

It is interesting to note, for example, that right on the heels of all the
furor about the "affluent society," our economists (and politicians) have
suddenly become greatly concerned about the problem of poverty. The
"other American" has become a more frequent topic of conversation than
the "affluent American." Other problems allied to the question of poverty
still remain to be solved. Despite the repeated reassurance of economists
that technological unemployment is only a bogey, automation continues to
haunt many workers. The long run, if that is all that is required to solve
the problem, still remains too long! More constructive thinking about the
role of leisure and the creative uses of men's time still remains to be
done. Equally perplexing has been the development of an economy simultaneously plagued by excessively large amounts of unemployment and
by inflationary pressures. Neither the Classical and Neoclassical doctrine
nor Keynesian economics seems to provide complete answers for this
problem.

Another dramatic change which has been taking place in our economy
in recent years, partly in response to the above changes, is the growth in
the distribution and service trades. The implications of this change for
economic thought have as yet received little consideration. Even if we
should succeed in solving all of these economic problems here at home
(and this still remains to be seen), the vast economic problems of much
of the rest of the world would remain before us. It is not surprising in the
light of these facts that the problems of economic development which
were largely left to the Marxians after the middle of the nineteenth century have returned to the mainstream of economic thought. Despite the
vast amount of literature already in the field, much work still remains to
be done. Neither the economics of laissez-faire nor the mathematical

growth models of Hicks and Domar based on the Keynesian analysis appear particularly applicable to the problems of these countries.

The growing preoccupation of economists with the issues of economic development has already marked two significant changes in economic thought. The role of government has been accorded a greater place in economic theory; no longer is it only the socialists and the totalitarians who write and speak of the merits of at least a certain amount of government planning. While a substantial number of economists in the United States are still reluctant to accept this trend, this hesitancy is far less pronounced among economists of the countries seeking rapid economic development. Many economists have also been reluctant to accept allied social sciences, such as sociology and anthropology, as the equal of economics, but the problems of economic development have pointed to the need for the economist to recognize various cultural and noneconomic factors as being as important or more important than the economic ones in the process of economic development.

Franklin P. Adams, the noted literary critic, along with a number of his colleagues, was once asked by a book review editor to state which book he had always wished to read. While his colleagues were naming some of the more massive tomes often owned but seldom read, Adams replied, "None. If there were one, I would read it." This author has sometimes felt a similar desire to answer the question of students, "Where is the history of economic thought going in the next twenty years?" with the response, "I don't know; if I knew, I would do the leading!" Despite this confession of uncertainty as to the future, it is still the author's hope that some of this book's readers will find the ideas sketched herein an inspiration to them to make further advancements in economic thought.

Bibliography

BIBLIOGRAPHY

CHAPTER I.   Introduction

BRANDIS, ROYALL, "Value Judgments and Economic Science," *Economics and Business,* Vol. 3, No. 2 (Summer, 1963), pp. 41–50.

SCHUMPETER, JOSEPH A., "Science and Ideology," *The American Economic Review* (March, 1949), pp. 345–359. An address by a former president of the American Economic Association at the annual meeting of that association.

STIGLER, GEORGE, "The Politics of Political Economists," *The Quarterly Journal of Economics* (November, 1959), pp. 522–532. An interesting article arguing that the study of economics makes men conservative. It uses great writers of the past for illustrative purposes.

CHAPTER II.   Early Economic Thinkers

Plato

PLATO, *The Republic,* trans. by Benjamin Jowett. New York: Random House, 1937.

Aristotle

ARISTOTLE, *Politics,* trans. by Benjamin Jowett. New York: Modern Library, 1942.

Mercantilists

HECKSCHER, ELI, *Mercantilism.* New York: Macmillan, 1955.

CHAPTER III.   Beginnings of Political Economy

Adam Smith

CLAPHAM, J. H., *A Concise Economic History of Great Britain from the Earliest Times to 1750.* Cambridge: Cambridge University Press, 1949. Useful historical background of the period leading up to Adam Smith.

CLARK, J. M., and others, *Adam Smith, 1776–1926.* Chicago: University Chicago Press, 1928. Adam Smith's economics as seen by a number of twentieth-century economists.

RAE, JOHN, *Life of Adam Smith.* New York: Macmillan, 1895. Old, but still one of the standard biographies of Smith.

SMITH, ADAM, *The Wealth of Nations.* New York: Modern Library, 1937.

SPENGLER, JOSEPH J., "Adam Smith's Theory of Economic Growth," *The Southern Economic Journal* (April, 1959), pp. 397–415; (July, 1959), pp. 1–12.

Mercantilism

JOHNSON, E. A. J., *Predecessors of Adam Smith.* New York: Prentice-Hall, 1957. An appraisal of ten pre-Smith economists.

VINER, JACOB, *Studies in the Theory of International Trade.* New York: Harper,

1937. Chaps. 1 and 2. One of America's leading economic views of Mercantilism.
Physiocrats

GIDE, CHARLES, and RIST, CHARLES, *A History of Economic Doctrines*. New York: Heath, 1949. Chap. 1. An earlier history of thought text presenting the Physiocrats from fellow countrymen's viewpoints.

HIGGS, HENRY, *The Physiocrats*. New York: Macmillan, 1897. One of the standard works on the subject.

CHAPTER IV.   Malthus—Pessimism Personified

BONAR, JAMES, *Malthus and his Work*. London: Allen and Unwin, 1924. Bonar was a biographer and expert on Malthus.

KEYNES, JOHN MAYNARD, *Essays in Biography*. New York: Macmillan, 1933. Chap. 2.

MALTHUS, THOMAS ROBERT, *Essay on Population*. New York: Everyman, 1933.

PENROSE, E. F., "Malthus and the Underdeveloped Areas," *Economic Journal* (June, 1957), pp. 219–239. The first part of this article is particularly interesting in its statement of Malthus' assumptions.

SPENGLER, JOSEPH J., "Malthus the Malthusian as Malthus the Economist," *Southern Economic Journal* (July, 1957), pp. 1–11.
Say

SAY, JEAN BAPTISTE, *A Treatise on Political Economy,* trans. by C. R. Prinsep, 2 vols. Boston: Wells and Lilly, 1821.

CHAPTER V.   Ricardo—The Pessimistic View Continued

BUCHANAN, DANIEL H., "The Historical Approach to Rent and Price Theory," reprinted from *Economica* (1929) in *Readings in Theory of Income Distribution,* Selections by the American Economics Association Homewood, Ill.: Richard Irwin, 1951. Ricardo's theory in contrast with others.

KNIGHT, FRANK, "The Ricardian Theory of Production and Distribution," *Canadian Journal of Economics and Political Science* (May, 1935).

PATTEN, SIMON N., "The Interpretation of Ricardo," *The Quarterly Journal of Economics* (April, 1893), pp. 322–352.

RICARDO, DAVID, *The Works and Correspondence,* Piero Sraffa (ed.). Cambridge: University Press for Royal Economic Society, 1951–1955. The monumental collection of Ricardo's writings.

STIGLER, GEORGE, "Ricardian Theory of Value and Distribution," *Journal of Political Economy* (June, 1952), pp. 187–207.

———, "Ricardo and the 93 Percent Labor Theory of Value," *American Economic Review* (June, 1958), pp. 357–367. A rejection of the interpretation of Ricardo as a simple exponent of the labor theory of value.

CHAPTER VI.   Mill and the Close of the Classical System

Bentham
HUTCHISON, T. W., "Bentham as an Economist," *Economic Journal* (June, 1956), pp. 208–306.

VINER, JACOB, "Bentham and J. S. Mill, The Utilitarian Background," *The American Economic Review* (March, 1949), pp. 360–382.

Cairnes

CAIRNES, J. E., *The Character and Logical Method of Political Economy*. New York: Harper and Brothers, 1875.

——, *Some Leading Principles of Political Economy Newly Expounded*. New York: Harper and Brothers, 1874.

Mill

BLADEN, VINCENT, "John Stuart Mill's Principles, A Centenary Appraisal," *The American Economic Review* (May, 1949), pp. 1–12.

MILL, JOHN STUART, *Autobiography*. Oxford: Oxford University Press, 1924.

——, *Principles of Political Economy*. Ashley ed. London: Longmans Green, 1920.

Senior

BOWLEY, MARION, *Nassau Senior and Classical Political Economy*. New York: Augustus Kelley, 1949.

SENIOR, NASSAU, *An Outline of the Science of Political Economy*. New York: Augustus Kelley, 1951.

CHAPTER VII.   Karl Marx and the Socialist Critics

Pre-Marxian Socialists

BERNSTEIN, EDWARD, *Evolutionary Socialism*. New York: Huebsch, 1909.

FOURIER, CHARLES, *Selections from the Works of Fourier*. Ed. by Charles Gide. London: S. Sonnenschein, 1901. Gide's preface presents Fourier in a far more sympathetic light than is usually the case.

GIDE, CHARLES, and RIST, CHARLES, *A History of Economic Doctrines*. Boston: Heath, n.d., pp. 170–255. Includes discussions of Sismondi, Saint-Simon, Owen, and Fourier.

OWEN, ROBERT, *A New View of Society*. New York: Everyman, 1927.

SELIGMAN, E. R. A., *Essays in Economics*. New York: Macmillan, 1925, pp. 23–31. An interesting interpretation of Owen's contribution.

Marx

COLE, G. D. H., *The Meaning of Marxism*. London: Golloncz, 1948.

FREEDMAN, ROBERT, ed., *Marx on Economics*. New York: Harcourt, Brace & World, 1961.

MARX, KARL, *Capital*. New York: Modern Library, n.d. This is only the first volume. Important parts of the other volumes and other parts of Marx's writings can be found in *Capital and Other Writings,* ed. by Max Eastman. New York: Modern Library, 1932.

MEHRING, FRANZ, *Karl Marx, The Story of His Life,* trans. by Edward Fitzgerald, ed. by Ruth and Heinz Norden. New York: Covici Friede, 1935.

SCHUMPETER, JOSEPH, "The Communist Manifesto in Sociology and Economics," *Journal of Political Economy,* vol. LVII (1949), pp. 199–212.

SWEEZY, PAUL M., *The Theory of Capitalist Development*. New York: Oxford, 1942. The views of America's leading Marxist scholar.

Lenin

LENIN, V. I., *Imperialism*. New York: International Publishers, 1939.

——, *The Teachings of Karl Marx*. New York: International Publishers, 1935.

George

DORFMAN, JOSEPH, *The Economic Mind in American Civilization*, 5 vols. New York: Viking, 1956–1959. The most complete study of American economic thought. Vol. III, pp. 142–149 contains a discussion of George.

GEORGE, HENRY, *Progress and Poverty*. New York: The Modern Library, n.d.

CHAPTER VIII.   The German Historical School

BÖHM VON BAWERK, E., "The Historical and the Deductive Method in Political Economy," *Annals of the American Academy of Political Science*, vol. I (1890–1891), pp. 244–271. An attack on the Historical School combined with a plea for a reconciliation.

LIST, FRIEDRICH, *National System of Political Economy*, trans. by S. S. Lloyd. London: Longmans Green, 1904.

ROSCHER, WILHELM, *Principles of Political Economy*. New York: Holt, 1877.

SOMBART, WERNER, *The Jews and Modern Capitalism,* trans. by M. Epstein. Glencoe, Ill.: The Free Press, 1951.

TAWNEY, R. H., *Religion and the Rise of Capitalism: A Historical Study*. New York: Harcourt, Brace, 1926.

WEBER, MAX, *The Protestant Ethic and the Spirit of Capitalism,* trans. by Talcott Parsons. London: Allen and Unwin, 1930.

CHAPTER IX.   The Concept of Marginal Utility

General Reference

HUTCHISON, T. W., *A Review of Economic Doctrine, 1870–1929*. Oxford: Oxford University Press, 1952.

STIGLER, GEORGE, *Production and Distribution Theories*. New York: Macmillan, 1941.

Böhm von Bawerk

BÖHM VON BAWERK, EUGEN, *The Positive Theory of Capital*. New York: Macmillan, 1891.

SCHUMPETER, JOSEPH, *Ten Great Economists*. New York: Oxford University Press, 1951. Chap. 6.

Clark

CLARK, JOHN BATES, *The Distribution of Wealth*. New York: Ginn, 1903.

——, *The Philosophy of Wealth*. New York: Macmillan, 1899.

HOMAN, PAUL T., *Contemporary Economic Thought*. New York: Harper, 1928. Chap. 2.

Jevons

JEVONS, WILLIAM STANLEY, *The Theory of Political Economy,* 4th ed. London: Macmillan, 1911.

KEYNES, JOHN MAYNARD, *Essays in Biography*. New York: Horizon Press, 1951, pp. 255–309.

Menger

MENGER, KARL, *Principles of Economics,* rev. ed. by James Dugwall and Bert Hoselitz. Glencoe, Ill.: Free Press, 1950.

SCHUMPETER, JOSEPH, *Ten Great Economists.* New York: Oxford University Press, 1951. Chap. 3.

Pareto

SCHUMPETER, JOSEPH, *Ten Great Economists.* New York: Oxford University Press, 1951. Chap. 5.

Walras

HARROD, R. F., "Walras, A Reappraisal," *Economic Journal* (June, 1956), pp. 307–316.

SCHUMPETER, JOSEPH, *Ten Great Economists.* New York: Oxford University Press, 1951. Chap. 2.

WALRAS, LÉON, *Elements of Pure Economics,* trans. by William Jaffe. Homewood, Ill.: Irwin, 1954. Only for those mathematically inclined.

von Wieser

VON WIESER, FRIEDRICH, *Natural Value,* trans. by Christian A. Wallach. London: Macmillan, 1893.

————, *Social Economics,* trans. by A. Ford Hinriche. New York: Adelphi, 1917.

Wicksell

WICKSELL, KNUT, *Lectures on Political Economy,* trans. by F. Glassen. London: Routledge and Kegan Paul, 1934.

CHAPTER X. Alfred Marshall and the Neoclassical System

Marshall

KEYNES, JOHN MAYNARD, *Essays in Biography.* New York: Norton, 1951, pp. 125–217.

MARSHALL, ALFRED, *Principles of Economics,* 8th ed. London: Macmillan, 1946.

SCHUMPETER, JOSEPH, *Ten Great Economists.* New York: Oxford University Press, 1951. Chap. 4.

SHOVE, G. F., "The Place of Marshall's Principles in the Development of Economic Theory," *The Economic Journal* (December, 1942), pp. 294–329.

VINER, JACOB, "Marshall Economics in Relation to the Man and His Times," *American Economic Review* (June, 1941), pp. 223–235.

Edgeworth

EDGEWORTH, FRANCIS Y., *Mathematical Psychics.* 2nd ed. London: Routledge and Kegan Paul, 1932. Not for those readers uninitiated into mathematical techniques.

KEYNES, JOHN MAYNARD, *Essays in Biography.* New York: Norton, 1951, pp. 218–238.

FISHER, IRVING, *The Theory of Interest.* New York: Macmillan, 1930.

————, *Stabilizing the Dollar.* New York: Macmillan, 1920.

Hobson

HOBSON, JOHN, *The Economics of Distribution.* New York: Macmillan, 1903.

————, *The Economics of Unemployment.* New York: Macmillan, 1931.

————, *Imperialism.* London: Allen and Unwin, 1938.

————, *The Industrial System.* New York: Scribners, 1910.

HOMAN, PAUL T., *Contemporary Economic Thought*. New York: Harper, 1928. pp. 281–374.

Pigou

PIGOU, A. C., *The Economics of Welfare*. London: Macmillan, 1932.

——, *The Theory of Unemployment*. London: Macmillan, 1933.

CHAPTER XI.   Three American Institutionalists

Veblen

DORFMAN, JOSEPH, *Thorstein Veblen and His America*. New York: Viking, 1934. A thorough study of Veblen's life and work by one of the leading experts on the subject.

LERNER, MAX, ed., *The Portable Veblen*. New York: Viking, 1948. A collection of Veblen's chief writings with an introduction by this noted social scientist.

VEBLEN, THORSTEIN, *The Engineers and the Price System*. New York: Viking, 1947.

——, *The Instinct of Workmanship*. New York: Huebsch, 1918.

——, *The Theory of Business Enterprise*. New York: Scribners, 1904. Now available in paperback.

——, *The Theory of the Leisure Class*. New York: Modern Library, 1934. Also available in a paperback edition.

Mitchell

BURNS, ARTHUR F., *Wesley Clair Mitchell: The Economic Scientist*. New York: National Bureau, 1952. Over a dozen leading economists pay their respects in this memorial volume.

MITCHELL, W. C., *The Backward Art of Spending Money*. New York: Augustus Kelley, 1950. A collection of Mitchell's best essays on a variety of topics.

——, *Business Cycles, the Problem and its Setting*. New York: National Bureau, 1927.

Commons

COMMONS, JOHN R., *The Economics of Collective Action*. New York: Macmillan, 1950.

——, *Institutional Economics*. New York: Macmillan, 1934.

——, *Legal Foundations of Capitalism*. New York: Macmillan, 1924.

——, *Myself*. New York: Macmillan, 1934.

GRUNCHY, ALLEN, "John R. Commons' Concept of the Common Man," *Journal of Political Economy* (December, 1940), pp. 823–849.

General

DORFMAN, JOSEPH, and others, *Institutional Economics; Veblen, Commons, Mitchell Reconsidered*. Berkeley: University of California Press, 1962. A valuable collection of essays appraising the work of all three of the major Institutionalists.

CHAPTER XII.   Monopolistic vs. Imperfect Competition

General

DEAN, JOEL, *Readings in the Social Control of Industry*. Philadelphia: Blakiston, 1942.

SRAFFA, PIERO, "The Laws of Returns Under Competitive Conditions," *Economic Journal* (December, 1926), pp. 335–350. Reprinted in *Readings in Price Theory*,

George Stigler, ed. Homewood, Ill.: Irwin, 1952. Other important journal articles are included in this collection.

Chamberlin

CHAMBERLIN, EDWARD H., *The Theory of Monopolistic Competition.* Cambridge: Harvard University Press, 1947.

Proceedings of American Economic Association, *American Economic Review* (May, 1964), pp. 28–57.

The interested student can find a wealth of references in the bibliographies compiled by Professor Chamberlin in *The Quarterly Journal of Economics,* August, 1948, pp. 629–638; November, 1956, pp. 613–643.

Robinson

ROBINSON, JOAN, *The Economics of Imperfect Competition.* London: Macmillan, 1933.

———, "Imperfect Competition Revisited," *Economic Journal* (September, 1953), pp. 579–593.

CHAPTER XIII. The Economics of Capitalism

Keynes

DILLARD, DUDLEY, *The Economics of John Maynard Keynes.* New York: Prentice Hall, 1948.

HANSEN, ALVIN H., *A Guide to Keynes.* New York: McGraw-Hill, 1953. A chapter-by-chapter interpretation of the *General Theory.*

HARRIS, SEYMOUR, ed., *The New Economics.* New York: Knopf, 1948. A series of essays by leading Keynesians around the world discussing the wide ramifications of Keynes' book.

HARROD, ROY F., *The Life of John Maynard Keynes.* New York: Harcourt, Brace & World, 1951. The most important study of Keynes' life, by a former colleague.

HUNT, W. H., *Keynesianism—Retrospect and Prospect.* Chicago: Henry Regnery, 1964. A highly critical view of Keynes' contributions.

KEYNES, JOHN MAYNARD, *The General Theory of Employment, Interest, and Money.* New York: Harcourt, Brace, 1936.

Clark

CLARK, JOHN MAURICE, *Alternative to Serfdom.* New York: Knopf, 1948.

———, *Economic Institutions and Human Welfare.* New York: Knopf, 1957.

———, *Preface to Social Economics.* New York: Farrar & Rinehart, 1936.

———, *Social Control of Business.* New York: McGraw-Hill, 1939.

———, *Studies in the Economics of Overhead Costs.* Chicago: University of Chicago Press, 1923.

Schumpeter

HARRIS, SEYMOUR E., ed., *Schumpeter: Social Scientist.* Cambridge: Harvard University Press, 1951. An excellent collection of appraisals by Schumpeter's friends and colleagues.

SCHUMPETER, JOSEPH A., *Capitalism, Socialism, and Democracy.* New York: Harper, 1950.

———. *The Theory of Economic Development.* New York: Oxford University Press, 1961.

Index